PSALMS I

1–50

THE ANCHOR BIBLE is a fresh approach to the world's greatest classic. Its object is to make the Bible accessible to the modern reader; its method is to arrive at the meaning of biblical literature through exact translation and extended exposition, and to reconstruct the ancient setting of the biblical story, as well as the circumstances of its transcription and the characteristics of its transcribers.

THE ANCHOR BIBLE is a project of international and interfaith scope: Protestant, Catholic, and Jewish scholars from many countries contribute individual volumes. The project is not sponsored by any ecclesiastical organization and is not intended to reflect any particular theological doctrine. Prepared under our joint supervision, THE ANCHOR BIBLE is an effort to make available all the significant historical and linguistic knowledge which bears on the interpretation of the biblical record.

THE ANCHOR BIBLE is aimed at the general reader with no special formal training in biblical studies; yet, it is written with the most exacting standards of scholarship, reflecting the highest technical accomplishment.

This project marks the beginning of a new era of co-operation among scholars in biblical research, thus forming a common body of knowledge to be shared by all.

William Foxwell Albright
David Noel Freedman
GENERAL EDITORS

THE ANCHOR BIBLE

PSALMS I
1-50

INTRODUCTION, TRANSLATION, AND NOTES
BY
MITCHELL DAHOOD, S.J.

Doubleday & Company, Inc.
Garden City, New York
1966

IMPRIMI POTEST
Rome, May 20, 1965
R. A. F. MacKenzie, S.J.
Rector of the Pontifical Biblical Institute

IMPRIMATUR
From the Chancery of Rome, September 16, 1965
✠ Luigi Traglia, Cardinal Vicar

Library of Congress Catalog Card Number 66–11766

Printed in the United States of America
First Edition

Dedicated to
William Foxwell Albright

PREFACE

A preface may serve various purposes. The author of a book that lately arrives for review attempts to disarm the would-be critic in his preface. He honestly sets forth the difficulties encountered in the composition of his work and candidly exposes the defects that mar the finished product. But he apparently overdoes it because one is inclined to ask, while glancing through the preface, the not impertinent question, "Then why was the book ever written?" The present volume, too, has need of asking the reader to concentrate more on its merits than on its defects, but—to forestall the embarrassing question—no list of its shortcomings or lapses from consistency will be given here. If the reader should arrive at the conclusion made famous by Henry Adams' dictum that "translation is an evil," his position will not essentially differ from mine, at least as regards the Hebrew Psalms.

Instead, I shall proceed directly to the agreeable office of expressing my gratitude to Professor D. N. Freedman, one of the General Editors, whose critical eye nailed more than one fallacy to the spot. His influence on this book is much more pervasive than the few explicit acknowledgments would suggest. For his unstinting help and for the timely assistance of his wife Cornelia I am genuinely grateful. I am likewise indebted to my colleagues of the Pontifical Biblical Institute for their even-minded criticism and to the students of the Institute whose seemingly columbine questions often concealed a serpentine penetration.

In the Borghese Gallery in Rome there is a painting of Judith and Holofernes by Giovanni Baglioni (1571–1644). The official guidebook of the Gallery, by P. della Pergola, explains that Baglioni—Caravaggio's fiercest rival—did not, in this painting, escape the powerful influence of the new style to which Caravaggio gave expression. In dedicating this work to my teacher, I am registering my thanks to a scholar who, early and steadily, realized the importance of Ugaritic for all phases of biblical research. He clearly saw that the sweet singers of Israel, like Baglioni before his adversary, were profoundly influenced by the Canaanite poets whose works and pomp they ostensibly renounced.

Candlemas, 1965

CONTENTS

Preface VII

Principal Abbreviations XI

Introduction XV

Selected Bibliography XLV

Translation and Notes

Psalm 1 (i 1–6) 1
Psalm 2 (ii 1–12) 6
Psalm 3 (iii 1–9) 15
Psalm 4 (iv 1–9) 22
Psalm 5 (v 1–13) 28
Psalm 6 (vi 1–11) 37
Psalm 7 (vii 1–18) 40
Psalm 8 (viii 1–10) 48
Psalm 9 (ix 1–21) 53
Psalm 10 (x 1–18) 60
Psalm 11 (xi 1–7) 68
Psalm 12 (xii 1–9) 72
Psalm 13 (xiii 1–6) 76
Psalm 14 (xiv 1–7) 80
Psalm 15 (xv 1–5) 83
Psalm 16 (xvi 1–11) 86
Psalm 17 (xvii 1–15) 92
Psalm 18 (xviii 1–51) 101
Psalm 19 (xix 1–15) 120
Psalm 20 (xx 1–10) 126
Psalm 21 (xxi 1–14) 130
Psalm 22 (xxii 1–32) 136
Psalm 23 (xxiii 1–6) 145
Psalm 24 (xxiv 1–10) 150

Psalm 25 (xxv 1–22) 154
Psalm 26 (xxvi 1–12) 160
Psalm 27 (xxvii 1–14) 165
Psalm 28 (xxviii 1–9) 171
Psalm 29 (xxix 1–11) 174
Psalm 30 (xxx 1–13) 181
Psalm 31 (xxxi 1–25) 185
Psalm 32 (xxxii 1–11) 193
Psalm 33 (xxxiii 1–22) 199
Psalm 34 (xxxiv 1–23) 204
Psalm 35 (xxxv 1–28) 208
Psalm 36 (xxxvi 1–13) 217
Psalm 37 (xxxvii 1–40) 225
Psalm 38 (xxxviii 1–23) 233
Psalm 39 (xxxix 1–14) 238
Psalm 40 (xl 1–18) 243
Psalm 41 (xli 1–14) 248
Psalm 42 (xlii 1–12) 254
Psalm 43 (xliii 1–5) 261
Psalm 44 (xliv 1–27) 263
Psalm 45 (xlv 1–18) 269
Psalm 46 (xlvi 1–12) 277
Psalm 47 (xlvii 1–10) 283
Psalm 48 (xlviii 1–15) 288
Psalm 49 (xlix 1–21) 295
Psalm 50 (l 1–23) 304

Index of Biblical Passages 313

Index of Hebrew Words 319

Subjects Index 325

PRINCIPAL ABBREVIATIONS

1. Publications

AfO	Archiv für Orientforschung
AJSL	American Journal of Semitic Languages and Literatures
ARW	Archiv für Religionswissenschaft
BA	Biblical Archaeologist
BASOR	Bulletin of the American Schools of Oriental Research
BCCT	*The Bible in Current Catholic Thought,* ed. J. L. McKenzie
BDB	F. Brown, S. R. Driver, and C. A. Briggs, eds., *A Hebrew and English Lexicon of the Old Testament*
BH^3	*Biblia Hebraica,* ed. R. Kittel, 3d ed.
BO	Bibliotheca Orientalis
BSOAS	Bulletin of the School of Oriental African Studies
BZ	Biblische Zeitschrift
BZAW	Beihefte zur Zeitschrift für die alttestamentliche Wissenschaft
CAD	*The Assyrian Dictionary,* Oriental Institute of the University of Chicago
CBQ	Catholic Biblical Quarterly
CECBP	*A Critical and Exegetical Commentary on the Book of Psalms,* by C. A. Briggs
CML	*Canaanite Myths and Legends,* by G. R. Driver
CPBP	*Canaanite Parallels in the Book of Psalms,* by J. H. Patton
CRAIBL	Comptes Rendus de l'Académie des Inscriptions et Belles Lettres
FuF	Forschungen und Fortschritte
GB	Gesenius-Buhl, *Handwörterbuch*
GHB	*Grammaire de l'Hébreu Biblique,* by P. Joüon
GK	*Gesenius' Hebräische Grammatik,* ed. E. Kautzsch
GLECS	Groupe Linguistique d'Études Chamito-Sémitiques
HTR	Harvard Theological Review
HUCA	Hebrew Union College Annual
ICC	International Critical Commentary
IDB	The Interpreter's Dictionary of the Bible
IEJ	Israel Exploration Journal

JAOS Journal of the American Oriental Society
JBL Journal of Biblical Literature and Exegesis
JCS Journal of Cuneiform Studies
JJS Journal of Jewish Studies
JNES Journal of Near Eastern Studies
JPOS Journal of the Palestine Oriental Society
JQR Jewish Quarterly Review
JRAS Journal of the Royal Asiatic Society
JSS Journal of Semitic Studies
JTS Journal of Theological Studies
KAI *Kanaanäische und Aramäische Inschriften,* by H. Donner and W. Röllig
KB L. Koehler and W. Baumgartner, *Lexicon in Veteris Testamenti Libros*
LKK *The Legend of King Keret,* by H. L. Ginsberg
OLZ Orientalistische Literaturzeitung
PCTNT *The Psalms Chronologically Treated with a New Translation,* by M. Buttenwieser
PEQ Palestine Exploration Quarterly
PNWSP *Proverbs and Northwest Semitic Philology,* by M. Dahood
PPG *Phönizisch-Punische Grammatik,* by Johannes Friedrich
1QIs^a The St. Mark's Isaiah Scroll, ed. M. Burrows
1QM Qumran War Scroll
1QS Qumran Manual of Discipline
Rendiconti Lincei *Atti dell'Accademia Nazionale dei Lincei, Rendiconti della classe di scienze morali, storiche e filologiche*
RHR Revue de l'histoire des religions
ThR Theologische Rundschau
TNSI *A Text-Book of North-Semitic Inscriptions,* by G. A. Cooke
TS Theological Studies
TSP *Tempora und Satzstellung in den Psalmen,* by Diethelm Michel
UT *Ugaritic Textbook,* 4th ed., 1965, of C. H. Gordon's *Ugaritic Grammar*
VT Vetus Testamentum
VTS Vetus Testamentum Supplements
WO Die Welt des Orients
WuS *Wörterbuch der ugaritischen Sprache,* by Joseph Aistleitner
ZA Zeitschrift für Assyriologie und vorderasiatische Archäologie
ZAW Zeitschrift für die alttestamentliche Wissenschaft
ZDMG Zeitschrift der deutschen morgenländischen Gesellschaft
ZDPV Zeitschrift des deutschen Palästinavereins
ZLH F. Zorell, *Lexicon Hebraicum*

2. Versions

AT	The Bible, an American Translation, 1931
ATD	Das Alte Testament Deutsch
CCD	Confraternity of Christian Doctrine Version
KJ	The Authorized Version of 1611, or the King James Version
LXX	The Septuagint
LXX[A]	Codex Alexandrinus
MT	Masoretic Text
RSV	The Revised Standard Version, 1946, 1952
Symm.	Ancient Greek translation of the Old Testament by Symmachus
Syr.	Syriac version, the Peshitta
Targ.	Aramaic translations or paraphrases
Vrs.	Ancient versions
Vulg.	The Vulgate

3. Other Abbreviations

Akk.	Akkadian
Ar.	Arabic
Aram.	Aramaic
Heb.	Hebrew
NT	New Testament
OT	Old Testament
Phoen.	Phoenician
Ugar.	Ugaritic

INTRODUCTION

An introduction should more properly be written when the study of all one hundred and fifty Psalms has been completed. A number of conclusions, however, have already emerged with sufficient clarity to warrant at this time a brief, preliminary formulation.

What with the recent spate of Psalms' translations and commentaries, a new work on the Psalter would appear almost as difficult to justify at this juncture as another book on the Scrolls of Qumran. But the translation offered here differs from earlier efforts in that it is not the fruit of a confrontation of the Hebrew text with the ancient versions, from which the least objectionable reading is plucked. Much less does it follow the method of the recent *Psalterii secundum Vulgatam Bibliorum Versionem Nova Recensio,* edited by Robert Weber (Clervaux, Luxembourg, 1961), *pro manuscripto,* which presents a Latin version based on a comparison of the Hebrew original with Jerome's Vulgate, the *Juxta Hebraeos,* and the *Psalterium Novum* of the Pontifical Biblical Institute. What is attempted here is a fresh translation, accompanied by a philological commentary, that lays heavy stress on the Ras Shamra-Ugarit texts and other epigraphic discoveries made along the Phoenician littoral. Though some thirty-five years have passed since the discovery and decipherment of the Ras Shamra-Ugarit texts, no subsequent translation of the Psalms[1] has yet availed itself of these clay tablets. In 1941, when reviewing C. H. Gordon's *Ugaritic Grammar* (the fourth edition under the title *Ugaritic Textbook* [abbr. UT] appeared in 1965 [Analecta Orientalia 38; Rome]),[2] W. F. Albright

[1] One monograph and numerous short articles have examined the Psalms in relation to the literary corpus from Ras Shamra; some of these will be referred to in the course of this study. The positive results of such studies have not as yet found their way into any better-known translations.

[2] In citing the Ugaritic texts, I follow the numbering and transliteration of UT.

wrote that "the tremendous significance of the North Canaanite religious literature of Ugarit for biblical research is becoming clearer every day. It is not too much to say that all future investigations of the Book of Psalms must deal intensively with the Ugaritic texts. . . . Thorough knowledge of Ugaritic grammar, vocabulary and style is an absolute prerequisite for comparative research on the part of biblical scholars. Moreover, the significance of Ugaritic for historical Hebrew grammar, on which will increasingly rest our reconstruction of the literary history of Israel, cannot be overestimated. Ugaritic was only dialectically different from ancestral Hebrew in the generations immediately preceding the Israelite occupation of Canaan. Ugarit and Canaanite Palestine shared a common literary tradition, which profoundly influenced Israel. For these reasons Gordon's *Ugaritic Grammar* is of greater lasting importance for OT research than any dozen assorted recent commentaries taken together."[3]

Nearly a quarter of a century has passed since Albright stressed the relevance of Ugaritic for Psalms' research, but most translators and commentators have continued to treat the Ras Shamra texts as, at best, only peripherally significant. To be sure, Sigmund Mowinckel, in his studies on the Psalms, has displayed a familiarity with the Ugaritic myths, but his failure to exploit the rich linguistic material at his disposition makes some of his conclusions philologically vulnerable.[4] H. J. Kraus, in his two-volume commentary on the Psalms that first began to appear in fascicles in 1957, does cite a few articles which seek to apply the new Ugaritic data to problems in the Psalter, but he is not convinced that Ugaritic is terribly important for a better understanding of the Psalms. His remarks in the *Einleitung* to the first volume of the 1961 revised edition are symptomatic: "Difficult or rare Hebrew words can sometimes be explained from Ugaritic poetry (cf., above all, Ps 68). . . . With great prudence one must check to see if individual words and expressions are open to new possible definitions because of Ugaritic."[5]

[3] In JBL 60 (1941), 438 f.

[4] To cite but one instance, Mowinckel, *The Psalms in Israel's Worship* (see Selected Bibliography), I, pp. 77 ff., has placed considerable emphasis upon Ps xlv 7, which he renders, "Thy throne, O god, is for ever and ever," as explicit evidence for the existence in Israel of a form of divine kingship. However, the translation and philological commentary proposed below remove this verse from among his proof-texts for divine kingship in Israel.

[5] *Psalmen,* 2d ed. (see Selected Bibliography), I, p. xii.

One may, however, legitimately ask whether Kraus is exercising *Vorsicht* vis à vis the new material, or an excess of caution with regard to the new canons of Hebrew philology being imposed by the Ras Shamra discoveries and by progress in Northwest Semitic philology. An example to illustrate. There are two textual difficulties in the second colon of Ps iv 7, *n^{e}sāh ʻālēnū ʼōr pānekā yhwh.* Kraus accepts G. R. Driver's proposal that *ʻālēnū* here denotes "from us," as in Phoenician and probably also in Ugaritic, but fails to appreciate that consonantal *nsh* (from *nūs*) is the verb "to flee," a synonym of *brḥ,* "to flee," precisely the verb with which *ʻl,* "from," is employed in Phoenician. Though his translation reflects the sense of the line, "The light of your face has departed from us," Kraus introduces the gratuitous emendation of consonantal *nsh* (to be pointed *nāsāh,* with archaic third-person masculine ending) to *nās^{e}ʻāh.* In other terms, he resorts to the method of emendation instead of fully availing himself of the Phoenician parallel which offers a smooth exit from the textual impasse and permits the clear and literal rendering, "The light of your face has fled from us, O Yahweh."[6]

The present work is not a commentary on the Psalms in the traditional sense of the word; a better term would perhaps be a prolegomenon to a commentary. The topics usually treated in a standard commentary, such as the name "Psalms," the title of the Psalms, their arrangement and use, the origin and authorship of the Psalms, etc., have been waived in the interest of the primary scope of this study, namely, a translation and philological commentary which utilizes the linguistic information offered by the Ras Shamra tablets. Psalms as such have not yet been unearthed at Ras Shamra so that the Ugaritic texts do not directly bear on such questions as literary classification or *Sitz im Leben;* the treatment of these problems therefore will also be cursory and incidental to the main purpose at hand. Numerous recent works examine such problems fully and competently, so there is no pressing need to rehearse them in the following pages. To judge from reviewers' comments, nothing is more depressing than having to read the long introductions which merely rehash issues that have already been well aired. However, a

[6] Similar criticism of Kraus's handling of this text has been made by J. H. Eaton in *Theology Today* 67 (1964), 356.

more ample discussion of the more important issues of literary criticism is foreseen for the second volume of Psalms in this series, covering Psalms 51–150.

Discoveries at Ras Shamra-Ugarit

The history of the discovery and subsequent excavations of Ras Shamra has been well summarized. The entry on "Ugarit" in *The Interpreter's Dictionary of the Bible* (abbr. IDB) (New York, 1962) runs to fifteen columns. Ugaritic has taken its place as a major language (or more properly, a dialect of Canaanite) in the Semitic family of languages.

About seven miles north of Latakia (ancient Laodicea ad Mare) on the north Syrian coast stands an artificial mound about sixty feet high and covering some seventy acres. Today called Ras Shamra (Fennel Promontory), this mound concealed the ancient city of Ugarit, known from Babylonian, Hittite, and Egyptian records. In the spring of 1928, a north Syrian peasant was plowing his field when the plow jammed against a stone slab which happened to form part of the ceiling of a corbelled tomb. Informed of this strike, the archaeological authorities commissioned C. F. A. Schaeffer of Strasbourg, who began excavations at the site in 1929 and has continued in that capacity to the present day. He has thus far conducted twenty-seven archaeological campaigns at Ras Shamra. The discoveries seem unlimited—each season's dig seems to yield a rich harvest. The discoveries include enormous quantities of pottery, weights, bronzes, jewelry, statuary, stelae, tombs, constructions such as temples, palaces, private homes, sanitation systems, and, above all, texts.

Since the initial discoveries in 1929, thousands of tablets in at least eight different languages have come to light. Our present interest focuses on those in a previously unknown cuneiform alphabet of twenty-nine or thirty signs. Many of the copies date to the reign of a certain King Niqmad of Ugarit, a contemporary of the Hittite king Shuppiluliuma (ca. 1375–1340 B.C.). Though copied in this period, the myths and legends recorded on the tablets are doubtless much older, the Baal Cycle reaching back, in all likelihood, to the third millennium B.C. The decipherment was worked out in less than a year's time by three scholars working independently: Hans Bauer in Germany, Édouard Dhorme in Jerusalem, and Charles Virolleaud in Paris.

The longest and most important composition is the Baal Cycle, a collection of episodes about the Canaanite gods, preserved in eight tablets and in a number of fragments; it numbers more than two thousand lines. Next in importance is the *Legend of King Keret,* a semi-historical poem, recorded on three tablets and several fragments which total some five hundred lines, while the Epic of Aqhat runs to about four hundred legible lines on four tablets. Two other mythological poems have been published, both of which seem to be complete. One is named after its invocation, *The Beautiful and Gracious Gods,* and describes the birth of the twin deities Dawn and Dusk. The other is a hymn celebrating the marriage of the goddess Nikkal to the Moon-god. Finally, there are tablets which list offerings to the gods, sacred and secular professions, rituals; some contain private letters, economic and juridical texts, and even medicinal formulas for curing ailing horses. In recent years a series of lexicographical tablets has been found, one of them a quadrilingual vocabulary containing some two hundred words, as well as a perfectly preserved incantation of seventy-five lines. The very variety of subjects treated in these texts makes them an inexhaustible source of information for the biblical philologist and exegete.

One need not be surprised, therefore, to encounter among the plates accompanying the text of C. F. A. Schaeffer's *The Cuneiform Texts of Ras Shamra-Ugarit* (London, 1939) a figure, taken from a fresco in the Church of Santa Maria Antica in the Roman Forum, which shows Hezekiah, king of Judah, sick in bed with his face turned toward the wall, while the prophet Isaiah, standing at the foot of the bed, talks to him. On page 41 the reader is informed that the biblical name of the remedy made of boiled figs that Isaiah recommended is identical with the name of a remedy used by the veterinary surgeons at Ugarit in the fifteenth and fourteenth centuries B.C.!

Since the decipherment of the texts in 1930, the linguistic classification of Ugaritic (as the language came to be called) has been a matter of dispute. The widely held view that Ugaritic is a Canaanite dialect whose closest affinity is to biblical Hebrew, especially in the poetic books, has been winning the day. The publication of new texts by Virolleaud in 1957 and 1965, and recent comparative studies disclosing added points of contact in the areas of phraseology, imagery, prosody, and thought, have corroborated the Canaanite classification of Ugaritic. The numerous equations and comparisons proposed in this volume point to the same classification, and though many of them are admittedly banal, their inclusion will enable the comparative Semitist to make a more accurate assessment.

Comparative Studies

The nineteenth century witnessed the rise and progress of Egyptian and Babylonian studies, a rise which was to exert a tremendous impact upon Old Testament research. In time, however, the legacy left by these two disciplines for a clearer understanding of the biblical text turned out to be much less than was imagined, say, thirty years ago.[7] History, then, cautions scholars to moderate their claims on behalf of a new discipline and its bearing on Old Testament inquiry. The raison d'etre of the following study is precisely to set forth the relevance of the Ugaritic texts for Psalms' research; that considerable risk is involved in such an ostensibly restricted approach to the Psalter and its problems does not, in the light of recent history, escape the present writer. But the positive results flowing from an application of Ugaritic grammatical and stylistic principles to the Hebrew text of Psalms appear to be sufficiently numerous and significant to merit detailed presentation. Not all the proposals submitted here will stand the test of present criticism or future discoveries, but if the present effort succeeds in showing what possibilities are open to the modern student of the Bible, the effort will have proved worth while. The evidence is registered throughout the notes accompanying the translation, but for the sake of general orientation, some observations on the areas of Psalms' research affected by Ugaritic and Northwest Semitic philology may not be out of place.

The Consonantal Text

Biblical poetry teems with textual cruxes, and the Hebrew text of Psalms is no exception. In fact, if one were to base his opinion

[7] This point has been more fully developed by the present writer in *Gregorianum* 43 (1962), 55–57 (see Selected Bibliography).

of the consonantal text upon those psalms, such as xiv and xviii, which are preserved in doublets, he would conclude that the text is corrupt and stands in need of constant emendation. But happily these doublets prove not to be typical, and the consonantal text of the first fifty psalms is remarkably well preserved; in my opinion, resort to emendation can be justified in fewer than a half a dozen instances. This does not mean that all the textual difficulties have been solved; it merely suggests that the rich thesaurus of forms and constructions in the Ugaritic and Phoenician texts severely restricts the freedom of the textual critic to emend the text. For example, in Ps xxiv 4, *napšī* is customarily emended to *napšō* since, as Kraus (*Psalmen*, I, p. 193) writes, "The context requires this correction," but now it turns out that Hebrew, like Phoenician and probably Ugaritic, also possessed a third-person singular suffix (masculine and feminine) in *-ī;* more than ninety examples, listed under Ps ii 6, have thus far been identified in the poetic books of the Bible. Biblical morphology has thus been enriched with a new morpheme and both the consonantal and punctualized texts have been vindicated in over eighty cases. The Masoretes almost certainly did not understand the morpheme, but they nonetheless preserved it. Or again, in a number of texts the presence of a *lamedh* has proved embarrassing and, to many, deletion was the only viable expedient. But the well-documented existence in Ugaritic of both *lamedh emphaticum* and *lamedh vocativum* considerably widens the choice a philologist can make when faced with such a problem. Consider, for instance, Ps cxl 7, *'āmartī l^eyahweh 'ēlī 'attāh ha'^azīnāh yhwh qōl taḥ^anūnay;* the Tetragrammaton in the second colon is, on the strength of the Syriac reading, deleted. When, however, the *lamedh* preceding *yhwh* in the first colon is parsed as vocative, the presence of *yhwh* in the second colon is rendered necessary by both parallelism and meter. Hence I translate, "I said, O Yahweh, you are my God; hear, O Yahweh, my plea for mercy." A similar situation obtains in Ps lxxiii 1, *'ak ṭōb l^eyiśrā'ēl '^elōhīm l^ebārē lēbāb,* where *l^eyiśrā'ēl* is often labeled the product of faulty word division and critics widely adopted the emendation first proposed by H. Graetz in the last century, *layyāšār 'ēl.* But the analysis of *l^e* in *l^eyiśrā'ēl* as *lamedh vocativum* produces this version, "Truly good, O Israel, is God to the pure of heart," a fine example of smoothly flowing enjambment. The fact that in Ugaritic the vocative *lamedh* is particularly frequent with personal names, enhances the likelihood that this is the particle preceding personified Israel.

Often enough, of two nouns in parallelism, one has a pronominal suffix and the other has none. Critics have generally supplied the lack, but the principle of double-duty suffix, employed by Canaanite poets for metrical or other reasons, shows that the inventiveness of textual critics has in this instance been misplaced. In brief, the textual critic is today obliged to familiarize himself with Northwest Semitic philology before venturing to set the biblical text to rights. Otherwise he may find himself writing in a vein similar to that of a well-known biblical scholar who confesses, "Indeed, this particular example serves the present writer a stern warning against hasty textual 'emendation'; for, when he began his researches into the Psalter along the lines indicated by 'The Role of the King in the Jerusalem Cultus,' he followed the usual practice of attempting to improve the reading, and only discovered later, as his work developed, that in so doing he was destroying a valuable piece of evidence and an important link in his argument."[8] A. E. Housman has written of Richard Bentley that "the best prize that Bentley missed, and the richest province left for his successors, is the correction of those verses of Manilius which he precipitately and despotically expelled." Quoted from *A. E. Housman: Selected Prose,* ed. John Carter (Cambridge University Press, 1961), p. 30.

The Masoretic Text

The reverence of the Masoretes for the consonantal text outstripped their knowledge of archaic Hebrew poetry: the result is that their vocalization, and even their word division, must sometimes be disregarded if one is to find the way back to the original sense. The *crux interpretum* in Ps xlv 5, *w^{e}'anwāh ṣedeq,* is a Masoretic creation; divide and point the same consonants in the light of Ps lxxxii 3, *'ānī wārāš haṣdīqū,* and the result is *w^{e}'ānāw haṣdēq,* "And defend the poor," an unimpeachable sequence to "Ride on in behalf of truth." The meaning of many substantives has been lost, with the inevitable consequence of false vocalization. A probable illustration presents itself in Ps ii 8, *mimmennī,* which is preferably

[8] Aubrey R. Johnson, *Sacral Kingship in Ancient Israel* (Cardiff, 1955), p. 81, n. 1.

pointed *m^emōnī,* "my wealth," while Ps xxxiii 7, *kannēd,* gives pellucid sense when pointed *kened,* "pitcher," a substantive known from Akkadian and Ugaritic. The resultant image is completely changed. Where KJ translates, "He gathereth the waters of the sea together as an heap," which evokes the imagery of Exod xv 8, "the floods stood upright as an heap" (KJ), we would read, "He gathers into a jar the waters of the sea."

The practice of using plural forms of names of dwellings, though with a singular meaning, seems to have escaped the Masoretes. In Ps xv 1, MT reads singular *b^e'oh^olekā,* but some manuscripts more correctly read the plural form *b^e'ōh^olekā.* The desire to avoid a graphic anthropomorphism may account for the dubious vocalization *r^eṣēh,* parallel to *ḥūšāh,* in Ps xl 14. Stylistic considerations favor the pointing *rūṣāh,* an energic imperative from *rūṣ,* "to run," the natural parallel to energic imperative *ḥūšāh,* from *ḥūš,* "to hasten."

An imperfect knowledge of archaic divine appellatives will explain the repeated confusion between *'ēl, 'ēlī,* "the Most High," and the prepositions *'al* and *'ālay,* respectively; cf. Pss vii 9, 11, xvi 6, lvii 3, lxviii 30, 35, cvi 7. From this imperfect knowledge stems the erroneous division of consonants in Ps lxxv 10, where MT reads grammatically incongruent *'aggīd l^e'ōlām* for *'^agaddēl 'ōlām,* "I shall extol the Eternal", parallel to "I shall sing to the God of Jacob." In other words, the real parallelism intended by the psalmist is between the God of Abraham, who in Gen xxi 33 is called *'ēl 'ōlām,* "El the Eternal," and the God of Jacob. The Masoretes missed the historical allusion. The LXX experienced difficulty with the consonantal division and read *'āgīl,* "I shall rejoice"; many modern versions have opted, ill-advisedly in my judgment, for the LXX emendation.

These observations should not, however, be construed as a warrant for setting the MT at nought whenever the text proves recalcitrant. In the temple and later in the synagogue, there must have been a strong tradition of prayer and singing which secured the pronunciation of the psalms even when the grammatical parsing of forms was not immediately evident. This living tradition was never interrupted for Judaism in its totality. In Ps xxxv 16, for example, the infinitive absolute *ḥārōq,* which fares badly at the hands of the critics (cf., e.g., Kraus, *Psalmen*), can handily be defended on the basis of the multiple functions of the infinitive absolute revealed in recent epigraphic discoveries. In view of the Ugaritic *plurale majestatis ilm,* predicated of the god *kṯr wḫss,* "Skillful and Cunning One," there is no need to alter the vocalization of Ps vii 7, *'ūrāh 'ēlay,* to singular *'ēlī*. The plural form is probably also found in Pss lxxvii 2–3 and cxxix 8. The frequent emendation of Ps iv 2, *hirḥabtā,* cannot be sustained; the form is precative perfect, which often substitutes for the imperative in the poetic books. Critics have found it necessary in scores of verses to change the pronominal suffix *-ī* to *-ō,* since the context desiderates the third person. If one admits, as now it seems one must, that Hebrew, like Phoenician, possessed a third-person singular suffix *-ī,*[9] one will see that the Masoretes, who probably did not understand the morpheme, nonetheless safeguarded the correct tradition. This explanation may sound much like "you name it, we have it," but the plain fact is that the Northwest Semitic morphological and lexical treasure-trove offers the biblical philologist choices unthinkable three decades ago.

The Ancient Versions

In the present study the ancient versions are cited infrequently, not because they have not been consulted, but because they have relatively little to offer toward a better understanding of the difficult texts. For such texts, the critic who seeks succor from the ancient translations will usually be disappointed. A significant corollary of Ugaritic studies will be the devaluation of the ancient versions. My consistent experience in studying Psalms (as well as Job and Proverbs) has been that Ugaritic embarrassingly exposes—at least in the poetic books—the shortcomings of the versions and seriously undermines their authority as witnesses to the original text. The *Bible de Jérusalem* can be taxed with a serious error in method when, in the poetic books in particular, it detours to the LXX whenever the Hebrew text throws up an obstacle. The numberless details of grammar which Phoenician and Ugaritic place at the disposal of the Hebraist allow him to ask anew: "How much grammar did the translators in antiquity understand? Were they familiar with the poetic vocabulary of the second millennium, the language often used by

[9] See above, p. xxi.

the biblical poets? How many mythological allusions did they seize?"

In response to the first query, Ps xlix 16 may serve as an object lesson: *'ak 'elōhīm yipdeh napšī miyyad še'ōl kī yiqqāḥēnī,* is rendered by the LXX, "But God will redeem my soul from the power of that mansion when it receives me," and by the Vulgate, "*Verumtamen Deus redimet animam meam de manu inferi, cum acceperit me*" ("But God will redeem my soul from the hand of hell, when he shall receive me"), while the *Psalterii Nova Recensio* of 1961 adopts the Vulgate reading except for the substitution of *acceperit* by *abstulerit.* Even the most casual reader will notice an imbalance that's uncharacteristic of biblical verse-structure. Four clear Ugaritic examples of an emphatic *kī,* which effects the post-position of the verb at the end of its colon, suggest the following translation and verse division: "But God will ransom me, from the hand of Sheol will he surely snatch me." The first colon thus ends with *napšī* and the second with *yiqqāḥēnī;* the rhyme was doubtless intended by the poet. In fact, none of the ancient versions grasped the nature of the construction in any of the passages where it is admittedly employed: Gen xviii 20; II Sam xxiii 5; Isa vii 9, x 13; Pss xlix 16, cxviii 10–12, cxxviii 2. They were equally strangers to the *waw emphaticum* in such texts as Pss iv 5, xi 6, xxv 11, xlix 11, lxxvii 2, etc.

Their knowledge of poetic vocabulary leaves much to be desired. The psalmists frequently used *'ereṣ,* "earth," in the poetic sense of "nether world," as in Akkadian and Ugaritic, but this nuance was lost on the ancient translators. Ps lxxv abounds in divine appellatives, but this could never be gathered from a perusal of the versions. Titles such as *'ōlām,* "the Eternal," *lē',* "the Victor," *mārōm,* "the Exalted One," *hammēbīn,* "the Observer," were simply not reproduced in antiquity and now must slowly be recovered with the aid of Northwest Semitic texts.

A poetic practice, notably clarified by recent discoveries, is the use of plural forms of nouns signifying "home, habitation," which, however, are to be translated as singular. Thus the ancient versions render *miškānōt* as plural in Pss xliii 3, lxxxiv 2 and cxxxii 5, 7, where the singular would appear more correct.

Many of the biblical images and metaphors do not come through in the ancient versions. A probable instance is the famous crux in Ps viii 3, *yāsadtā 'ōz, lemā'ōn* (MT *lema'an*), "You built a fortress for your habitation," where *'ōz* is a poetic name for "heaven," precisely as in Ps lxxviii 26, *yassa' qādīm baššāmāyim wayᵉnahēg bᵉ'uzzō tēmān,* poorly reflected in LXX, "He removed the southeast wind out of heaven, and by his power brought on the southwest wind." This rendition can scarcely be correct since it fails to preserve the synonymous parallelism which characterizes the preceding and following verses. The more plausible reading would be, "He let loose the east wind from heaven, and led forth the south wind from his stronghold."

The ancient versions do, however, make a positive contribution to textual criticism in their flexible attitude toward prepositions, an attitude which modern translators might well adopt. They often translated according to the needs of context, rendering *bᵉ* "from" when the context required this meaning. Contrast the translation of Deut i 44, *bᵉśē'īr 'ad ḥormāh,* "from Seir to Hormah," as rendered by LXX, Vulgate, and Syriac, with the less felicitous efforts of CCD and RSV (CCD: "in Seir as far as Horma"; RSV: "in Seir as far as Hormah"). Notice their handling of *baššāmāyim* in Ps lxxviii 26, cited above. This sense has amply been confirmed by Ugaritic where *b* and *l* denote precisely this in many cases; in Canaanite poetry *min* was unknown and its function was filled by *b* and *l*. The introduction of *min* into biblical Hebrew did not completely deprive *b* and *l* of their older function. Here the testimony of the LXX, Vulgate, and Syriac can be extremely valuable. But the overall judgment that the ancient versions invite in view of the new testimony is that they are not always reliable witnesses to what the biblical poets intended.

Comparative Literatures

Just as Canaanite literary documents of the second millennium cast some doubt on the authority of the ancient versions, so do they also reduce the immediate relevance of Egyptian and Mesopotamian literatures for the direct elucidation of biblical poetry. While the literatures of Egypt and Babylonia will continue to retain their value *ad complementum doctrinae,* they must, in the area of comparative studies, yield pride of place to the clay tablets of Ras Shamra. James A. Montgomery has written,[10] "The Assyro-Baby-

[10] In his review of J. H. Patton, *Canaanite Parallels in the Book of Psalms* (abbr. CPBP) (John Hopkins Press, 1944), in JBL 63 (1944), 418 f.

lonian and Egyptian literatures have for long been easily accessible to all students. But here is a literature far more closely related, geographically, linguistically, and culturally, to the Hebrew Scriptures, and even its gross polytheistic contents present a thesaurus of theological terminology which became the traditional inheritance of the thought and language of Israel's unique religion. . . . Canaan, i.e. Palestine-Syria, now no longer appears as a land backward in culture and literature, but is revealed as making its contributions to high literature in poetry and drama, during the age before Moses."

On the level of lexicography, a reassessment of the conclusions set forth in Heinrich Zimmern's *Akkadische Fremdwörter als Beweis für babylonischen Kultureinfluss*, 2d ed. (Leipzig, 1917), on the basis of the available Canaanite glossary (more than twenty-seven hundred roots are listed in the Glossary of C. H. Gordon's UT) would produce some highly interesting results which might serve as a gauge for measuring the other relationships between Babylonian and Hebrew cultures. How many Hebrew words described as *Akkadische Lehnwörter* in the authoritative *Handwörterbuch* of Gesenius-Buhl (abbr. GB), 17th ed. (Leipzig, 1921), retain their authenticity today?[11] Textual studies which try to explain difficult texts in the Bible on the basis of Akkadian words must now show, to be genuinely convincing, that the Akkadian word is also reported in non-biblical West Semitic texts. For example, the correspondence of Ps xxxiii 7, *kened* (MT *kannēd*), "pitcher," to Akk. *kandu*, "jug, pitcher," takes on new suasive force with the knowledge that *knd* was current in the economic texts of Ras Shamra. In passing it may be noted that Zimmern[12] identified Akk. *kandu* with Heb. *kad*, but the fact that Ugaritic distinguished between *kd* and *knd* indicates that the same distinction must be maintained in Hebrew. As S. Kirst has observed[13] in connection with his discussion of *t*ᵉ*hōm* in Hebrew, Ugar. *thmt*, "It is no longer strictly necessary to maintain that the Hebrew word is directly borrowed from Akkadian, even though in Akkadian the primordial flood Tiamat imaginatively stood for the female element of chaos"

[11] No less interesting would be a restudy of the data in E. Kautzsch, *Die Aramäismen im Alten Testament* (Halle, 1902) in light of the Northwest Semitic thesaurus that is available today.

[12] *Akkadische Fremdwörter als Beweis für babylonischen Kultureinfluss*, p. 33.

[13] In FuF 32 (1958), 218.

(*"Damit ist eine direkte Entlehnung des Wortes aus dem akkadischen Sprachbereich fürs Hebräische keine zwingende Notwendigkeit mehr, obwohl auch dort die Tiāmat als die Urflut das weibliche Chaoselement versinnbildlicht"*). How important for the correct interpretation of a text is the just appreciation of the relationships that might be found among the different Semitic languages is illustrated by C. Virolleaud's treatment of the unusual form *lšnm* encountered in the Ugaritic tablets published in 1957.[14] Virolleaud's reasoning goes like this: the Hebrew plural of *lāšōn,* "tongue," is feminine *l^e^šānōt,* while Akkadian preserves two plural forms, feminine *lišanāti* and masculine *lišānū;* accordingly, Ugaritic *lšnm* must be a masculine plural form. His own oft-stated conviction that Ugaritic is a Canaanite dialect closely related to Hebrew should have cautioned him against using Akkadian morphology to account for a newly attested West Semitic form. Hence W. F. Albright,[15] followed by Otto Eissfeldt,[16] had no difficulty in refuting Virolleaud's analysis by showing that *lšnm,* parallel to dual *ḏnbtm,* "two tails," was a dual form, like Ugaritic *ydm* or *kpm,* denoting a "double or forked tongue"; cf. Ps lv 10.

Hermann Gunkel's identification of numerous mythological motifs in OT poetry is a major contribution to biblical theology. But even this contribution must be reassessed in the light of the Ugaritic texts. While Gunkel seeks to make the biblical poets directly dependent upon Mesopotamian mythology,[17] the Ugaritic myths and legends show that the biblical exegete need not go so far afield to locate the source of Hebrew mythopoeic thought and expression.[18] Or again, while one cannot quarrel with H. Wheeler Robinson's statement that "The *ultimate* (my italics) origin of the conception of Yahweh's council is doubtless to be found in Babylonia; we hear of the deliberations of the gods in the story of creation,"[19] the existence of such Ugaritic phrases as *'dt ilm,* "the assembly of the gods," which scholars recognize as the equivalent of Ps lxxxii 1, *'^a^dat 'ēl,* shows that in the search for the immediate origin of mythological motifs in the Bible a new orientation is needed.

[14] *Palais royal d'Ugarit,* II (Paris, 1957), p. 12.

[15] In BASOR 150 (1958), 36, n. 5.

[16] In JSS 5 (1960), 34.

[17] See his *Schöpfung und Chaos in Urzeit und Endzeit* (Göttingen, 1895), pp. 106 ff.

[18] Cf. the sound observations of Kraus, *Psalmen,* II, p. 649.

[19] See his article, "The Council of Yahweh," in JTS 45 (1944), 152, n. 1.

The origin of the theological wordplays registered in such passages as Pss xlvii 3, 6, xcvii 7—often credited to the influence of the Akkadian epics in which this practice is a recognized feature (the puns on many of Marduk's fifty names suggest themselves)—can be more fruitfully sought among the Canaanites, who are known to have indulged in such paronomasia: for example, UT, 77:17–18, *tn nkl yrḫ ytrḫ*, "Give Nikkal that the Moon-god might marry."

THE DATING OF THE PSALMS

The work of Sigmund Mowinckel in stressing the cultic background of most of the psalms makes it impossible today to write a commentary along the lines of Moses Buttenwieser's, *The Psalms Chronologically Treated with a New Translation* (abbr. PCTNT) (see Selected Bibliography). Buttenwieser sought to arrange the psalms in chronological order, using several criteria, principally the purported historical allusions and the literary dependence of the psalmists upon historically datable writings, especially the prophets. By showing that many of the supposed historical phrases are cultic expressions whose origins cannot be dated with any meaningful precision, Mowinckel has seriously undermined Buttenwieser's primary presupposition. The Ugaritic texts now conspire to drain the method of literary dependence of much of its plausibility by introducing the possibility that both the psalmist and, say, the prophet were indebted to a literary tradition long resident in Canaan. For instance, Buttenwieser, on the basis of their literary resemblances to Isa lxiii 1–6, would date Psalms ii and cx to the post-Exilic period, while at the 1964 annual meeting of the Catholic Biblical Association of America one speaker proposed that Psalm cx is a product of the period of the Chronicler or Qoheleth (400–200 B.C.). An examination of the vocabulary of these psalms reveals that virtually every word, image, and parallelism are now reported in Bronze-Age Canaanite texts; the present writer would tentatively date Pss ii and cx to the tenth century B.C. If they are poems composed shortly prior to the LXX, why is it that the Alexandrian Jewish translators understood them so imperfectly? Roughly contemporary works should fare better than they did in translation.

Pursuing the method of literary affiliation, Pierre Bonnard, *Le Psautier selon Jérémie* (Paris, 1960), p. 39, concludes that the psalms containing the phrase *bōḥēn libbōt ūkᵉlāyōt,* "he who tests minds and hearts," are dependent upon Jeremiah, where the phrase appears characteristic. But the occurrence of part of the phrase, *klyth wlbh,* in a Ugaritic text of incantatory type strongly suggests that both psalmist and prophet drew from a common source. The appearance of part of the clause in an incantatory text hints that the entire expression *bōḥēn libbōt ūkᵉlāyōt* may have been used in incantations; the discovery of inscribed liver models during a recent campaign at Ras Shamra may resolve the problem. One may proceed further and submit that Ps vii, where the phrase in question occurs, appears to be linguistically too archaic and too difficult to have been composed in the Exilic or post-Exilic period, that is, after Jeremiah.

The tendency in recent years to assign earlier rather than later dates to the composition of the psalms comports with the evidence of the Ras Shamra texts. These show that much of the phraseology in the Psalter was current in Palestine long before the writing prophets, so the criterion of literary dependence becomes much too delicate to be serviceable. On the other hand, the inadequate knowledge of biblical poetic idiom and, more importantly, of biblical images and metaphors displayed by the third-century B.C. translators of the LXX, bespeaks a long chronological gap between the original composition of the psalms and their translation into Greek. Even the admittedly later poems in the Psalter are considerably older than the Hodayot (hymns of praise) from Qumran, which freely borrowed the phraseology, the imagery, and the central ideas of the Book of Psalms. These considerations thus point to a pre-Exilic date for most of the psalms, and not a few of them (e.g., Pss ii, xvi, xviii, xxix, lx, lxviii, lxxxii, cviii, cx) may well have been composed in the Davidic period.

The Structure of the Psalter

The psalms can be grouped in various ways, according to different points of view. One classification, somewhat extrinsic and artificial, divides the one hundred and fifty Psalms into five books, a division generally held to be a conscious imitation of the fivefold partition of the Pentateuch. A Midrash from the Talmudic period on Psalm 1 states that "as Moses gave five books of laws to Israel, so David gave five Books of Psalms to Israel, the Book of Psalms entitled *Blessed is the man* (Ps i 1), the Book entitled *For the leader: Maschil* (Ps xlii 1), the Book, *A Psalm of Asaph* (Ps lxxiii 1), the Book, *A prayer of Moses* (Ps xc 1), and the Book, *Let the redeemed of the Lord say* (Ps cvii 2)." (Cf. William G. Braude, *The Midrash on Psalms* [New Haven, 1959], I, p. 5.) Each of the five books ends with a doxology or benediction, and though these doxologies are found in the Greek translation of the second century B.C., this is not explicit evidence that the translators considered these benedictions as closing out individual Books of the Psalter. Perhaps the oldest explicit testimony to the fivefold partition of the Psalter occurs in a poorly preserved liturgical fragment 1 Qumran 30 dating to the turn of the Christian era. (Cf. D. Barthélemy and J. T. Milik, *Qumran Cave I* [*Discoveries in the Judaean Desert,* I; Oxford, 1955], p. 133, and Anton Arens, *Die Psalmen im Gottesdienst des Alten Bundes* [Trier, 1961], p. 107.)

Though the contents of Book I (Pss i–xli) are extremely varied, nearly all the psalms are bound together by two characteristics: the use of the divine name "Yahweh" and the occurrence of the expression "of David" in their superscriptions. The exceptions are i, ii, and xxxiii, which are not ascribed to David. The lack of superscription in Ps xxxiii does not make this psalm a later addition to Book I, as often maintained. The consideration that Ps xxxii 11 closes with the two vocatives *ṣaddīqīm* and *yišrē lēb* in parallelism, while the next verse (Ps xxxiii 1) likewise pairs the two vocatives *ṣaddīqīm* and *layᵉšārīm* (with vocative *lamedh*), indicates that Ps xxxiii is not a later addition and at the same time explains its lack of superscription.

The second collection (xlii–lxxii) prefers the designation "Elohim" for God. This is particularly noteworthy in liii and lxx which are in other respects identical with xiv and xl 13–17. Six of the psalms in Book II are connected with the "sons of Korah" (xliv–xlix), eighteen with David (li–lxv, lxviii–lxxi), while l is labeled an "Asaph" Psalm in lxxii introduced by *lšlmh,* "of Solomon."

Book III (lxxiii–lxxxix) is mainly Elohistic. It numbers the Asaph psalms (lxxiii–lxxxiii), four Korah psalms (lxxxiv–lxxxv, lxxxvii–lxxxviii), a hymn of Ethan (lxxxix), and one David psalm (lxxxvi).

In Books IV–V (xc–cl) the outlines of the earlier groupings are not so easily discerned. Psalms xciii–xcix are hymns celebrating Yahweh's kingship, c is a hymn of classic simplicity, cv, cvi, cxi–cxvii, cxxxv, cxlvi–cl are "Hallelujah Psalms." cxx–cxxxiv are "Songs of Ascent" or "Pilgrim Psalms," while ci, ciii, cviii–cx, cxxii, cxxiv, cxxxi, cxxxiii, cxxxviii–cxlv are designed "of David."

The timeless nature of many of the psalms makes it impossible for us now to trace the history of these collections or the process by which they were combined. Though direct evidence enabling us to date the completion of the entire collection is lacking, the vast difference in language and prosody between the canonical Psalter and the Qumran Hodayot makes it impossible to accept a Maccabean date for any of the Psalms, a position still maintained by a number of critics. Nor is a Hellenistic date more plausible. The fact that the LXX translators were at a loss before so many archaic words and phrases bespeaks a considerable chronological gap between them and the original psalmists. The earlier the composition date of the Psalms, the greater the likelihood that the grouping into five Books was early rather than late.

Literary Genus

No psalms, strickly speaking, have been identified among the Ras Shamra texts hitherto published, but the frequent citations of Canaanite hymns in the El Amarna Letters[20] evince the popularity of hymnal literature in Late Bronze Age Palestine-Syria (1500–1200 B.C.). On occasion one does encounter in the Ugaritic myths a strophe which may have formed part of a longer hymn. The main contribution, however, to the vexed questions of literary genus and *Sitz im Leben* that the Ras Shamra texts have to make is indirect. By rendering possible a more precise translation of what may turn out to be a crucial term or phrase for literary classification, they not infrequently bear on an accurate translation of Psalms. From the indirect light they shed on the specific sense of *ṭōb,* it may be concluded that Pss iv, lxv 10–14, lxvii, and lxxxv are prayers for rain, while the drastically revised translation of Ps xvi, supported by Ugaritic linguistic data, shows it to be the work of a Canaanite convert to Yahwism, expressing his profession of faith in Yahweh and his abjuration of the false gods he once served. What appears to be an

[20] Cf. A. Jirku, JBL 52 (1933), 108 ff. (see Selected Bibliography).

improved rendition of Ps xvii 2–5 confirms the widely held view that this is a psalm of innocence, while the elucidation of a pivotal phrase in Pss v 6, xxvi 9, and cxxxix 22 corroborates the opinion that these also are psalms of innocence.

Poetic Principles

The dominating principle of both Ugaritic and biblical poetry is the same, namely, that of balance or symmetry, the famous *parallelismus membrorum.* The Ugaritic texts are mainly in the 3+3 pattern, as would be expected in epic poetry; the 2+2 sequence is also common and there are numerous instances of mixed patterns, of 3+3 and 2+2.

The fixed pairs of synonyms or related words appearing in parallelism that characterize Ugaritic poetry also typify biblical poetry; U. Cassuto and Moshe Held[21] have collected about a hundred such pairs. This poetic practice points up the close kinship between Ugaritic and Hebrew and the consequent relevance of Ugaritic for the clarification of an obscure biblical text and vice versa. As Gordon writes,[22] "Nowhere does the proximity of Heb. and Ugar. manifest itself more plainly than in the pairs of synonyms used parallelistically in both languages." Thus the Ugaritic fixed pairs *lb-kbd,* "heart-liver," and *šmḫ-gīl,* "rejoice-exult," make it highly probable that Ps xvi 9 should read, *śāmaḥ libbī wayyāgel k*ᵉ*bēdī* (MT *k*ᵉ*bōdī*), "And so my heart rejoices, and my liver leaps with joy," instead of "Therefore my heart is glad, and my glory rejoiceth" (KJ).

The Ugaritic practice of pairing a concrete noun with one that is abstract (but both to be understood and translated concretely) forecloses emendation in a score of texts that scholars had considered lacking the proper balance. The Canaanite pairs *ib-ṣrt,* "foe-adversary," *ḫbr-dʿt,* "colleague-friend," *šbʿ-trš,* "wheat-wine" show that Ps xii 2, *ʾ*ᵉ*mūnīm,* which is abstract, assumes a concrete meaning by reason of its balance with *ḥāsīd,* "devoted one," and accordingly should be rendered "faithful ones"; Ps xxxvi 12, *yad r*ᵉ*šāʿīm,* "the

[21] M. D. Cassuto, *The Goddess Anath* (in Hebrew) (Jerusalem, 1951), pp. 24–28; Moshe Held in an unpublished doctoral dissertation on file in the Johns Hopkins University Library. Cf. Stanley Gevirtz, "The Ugaritic Parallel to Jeremiah 8:23," JNES 20 (1961), 41–46.

[22] UT, p. 145.

hand of the wicked," discloses the true force of *regel ga'ᵃwāh* as "the foot of the arrogant," not "the foot of arrogance."

For the sake of meter, rhyme, assonance, or some other quality, Canaanite poets enjoyed the license of making one pronominal suffix do duty for a brace of nouns in parallelism. Thus they could write, *spsg ysk lriš ḥrṣ lẓr qdqdy,* "Glaze will be poured upon my head, plaster upon my skull" (UT, 2 Aqht:VI:36–37), or they pair *ṯlḥny,* "my table," with *ks,* "my cup," and *mlk,* "my kingship," with *drkty,* "my dominion." Biblical poets widely availed themselves of this privilege so that several scores of nouns that have been gratuitously furnished with suffixes by the critics are now seen to stand in no such need. As P. Joüon has sagely remarked, *"Les métriciens semblent généralement oublier que les anomalies de syntaxe et de morphologie pourraient être d'un grand secours dans l'établissement de leurs hypothèses. Dans toute poésie, la contrainte métrique oblige à des déviations de l'usage prosaïque, qui peuvent être révélatrices du mètre."*[23] Examples of the double-duty suffix occur *passim* throughout the Psalter; for example, Ps xxxiv 7, *šāmēᵃ',* "he heard him," parallels *hōšī'ō,* "he saved him," while in vs. 18 *šāmēᵃ',* "he hears them," balances *hiṣṣīlām,* "he rescues them."

The employment of double-duty interrogatives, illustrated by the question, *mnm ib yp' lb'l ṣrt lrkb 'rpt,* "What foe has risen up against Baal, what adversary [note *ib* balanced by abstract *ṣrt*] against the Mounter of the Clouds?" (UT, 'nt:IV:48–49) suggests that in Ps iii 2, *māh rabbū ṣāray,* "How many are my adversaries?", the force of *māh* carries over into the following two cola and should appear in translation. Summarily, the double-duty negatives, vocatives, prepositions, etc., used by the Canaanite poets, are valuable criteria which the biblical metrician can follow with greater assurance, thanks to the Ras Shamra texts.

Without invoking the testimony of the tablets, E. Z. Melamed[24] has demonstrated the value for exegesis of a knowledge of the poetic technique which he calls the "break-up of stereotype phrases." The biblical poets habitually separate compound linguistic stereotypes into their components, placing one in the first half of the verse and the other in the second, with the result that both halves become more tightly interlocked. Compound divine names such as

[23] *Grammaire de l'Hébreu Biblique* (abbr. GHB), 2d ed. (Rome, 1947), pp. 449–50, n. 2.

[24] In *Studies in the Bible,* ed. Chaim Rabin (Scripta Hierosolymitana, VIII; Jerusalem, 1961), pp. 115–53.

yahweh ʿelyōn, "Yahweh Most High," readily lend themselves to this practice, as for example in Ps xxi 8, "For the king trusts in Yahweh, and from the love of the Most High (*ʿelyōn*) he will never swerve." The same usage can be noticed in UT, 2 Aqht:v:10–11, *hlk kṯr ky'n wy'n tdrq ḫss*, "The gait of the Skillful One indeed he sees, and he sees the tread of Sir Cunning." Here the composite divine name *kṯr wḫss*, "the Skillful and Cunning One," is separated into its components that are placed in different halves of the verse. This principle produces some arresting results when applied to such passages as Ps xiii 6, "Then shall I sing to Yahweh since the Most High (*ʿēlī*, MT *ʿālāy*) is a benefactor," and Ps xxxii 5, "I shall confess, O Most High, my transgressions, O Yahweh." A neat instance of enjambment emerges from reading *ʿēlī* for MT *ʿālāy* and from parsing the *lamedh* of *leyahweh* as *vocativum*. What is more, it eliminates the construction *ʾōdeh ʿālāy* that is elsewhere unwitnessed.

Biblical Theology

To forestall possible misunderstanding, we might recall that the adaptation of mythological motifs by prophets and psalmists does not diminish the significance or the originality of prophecy and psalmody. Leviathan, Tehom, Mot, Resheph, and other figures of pagan religion were not for the biblical poets religious verities as they were for the Babylonians and Canaanites, but merely mythological references to set off, as the case may be, the omnipotence and majesty of Yahweh.[25]

[25] The relationship between the biblical writers and the Canaanite poets from whom they borrowed is analogous to that existing between Christian Rome and Pagan Rome. On this latter point one cannot do better than cite, at some length, G. K. Chesterton, *The Resurrection of Rome* (New York, 1930), pp. 125 f.: "Christian Rome boasts of being built on Pagan Rome, of surmounting and transcending, but also of preserving it. From the thousand carven throats of the city, from the hollow wreathing horns of the Tritons, from the golden mouths of the trumpets, from the jaws of flamboyant lions and the lips of rhetorical attitudinizing statues, from everything that can be imagined to speak or testify, there is as it were one solid silent roar of exaltation and victory: 'We have saved Old Rome; we have resurrected Old Rome; we have resurrected Pagan Rome, so that it is more Roman for not being Pagan.' There is no question of hiding the connection between the two epochs; the new epoch emphasizes every point at which it touchs the old. Nearly every Christian Church is carefully built on the site of a Pagan temple. In one place it distinguishes a particular church by combining the name of Maria with that of Minerva."

Perhaps the most significant contribution to biblical theology that flows from the translations based on the new philological principles concerns the subject of resurrection and immortality. If the translations and exegesis propounded for such passages as Pss i 3–6, v 9, xi 7, xvi 10–11, xvii 15, xxi 7, xxvii 13, xxxvi 9–10, xxxvii 37–38, xli 13, lvi 14, lxxiii 23–24, bear up under criticism, then the treatment of these topics in standard biblical theologies will need drastic revision. The mythological motif of the Elysian Fields[26] that stands forth from the translations offered in Pss v 9, xxxvi 9–10, lvi 14, xcvii 11, cxvi 9 and Isa xxvi 11, is the clearest example of a theological verity finding expression in the idiom of mythological poetry; the opinion of Sigmund Mowinckel[27] that "neither Israel nor early Judaism knew of a faith in any resurrection nor is such a faith represented in the psalms" will not survive serious scrutiny.

The identification of the "Foe" in several of the psalms as Mot or Death (vii 6, xiii 3, xviii 4, xxvii 12, xxxi 9, xli 3, lxi 4), and the elucidation of some terms as poetic names for the nether world (xli 3, lvi 4, lxi 3, etc.) reveal a preoccupation with death only less acute than that of the author of Job, where some fourteen new names for Sheol or the nether world have been detected; these findings are as yet unpublished.

The large number of divine appellatives employed by the psalmists offers material for a separate study. The Canaanite appellative *aliyn b'l,* "Baal the Victor," from the root *liy,* "to prevail," is reflected in biblical *lē',* a stative participle from this root, which is Yahweh's title in Pss xxii 30, xxvii 13, lxxv 7, lxxxv 7, c 3. Ugaritic *'ly,* another title of Baal, which has been identified in Pss vii 9, xvi 6, xxxii 5, lvii 3, cvi 7, is now documented in the by-form *'l* in the Ugaritic personal name *yrm'l,* in which the theophoric element is *'l,* "Most High," as comparison with *yrmb'l* clearly indicates. Biblical poets used the same appellative of Yahweh in Pss vii 11, xviii 42, lxii 8 (long recognized by H. S. Nyberg), lxviii 30, 35, cxxxix 14, cxli 3 and II Sam xxiii 1 (also long admitted). Since these ephithets

[26] The term "Elysian Fields" may seem out of place in a Semitic context, but the images which such a phrase elicits are sufficiently close to Semitic ideas of the future life to justify its use in a work on Psalms. Recent studies, moreover, show that the common bonds between Greek and Semitic cultures were more numerous and deep-seated than earlier generations of scholars had suspected.

[27] *The Psalms in Israel's Worship,* I, p. 240.

can easily be confused with the prepositions *ʿal* and *ʿ*^{a}*lē,* it is very likely that numerous other examples will come up. A semantically related title is *mārōm,* "the Exalted One" (Pss vii 8, x 5, lvi 3, lxxv 6, xcii 9; Isa xxxviii 14; Jer xxxi 12), which apparently followed the same line of conceptual development as *ṣūr,* "mountain," but also serving as a divine title, and Ugar. *ṣpn,* the name of the sacred mountain of the storm-god, *bʿl ṣpn,* but which later became an epithet of the god himself. In Ps x 12, the original full title of Yahweh, *yhwh ʾēl,* often altered by the critics, is now confirmed by the recognition of the same full title in Ps xxxi 6, where faulty stichic division obscured its presence, and in Ps xviii 3, where the compound name is separated into its components in the parallel half verses. Surprisingly unremarked by commentators is the title *ṣaddīq,* "the Just One," in Pss xi 3 and lxxv 11, and in the composite forms *ʾ*^{e}*lōhīm ṣaddīq* ("God, the Just One") in Pss vii 10 and xiv 5, and *yhwh ṣaddīq* ("Yahweh, the Just One") in Pss xi 5, cxxix 4. There is further the archaic appellation *ṣaddīq ʿattīq* (MT *ʿātāq*), "the Ancient Just One," in Ps xxxi 19, which recalls the "Ancient of Days" in Dan vii 9, 13, 22. Though they preserved the correct vocalization, the Masoretes probably did not recognize the divine appellative *ʿōlām,* "the Eternal," in such passages as Pss xxiv 7, 9, lii 11, lxvi 7, lxxiii 12, lxxv 10, lxxxix 3. The homographs *māgēn,* "shield," and *māgān,* "suzerain, sovereign" (vocalization based on the Punic name for "emperor," *māgōn*) have been fused and subsumed under *māgēn,* "shield," but in Pss vii 11, xviii 31, xlvii 10, lix 12, lxxxiv 10, 12, the vocalization *māgān,* from the verb *māgan,* "to bestow," is distinctly preferable.

Recent progress in the study of covenant terminology helps the exegete to identify some passing allusions to this idiom in Pss vii 5, xviii 2, xxi 8, xxv 3, xli 10 and lxxviii 56–57.

Hebrew Grammar

The Hebraist can today bring to bear linguistic information on intractable texts that was not available before the Ras Shamra finds. Though some of these data were known from Akkadian and Arabic, their direct application to the biblical text often left the scholar uneasy unless documented in West Semitic sources. The Ugaritic tablets admirably fill that lacuna. With the grammatical information they contain the philologist can bring to difficult passages grammatically impeccable analyses; though much has been achieved in this regard, much more remains to be accomplished, especially in the Psalter. The present study, in attempting to resolve some problems, will raise many others.

I shall touch upon the more important grammatical phenomena which require further formal investigation:

The significance of defective orthography for textual criticism has been spotlighted by the studies of F. M. Cross, Jr., and D. N. Freedman. The defective spelling in Ps xvi of *'mrt,* "I said," in vs. 2 and of *mnt,* "you have portioned out," in vs. 5, corroborates the conclusion, based on the contents, that this psalm was composed by a Phoenician convert to Yahwism employing his native *scriptio defectiva.*

Contracted Northern dual forms, as in Ugaritic-Phoenician, make their appearance in about a dozen biblical texts, among them Ps xvi 4, *middēm* (MT *middām*), "from my hands," parallel to dual *śᵉpātāy,* "my lips." This pairing further illustrates the principle of the double-duty suffix cited above. In Ps xvii 4, *'ādēm* (MT *'ādām*), "your hands," balances *śᵉpātekā,* "your lips." Thus the presence of contracted forms bears out the correctness of Ps lxviii 26, *tōk,* which textual critics generally emend to *tāwek; tōk* is the normal absolute form in Ugaritic-Phoenician, since all diphthongs were contracted.

The Canaanite *qatala* form of the third-person singular masculine is still in evidence in Pss iv 7, xvi 6, xviii 35, xx 10, lxxxix 8; Prov ix 4; Eccles vii 27, and doubtless will be identified in other passages.

The fact that the LXX and Vulgate in numerous passages (e.g., Pss x 11, xxii 25, xxvii 10, xliv 25, lxxxix 47, cii 3) translated *histīr* as though it derived from *sūr,* "to turn aside," permits the inference that the infixed *-t-* conjugation, so vigorous in Ugaritic and sporadically attested in Phoenician and Moabite, was much more frequent in biblical Hebrew than the standard grammars allow.[28]

The frequency of the energic mode in Ugaritic proves to be an unerring indicator concerning the frequency of the form in Hebrew. Such anomalous readings as Ps xx 4, *yᵉdaššᵉneh,* yield to coherent

[28] The traditional view finds expression in Giovanni Garbini, *Il Semitico di Nord-Ovest* (Napoli, 1960), p. 130; contrast my view in *Orientalia* 32 (1963), 498. A monograph study of this question is badly needed, especially since the traditional and erroneous view is repeated in the very recent *An Introduction to the Comparative Grammar of the Semitic Languages, Phonology and Morphology,* ed. Sabatino Moscati (Wiesbaden, 1964), § 16.18, p. 127.

parsing when pointed *yᵉdaššannāh,* "may he consider generous," an energic form, and perhaps the famous crux in Ps viii 2, *'ᵃšer tᵉnāh,* becomes intelligible when the two words are joined and parsed as energic *'ᵃšarᵉtannāh,* "I shall serve," from *šārat.*

The treatment of the precative or optative perfect was much more satisfactory in the nineteenth-century grammars of Ewald and Böttcher than in more recent treatises. Israel Eitan and Moses Buttenwieser in this century followed the teaching of Ewald and Böttcher concerning the precative perfect, but their efforts have gone unrecognized by later translators. In fact, Buttenwieser devoted an *Excursus* to this topic in his 1938 commentary on the psalms (PCTNT), citing more than a score of convincing examples. That the doctrine propounded there has made little headway may be gauged by the translation of Ps iv 2 proffered by *La Bible de la Pléiade* (1959), *"Quand je crie, réponds-moi, Dieu de ma justice, dans la détresse tu m'as mis au large, aie pitié de moi, écoute ma prière."*[29] Similarly, RSV (1952), "Answer me when I call, O God of my right! Thou hast given me room when I was in distress. Be gracious to me, and hear my prayer." The preterite statement, "Thou hast given me room," lodged between the two imperatives, creates a logical difficulty which is dissolved by the analysis of *hirḥabtā* as a precative perfect, as proposed by Eitan and Buttenwieser. The Ugaritic attestation of this usage confirms their analysis based upon Arabic and Aramaic analogues. A wider recognition of this stylistic variation will change the complexion of many passages and may bear on the literary classification of a psalm.

The much-canvassed question of verbal tenses is affected by Ugaritic usage of the *yqtl* form as the normal expression of past action. This practice is most evident in Hebrew poetry where *yiqtōl* often is paired with *qatal,* with both expressing past actions; for example, Pss viii 7, xxxviii 12. But there are instances where *yiqtōl* occurs in both parts of the verse and expresses past time. The need for detecting this usage is particularly crucial when the determination of the literary genus is on the agenda; cf. Ps xx 7–10.

The frequent interposition of an enclitic *mem* between the *nomen regens* and the genitive in a construct chain that is witnessed in the Ugaritic texts and, as noted by many scholars, in biblical Hebrew makes inroads into the traditional view of the construct chain as ad-

[29] *La Bible de la Pléiade,* ed. É. Dhorme (Paris, 1959), II, p. 895.

mitting of no intervening particles. One can no longer subscribe to the teaching expressed by Buttenwieser,[30] "It should be emphasized that there neither is nor can be any exception to the rule that the genitive cannot be separated from the *nomen regens* by a pronominal suffix." To be sure, no clear case of such has turned up in Ugaritic, but the fact that an enclitic *mem* could and often did interpose in a construct chain is suasive proof that many instances like Ps lxxi 7, *maḥ^{a}sī 'ōz,* "my refuge of strength," which Buttenwieser emends away, are marked by an intervening pronominal suffix. This observation opens up some interesting possibilities in Pss xvii 9, xviii 18, xxxv 16, 19, xxxviii 20, xlviii 15, lxviii 34, lxxiv 12, cx 4.

A subject calling for special study is the biblical use of the vocative *lamedh,* amply witnessed in Ugaritic literature. Clearly to differentiate between the preposition *l^{e}* and the *lamedh vocativum* is not a light task, but sense and parallelism can provide sure guidance. Three examples to illustrate: Ps lxviii 33, *maml^{e}kōt hā'āreṣ šīrū lē'lōhīm zamm^{e}rū '^{a}dōnay,* "O kings of the earth, sing! O gods, hymn the Lord!" Ps xcii 2, *ṭōb l^{e}hōdōt l^{e}yahweh ūl^{e}zammēr l^{e}šim^{e}kā 'elyōn,* "It is good to give thanks, O Yahweh, and to hymn your name, O Most High." Ps cxl 7, *'āmartī l^{e}yahweh 'ēlī 'attāh ha'^{a}zīnāh yahweh qōl taḥ^{a}nūnay,* "I said, O Yahweh, you are my God; hear, O Yahweh, my plea for mercy." In all three verses sense, parallelism and meter are well served by this analysis of *lamedh,* while the emendations of *'^{a}dōnay* to *la'^{a}dōnay* in Ps lxviii 33 and the deletion of *yahweh* in the second colon of Ps cxl 7, as proposed by many, become expendable.

The new insights into the nature and function of prepositions afforded by Canaanite usage greatly facilitate the task of the translator. Familiarity with the usage permits the Hebraist to treat prepositions as words expressing relationships whose more specific sense must be determined by the verb they serve. As C. H. Gordon has correctly judged, "The most interesting feature of Ugar. prepositions is the meaning 'from' for both *b* and *l.*"[31] The judgment is not hazardous that the most palpable improvement and refinement of existing translations of the Bible will proceed *pari passu* with progress made in grasping the precise nuance of Hebrew prepositions.

[30] PCTNT, p. 597, n. 199.
[31] UT, § 10.1, p. 92.

What possibilities can ensue from such progress may be exemplified by the proposal to render Ps xviii 20, *wayyōṣī'ēnī lammerḥāb,* "And he brought me out of the broad domain." Further inquiry reveals that in Pss xxxi 9 and cxviii 5, *merḥāb* is likewise a poetic name for the nether regions; a new motif has probably been uncovered.

Lexicography

The lexical bearing of Northwest Semitic texts on the Psalter does not readily lend itself to summary statement, but several general observations may be apposite. By apprising himself of the lexical tendencies and preferences at work in the Canaanite dialects, the Hebraist will be better prepared to judge what remedies can be applied to an unruly text. The frequent Canaanite coining of denominative verbs from nouns denoting numerals, such as *yḫmš,* "he does for a fifth time," authorizes him to propose that Ps xxii 26, *mē'itt*ᵉ*kā,* should be pointed *mi'ētīkā,* "I repeated to you a hundred times"; its syntax is identical with Ugar. *aṯnyk,* "I shall repeat to you." The existence of composite nouns in Ugaritic, whose presence in Hebrew is sometimes doubted, allows the critic to proceed less gingerly in this area and to suggest that Ps v 5, *kī lō' 'ēl ḥāpēṣ reša' 'attāh lō' y*ᵉ*gūr*ᵉ*kā rā',* is correctly rendered, "A no-god delights in evil, but you—no evil man can be your guest." This solution discountenances the deletion of *'ēl* in the composite noun *lō'-'ēl,* also found in Deut xxxii 21.

The phonetic conservatism of Ugaritic and its lexical richness facilitate the systematic study of dialectal elements preserved in the Bible; a recognition of these may tell us something about the place of origin of a biblical writing. Thus the contracted dual *middēm* in Ps xvi 4 and the *scriptio defectiva* of *'mrt* in vs. 2 and of *mnt* in vs. 5 suggest a Northern origin.

For the last several years James Barr has been inveighing against those biblical theologians who appeal to the etymology of a word in support of a theological theory. While many of his criticisms are valid, there remain a goodly number of exegetes who will continue to follow the method partially discredited by Barr. If one wants to credit an etymology, one will have to check it against the roots that have been attested in the dialect of Ras Shamra. In a recent commentary on Proverbs, the exegetical comment to a verse containing the word *šulḥān,* "table," reads thus: "The word for TABLE refers to some material, leather or straw, spread out on the ground." This explanation is obviously founded upon the Arabic etymon *sulāḫatun,* "piece of hide stripped off"; Ugar. *ṯlḥn* undermines the Arabic etymology and the exegesis based upon it. By the same token, the LXX rendition of Ps cxxix 3, "Upon my back the wicked hammered, they prolonged their iniquity," is rendered suspect by the Ugaritic phrase *'nt mḥrṯt,* "the furrows of the plowland," which collocates the two roots that appear in the biblical verse: *ḥārᵉšū ḥōrᵉšīm,* derives from the root *ḥrṯ,* "to plow," not from *ḥrš,* "to work metal, to hammer," while the balancing phrase *he'ᵉrīkū lᵉmō 'ᵃnōtām* (MT *lᵉma'ᵃnīwtām*) contains the root found in Ugar. *'nt.* Hence render, "Upon my back the plowmen plowed, upon it they made their furrows long."

Having reached this point, the reader doubtless feels dissatisfied with the inconclusive character of the replies given to some of the central questions of the Psalter, and disappointed that others have been partially or completely sidestepped. An introduction should pave the way for a smooth journey through a biblical book, but the remarks hitherto submitted may well give the impression that we are moving into uncharted territory. They may even be interpreted as a negative judgment upon the work of our predecessors: the versions, ancient as well as modern; the commentators, ancient as well as modern. One might be reminded of the young doctoral candidate who, after a month's work on his dissertation, arrives at the conclusion that everyone who previously treated his question was incompetent—be his name St. Thomas or John Calvin—and that providence had chosen him to set things straight. That the present Introduction has not hewed very closely to the paths traced by the classic commentaries on Psalms is due more to chance than to choice. The current generation of biblical scholars has fallen heir to such an embarrassment of epigraphic riches that one finds scholars debating in learned journals whether Ras Shamra or Qumran has contributed more to an understanding of the Old Testament. That very few researchers have availed themselves of the Ugaritic material in their studies on Psalms has already been indicated. To claim that the present application of this new information to the biblical text is judicious in every instance would be patently absurd. What is maintained is that the extensive impact of recent finds has produced such a state of fluidity in Psalms' research that a formal, full discussion of the problems traditionally handled in an introduction must be deferred until more of the evidence has been sifted.

Unsupplied with adequate and precise information regarding the headings of the Psalms, their dates, their historical background, the cultic setting from which the individual Psalms arose or to which they were addressed, the reader will perhaps feel at a disadvantage when perusing this translation. The limited consideration of form-critical questions and of the theology of the Psalter may create the impression that these are unimportant. That one should make such an inference is at the furthest possible remove from my intention. But the reader should be informed that some of the "assured" results of collective scholarship in Psalms are nothing of the sort. Research on the first fifty Psalms has convinced me that the textual discoveries of recent decades impinge on more than text-critical questions. As yet unable to work out these implications for higher criticism, I hesitate to take a stand on a number of critical issues until research on all one hundred and fifty Psalms has been completed.

For these reasons, an introduction embodying the results of this research is envisioned for the second volume. The initial, tentative observations stated above concerning dating, literary genus, *Sitz im Leben,* etc., will be expanded and developed; where needed, they will be corrected or modified. An evaluation of the cultic school of interpretation, which has enjoyed a central position in criticism for the past generation, will be attempted in the light of philological advances. The theology of the Psalter, especially as revealed in the numerous divine appellatives that have come to light, and in the new translations of texts dealing with life and death, will receive more attention than it has received thus far. Finally, there are plans for an excursus on the salient features of grammar and style, with the aim of bringing out both the originality of the psalmists and their skill in adapting older material.

SELECTED BIBLIOGRAPHY

Commentaries

Briggs, C. A., *A Critical and Exegetical Commentary on the Book of Psalms* (abbr. CECBP) (International Critical Commentary, 2 vols.). Edinburgh, 1906.

Buttenwieser, Moses, *The Psalms Chronologically Treated with a New Translation* (abbr. PCTNT). University of Chicago Press, 1938.

Castellino, Giorgio, *Libro dei Salmi*. Torino-Roma, 1955.

Delitzsch, Franz, *Biblischer Kommentar über Die Psalmen*. Leipzig, 5th rev. ed., 1894. Edited by Friedrich Delitzsch.

Gunkel, H., *Die Psalmen* (Handkommentar zum Alten Testament). Göttingen, 1926.

Gunkel, H., and Begrich, J., *Einleitung in Die Psalmen. Die Gattungen der religiösen Lyrik Israels* (Handkommentar zum Alten Testament). Göttingen, 1933.

Kraus, H. J., *Psalmen* (Biblischer Kommentar Altes Testament, 2 vols.). Neukirchen Kreis Moers, 2d ed., 1961.

Mowinckel, Sigmund, *Psalmenstudien,* I–VI. Kristiania, 1921–24.

———, *The Psalms in Israel's Worship. A Translation and Revision of* Offersang og Sangoffer, by D. R. Ap-Thomas. Oxford, 1963. 2 vols.

Nötscher, F., *Die Psalmen* (Echter-Bibel). Würzburg, 1947.

Podechard, E., *Le Psautier. Traduction littérale et explication historique. Psaumes 1–75*. Lyon, 1949. 2 vols.

Schmidt, H., *Die Psalmen* (Handbuch zum Alten Testament). Göttingen, 1934.

Weiser, Artur, *Die Psalmen* (Das Alte Testament Deutsch). Göttingen, 5th ed., 1959. Now available in English. *The Psalms: A Commentary* (Old Testament Library). London-Philadelphia, 1962.

ARTICLES

Albright, W. F., "The Old Testament and Canaanite Literature and Language," CBQ 7 (1945), 5–31.

———, "The Psalm of Habakkuk," *Studies in Old Testament Prophecy. Essays presented to Theodore H. Robinson.* Ed. by H. H. Rowley (Edinburgh, 1950), pp. 1–18.

———, "A Catalogue of Early Hebrew Lyric Poems (Psalm LXVIII)," HUCA 23 (1950), 1–39.

———, "Notes on Psalms 68 and 134," *Norsk teologisk Tidsskrift* 56 (1955), 1–12.

Coppens, J., "Les parallèles du Psautier avec les textes de Ras-Shamra-Ougarit," *Muséon* 59 (1946), 113–42.

Cross, F. M., Jr., and Freedman, D. N., "A Royal Song of Thanksgiving: II Samuel 22=Psalm 18," JBL 72 (1953), 15–34.

Dahood, M., "Ugaritic Studies and the Bible," *Gregorianum* 43 (1962), 55–79.

Jirku, A., "Kana'anäische Psalmenfragmente in der vorisraelitischen Zeit Palästinas und Syriens," JBL 52 (1933), 108–20.

Johnson, A. R., "The Psalms," *The Old Testament and Modern Study,* ed. H. H. Rowley (Oxford, 1951), pp. 162–209.

O'Callaghan, Roger T., "Echoes of Canaanite Literature in the Psalms," VT 4 (1954), 164–76.

Robinson, T. H., "Basic Principles of Hebrew Poetic Form," *Festschrift Alfred Bertholet,* ed. W. Baumgartner and others (Tübingen, 1950), pp. 438–50.

Stamm, J. J., "Ein Vierteljahrhundert Psalmenforschung," ThR 23 (1955), 1–68.

PSALMS I

1–50

PSALM 1

(i 1–6)

1 How blest the man who has not entered
the council of the wicked,
Nor in the assembly of sinners stood,
nor in the session of scoffers sat.
2 But from the law of Yahweh is his delight,
and from his law he recites day and night.
3 So shall he be like a tree
transplanted near streams of water;
Which yields its fruit in its season,
and whose leaves never wither.
Whatever it produces is good.
4 Not so the wicked:
rather are they like the winnowed chaff
that the wind drives along.
5 And so the wicked shall not stand
in the place of judgment,
Nor sinners in the congregation of the just.
6 But Yahweh shall safekeep
the assembly of the just,
While the assembly of the wicked shall perish.

NOTES

i. A Wisdom psalm contrasting the assembly of the just with the assembly of the wicked. Happiness awaits the good, the nether world the impious. This psalm is more than an introduction to the Psalter; it is rather a précis of the Book of Psalms.

1. *How blest.* The interjection *'ašrē* is an important criterion in the classification of psalms.

the council of the wicked. Like *sōd,* which signifies both "counsel" and "council" (GB, p. 538a), *'ēṣāh,* "counsel," can also denote "council." The clearest evidence comes from 1QS 5:7; 6:3, etc., where *'ṣt hyḥd* means "the council of the community"; see P. Wernberg-Møller, *The Manual of Discipline. Translated and Annotated with an Introduction* (Leiden, 1957), p. 58; *idem,* JSS 7 (1962), 127. In Ps xiv 6 *'aṣat 'ānī,* "the council of the poor," is associated with *dōr ṣaddīq,* "the family of the just," while Ps lxxiii 24, *ba'aṣāt ekā tanḥēnī we'aḥar kābōd tiqqāḥēnī* means, "Into your council will you lead me and with glory will you receive me." In Job x 3, xxi 16, and xxii 18, *'aṣat rešā'īm* should be interpreted in the light of Job xviii 7, *tašlīkēhū 'aṣātō,* "His own council will eject him," a clause that is chiastically parallel to Job xviii 6, *'ōr ḥāšak be'ohelō,* "The light grows dark in his tent." Cf. Sirach xxx 21.

assembly of sinners. Preceded by *'ēṣāh,* "council," and followed by *mōšāb,* "session," *derek* can scarcely signify "way." The Syriac version was alive to the incongruity of "standing in the way," and accordingly transposed *'ṣt* and *drk.* The philological basis for our proposal is proffered by Ugar. *drkt,* "dominion, power, throne," senses preserved in a number of biblical passages; cf. W. F. Albright in JBL 63 (1944), 219, 225; P. Nober in *Verbum Domini* 26 (1948), 351–53; M. Dahood, "Ugaritic DRKT and Biblical DEREK," in TS 15 (1954), 627–31; H. Zirker in BZ 2 (1958), 291–94, with full bibliography; M. Dahood, "Hebrew-Ugaritic Lexicography II," in Biblica 45 (1964), 404. On *drkt,* "throne," a definition usually overlooked by Ugaritic specialists, see Joseph Aistleitner, *Wörterbuch der ugaritischen Sprache* (abbr. WuS) (Berlin, 1963), No. 792, pp. 82 f., and for the biblical occurrence of *derek,* "throne," Ps cx 7, *manḥīl* (MT *minnaḥal*) *bederek yešītēhū,* "He has set him as ruler upon the throne." The semantic transition from "dominion" to the place where dominion is exercised can be illustrated by *mišpāṭ,* "justice, right," but also "court of judgment"; *A Hebrew and English Lexicon of the Old Testament,* eds. F. Brown, S. R. Driver, and C. A. Briggs (abbr. BDB) (Boston, 1906), p. 1048 a–b, and vs. 5 below. Modern languages offer instructive analogies; thus English "throne" denotes both "the seat of a sovereign" and, synecdochically, "sovereign authority." Finally, in vs. 6, *derek ṣaddīqīm* is synonymously parallel to vs. 5, *'adat ṣaddīqīm.* Cf. also Amos viii 14 and Job xxiv 4.

nor . . . stood. Like Akk. *uzuzzu, 'āmad* here has a technical sense, i.e., "to participate as a member." Cf. Jer xxiii 22; Zech iii 3; and F. M. Cross, Jr., in JNES 12 (1953), 274, n. 3.

session of scoffers. The political nuance of *mōšāb* recurs in Ps cvii 32. The synonymy of *lēṣīm,* "scoffers," and *rešā'īm,* "wicked," equivalently appears in Karatepe I:9–10, *wšbrt mlṣm wtrq 'nk kl hr' 'š kn b'rṣ,* "And I crushed the scoffers and cleared out all the evil that was in the land." The reason why King Azitawaddu was so eager to rid his kingdom of all the critics and deriders may be gathered from Prov xxii 10, "Expel the insolent man and discord will leave with him, / Disputes and name-calling will cease" (R. B. Y. Scott, *Proverbs & Ecclesiastes* [The Anchor Bible, vol. 18; New York, 1965]).

2. *from his law.* The precise force of *b,* "in, from," depends upon the verb with which it is employed. See NOTE on Ps ii 4.

he recites. The frequent Hebrew balance of *hāgāh* with verbs of "speaking" or "uttering" suggests some sort of oral activity. Ugaritic usage points to the same conclusion; UT, Krt:90–91, *ḫpṯ dbl spr ṯnn dbl hg,* "serfs beyond number, archers beyond counting," and 1001:rev:13, *k'ṣm lttn kabnm lthggn,* "when trees do not give forth (their voice), when the stones do not speak." In Damascus Covenant 10:6; 13:2, the phrase *spr hgw* may signify, "the book of recitation." Cf. NOTE on Ps ii 1 for similar use of *hāgāh.*

day and night. Compare 1QS 6:6–8, "There is not to be absent from them one who can interpret the Law to them at any time of day or night, for the harmonious adjustment of their human relations. The general members of the community are to keep awake for a third of all the nights of the year reading book(s), studying the Law and worshiping together." Translation of Theodor H. Gaster, *The Dead Sea Scriptures in English Translation* (New York: Doubleday Anchor Books, 1957), pp. 49 f.

3. *So shall he be.* The *waw* of *wᵉhāyāh* is naturally parsed as perfect consecutive. Diethelm Michel, *Tempora und Satzstellung in den Psalmen* (abbr. TSP) (Bonn, 1960), § 15, pp. 108–11, devotes a special excursus to Psalm 1, whose use of tenses is a source of great difficulty to Michel. He puzzles before the use of the perfect in vs. 1, the imperfect in vs. 2, and the perfect consecutive in vs. 3. He deplores the fact that the standard commentaries skirt the problem of tenses in this poem and then proceeds to propound his solution. He seems to have created a false problem which issues from a misunderstanding of the contents of the poem. The *qāṭal* forms of vs. 1 (*hālak, 'āmad,* and *yāšab*) refer to past time; the nominal sentence of vs. 2a and the *yiqṭōl* form (*yehgeh*) of vs. 2b signify the present, while vs. 3 *wᵉhāyāh* refers to future time, namely, when the just man, like a tree, shall be transplanted to the Elysian Fields. For the theme of the Elysian Fields, see NOTES on Ps xxxvi 9–10.

tree transplanted. Commentators are correct in insisting that *šātal* properly means "to transplant," rather than "to plant." Eschatological connotations of this verb emerge from a new proposal at Ps lxxiii 18, *'ak baḥᵃlāqōt tišťᵉlēmō* (MT *tāšīt lāmō*) *hippaltām lᵉmaššū'ōt,* "But to Perdition transplant them, make them fall into Devastation!" The theme of transplanting one's foes to the underworld appears in UT, 76:II:24–25, where the verb, however, is *nṭ',* "to plant": *nṭ'n barṣ iby wb'pr qm aḫk,* "We have planted my foes in the nether world, and in the mud those who rise up against your brother." The documented motif of planting or transplanting foes in the underworld permits the conclusion that *šātal* could also be used for the transference of the just to the abode of the blest.

near streams of water. C. A. Briggs, *A Critical and Exegetical Commentary on the Book of Psalms* (abbr. CECBP) (see Selected Bibliography), I, p. 6, is doubtless right in his view that the psalmist, in adapting and combining from Jer xvii 8, probably had in mind the story of the streams of Eden, the land of bliss (Gen ii). This opinion is supported by the observation that in Ps xxxvi 9, which is a description of the region of eternal happiness, the poet used the phrase *naḥal ʿadānekā*, "the stream of your delicacies," with the intention of evoking the description of the Garden of Eden. For *ʿal*, "near," cf. UT, 1 Aqht:152–53, *ylkm qr mym dʿlk mḫṣ aqht ǵzr*, "Woe to you, fountain of water, for near you was Aqhat the lad struck down." That *peleg* can carry cosmic overtones is reasonably clear from Ps xlvi 5, as interpreted below.

whose leaves never wither. A symbol of immortality. C. Virolleaud in CRAIBL, 1962 (appeared in 1963), 108, reports that a Ugaritic fragment describes the banishment of the god Horon to the wilderness where he planted a tamarisk (*ʿrʿr*), which is called *ʿṣ mt*, "the tree of death."

Whatever it produces. Though ancient and modern versions assume that the subject changes from "tree" to "the just man," the shift is abrupt and unnecessary. The verb *ʿāśāh*, "to produce, yield," is predicated of trees, grain, vines, etc., while Ezek xvii 10, in a similar metaphor, employs the phrase *šᵉtūlāh hᵃtiṣlāḥ*, "when transplanted, can it (the vine) thrive?"

is good. The frequent revocalization of *yaṣlīᵃḥ* as *yiṣlaḥ* does not impose itself in view of *yipraḥ*, "it flourishes," and *yaprīᵃḥ* with the same sense in Job xiv 9.

4. *the wind drives along*. Cf. the description of the wicked being driven into Sheol in Ps xxxv 5–6.

5. *shall not stand*. Formally construed with *bammišpāṭ* and logically also with *baʿadat*, *yāqūmū* must bear a meaning that is apt with both. Hence the frequent version "shall not rise" seems less probable. Cf. UT, 51:III:13–14, *yqm wywpṯm btk p[ḫ]r bn ilm*, "He stands and spits in the midst of the assembly of the gods."

the place of judgment. This phrase is denoted by *mišpāṭ* in Deut xxv 1; I Kings vii 7; Isa xxviii 6, xxxii 7; Prov xviii 5, xxiv 23. As the final judgment will take place in the heavenly council, to which the wicked will not be admitted, they will be condemned *in absentia*. Cf. Ps lxxxii 1, "God stands in the divine council; in the midst of the gods he passes judgment." The psalmist has adapted an ancient Canaanite mythological motif to his Yahwistic, ethical purposes.

The proposed exegesis assumes a rather advanced concept of resurrection and immortality, but there is ample basis in the Psalter for this supposition. Passages where these concepts appear include v 12, xvi 10–11, xvii 15, xxii 30, xxvii 4, 13, xxxvi 9–10, xxxvii 37–38, xlix 16, lxxiii 23–26, cxxxix 18, 24. For a brief but competent orientation, see E. Jacob, "Immortality," in IDB, II, pp. 688–90; Briggs, CECBP, I, pp. 6f.

congregation of the just. This is an ethical adaptation of a mythological phrase which originally described the council of the gods in Canaanite religion; e.g., UT, 128:III:7, *'dt ilm.* For collection of texts, see Gerald Cooke, "The Sons of (the) God(s)," in ZAW 76 (1964), 22–47, with rather full bibliography; F. M. Cross, Jr., "The Council of Yahweh in Second Isaiah," in JNES 12 (1953), 274–77.

6. *safekeep. yāda'* connotes "to care for, protect" in Pss ix 10, xxxi 8, xxxvii 18, l 11; Hos xiii 5; Amos iii 2, etc.; see D. Winton Thomas, *The Text of the Revised Psalter* (London, 1963), p. 1; BDB, p. 394a.

assembly of the wicked. derek rᵉšā'īm is synonymous with vs. 1, *derek ḥaṭṭā'īm,* and with it forms an *inclusio,* a rhetorical device also called "cyclic composition," in which the author returns to the point where he began.

PSALM 2
(ii 1–12)

1 Why do the nations forgather,
and the peoples number their troops?
2 Why do kings of the earth take their stand,
and the princes make common cause
Against Yahweh and against his anointed?
3 Let us snap their bonds,
and throw off their yoke from us.
4 The Enthroned laughs down from heaven,
the Lord makes sport of them.
5 Then he drives away their lieutenants in his ire,
and in his fury discomfits them.
6 But I have been anointed his king,
upon Zion his holy mountain.
7 Let me recite the decree of Yahweh;
he said to me:
"You are my son,
this day have I begotten you.
8 Ask wealth of me and I will give it;
the nations will be your patrimony,
and your possessions the ends of the earth.
9 You will break them with a rod of iron,
shatter them like a potter's jar."
10 And now, O kings, be prudent,
take warning, you rulers of the earth.
11 Serve Yahweh with reverence,
and live in trembling, O mortal men!
12 Lest he grow angry and your assembly perish,
for his ire flares up quickly.
How blest are all who trust in him!

Notes

ii. A royal psalm, composed for a coronation. It readily divides into three sections: vss. 1–3 describe the rebellion of local kings against the new overlord; vss. 4–9 relate the reaction of God to their behavior (4–5) and the reaction of the new king, who vindicates his royal authority (6–9); vss. 10–12 explain the reconciliation to be effected. Punishment awaits the intractable, reward the obedient.

The import of recent discoveries for the literary study of the Psalter may be illustrated by citing, with no captious intent, a judgment expressed by Briggs, CECBP, I, p. 13, at the beginning of the century: "There is no dependence on other Lit.; the Ps. is throughout original in conception." The genuinely archaic flavor of the language suggests a very early date (probably tenth century). My linguistic analysis thus points to a conclusion at a great remove from the opinion of André Robert, "Considérations sur le messianisme du Ps. II," in *Recherches de Sciences Religieuses* 39 (1951–52), 86–99, who maintains that *"Tous les versets du Psaume, sauf 6 et 12, renferment des termes charactéristiques de la langue postexilienne"* (p. 97).

1. *the nations forgather.* That *rāgaš* denotes "to forgather" has been amply demonstrated by Briggs, CECBP, I, pp. 17 f. Its chiastic parallelism with vs. 2, *nōsᵉdū yaḥad,* corresponds to the balance of *rgš* with *sōd,* "council, counsel," in Pss lv 15 and lxiv 3. The close association of *rgš* with *sōd* in each of its three biblical occurrences is a safer guide to the meaning of *rgš* than the Syriac etymology which has served as the basis for traditional "be in tumult, to rage."

number their troops. In addition to signifying "to mumble, utter, speak," *hāgāh* also denotes "to number, count [out loud]," a nuance brought out by UT, Krt:90–91, where the three million troops mustered by King Kirta are said to be, *ḫpṯ dbl spr ṯnn dbl hg,* "serfs beyond number, archers beyond counting." The Ugaritic occurrence of *hg* in a military context may speak volumes for the significance of *yehᵉgū* in this verse. In passing, one may note that the Canaanite pairing of *spr* and *hg* has served to uncover a similar pairing in Eccles xii 12; see M. Dahood, *Biblica* 33 (1952), 219, and John Gray, *The Legacy of Canaan* (VTS, V; Leiden, 1957), p. 201. J. D. Shenkel (oral communication) finds parallel terminology in Luke xiv 31.

The meaning of *rīq,* "troops," is based primarily upon Gen xiv 14, *wayyāreq 'et ḥᵃnīkāyw,* "And he mustered his retainers." Ps xxxv 3, *hārēq ḥᵃnīt,* frequently rendered "ready the spear," should probably be attached to the root being considered here. See Ps xxxii 6. The troops of Abimelech (Judg ix 4) and of Jephthah (Judg xi 3) are labeled *'ᵃnāšīm rīqīm,* usually translated "worthless fellows" or "vagabonds," but the term probably signifies "enlisted men" or something similar. Morphologically, *rīq* is a passive participle like *śīm;* Joüon, GHB, § 58c.

2. *Why do kings.* The force of vs. 1, *lammāh* is taken to extend to vs. 2. Similar ellipsis is evident in Ps iii 2, *māh rabbū,* where the force of *māh* carries over into the two following half verses. Frequent ellipsis in Ugaritic poetry and prose makes it *a priori* likely that this practice obtained far more widely in biblical Hebrew than heretofore recognized. See H. L. Ginsberg, *The Legend of King Keret* (abbr. LKK) (New Haven, 1946), p. 47. Cf. UT, 'nt:IV:48, *mnm ib yp' lb'l ṣrt lrkb 'rpt,* "What foe has risen up against Baal, what adversary against the Mounter of the Clouds?" In this passage *mnm* and *yp'* are omitted in the second colon.

kings . . . princes. The pair *melek* and *rōzen,* recurring in Judg v 3; Hab i 10; Prov viii 15, xiv 38, xxxi 4, appears in Phoenician Karatepe III:12; cf. Stanley J. Gevirtz, *Patterns in the Early Poetry of Israel* (Chicago, 1964), p. 3, n. 11.

There is no point in trying to identify the kings historically. By the time of the composition of this psalm (probably tenth century) they had become stock literary figures who belong to the genre of royal psalms. They should be classed with the kings of Ps xlviii 5. If an historical background must be sought, the El Amarna period in Syria-Palestine would be a strong candidate. The El Amarna correspondence offers graphic descriptions of the plottings and intrigues of the petty kings of Syria-Palestine against the Egyptian suzerain and against one another.

take their stand. I.e., for pitched battle.

and against his anointed. RSV appears ill-advised in omitting the second *'al* in their translation, "against the Lord and his anointed." In view of the elliptical nature of the psalmist's language, the repetition of the preposition in the Hebrew text must have served a purpose (perhaps metrical) and should be reflected in translation. The root of "his anointed" occurs in an unpublished Ras Shamra tablet, [*šm*]*n mšḥt kṯpm,* "oil for the anointing of sorcerers."

3. *snap their bonds.* This phrase may be a metaphorical reference to their obligations as vassals of Yahweh and his anointed.

throw off their yoke from us. LXX and Vulg. are probably correct in taking *'ābōt,* "cords," as metonymy for "yoke," which the ropes held in place. The same semantic transition appears in Ps cxxix 4, *qiṣṣēṣ 'ᵃbōt rᵉšā'īm,* "He snapped the yoke of the wicked." In Jer ii 20, *'ōl,* "yoke," pairs with *mōsārōt,* "bonds," to create the parallelism proposed for this verse. Another instance of metonymy can be seen in Ps xxxv 3, where *sᵉgōr,* "the socket of a javelin," signifies the "javelin" itself.

4. *The Enthroned.* Literally, "he who sits," but *yōšēb* often pregnantly

connotes "throne-sitter, king." So in I Kings viii 25; Amos i 5, 8, etc. Cf. F. M. Cross, Jr., and D. N. Freedman, JNES 14 (1955), 248; J. M. Allegro in JBL 75 (1956), 174, n. 4. Similar usage occurs in UT, 52: 8–9, *mt wšr yṯb bdh ḫṭ ṯkl bdh ḫṭ ulmn,* "Death and Corruption sits enthroned; in his hand is the scepter of bereavement, in his hand the scepter of widowhood."

from heaven. The ambivalence of *baššāmayim,* "in/from heaven," is relieved by parallel *yil'ag lāmō,* which points to *actio ad extra.* A similar problem arises in Ps lxviii 6, "The father of orphans and the protector of the widow is God *bīmeʿōn qodšō.*" Since God is thought to operate outward from heaven, *bīmeʿōn qodšō* is more properly understood as "from his holy habitation," i.e., "from heaven." In fact, LXX took it this way and some MSS read *mimmeʿōn.* Since *b* very often denotes "from" in Ugaritic and Hebrew, emendation becomes gratuitous.

5. *he drives away.* I.e., makes them flee the field of battle. The verb *yedabbēr* equals El Amarna Akk. *duppuru* (*dubburu*), "to pursue, drive away," senses preserved in Pss lvi 6 and cxxvii 5, *lō' yēbōšū kī yedabberū 'et 'ōyebīm baššā'ar,* "They will not be humiliated but will drive their foes from the gate." See my remarks in TS 14 (1953), 87–88; CBQ 17 (1955), 23 f., on Ps cxvi 10; *Biblica* 38 (1957), 95, on Prov xxi 28; *Biblica* 45 (1964), 401, on Lam v 9 and Jer ix 20–21, "cutting off the children from the streets, banishing (*dabbēr*) the young men from the squares."

The failure to name a place from which God drives away the lieutenants should cause no difficulty in view of the usage in El Amarna, 104:27, *annū inanna dubiru rabiṣaka,* "Look, they have now driven away your lieutenant"; [Chicago] *The Assyrian Dictionary* (abbr. CAD) (Oriental Institute of the University of Chicago, 1956–), III (D), p. 188a.

their lieutenants. 'ēlēmō is not a preposition plus suffix, but the substantive *'ayil,* spelled defectively *'l* (one would expect *'yl*) as in Job xix 22, *lāmmāh tirdepūnī kemō 'ēl,* "Why do you pursue me like a ram?", (contrast Marvin H. Pope's translation "Why do you pursue me like God?" in *Job* [The Anchor Bible, vol. 15; New York, 1965]) used in a metaphorical sense as in Exod xv 15; II Kings xxiv 15; Ezek xvii 13, etc. The most relevant passage is Exod xv 15, *'āz nibhalū 'allūpē 'edōm 'ēlē mo'āb yō'ḥazēmō rā'ad nāmōgū kol yōšebē kenā'an,* "Then were the chieftains of Edom discomfited; the lieutenants of Moab—trembling seized them; all the kings of Canaan melted away." Notice the similarity of language: *'āz, nibhālū, 'ēlē,* and *yōšēb* all occur in Ps ii. Ps lxxxiii 16 is instructive in balancing *bāhal* with *rādap,* "to pursue," the same two ideas that are paired in the present verse. See also II Kings xxiv 15, "He exiled the lieutenants of the land" (*'ēlē hā'āreṣ*). The widespread biblical use of animal names in a metaphorical sense (some twenty-five have already been identified) is now seen to have had Canaanite antecedents;

see M. Dahood, "The Value of Ugaritic for Textual Criticism," *Biblica* 40 (1959), 161 f.; Patrick Miller, Jr., in HTR 57 (1964), 239.

The antecedent of the suffix in *'ēlēmō* is probably the kings and princes of vs. 2 rather than the nations and peoples of vs. 1. Once the field lieutenants take to flight, the entire host is discomfited.

The metaphorical use of *'ēl,* "ram," is found in the Phoenician Inscription from Ma'ṣub, line 2, *'š bn h'lm ml'k mlk'štrt,* "which the leaders, the envoys of Milkashthart, built"; cf. G. A. Cooke, *A Text-Book of North-Semitic Inscriptions* (abbr. TNSI) (Oxford, 1903), pp. 48 f.; Edward Meyer in ZAW 49 (1931), 3.

6. *But I.* This begins the description of the king's reaction to the conspiracy. The subject changes from God to his anointed, as is patent from the use of the *waw adversativum;* see Joüon, GHB, § 172a.

have been anointed. Pointing *nᵉsūkōtī,* from *sūk,* "to anoint," for MT *nāsaktī.* In Prov viii 23 likewise vocalize *nᵉsūkōtī,* "From eternity I (Wisdom) was anointed." Biblical usage, to be sure, seems to reserve *sūk* as a term for mere cosmetic anointing, employing *māšaḥ* for ritual unction, but both Ps ii and Prov viii contain elements reflecting pre-Israelite usage and culture. The traditional view can be found in the recent monograph of Ernst Kutsch, *Salbung als Rechtsakt* (BZAW 87; Berlin, 1963), p. 7. Recognition of this root in Ugaritic leads to a better translation and a more satisfactory syntactical analysis of UT, 'nt:II:40–44, *ṭl šmm tskh rbb tskh kbkbm,* "With dew the heavens anoint her, with spray anoint her the stars." Parse *ṭl* and *rbb* as accusatives of material-with-which, as in UT, 'nt:II:39, *wtrḥṣ* [*ṭ*]*l šmm šmn arṣ,* "And she is washed by the dew of heaven, the oil of earth," and in Deut xxviii 40, *wᵉšemen lō' tāsūk,* "But you shall not anoint yourself with oil." Grammatically, this version seems superior to that of H. L. Ginsberg in *Ancient Near Eastern Texts Relating to the Old Testament,* ed. J. B. Pritchard, 2d ed. (Princeton, 1955), p. 136c, which assumes Aramaic syntax: "Dew that heavens do shed, [spray] that is shed by the stars." The syntactic problem can be felt in the version proposed by G. R. Driver, *Canaanite Myths and Legends* (abbr. CML) (Edinburgh, 1956), p. 89b, "[She] poured the dew of heaven (and) the showers that she poured (were as many as) the stars."

his king . . . his holy mountain. The suffix of *malkī* and *qodšī* is the third-person singular masculine, equivalent to Phoen. *-y,* "his, her." This suffix is also found in Ugaritic, though specialists have not recognized it; good examples include UT, 51:VIII:12–13 = 67:II:15–16; 1001:10 = rev:8.20. Though the existence of Phoen. *-y* is undoubted, its pronunciation and origin remain a matter of dispute; cf. F. M. Cross, Jr., and D. N. Freedman, "The Pronominal Suffixes of the Third Person Singular in Phoenician," JNES 10 (1951), 228–30. The remarks concerning the pronunciation of *-y* in Johannes Friedrich, *Phönizisch-Punische Gram-*

matik (abbr. PPG) (Roma, 1951), §§ 23, 112, have been retracted in his article "Punische Studien," ZDMG 107 (1957), 282–98, especially pp. 287, 290. To judge from MT, the pronunciation coincided with that of the first-person singular suffix; see Hans Bauer in ZDMG 68 (1914), 599.

Since the existence of this suffix is of such text-critical importance, a full listing of the examples hitherto recognized seems in order: Pss ii 6, xiv 4, xvi 7, 8, xviii 33, 34, xxii 29, xxiv 4, xxvii 8, xxxvi 2, xlii 5, l 5 (thrice), li 5, lxi 3, lxviii 34, 36, lxxviii 49, lxxxix 51, cv 6, 18, 28, cix 31, cxiii 8, cxxxi 2, cxxxv 1, cxli 6, cxlii 8, cxlvii 20; Judg ix 9; Isa iii 13, xiv 30, xv 5, xxxviii 15, xli 25, xlvi 11, xlix 11, liii 10, lix 3, lx 21; Jer xvii 13, xxiii 18, xxxi 3; Hos v 13, x 6, xiv 9; Jon ii 3; Mic ii 7; Hab ii 1, iii 19; Zech ii 15; Job iii 10, vi 13, ix 15, x 1, xiii 17, xiv 3, xvi 10, 18, xix 17, 27, xxii 18, xxiii 2, 12, 14, xxiv 15, xxxi 18, xxxiii 28, xxxviii 10, xli 2, 3; Prov vii 6, viii 35, xxviii 23; Eccles ii 25, xi 3; Lam i 3, 14; Neh iii 30. Admittedly, not all these examples will bear up under further inquiry, but the number that will have to be eliminated from this list will surely be smaller than that of new examples which will eventually turn up. One may also voice the objection that in these passages there is the usual orthographic confusion between *yod* and *waw*, but this difficulty founders on the paleographic fact that in the Qumran Scrolls these letters can hardly be confused except during a limited period when they were difficult to distinguish.

In brief, just as the Phoenician dialects possessed third-person singular suffixes *-ō*, *-h*, and *-y*, so Hebrew used all three; the possible ambiguity was resolved by context and was no more acute than, say, in *lāmō*, "for him/for us/for them." For *lāmō*, "for us," see NOTE on Ps xxviii 8.

holy mountain. Cf. UT, ʻnt:III:25–28, *btk ǵry il ṣpn bqdš bǵr nḥlty*, "in the midst of my towering mountain Zaphon, in the sanctuary, the mountain of my patrimony."

7. *decree of Yahweh.* G. von Rad ("Das judäische Königsritual," in *Gesammelte Studien zum Alten Testament* (München, 1958), especially pp. 210 f.), discusses *ḥōq, das Königsprotokoll,* citing Egyptian analogies. Cf. likewise R. de Vaux, "Le roi d'Israël, vassal de Yahvé," in *Mélanges Eugène Tisserant,* I (Studi e Testi, 231; Città del Vaticano, 1964), pp. 119–33, especially p. 127. The divine decree, which established the king's legitimacy, contained a list of his titles. That the custom was also Canaanite appears from a brief, partially preserved tablet, whose importance remains to be appreciated. The text enumerates some of the titles of King Niqmepa, the son of Niqmad; UT, 1007:4–7, *bʻl ṣdq skn bt mlk ṯǵr mlk bny*, "Legitimate lord, governor of the palace, king of the city, builder king." (With the title *skn bt* compare Isa xxii 15.)

You are my son. Implying through adoption; cf. II Sam vii 14; Ps lxxxix 27–28. In Canaanite culture the king was believed to be an offspring of the gods and to have been suckled at divine breasts. The former belief finds literary expression in UT, 125:10–11, *[k]rt bnm il špḥ lṭpn wqdš,* "Kirta is the son of El, the offspring of Lutpan and Qudshu (Asherah)," while the latter credence receives artistic representation on an ivory panel depicting two princes sucking the breasts of a goddess (probably Anath). See C. F. A. Schaeffer, *Syria* 31 (1954), Pl. VIII, and C. H. Gordon, "Language as a Means to an End," *Antiquity* 29 (1955), 147–49, who illustrates the connection between UT, 51:VI: 56, *mrǵtm ṯd* and the scene shown on the ivory panel. In biblical literature, on the other hand, no claims are made for the king's divinity, nor did prophetic Yahwism ever attack Hebrew kings and kingship on this score; consult Gerald Cooke, "The Israelite King as Son of God," ZAW 73 (1961), 202–25.

8. *Ask wealth of me.* Reading for MT *mimmennī, māmōnī,* literally "my wealth," but the dative notion is sometimes expressed by the possessive suffix; see Joüon, GHB, § 129h. Instructive examples occur in Pss xvi 4, xx 3, l 5, lxv 3. The reader will recognize similar usage in UT, 51:v:89, *bšrtk yblt,* "I bring you good tidings," literally "I bring your good tidings"; UT, 137:37, *hw ybl argmnk,* "He will bring you tribute," literally "He will bring your tribute." Contrast UT, 51:v:93–93, *tblk ǵrm mid ksp,* "The mountains will bring you much silver." In Hebrew, the substantive *māmōn* occurs in Sirach xxxi 8, as noted by F. Zorell, *Lexicon Hebraicum* (abbr. ZLH) (Rome, 1955), p. 444b, and in a cognate form *'āmōn* in Ps xxxvii 3. According to St. Augustine, *De Sermone Domini in Monte,* in *Patrologia Latina,* ed. J. P. Migne (Paris, 1878–90), vol. 34, col. 1290, *māmōn* (or *mammōn*) is a Punic word. Its appearance in Canaanizing Ps ii seems to bear out his statement. It is also found in 1QS 6:2; Damascus Covenant 14:20; as well as in Mishnaic Hebrew. Cf. A. M. Honeyman, "The Etymology of Mammon," in *Archivum Linguisticum* 4, 1 (Glasgow, 1952), 60–65 (not consulted by me). In NT (Matt vi 24; Luke xvi 9, 11, 13), the word was known well enough to need no explanation. Most recent study of *māmōn* is that of Giovanni Rinaldi in *Bibbia e Oriente* 7 (1965), 19–20.

and I will give it. Reading *modus energicus wᵉ'ettannāh* for MT *wᵉ'ettᵉnāh.* Cf. NOTE on Ps viii 2. Compare this phrase with UT, 2 Aqht:VI:17, *irš ksp watnk,* "Ask for silver and I will give it to you." To all appearances, the accusative object of *atn,* that refers to the silver, is omitted, precisely as in my parsing of biblical *'ettannāh,* since the final *-k* of Ugar. *atnk* is a dative suffix. However, it is possible, though less likely, that the accusative object *-n* has been assimilated by the final *-k,* as occasionally happens in Hebrew. Cf. further 2 Aqht:VI:27, *irš ḥym watnk,* "Ask for life eternal and I will give it to you." This analysis of vs. 8 results in a 3+3+2 beat that forms a kind of chiasm with vs. 7b that scans into 2+2+3.

your patrimony. For this meaning of *naḥᵃlāh,* see Friedrich Horst, "Zwei Begriffe für Eigentum (Besitz): *nḥlh* und *'ḥwzh,"* in *Verbannung und Heimkehr: Festschrift für Wilhelm Rudolph,* ed. A. Kuschke (Tübingen, 1961), pp. 135–56; Abraham Malamat, "Mari and the Bible," JAOS 82 (1962), 143–50, especially p. 149.

9. *You will break them.* Retaining MT *tᵉrō'ēm,* the balance with *nāpaṣ* "to shatter," and the kinship with royal Ps cx 2, *ruddāh* (MT *rᵉdāh*) *biqrāb* (MT *bᵉqereb*), *'ōyᵉbekā,* "Cudgel in combat your foes," may be cited in favor of this version as against "You shall rule them."

10. *kings . . . rulers.* The frequent biblical pair *melek-šōpēṭ* appears in UT, 51:IV:43–44, *mlkn aliy[n] b'l ṯpṭn win d'lnh,* "Our king is Victor Baal, our ruler, and there is none above him." The basic sense of *špṭ* is "to exercise authority" in various matters; see E. A. Speiser, *Genesis* (The Anchor Bible, vol. 1; New York, 1964), p. 134; Werner Schmidt, *Königtum Gottes in Ugarit und Israel* (BZAW 80; Berlin, 1961), pp. 27–34. The balance of *ḥṭr mšpṭh,* "the scepter of his authority," with *ks' mlkh,* "the throne of his kingship," occurs in Phoenician Ahiram, line 2.

take warning. Cf. UT, 127:26, *wywsrnn ggnh,* "And his innards instruct him."

11. *live in trembling.* The root is probably *gīl,* recurring in Ps xxii 9, *gāl 'el yhwh,* "He lived for Yahweh"; Ps xliii 4, *śimḥat gīlī,* "the happiness of my life"; and Ps cxxxix 15, *gīlay,* "my life stages." See Dahood, *Biblica* 40 (1959), 168 f. In Dan i 10, *gīl* means "era, stage of life," like old South Arabic *gyl,* "course of the year"; see W. W. Müller, in ZAW 75 (1963), 308. This root may be present in the unexplained personal names *'ᵃbīgayil* and *'ᵃbīgāl.*

O mortal men. Reading, with no consonantal changes, *nᵉšē qāber,* literally "men of the grave," for much-canvassed MT *naššᵉqū bar.* Compare the phrases *'īš māwet* (I Kings ii 26), "a man appointed for death"; *bᵉnē māwet* (I Sam xxvi 16), "sons deserving to die"; *bᵉnē tᵉmūtāh* (Pss lxxix 11, cii 21), "men exposed to death." The form *nāšīm,* "men," is well documented in Ugaritic, e.g., UT, 2 Aqht:VI:45, *'mq nšm,* "the strongest/wisest of men," and in Prov xiv 1, *ḥakmōt nāšīm,* "the wisest of men"; see M. Dahood, *Proverbs and Northwest Semitic Philology* (abbr. PNWSP) (Rome, 1963), p. 30. These two biblical occurrences of *nāšīm,* against normal *'ᵃnāšīm,* should be classed with the rare Phoenician plural of *'īš,* namely *'īšīm,* recorded in Ps cxli 4; Isa liii 3; and Prov viii 4.

The stichometric division is two parallel cola, the first with 9 syllables and 3 beats, the second with 10 syllables and 3 beats. On the utility of syllable-counting as a textual criterion, see D. N. Freedman in ZAW 72 (1960), 102.

With the vocative, "O mortal men," the Yahwist king is portrayed as railing against the Canaanite concepts of divine kingship, reminding the rebel Canaanite kings of vss. 1–2 that they too are appointed for the inevitable hour. They should accordingly acknowledge the supreme suzerainty of Yahweh and live in fear of incurring his wrath.

In an unpublished king-list from Ras Shamra, *il,* "god," which means that the deceased king has been made divine is placed in the right column before the king's name; cf. C. F. A. Schaeffer in AfO 20 (1963), 215, and in CRAIBL, 1962 (appeared in 1963), 204 f. The recent proposal of Henri Cazelles, "NŠQW BR (Ps., ii, 12)," in *Oriens Antiquus* 3 (1964), 43–45, who translates *"Saluez le Brillant,"* on the basis of Ugar. *brr,* "to shine," is possible though it requires further confirmation.

12. *your assembly perish.* See NOTE on Ps i 1; *derek,* "assembly," forms an *inclusio* with vs. 1, *rāgᵉšū,* "forgather."

who trust in him. I.e., as Suzerain, to judge from the contents of the poem and from Ps xviii 31, *māgān hū' lᵉkol haḥōsīm bō,* "Suzerain is he to all who trust in him." See NOTE on Ps iii 4.

PSALM 3

(iii 1–9)

1 *A psalm of David, when he fled from his son Absalom.*

2 O Yahweh, how many are my adversaries!
How many who rise up against me!
How many who eye my life! [2]*
3 "No salvation for him from God." *Selah*
4 But you, O Yahweh, are my Suzerain as long as I live, [3]
my Glorious One who lifts high my head.
5 If with full voice I call to Yahweh, [4]
he answers me from his holy mountain. *Selah*
6 If I lie down to sleep, [5]
I shall wake up, for Yahweh sustains me.
7 I fear not the shafts of people, [6]
deployed against me on every side.
8 Rise up, O Yahweh, save me, my God! [7]
O that you yourself would smite
All my foes on the jaw!
Smash the teeth of the wicked!
9 O Yahweh, salvation! [8]
upon your people your blessing! *Selah*

* Verse numbers in RSV.

NOTES

iii. A personal lament in which the psalmist prays for deliverance from his calumniators.

1. The superscriptions of seventy-three psalms contain the phrase *l^{e}dāwīd* whose exact meaning—"from David," "concerning David," like Ugar. *lbʿl,* "concerning Baal"—remains to be determined. A number of psalms contain allusions to certain events in David's life, as in the present

instance; the historical significance of these superscriptions is still a matter of dispute.

2. *How many who rise.* The force of *māh* in *māh rabbū* affects the following two cola; cf. NOTE on Ps ii 1. With rare exceptions, the Vrs. fail to note the ellipsis. A recent translation which recognizes it is *The Psalms, A New Translation* (Fontana Books; London, 1962), p. 13.

The parallel pair *ṣāräy* ‖ *qāmīm* are semantic equivalents of UT, *'nt*:IV:48, *mnm ib yp' lb'l ṣrt lrkb 'rpt,* "What foe has risen up against Baal, what [note ellipsis of *mnm*] adversary against the Mounter of the Clouds?"

who eye my life. Suggesting hostile intent. In a number of texts *'āmar,* "to say," bears its original meaning "to see," as in Akkadian and Ugaritic. These include Pss xi 1, xxix 9, lxxi 10, lxxvii 9, xciv 4, cv 28. For present purposes the most enlightening is lxxi 10, *kī 'āmᵉrū 'ōyᵉbay lī wᵉšōmᵉrē napšī nō'ᵃṣū yaḥdāw,* "For my foes eye me, and they who are on the lookout for my life consult together." Here the parallelism appears convincing; in fact, Hermann Gunkel, *Die Psalmen* (see Selected Bibliography), p. 302, accepts Lagarde's emendation of *'āmᵉrū* to *'ārᵉbū,* "they lie in wait," since *sie reden von mir ist etwas blass.* The note of hostile intent carried by *'āmar* is well illustrated by the analogous verb *'īn* "to eye suspiciously" in I Sam xviii 9, *wayᵉhī šā'ūl 'ōwēn 'et dāwīd,* "And Saul was suspiciously eyeing David." See Zorell, ZLH, p. 590b. For the thought, cf. Ps xxxvii 32, "When the wicked man spies on the just." The unexplained personal name *'ītāmār* may well be infixed *-t-* form of this root which is attested in UT, 137:32, *išt ištm yitmr,* "One fire, two fires appear."

3. *from God.* The most significant feature of Ugaritic prepositions is the meaning "from" for both *b* and *l;* cf. Gordon, UT, § 10.1. The problem of ambiguity in the Ras Shamra texts is thus acute. While the acuteness has been considerably alleviated in Hebrew by the introduction of *min,* the problem nonetheless exists, especially in poetic texts. In the Psalter the difficulty obtrudes too often for confident translation, twice in this brief lament of nine verses. Consult NOTE on Psalm ii 4.

4. *my Suzerain.* The need for distinguishing between *māgēn,* "shield," and *māgēn* (to judge from Punic *māgōn,* the correct Hebrew vocalization appears to be *māgān*), "suzerain," has been examined by M. Dahood in "Ugaritic Lexicography," *Mélanges Eugène Tisserant,* I, pp. 81–104, especially p. 94. The argument proceeds from Ps lxxxiv 12, which virtually defines a suzerain: *kī šemeš ūmāgān yhwh 'ᵉlōhīm ḥēn wᵉkābōd yittēn,* "For Sovereign (*šemeš* = Ugar. *špš,* the title of the Pharaoh or the Hittite overlord; El Amarna *šamšu*) and Suzerain is Yahweh; God bestows favors and honors." The root concept is *māgan* "to give, bestow, hand over," very frequent in Ugaritic and found also in Phoenician. The virtual balance between *māgān* and

yittēn in Ps lxxxiv 12 corresponds to the parallelism in Prov iv 9, *tittēn lerō'šekā ḥēn 'aṭeret tip'eret temaggenekā,* "She will give your head a chaplet of grace; a crown of glory will she bestow upon you." In Ps lxxxiv 10, *māgān* is parallel to *māšīaḥ* "the anointed"; in Ps lxxxix 19 it balances *melek,* "king." This divine title also recurs in Pss vii 11, xviii 31, xlvii 10, lix 12; Gen xv 1; Prov ii 7, xxx 5.

This definition reveals the theological wordplay (discussed in NOTES on Ps xlvii 6, 10) in Gen xiv 20 and xv 1. In the former verse one reads, "Praised be God Most High who has delivered (*miggēn*) your adversaries into your hand," and in xv 1, "Fear not, Abraham, I am your Suzerain (*māgān* [MT *māgēn*] *lāk*) who will reward you [point as participle *śōkērekā*] very greatly." In Punic the Carthaginian generals are given the title *māgōn,* which Latin inscriptions reproduce by *imperator,* "suzerain," or *dux;* see Louis Maurin, "Himilcon le Magonide. Crises et mutations à Carthage au début du IVe siècle avant J.-C.," *Semitica* 12 (1962), 5–43. The conceptual relationship between "suzerain" and "benefactor" comes out in Luke xxii 25, "The kings of the heathen lord it over their subjects, and those in authority are called Benefactors."

In the historical prologues of suzerainty or vassal treaties, emphasis was laid upon the past benevolent acts of the great king, and the advantages that would accrue to the vassal who accepted the treaty were set forth. In other words, the great king represented himself as a benefactor, so that the transition from *māgān,* "benefactor," to "suzerain," may have occurred within this terminological framework.

The possessive suffix of *māgān,* "my Suzerain," is logically to be supplied from *kebōdī,* "my Glorious One," on the principle of the double-duty suffix. This literary device deserves a word of comment. Identified in the last century by Franz Delitzsch (*Biblischer Kommentar über Die Psalmen,* 5th rev. ed. [see Selected Bibliography], p. 666), who recognized the usage in Pss cvii 20 and cxxxix 1, the extent and importance of its usefulness for stylistic analysis was not fully appreciated until numerous Ugaritic instances clarified this poetic practice. On the basis of Ugaritic usage—where the sense of the possessive pronoun must not infrequently be carried from the noun that has it to the parallel noun without it, as in UT, 127:37–38, *mlk* ‖ *drktk;* 'nt:I:16–17, *bḫmr* ‖ *bmskh;* 2 Aqht:I:26–27, *bt* ‖ *hklh;* II:11–12, *p'n* ‖ *gh;* and VI:36–37, *spsg ysk*[*l*]*riš ḥrṣ lẓr qdqdy,* "Glaze will be poured upon my head (*riš*), plaster upon my skull (*qdqdy*)"—G. R. Driver in JRAS (1948), 164–65, was able to show that a number of biblical texts that had been emended for lack of a suffix stood in no such need. Among his examples are Pss xxx 13, xxxv 5–6, lxxvii 9, lxxxv 10. See also M. Dahood, *Biblica* 37 (1956), 338–40, and 42 (1961), 384; and D. N. Freedman, IEJ 13 (1963), 125 f., who effectively applies this principle in Deut xxxiii

28; and most recently Chr. Brekelmans, "Pronominal Suffixes in the Hebrew Book of Psalms," in *Jaarbericht van het Vooraziatisch-Egyptisch Genootschap Ex Oriente Lux, Annuaire de la Société Orientale "Ex Oriente Lux"* (Leiden); *Ex Oriente Lux* 17 (1963, appeared in January 1965), 202–6.

Numerous new instances will be cited in due sequence: e.g., Pss iv 4, ix 2, xi 2, xiii 4, xvi 4, xvii 1, 2, 3, 4, 7, 8, xviii 15, xix 6, 8, 9, 15, xx 7, xxi 10, xxv 9, xxvi 7, xxxi 24, xxxiv 7, 18, xxxvi 10, xxxvii 14, xxxix 12, xlvi 5, xlviii 4, l 17, 23, li 14, liv 9, lv 13, lxii 5, lxvi 18, 19, lxviii 10, lxix 23, lxxiii 7, lxxvii 18, 19, lxxviii 69, lxxxix 37, xc 12, xcviii 1, cix 19, cxviii 14, cxxxv 7, cxxxix 6.

This poetic usage, a type of ellipsis, is analogous to the use of double-duty prepositions (see NOTE on Ps xxxiii 7), conjunctions (NOTE on Ps xxxvi 7), negatives (NOTE on Ps ix 19), interrogatives (NOTES on Pss ii 1 and iii 2), and vocatives (NOTE on Ps xxxiii 1). Though ellipsis has long been recognized in biblical poetry, its pervasiveness was not fully appreciated till the discovery of ancient Canaanite poetic texts.

as long as I live. Reading *b^{e}'ōdī* for MT *ba'^{a}dī;* the mispointing may indicate a *Vorlage* employing *scriptio defectiva.* A similar explanation may account for MT *ba'^{a}dī,* which appears to be the inferior reading, in Ps cxxxviii 8, where one may propose, *yhwh yigmōr b^{e}'ōdī yhwh ḥasd^{e}kā l^{e}'ōlām,* "Yahweh will deal bountifully as long as I live; your kindness, O Yahweh, is to eternity." Cf. Pss civ 33 and cxlvi 2.

my Glorious One. *k^{e}bōdī* is apparently a divine appellative, as in Pss iv 3, lxii 8, lxvi 2, which lends its suffix to parallel *māgān;* cf. preceding NOTE on *my Suzerain.* In Exod xxxiii 18, 22; Ps cxiii 4, *kābōd* denotes *ipsa Dei essentia,* according to Zorell, ZLH, p. 345b. If this explication of *kābōd* is correct, it will be analogous to *'ōlām,* "eternity," which also became an appellative, "the Eternal One," in Pss xxiv 7, 9, lxvi 7, lxxv 10, etc.; see F. M. Cross, Jr., "Yahweh and the God of Patriarchs," HTR 55 (1962), 225–59, especially pp. 236 ff.

who lifts high my head. I.e., defends my honor and gives me victory over my adversaries. The copula of *ūmērīm* could be appositional as in Prov xxx 16 and in the Ugaritic title *kṯr wḫss,* "Kothar who is Hasis," as explained by W. F. Albright in BASOR 164 (1961), 36; *Wilhelm Gesenius' Hebräische Grammatik* völlig umgearbeitet von E. Kautzsch (abbr. GK), 28th rev. ed. (Leipzig, 1909), § 154a. An equivalent phrase is used of the Pharaoh (hence "suzerain") in Gen xl 20, "And he lifted up the head of the chief cup-bearer"; there may be some significance in the fact that Ps lxxxix 18, "In your favor you lift high our horn," immediately precedes the proclamation, "For Yahweh himself is our Suzerain, and the Holy One of Israel our King." Compare also Ps cx 7, where the great king Yahweh is said to raise high (*yārīm rō'š*) the head of his anointed king of Israel.

5. *If with full voice.* A conditional sentence without morphologic indicator, as correctly remarked by Gunkel, *Die Psalmen,* p. 14; cf. GK, § 159b. Similar usage occurs in UT, 1019:12–16, *ttn wtn wlttn wal ttn tn ks yn wištn,* "If you give, then give; if you don't give, then don't give; if you give a cup of wine, I will drink it"; cf. UT, § 13.79.

he answers me. wayyaʿanēnī is a consecutive imperfect after an imperfect; see Michel, TSP, pp. 26 f. This expression of confidence is a constitutive element of personal laments.

from his holy mountain. This sentiment supports the version proposed in vs. 3, "from God."

6. *If I lie down.* Conditional sentence without conditional particle.

7. *the shafts of people.* Customarily rendered "myriads of people," *rībebōt ʿām* yields better sense when studied along with Pss xviii 44 and lxxxix 51. The sense of these latter two texts is also disputed, but a derivation from *rbb,* "to shoot arrows," produces a consistent image in all three texts. Thus lxxxix 51, *zekōr ʾadōnay ḥerpat ʿabādekā śeʾētī beḥēqī kol rabbē-m ʿammīm* (MT *rabbīm ʿammīm*), "Remember, Lord, the insults to your servant, his bearing in his bosom all the shafts of peoples." This evokes the motif of Job xvi 13, *yāsōbbū ʿālay rabbāyw yepallaḥ kilyōtay welōʾ yaḥmōl,* "His arrows encompass me, he pierces my entrails without pity." The balance with *ḥerpāh* "insults," indicates that *rabbē-m ʿammīm* refers to the sarcastic shafts of nations; this too is the sense suggested in Ps iii, the lament of an individual who has been sorely calumniated. The imagery which represents detractors as archers may be seen in Gen xlix 23, as recognized by LXX, "Against whom the calumniators brought false accusations, though the masters of bows took aim at him" and by Speiser, "Archers in their hostility / Harried and attacked him" (The Anchor Bible, vol. 1).

deployed against me. The syntax of *šātū ʿālāy* has long presented a problem. BDB, p. 1011b, for instance, call it internally transitive, but progress in the study of the use and extent of the *qal* passive conjugation suggests that *šītū* would be the most probable vocalization. The military sense of *šīt* recurs in Isa xxii 7 where a *qal* passive pointing bids fair to resolve the syntactic problem. Cf. NOTE on Ps xvii 10.

8. *O that.* Explaining *kī* as an emphatic particle used with the precative or optative perfect (see NOTE below on *would smite . . . smash.*). Compare the construction *kī hikkītā* with Pss ix 5, *kī ʿāśītā mišpeṭī wedīnī,* "O that you would defend my right and my cause!"; xxxix 10, *kī ʾattā ʿāśītāh,* "O that you yourself would act!"; lxi 4, *kī hāyītā maḥseh lī,* "O that you would be my refuge!" Cf. also Pss x 14, lv 10, lxi 6, lxiii 8, and James Muilenburg, "The Linguistic and Rhetorical Usage of the Particle *kī* in the Old Testament," HUCA 32 (1961), 135–60.

you yourself. The single *nota accusativi* in this psalm, which many would delete as otiose, should be pointed *'attā,* the independent personal pronoun occasionally found with the precative perfect. Cf. Pss x 14, *rā'ītāh kī 'attāh 'āmāl,* "See for yourself the misery"; xxxix 10 (cited in previous NOTE); lvi 9, *nōdī sāpartāh 'attāh,* "You yourself write down my tears"; lxi 6, *kī 'attāh 'ᵉlōhīm šāma'tā līnᵉdāray,* "O that you yourself, O God, would hear my vows!"

would smite . . . Smash. Parsing *hikkītā* and *šibbartā* as precative perfects which balance the two imperatives of vs. 8a, *qūmāh* and *hōšī'ēnī.* The presence of imperatives or jussives in the immediate context is the surest clue to the precative mode. In Ps iv 2, e.g., precative *hirḥabtā* is preceded by one imperative and followed by two others.

GK seem not to have recognized this construction, so well known from Arabic, even though Ewald and Böttcher in the last century had noted a few instances in the Bible. Joüon, GHB, § 112k, is alive to the niceties of style when he submits that in poetry (Psalms, Job) and in elevated prose *qatal* carries an optative nuance; he cites I Chron xvii 27 ‖ II Sam vii 29; Ps lvii 7; Job xxii 18. The greatest contribution, however, was made by Moses Buttenwieser, who, in his 1938 commentary on the Psalms, devoted a special excursus to the subject and cited more than a score of convincing examples in the Psalter alone; see p. 905 of his PCTNT for a complete listing. To his number thirteen may be added: iv 8, ix 18, xvii 3, xxii 22, xxxix 10, xliv 27, lvi 9, lxiii 3, lxvii 7, lxxiii 23, xciv 17, cx 3, cxix 121.

Briggs, CECBP, I, p. 33, hesitated to accept the precative perfect in Hebrew even though it was a recognized Arabic construction. Such hesitation can no longer be defended since Ugaritic confirms the presence of this usage in Northwest Semitic and further points up the strict linguistic relationship of Ugaritic to Hebrew. Cf. UT, 76:II:20, *ḥwt aḫt,* "May you live, O my sister," a formula which appears in a modified form in the letter published in UT, 2008:10, *mlkn b'ly ḥw[t],* "Our king, my lord, may you live!" Further, in UT, 52:7, *šlmt mlk,* "May you prosper, O king!"; 77:38–39, *ar yrḫ wyrḫ yark,* "May the moon shine, and may the moon shine for you!"; 117:17–18, *w pn mlk nr bn,* "And may the face of the king be radiant upon us!"; 128:III:13, *mid rm krt,* "May Kirta be greatly exalted!" On Phoenician Karatepe III:2–3, *b'l brk . . . 'yt 'ztwd,* "May Baal bless . . . Azitawaddu!", see Friedrich, PPG, § 262.4, and G. Levi Della Vida in *Rendiconti Lincei* 8 (1949), 286.

on the jaw. Implying that they will no longer be able to calumniate the psalmist. This is perfectly in keeping with the metaphor of the slanderous shafts of vs. 7. In the Canaanite Legend of Aqhat, one of the obligations of a dutiful son toward a deceased father was to silence those who would calumniate his dead father. The text, which has lent itself to widely diverging translations, can be rendered meaningfully by recourse to Ar. *ṭabaqa,* "to shut," used of mouth, eyes, etc. The text is UT, 2

Aqht:I:29–30, *ṯbq lḥt niṣh,* "who will shut the jaws of his detractors." The noun *lḥt* is the plural of *l*ᵉ*ḥī,* Ugar. *lḥy*. Cf. Ps lxiii 12, "The mouth of those telling lies will be shut."

9. *O Yahweh.* Interpreting *l* of *l*ᵉ*yahweh* as *lamedh vocativum,* widely used in Ugaritic; a convenient list of occurrences can be found in Aistleitner, WuS, No. 1425, pp. 163 f. Biblical examples include Pss vii 8, xiii 6, xvi 2, xxxi 3, xxxii 4–5, xxxiii 1, xlii 10, xlvii 2, lii 11, lxviii 5, 33, lxxi 1, 18, lxxiii 1, lxxv 5 (twice), xcii 1, cxxii 4, cxl 7; Gen xxiii 11; Isa xxxviii 14, lii 7; Jer xxxi 7. For the vocative particle in the Hebrew name **rūmlāyāhū* in Isa vii 1, 4, 5, 9 (MT *r*ᵉ*malyāhū*), see Dewey M. Beegle in BASOR 123 (1951), 28, who interprets it as "Be exalted, O Yahweh"; cf. further, William H. Brownlee, *The Meaning of the Qumran Scrolls for the Bible* (New York, 1964), p. 167. For the Phoenician vocative particle in Arslan Tash, I:4, *lḥnqt 'mr,* "O Strangler of Lamb(s)," see H. Donner and W. Röllig, *Kanaanäische und Aramäische Inschriften* (abbr. KAI), II: Kommentar (Wiesbaden, 1964), p. 44. In this analysis, vocative *yhwh* corresponds to vocatives *yhwh* and *'*ᵉ*lōhay* in vs. 8 and further point up the chiastic arrangement of vss. 8–9, so ably studied by N. W. Lund in AJSL 49 (1933), 299.

Selah. A liturgical direction; its meaning and etymology still elude scholars.

PSALM 4

(iv 1–9)

1 *For the director; with stringed instruments. A psalm of David.*

2 When I call, answer me, O God of my vindication;
in distress, set me at large;
Have pity on me and hear my prayer.
3 O men of rank, how long must my Glorious One be
insulted? [2]*
How long will you worship inanities
or consult idols? *Selah*
4 And recognize that [3]
Yahweh will work wonders for the one devoted to him,
Yahweh will hear me when I call to him.
5 Be disquieted, but do not sin, [4]
examine your conscience,
upon your beds weep. *Selah*
6 Offer legitimate sacrifices and trust in Yahweh. [5]
7 Many keep saying, "Who will show us rain? [6]
The light of your face has fled from us, O Yahweh."
8 Put happiness in my heart; [7]
now let their wheat and their wine increase.
9 In his peaceful presence, [8]
I shall lie down and sleep;
For you alone, O Yahweh,
make my repose secure.

* Verse numbers in RSV.

NOTES

iv. A prayer for rain. Drought is in the land; the psalmist (a *ḥāsīd*) is much distressed, while the pusillanimous leaders of the people criticize Yahweh and seek rain from the nature deities. The psalmist reminds those of little faith that Yahweh will hear their prayer if they but examine their consciences, weep for their sins, and offer legitimate sacrifices. The correct exegesis of some of the phrases flows from the comparison with similar phrases and contexts in the other psalms that are prayers for rain, such as lxv 10–14, lxvii, lxxxv.

2. *God of my vindication.* This connotation of *ṣedeq* is present in Pss xvii 1, xxxv 27; Isa l 8, liii 11; Job xxxiii 32. If the psalmist's prayer goes unheeded, his reputation as a *ḥāsīd* will suffer; hence he is eager to be vindicated and purposely invokes God with the epithet, "God of my vindication." In Ps xvii 1, where the epithet occurs anew, the vindication of the poet consists in being acquitted of false accusations.

set me at large. With Israel Eitan in AJSL 46 (1929), 25, parsing *hirḥabtā* as a precative or optative perfect in parallelism with the imperatives *ʿᵃnēnī, ḥonnēnī,* and *šᵉmaʿ;* see NOTE on Ps iii 8. Michel, TSP, p. 246, labels a *qatal* form in the midst of three imperatives *"merkwürdig,"* and accordingly adopts Gunkel's emendation of the three imperatives into *qatal* forms; this is text-critical aberration with a vengeance. One may here remark that much of Michel's volume on the tenses in the Psalter is vitiated by his failure to recognize the existence of the precative perfect; there are more than thirty instances of this usage in the Psalter, all unremarked by Michel.

Have pity on me. The apparatus of BH³ recommends that *ḥonnēnī* be deleted, but this wayward proposal forfeits claims to further consideration with the observation that the equivalent jussive form *yᵉḥonnēnū* occurs in Ps lxvii 2, which is also a prayer for rain.

3. *men of rank.* In Pss xlix 3 and lxii 10, men of high degree are contrasted with those of no rank.

my Glorious One. Consult NOTE on Ps iii 4. The Glorious One is contrasted with the inanities (*rīq*) and the idols (*kāzāb*) to which men of rank have resorted.

be insulted. Literally "for insult, dishonor." By turning to false gods, the Israelites dishonor Yahweh.

worship inanities. This nuance of *'āhēb* occurs in Jer viii 2 (the parallel verbs appear decisive) and Hos iv 8; BDB, p. 13a.

consult idols. I.e., to find out when the rain will come. The substantive *kāzāb,* "idol" (*res ementita*), recurs in Ps xl 5 and Amos ii 4. This may well be the sense in Sirach xv 8 where *'anšē kāzāb,* "idolaters," is chiastically balanced by vs. 7, *m^etē šāw'*, "men of the idol." Gunkel, *Die Psalmen,* p. 17, writes that *"kāzāb ist nach anderen hier ein Schimpfname der Götzen Amos 2:4 vgl Ps 40:5"* ("According to others, *kāzāb* is a nickname for idols; Amos ii 4, cf. Ps xl 5.").

4. *And recognize that.* This stichometric division was suggested by D. N. Freedman, who noticed that the introductory formula *d^e'ū kī* operates with both halves of the verse.

will work wonders. hiplāh is an alternate spelling of *hiplā',* found in many MSS. Perfect *hiplāh* is balanced by imperfect *yišma',* a very common sequence in Ugaritic and Hebrew poetry. Good examples occur in Pss vi 10, vii 13, 14, viii 7, ix 8, xx 10, xxxviii 12, xlvi 5, l 19, xciii 3.

the one devoted to him. The psalmist refers to himself in the third person as *ḥāsīd,* just as the author of Ps v identified himself with the *ṣaddīq* in vs. 13. In other words, *ḥāsīd* is used much like *'ebed,* which sometimes functions as a polite substitute for the personal pronoun; cf. NOTE on Ps xix 12.

will hear me. The principle of the double-duty suffix operates with *yišma';* see NOTE on Ps iii 4. To judge from the recognized examples, the omission of the suffix with forms of *šāma'* was uncommonly frequent; e.g., Pss xxi 25, xxxiv 7, 18, lxvi 18, 19.

when I call. b^eqor'ī forms an inclusion with vs. 2, *b^eqor'ī.*

5. *Be disquieted.* I.e., by the lack of rainfall. The verb *rgz* is found in Phoenician Tabnit Inscription, *rgz trgzn,* "(If you) at all disquiet me."

examine your conscience. Literally "look into your heart." On *'āmar,* "to see, look," cf. NOTE on Ps iii 3 and M. Dahood, "Hebrew-Ugaritic Lexicography I," *Biblica* 44 (1963), 295 f. The sins of the people were thought to be the cause of the drought. Jer v 24 is especially instructive for the exegesis of this phrase in that the phrase occurs there in a context explicitly dealing with "the theology of rain."

upon your beds weep. As I proposed, on the basis of Ugar. *dmm,* parallel to *bky,* "to cry," in CBQ 22 (1960), 400–3, and accepted by C. H. W. Brekelmans, *Ras Sjamra en het Oude Testament* (Nijmegen, 1962), pp. 10 f. The cluster *w^edommū* illustrates a point of Hebrew syntax and a new Hebrew root. The conjunction *w^e* is here emphatic, a function put into clear light by UT, 51:v:107–8, *št alp qdmh mra wtk pnh,* "Set an ox before him, a fatling right in front of him." The particle has been studied by Marvin H. Pope in JAOS 73 (1953), 95 ff.; P. Wernberg-Møller in JSS 3 (1958), 321–26; M. Dahood in *Gregorianum* 43 (1962), 65–67; and by Leo Prijs in BZ 8 (1964), 105–9, whose point of departure was Arabic usage and who only at the end of his article recognized the relevance of the Ugaritic text cited above.

The position of *dommū* at the end of its clause may possibly be ascribed to the emphasizing nature of *waw,* much like emphatic *kī* in Ugaritic and Hebrew. Emphatic *lamedh* produces a similar effect; see

NOTE on Ps viii 3. For other instances of postposition with emphatic *waw*, see Pss v 4, vii 2, xlix 21, lxxvii 2, lxxxix 20; Job xxiii 12; Lam i 13.

In recent years the root *dmm* has been the object of several studies, the latest being that of Norbert Lohfink in VT 12 (1962), especially pp. 275–77, where G. R. Driver in *Sepher Tur Sinai* (Jerusalem, 1960), p. 2*, might be added to the bibliographical references. Though scholars dispute whether *dmm* denotes "to moan" or "to weep," the synonymy of *dmm* with *bky* in UT, 125:25–26, and the fact that the pun in Jer viii 14 depends precisely on the meaning "to weep," weight the balance toward the second meaning. For full treatment of the wordplay, see Dahood, *Biblica* 45 (1964), 402.

That one's bedroom is a fitting place for shedding tears is clear from Gen xlviii 30; Ps vi 7, "I bathe my couch with tears," and UT, Krt: 27–29, "His tears drop like shekels to the floor, like pieces-of-five to the bed." See also Matt vi 6.

6. *legitimate sacrifices.* I.e., as opposed to sacrifices to idols. On *zibḥē ṣedeq,* which recurs in Ps li 21, see Roger T. O'Callaghan in VT 4 (1954), 170 (see Selected Bibliography).

7. *show us rain.* The explanation of the sense of *ṭōb* appears crucial for determining the literary genus of the poem. The "good" par excellence in Palestine is the rain, so that in a number of texts *ṭōb* without further modification concretely signifies "rain." Deut xxviii 12, "Yahweh will open for you his treasury of rain (*'ōṣārō haṭṭōb*) the heavens, to give your land its rain in due season." For other instances of a pronominal suffix intervening in a construct chain as in *'ōṣārō haṭṭōb,* see Gevirtz, *Patterns in the Early Poetry of Israel,* p. 80. Cf. Jer v 25, "And your sins have withheld the rain from you (*haṭṭōb mikkem*)"; Jer iii 3, "So that the showers (*rᵉbībīm*) were withheld," and Amos iv 7, "I withheld from you the rain (*gešem*)." See also Ps lxxxv; Deut xxviii; and I Kings viii 35, which explain the relationship between sin and rain. Jer xvii 6, "He shall be like the scrub in the desert unable to see the coming of the rain (*ṭōb*)," becomes fully intelligible in the light of the antithetic statement in Jer xvii 8 describing the condition of the man who trusts in God: "For he is like a tree that is planted near water . . . That fears not the coming of heat." (John Bright, The Anchor Bible, vol. 21). The antithesis with "heat" shows that *ṭōb* denotes "rain." The frequently proposed emendation of *ṭōb* to *roṭeb,* "moisture," becomes dispensable. Finally, Ps lxxxv 13, *gam yhwh yittēn haṭṭōb wᵉ'arṣēnū tittēn yᵉbūlāh,* "With a loud voice Yahweh gives his rain, and our land gives its produce." Some medieval rabbis correctly interpreted *ṭōb* here to mean "rain." Further examples are cited in *Biblica* 45 (1964), 411. The connection between *ṭōb* and "rain" already appears in Bronze Age Canaanite litera-

ture, in UT, 1 Aqht:I:45–46, *bl šrʻ thmtm bl ṭbn ql bʻl,* "May there be no surging of the two deeps, no rain with Baal's thunder."

The light of your face. As a sign of beneficence, this phrase is an ancient metaphor of frequent occurrence in the El Amarna and Ugaritic correspondence, as in UT, 1126:6, *wpn šmš nr by mid,* "And the face of the Sun [i.e., Pharaoh] shone brightly upon me." The comparison of our clause, "The light of your face has fled from us," with Ps lxvii 2, *yāʼēr pānāyw ʼittānū,* "May he make his face shine upon us," further reveals that Ps lxvii, whose literary classification has been a matter of dispute, is a prayer for rain and should be classed with Ps iv. Both phrases may serve as commentary upon Ps lxxxv 5, *šūbēnū ʼēl,* "Return to us, O God." Cf. NOTE on vs. 2 for another connection with Ps lxvii.

has fled from us. Vocalizing *nāsāh* for MT *nesāh.* The statement, *nāsāh ʻālēnū ʼōr pānekā yhwh,* becomes intelligible with the knowledge that in Northwest Semitic (Ugaritic, Phoenician, Hebrew, Aramaic, and Moabite) *ʻal* with verbs of fleeing can denote "from." The evidence has been assembled in Dahood, TS 14 (1953), 85–86. Among the probative texts cited there is Phoenician Ahiram, *wnḥt tbrḥ ʻl gbl,* "And may peace flee from Byblos." On the possible Ugar. *ʻl,* "from," see Driver, CML, p. 141b, and for Moabite usage, S. Segert in *Archiv Orientální* 29 (1961), 228. The evidence for *ʻal,* "from," has been gathered anew by G. R. Driver in JSS 9 (1964), 349.

The reading *nāsāh,* from *nūs,* represents an archaic third-person masculine singular of the Canaanite *qatala* type as in Ugaritic; metrical considerations may account for its presence here. Other instances of this archaic ending include Pss xi 5, *ʼōhēb ḥāmās śāneʼāh napšō,* "Who loves injustice hates himself"; xviii 35, *niḥatāh,* "He lowered," where the doublet II Sam xxii 35 reads *niḥat,* obviously a modernized reading; xx 10, *hōšīʻāh,* "He has given victory"; and lxxxix 8, *rabbāh,* "He is great." These examples offer a solid basis for arguing that Eccles vii 27, *ʼāmerāh qōhelet,* "Qoheleth said," is the correct reading and that xii 8, *ʼāmar haqqōhelet,* should be redivided to read *ʼāmerāh qōhelet,* since *qōhelet* is to be considered a proper name and hence does not need determination with the article. Cf. further Ps xvi 6 and Prov ix 4.

8. *Put happiness.* Parsing *nātattāh* as precative perfect (cf. vs 2 and NOTE therewith), precisely as in Ps lx 6, *nātattāh līrēʼekā nēs,* "Give a banner of victory to those who fear you." The *scriptio plena* of the final syllable *-āh* may correspond to the energic ending of the imperative, especially since an impressive number of precative perfects are written fully in the final syllable: Pss x 14, xxxi 6, xxxv 22, xliv 27, lvi 9, lx 6, cxl 8; Prov ix 4; Lam iii 59, 60. This analysis bears importantly on the parsing of Ps lxvii 7, *ʼereṣ nātenāh yebūlāh yebārekēnū ʼelōhīm ʼelōhēnū,* "May the earth give her produce, may God, our God, bless

us." The psalm is thus a prayer for rain rather than a hymn of thanksgiving for blessings bestowed; the presence of the jussive *y*^{e}*bār*^{e}*kēnū* points to the same conclusion.

in my heart. Adding the *mem* of *mē'ēt* to *libbī* as enclitic; cf. the enclitic *mem* with *lēb* in Ps x 17.

now let their wheat. Reading (for MT *'ēt,* "time") the adverb *'attā* written defectively as in Ps lxxiv 6 and Ezek xxvii 24, where critics agree that *'ēt* should be pointed *'attā.* Cf. the usage in Ps xx 7. The reading *d*^{e}*gānām* seems assured by the appearance of the same form in the petition for rain in Ps lxv 10.

their wine increase. Like *nātattāh* at the beginning of the verse, *rabbū* is also a precative perfect, thus creating a fine syntactic balance, while, etymologically, *rabbū* encloses the inclusion beginning with *rabbīm,* the first word of vs. 7. Though the majority of precative perfects are second person, there are a number of clear third-person precatives: Pss ix 18, x 16, lvii 7; Isa xliii 9; Prov ix 4.

Though well attested in other books of the Bible and in Ugar. *trṯ, tīrōš,* "wine, must," is a hapax legomenon in the Psalter.

9. *his peaceful presence.* Literally "in the peace of his face," an example of hendiadys which might be compared with UT, 'nt:IV:47, *lnḫt lkḥṯ drkth,* "on the peaceful bench of his authority." Cf. W. F. Albright in JAOS 67 (1947), 156, n. 26, on the Ugaritic hendiadys.

Commenting on *yaḥdāw,* Briggs, CECBP, I, p. 37, remarks that this is the only text in which it denotes "at one and the same time," joining both verbs in action of same persons, which suggests that a solution must be sought elsewhere. One could explain *yaḥdāw* as the substantive "face," from dialectal *ḥdy,* "to see, gaze," Heb. *ḥāzāh,* which is discussed at Ps xxi 7. Cf. Isa xl 5, *w*^{e}*niglāh k*^{e}*bōd yhwh w*^{e}*rā'ū kol bāśār yaḥdāw,* "And the glory of Yahweh shall be revealed, and all flesh shall see his face." For this version, see M. Dahood, CBQ 20 (1958), 46–49.

PSALM 5

(v 1–13)

1 *For the director; for the flutes. A psalm of David.*

2 Give ear to my words, O Yahweh,
attend to my utterance.
3 Give heed to the sound of my cry, [2]*
my King and my God;
For to you am I praying, O Yahweh.
4 At dawn hear my voice, [3]
at dawn I will draw up my case,
for you will I watch.
5 A no-god delights in evil, [4]
but you—no evil man can be your guest.
6 Let no boasters stand before you. [5]
I hate all evildoers,
7 destroy those who tell lies! [6]
The man of idols and figurines
Yahweh detests.
8 But through your great love [7]
I will enter your house;
I will worship in your holy temple,
among those who fear you, O Yahweh.
9 Lead me into your meadow [8]
because of my rivals,
Your way make level before me.
10 For there is nothing firm in his mouth, [9]
his belly is an engulfing chasm;
A grave wide-open is their throat,
with their tongue they bring death.
11 Make them perish, O God, [10]
let them fall because of their schemes;

* Verse numbers in RSV.

For their numerous crimes
hurl them down,
Since they have challenged you.
12 While all who seek refuge in you will rejoice, [11]
forever singing with joy;
And you will shelter them,
that they who love your name
may exult in you.
13 For you will bless the just man yourself, O Yahweh, [12]
as with a shield
you will surround him with your favor.

Notes

v. Though usually classified as an individual lament comprised of five strophes which alternately contrast the just with the wicked, this psalm maintains distinct points of contact with the psalms of innocence, especially with Pss xxvi and cxxxix, and can with equal validity be placed in that category.

2. *my utterance.* Zorell, ZLH, p. 184b, appears to be correct in subsuming *hāgīg* and *hāgāh,* "to utter," under the same root against BDB, GB, and Koehler who distinguish two roots. Zorell's view is sustained by UT, 1001:rev:13, *k'ṣmm lttn kabnm lthggn,* "When the trees do not give forth (their voice), when the stones do not utter," a variation on the theme of UT, 'nt:III:19–20, *rgm 'ṣ wlḫšt abn,* "word of tree and whisper of stone." The reduplicated conjugation of *thggn* may contribute to the explanation of the morphology of biblical *hāgīg* which is a dis legomenon.

3. *O Yahweh.* Customarily attached to vs. 4, vocative *yhwh* is for metrical and stylistic reasons to be joined to vs. 3. This redivision, which results in two 3+3 cola followed by two 2+2 cola in vss. 3b and 4, permits each of the two cola in vs. 4 to begin with *bōqer,* "at dawn," and uncovers an inclusion starting with *'ēlekā 'etpallāl,* "to you am I praying," and closing with *lᵉkā wa'ᵃṣappeh,* "for you will I watch."

4. *hear my voice.* Following the imperatives of vss. 2–3, *tišma',* though morphologically imperfect, serves an imperative function. Cf. Joüon, GHB, § 113m, who lists seven texts (but not the present one) from the Psalter, and add Pss x 15, xxxii 7, lxi 3. Albrecht Goetze in *Studia Orientalia Ioanni Pedersen Septuagenario A.D. VII Id. Nov.*

Anno MCMLIII a Collegis, Discipulis, Amicis Dicata, ed. Flemming Hvidberg (Copenhagen, 1953), p. 117, n. 8, has noted the same construction in UT, 51:VIII:7–9, *wrd bṯḫpṯt arṣ tspr byrdm arṣ,* "And go down to the house of beds, the nether world, count yourself among those who have gone down to the nether world." In this passage *tspr* is a jussive with the same modal force as the parallel imperative *rd.* This identical usage in Hebrew and Ugaritic speaks volumes for the Canaanite classification of Ugaritic. Recognition of this stylistic variation may result in smoother renditions of certain biblical passages. For example, Deut xxxii 1, *ha'^{a}zīnū haššāmayim wa'^{a}dabbērāh w^{e}tišm^{e}'ī* (understand consonantal *tšm'* as *scriptio defectiva* for normal *tšm'y*) *he'āreṣ* (MT *hā'āreṣ*) *'imrē pī,* "Give ear, O heaven, and I shall speak, and hear, O earth, the words of my mouth." RSV and other versions retain MT *w^{e}tišma' hā'āreṣ,* "And let the earth hear," but related formulas such as Isa i 2 suggest that imperative *ha'^{a}zīnū* and vocative *haššāmayim* be matched by a second-person jussive, and that consonantal *h'rṣ* contains the vocative particle rather than the article.

I will draw up my case. *'e'^{e}rōk* is a forensic term used absolutely in Ps l 21; Job xxxiii 5, xxxvii 19. Such usage suggests that the poet has formally been accused of a crime (idolatry, see NOTE on vs. 6) and is now preparing his case.

for you will I watch. Dividing second half of vs. 4 to read *bōqer 'e'^{e}rōk l^{e}kā wa'^{a}ṣappeh* (2+2), and parsing *wa* as *waw emphaticum,* which often precedes a verb placed at the end of a sentence for reasons of emphasis; cf. NOTE on Ps iv 5. This stichic division obviates the need for supplying *l^{e}kā* or *'ēlekā* after *wa'^{a}ṣappeh,* as proposed in the apparatus of BH^{3}.

5. *A no-god. lō' 'ēl* is a composite noun occurring in Deut xxxii 21 and equivalently found in Deut xxxii 17 and Jer v 7. Ugaritic compounds such as *blmt,* "immortality" (equals Prov xii 28, *'al māwet* as proposed by M. Dahood, *Biblica* 41 [1960], 176–81), *aplb,* "surface of the chest" (UT, § 8.74), make it very likely that composite nouns are of more frequent occurrence than recent Hebrew grammars allow and that the doctrine found in J. Olshausen, *Lehrbuch der hebräischen Sprache* (1861), § 225i, p. 445, more accurately reflects the real situation. Accordingly, *lō' kēn* (Akk. *la kettu*) in Isa xvi 16 (cf. Jer xlviii 30) and in Prov xv 7 should be analyzed as a composite noun and defined as "injustice." On *lō' ṭōb,* "evil, crime," see NOTE on Ps xxxvi 5, and for composite *ṣalmāwet,* "utter darkness," D. Winton Thomas in JSS 7 (1962), 199 f. Composite *'ōlām wā'ed* is discussed in the NOTE on Ps x 16.

The immorality of the Canaanite gods, richly illustrated by the Ras Shamra tablets, is contrasted with the absolute holiness of Yahweh, in whose sight even the stars are not pure. An unpublished Ugaritic tablet graphically describes the excesses of El, the head of the Canaanite pantheon, while he is at table. As a result of his intemperance, El ends up wallowing *bḫrih wṯnth,* "in his excrement and his urine."

can be your guest. Note the kindred concept in Ps xv 1–2. The construction *y*ᵉ*gūr*ᵉ*kā,* with dative suffix (cf. NOTE on Ps xxi 4), resembles the usage in Ps xciv 20, *hay*ᵉ*ḥobr*ᵉ*kā,* "Can he be a friend of yours?"

6. *boasters. hōl*ᵉ*līm,* parallel to *r*ᵉ*šā'īm* in Pss lxxiii 3 and lxxv 5, may possess pagan overtones which today escape us. In UT, 77:40–41, *bnt hll,* "the daughters of shouting," is the name of the professional songstresses.

stand before you. I.e., in the law court to press their charges against the psalmist. What prompts the forensic interpretation of *yityaṣṣ*ᵉ*bū* is the presence of the legal term *'ārak* in vs. 4 and the collocation of both these verbs in the legal context of Job xxxiii 5, *'im tūkal h*ᵃ*šībēnī 'er*ᵉ*kā l*ᵉ*pānay hityaṣṣābāh,* "If you are able, refute me; draw up your case and stand before me."

I hate all evildoers. Pointing *śn't* as first person *śānē'tī* rather than second person *śānē'tā* with MT. The defective spelling of the first person is duplicated in Pss xvi 2 (*'mrt* for normal *'mrty*), xxxviii 9, and cxl 13. First person *śānē'tī* appears to be a *terminus technicus* employed in the formula of repudiation of false gods when one was accused of idolatry. The term is characteristic of psalms of innocence: xxvi 5, *śānē'tī q*ᵉ*hal r*ᵉ*šā'īm,* "I have hated the company of evildoers"; xxxi 6–7, *'*ᵉ*met śānē'tī haššōm*ᵉ*rīm hablē šāw',* "Truly I hate those who keep worthless idols"; ci 3, *'*ᵃ*śōh sēṭīm śānē'tī lō' yidbaq bī,* "I hate the making of images; may it never cling to me"; cxxxix 22, *taklīt śin'āh ś*ᵉ*nē'tīm,* "With perfect hatred I hate them" (the men of idols in vs. 19).

7. *destroy.* Being parallel to jussive implicit in *lō' yityaṣṣ*ᵉ*bū, t*ᵉ*'abbēd* has the force of an imperative; cf. NOTE on vs. 4a.

who tell lies. I.e., those who falsely accuse the psalmist of idolatry. Cf. the psalm of innocence xvii 1, *ballē'* (MT *b*ᵉ*lō'*) *śiptē mirmāh,* "Destroy deceitful lips," in a context where the poet makes a protestation of innocence when accused of idol-worship.

man of idols. One should distinguish, it would seem, between *'īš dāmīm,* "a man of blood," and *'īš dāmīm* [vocalization doubtful], "a man of idols." The root of the latter would be *dāmāh,* "to be like" (cf. especially Isa xiv 14), while Latin *similis,* "similar," and *simulacrum,* "image," illustrate the semantic nexus between the root and the substantive. Cf. Ar. *dumyatu,* "image, effigy," and the following biblical texts: Ps xxvi 9–10, "Snatch me not away with sinners, nor my life with men of idols (*'anšē dāmīm*), in whose left hand is idolatry (*zimmāh*), and whose right hand is full of bribes"; Ps cxxxix 19–20, "O that you would slay the wicked, O God! O men of idols (*'anšē dāmīm*) turn away from me!

Who look upon you as an image (*m^e^zimmāh*); 'Your protector is honored as an idol'"; Hos iv 2, *dāmīm b^e^dāmīm nāgā'ū,* "Idols touch idols"; and possibly Ps cvi 38, "Whom they sacrificed to the statues of Canaan, and they defiled the land with idols (*dāmīm*)." Here there is probably a play on the double sense of *dāmīm,* "idols/blood." Cf. also Ps lv 24.

and figurines. mirmāh, "deceit, fraud," concretely denotes "figurine" or "idol" in Ps xxiv 4, where it is parallel to *šāw',* "idol," in Job xxxi 5, and, most clearly, in Jer v 27, *kik^e^lūb malē' 'ōp bottēhem m^e^lē'īm mirmāh,* "Like a cage full of birds, their houses are full of figurines," and ix 5, *šibt^e^kā b^e^tōk mirmāh b^e^mirmāh,* "Your dwelling is among figurine upon figurine."

Yahweh detests. The interpretation of *'īš dāmīm ūmirmāh* set out in preceding NOTES finds some confirmation in Ps cvi 40, where Yahweh is said to detest (*y^e^tā'ēb*) Israel because of its idols.

8\. *through your great love.* The love is to be manifested by declaring the poet innocent of the charges preferred against him.

I will enter your house. 'ābō' bēteka compares with UT, 127:3, *bt krt bu tbu,* "They enter Kirta's house," and with Phoenician Arslan Tash Incantation, 5–6, *bt 'b' 'l tb'n,* "The house I enter you shall not enter."

If he were not declared innocent, the psalmist would have been barred from the temple. Notice a similar sequence of ideas in Ps xxvi where after renouncing the pagans and their idols (vs. 5), the psalmist describes his love for the house of Yahweh (vss. 6–8).

among those who fear you. yir'ātekā in the present context means those who have not been guilty of idolatry and contrasts with the terms that describe the pagans in vss. 5–7.

Morphologically, *yir'ātekā* is an abstract noun which assumes a concrete signification by reason of its parallelism with a concrete substantive, just as *yad,* "hand," sometimes comes to mean "left hand" when in balance with *yāmīn,* "right hand" (cf. NOTE on Ps xxvi 10). This very frequent stylistic device deserves a word of comment. The practice is well documented in Ras Shamra literature, with some five instances recognized. UT, 62:48–49, *ḥbr,* "colleague," is matched with abstract *d't* concretely signifying "friend"; 68:9 = 'nt:IV:48, *ib,* "foe" balances abstract *ṣrt,* "hostility," but with concrete meaning "adversary." 137:22, *mlak ym,* "messengers of Yamm," are the counterpart of *t'dt,* "emissaries," while in 1012:35, *mlakty* probably connotes "my two messengers," even though the form is abstract. This device is attested in Phoenician Karatepe III:7, *šb' wtrš,* "wheat and wine," the same balance as in Prov iii 10. Donner and Röllig, KAI, II, p. 38, overlooked this literary nicety in their literal translation "Satiety and wine," *"Sättigung und Wein."* Biblical attestations of this phenomenon appear in Pss xii 2, xxii 12, 29, xxv 19, xxvii 9, xxxi 24, xxxvi 12, xxxvii 28, liv 9, lxxxix 9, xc 11, cix 2, cxix 38, 139, cxli 4; Exod xv 11; II Sam xxiii 3; Isa iii 35; Nah i 8–9; Job xv 34; Prov ii 8, iii 10, viii 12, 13, xiii 6, xiv 25, xxi 26, xxii 12, xxiii 17, xxiv 9, xxxi 30; Song of Sol ii 7; Eccles ii 8.

For our present purpose the most relevant is Ps cxix 38, *hāqēm lᵉʿabdᵉkā ʾimrāteka ʾᵃšer lᵉyīrāʾtekā,* "Confirm the promise to your servant, which is for those who fear you." The frequent emendation to *līrēʾekā* establishes our analysis. Cf. II Sam xxiii 3, *mōšēl bāʾādām ṣaddīq mōšēl yirʾat ʾᵉlōhīm,* "The ruler over men is the just man, the ruler is he who fears God." No need for the emendation *yārēʾ*. This principle proves especially valuable in Prov xxiii 17, *ʾal yᵉqannēʾ libbekā baḥaṭṭāʾīm kī ʾim bᵉyirʾat yhwh kol hayyōm,* "Let not your heart envy sinners, but rather those who fear Yahweh always." The antithesis to "sinners" reveals the true sense of the abstract form. See also Ps xc 11, *mī yōdēᵃʿ ʿoz ʾappekā ūbᵉyīrātᵉkā* (MT *kᵉyirāʾtᵉkā*) *ʿebrātekā,* "Who can understand the power of your anger or your wrath against those who fear you?"

O Yahweh. Transferring *yhwh* from the beginning of vs. 9 to the end of vs. 8. Vs. 8 thus scans into 3+2, while vs. 9 divides into 2+2+3. This division undermines the position of those (e.g., Gunkel) who maintain that a half verse is missing after vs. 9c.

9. *Lead me.* Imperative *nᵉḥēnī* pregnantly signifies "to lead into Paradise" as comparison with the following texts suggests: (a) Pss xxiii 3, *yanḥēnī bᵉmaʿgᵉlē ṣedeq,* "He will lead me into green pastures," an expression of confidence that eternal life awaits the psalmist; (b) lxxiii 24, *baʿᵃṣatᵉkā tanḥēnī wᵉʾaḥar kābōd tiqqaḥēnī,* "Lead me into your council and with honor receive me"—here the heavenly council is meant since many commentators agree that there is an allusion to the assumption of Enoch and Elijah because *lqḥ* has the technical sense "to assume, take to oneself"; (c) cxxxix 24, *nᵉḥēnī bᵉderek ʿōlām,* "Lead me into the eternal assembly" (this sense of *derek* is treated in NOTE on Ps i 1).

Verse 9 thus records the prayer uttered by the psalmist when he worshiped in the temple (vs. 8); he requested eternal happiness with Yahweh, far from his enemies. Cf. Gerard Manley Hopkins, "I have desired to go / Where springs not fail, / To fields where flies no sharp and sided hail / And a few lilies blow."

your meadow. That *ṣᵉdāqāh* means approximately "meadow," and relates to the theme of the Elysian Fields discussed in the NOTE on Ps xxxvi 10, is based on these texts: (a) Pss xxiii 3 (cf. preceding NOTE); (b) lxix 28–29, "Add to them punishment upon punishment and let them not enter your meadow (*wᵉʾal yābōʾū bᵉṣidqātekā*). Let them be blotted out of the book of the living, and let them not be enrolled among the just"—since the entire context is eschatological, ṣᵉdāqāh must be a poetic term for Paradise; (c) cxliii 10b–11, rūḥᵃkā ṭōbāh tanḥēnī bᵉ'ereṣ mīšōr lᵉma'an šimᵉkā yhwh tᵉḥayyēnī bᵉṣidqātekā [join final colon of MT to next verse], "With your good spirit lead me into the level land; for your name's sake, O Yahweh, grant me life in your meadow"—this couplet balances 'ereṣ mīšōr with ṣidqātekā just as Ps v 9 associates ṣidqātekā with hōšar, "make level." In Prov xxi 21 there is a play on words based upon the different sense of ṣᵉdāqāh: rōdēp ṣᵉdāqāh wāḥāsed yimṣā' ḥayyīm ṣᵉdāqāh wᵉkābōd, "He who pursues justice [ṣᵉdāqāh] and mercy will find life eternal, the meadow [ṣᵉdāqāh], and honor." On ḥayyīm, "life eternal," Ugar. ḥym, with the same meaning, cf. Biblica 41 (1960), 176–81, and NOTE on Ps xxxvi 10.

This sense of ṣᵉdāqāh may have developed out of the notions of abundance and prosperity that are resident in the root ṣdq; cf. NOTE on Ps xxiv 5. Hence ṣᵉdāqāh would be a field of luxuriant growth.

The language of vs. 10 is mythical in origin, originally having been used in the description of the chasm-like maw of Mot; the description has been demythologized and predicated of slanderers whose throats are as pernicious as that of Death. Cf. NOTE on Ps xxvii 12.

10. *nothing firm in his mouth.* In other words, a mealy-mouthed character. The metaphor is probably taken from the Canaanite myth about Mot (Death), whose throat is called mhmrt (cf. Ps cxl 11), "the miry gorge," (Driver, CML, p. 103b), while his city, the nether world, is named hmry, "Mudville." Cf. Biblica 40 (1959), 166 ff.; U. Cassuto, "Baal and Mot in the Ugaritic Texts," IEJ 12 (1962), 77–86 (reprint of article that first appeared twenty years earlier). Other allusions to this motif are in Pss xlvi 3 and lxix 3. On mud in the underworld, see T. H. Gaster, Thespis, 2d ed. (New York, 1961), pp. 303 f. Philo Byblius writes that according to some, Mot signifies "mud," while others see in the name "foulness of a watery mixture." Cf. M. H. Pope in Wörterbuch der Mythologie, ed. H. W. Haussig (Stuttgart, 1962), p. 301.

his mouth, his belly. Balancing pīhū, "his mouth," consonantal qrbm should probably be pointed qirbō-m, with enclitic mem, a stylistic balance that recurs in Ps cix 13, 15; Job xv 29, xxxvi 15; cf. M. Dahood in The Bible in Current Catholic Thought (abbr. BCCT) ed. J. L. McKenzie, (New York, 1962), p. 61. There remains the possibility that qrbm is simply the substantive followed by enclitic mem, whose suffix is forthcoming from pīhū on the principle of the double-duty suffix examined in the NOTE on Ps iii 4.

A grave wide-open. The wordplay on qirbō-m, "his belly," and qeber, "grave," should be noticed.

their throat. The disconcerting shift from singular "his belly" to plural "their throat" is characteristic of impassioned style; the poet now lashes out against a particular enemy, now against all of them. This shift in number can be observed in Pss vii 2–3, xvii 11–12, xxxv 7–8, lv 20–21, cix 5–6. The practice is analogous to the unexpected change from the second to the third person sometimes encountered in Northwest Semitic curses. For example, Aramaic Nerab II, 8–10, "And whoever you are (who) shall injure and remove me, may ŠHR and NKL and NŠK make odious his death and may his future perish"; cf. C. C. Torrey, JAOS 57 (1937), 405 f.; S. Gevirtz, VT 11 (1961), 147, n. 4.

with their tongue. Parsing *lešōnām* as an accusative of means preceding its verb; see NOTE below on vs. 13. To judge from the examples available, the practice of placing the accusative of means or material before the verb is a characteristic of the style of the psalmists: xvii 10, xviii 36 (twice), xxxii 10, xxxiii 5, xxxv 7, xlviii 12, l 19 (twice), li 14, lxxv 9, lxxxviii 8, civ 15 (twice), cxliii 10. In some passages a recognition of this stylistic feature results in a translation that differs from the traditional versions; e.g., Ps civ 15, *weyayin yeśammaḥ lebab 'enōš,* "And with wine he gladdens the heart of man." With the appreciation that Ps civ is a hymn praising God for his wonderful works and that the subject of the immediately preceding verbs is Yahweh himself, this parsing seems superior to that of RSV, "And wine to gladden the heart of man."

For our present purpose the most relevant parallel is Ps l 19, *pīkā šālaḥtā berā'āh ūlešōnekā taṣmīd mirmāh,* "With your mouth you forge evil itself, with your tongue you weave deceit."

Canaanite poets exhibit the same stylistic trait in such examples as UT, 'nt:II:15, *mṭm tgrš šbm,* "With two clubs she drives out the *šbm,"* and 40–44, *ṭl šmm tskh rbb tskh kbkbm,* "With dew the heavens anoint her, with spray anoint her the stars" (cf. Amos vi 6).

they bring death. Deriving *yaḥalīqūn* from *ḥālaq,* "to die, perish," Ugar. *ḫlq,* parallel to *mt.* The root is found in Pss xii 4, xvii 14, xxxvi 3, lxxiii 18; Hos x 2; Job xxi 17; Lam iv 16. Cf. *Biblica* 44 (1963), 548; 45 (1964), 408. Of course, "they bring death" makes a fine parallel to "a grave wide-open." Cf. Pss xii 4, *śiptē ḥalāqōt,* "pernicious lips"; xxxvi 3, *kī heḥelīq 'ēlāyw be'ēnāyw,* "For his God will bring him death with his glance," and James iii 5 ff.

11. *Make them perish.* That a root *'šm,* "to perish," exists in Hebrew is the conclusion imposed by these texts: Ps xxxiv 22, 23; Isa xxiv 6; Jer ii 3; Ezek vi 6; Hos v 15, x 2, xiv 1; Joel i 18; Prov xxx 10. In Ezek vi 6, for instance, Vulg. renders *weye'šemū* by *et interibunt* and in Joel i 18 by *disperierunt.* In Hos xiv 1, *te'šam* is synonymous with *baḥereb yippōlū; 'āšam* and *nāpal,* it will be noted, are the same verbs that appear in the verse here. Ps xxxiv 22 pairs *temōtēt* "(evil)

will slay," with *ye'šāmū,* "(those who hate the just man) will perish," while Hos x 2 balances *ḥālaq,* "to die, perish," discussed in the previous NOTE, with *'āšam: ḥālaq libbām 'attāh ye'šāmū,* "Their heart has died, now let themselves perish." With the phrase *ḥālaq libbām* compare I Sam xxv 37, *wayyāmot libbō beqirbō,* "And his heart died within him."

let them fall. I.e., into Sheol; cf. Pss xxxi 18 and lv 16.

because of their schemes. I.e., their schemes to have the psalmist condemned for idolatry.

hurl them down. The congeners *nādaḥ* and *dāḥāh,* "to thrust," sometimes pregnantly signify "to thrust into Sheol." In fact, in Ps lvi 14, *deḥī,* parallel to *māwet,* "Death," is a poetic name for the underworld. For the exegesis of this verse Jer xxiii 12 may prove relevant: *ba'apēlāh yiddāḥū wenāpelū bāh,* "Into Darkness let them be hurled and let them fall into it." Cf. NOTES on Pss xxxv 5 and xxxvi 13.

12. *forever singing.* In contrast to the defiant who will be cast into eternal darkness, those who reverence Yahweh will eternally rejoice in the celestial meadows whither God will lead them (vs. 9).

13. *the just man.* The poet is probably referring to himself, unjustly accused by his rivals. In Ps iv 4 the psalmist calls himself a *ḥāsīd,* "a devoted one."

as with a shield. The *ṣinnāh* was a large rectangular shield that protected most of the body.

with your favor. Though formally lacking a suffix, *rāṣōn* receives one in translation because of its association with *šemekā,* "your name," in the preceding verse. In Ps xix 15, *rāṣōn* is entitled to a suffix by reason of its balance with *pānekā,* "your will"; cf. NOTE on Ps iii 4.

Syntactically, *rāṣōn* in the present verse is an accusative of means preceding its verb, a stylistic trait noted under vs. 10.

PSALM 6

(vi 1–11)

1 *For the director; with stringed instruments; upon "the eighth." A psalm of David.*

2 O Yahweh, do not reprove me in your anger,
nor in your wrath chastise me.
3 Have pity on me, O Yahweh, for I am spent, [2]*
heal me, O Yahweh, for my bones are racked.
4 My spirit is greatly racked, [3]
but you, O Yahweh,—how long?
5 Return, Yahweh, rescue my life, [4]
save me as befits your kindness.
6 For no one in Death remembers you, [5]
in Sheol, who praises you?
7 I am weary with sobbing; [6]
Each night I soak my bed,
with tears my couch I drench.
8 My eye is dimmed with sorrow, [7]
my heart has grown old from pining.
9 Depart from me, all evildoers, [8]
for Yahweh has heard the sound of my weeping.
10 Yahweh has heard my plea, [9]
Yahweh has accepted my prayer.
11 Let all my foes be humbled and greatly shaken, [10]
let them return, be humbled in Perdition.

* Verse numbers in RSV.

NOTES

vi. A prayer for healing from a wasting disease; a lament. The first of the seven Penitential Psalms of the liturgy of the Church (Pss vi, xxxii, xxxviii, li, cii, cxxx, cxliii).

1. *the eighth.* The Hebrew term *šᵉmînît,* occurring also in Ps xii 1, is probably a musical notation; both LXX and Vulg. understood it as *pro octava,* "on the octave." This may well be correct, as it accords with I Chron xv 21 which refers to the lower octave or the bass voice.

6. *no one in Death.* There is no need to vocalize MT *zikrekā* as a participle; what we have here is probably the phenomenon noted at Ps v 8 of an abstract ("memory") balancing a concrete noun ("Who praises you?"), but both of which are to be understood concretely. "Death" here connotes the realm of death, namely, the nether world, as in Job xxviii 22, xxx 23; Prov v 5, vii 27.

As noted by Brevard S. Childs, *Memory and Tradition in Israel* (London, 1962), p. 71, the psalmist suffers not because of the inability to remember Yahweh in Sheol, but from being unable to share in the praise of Yahweh which characterizes Israel's worship.

7. *Each night I soak.* Briggs, I, p. 50, finds this metaphor overly extravagant for his tastes and recommends the emendation *'āśîḥāh,* "I must complain." Exegesis must be governed by other criteria, as appears from similar extravagant language in UT, Krt:28–30, *tntkn udm'th km ṯqlm arṣh kmḫmšt mṭth,* "His tears are poured forth like shekels upon the ground, like pieces-of-five upon the bed."

8. *my heart has grown old from pining.* Reading *'ātᵉqāh bᵉkālā ṣrry* for MT *'ātᵉqāh bᵉkol ṣōrᵉray,* and identifying consonantal *ṣrry* with Akk. *ṣurru,* Ugar. *ṣrrt,* "heart, innards"; see Driver, CML, p. 150, n. 18. This provides an unexceptionable parallel to *'ēnî,* "my eye." Cf. Pss x 5, xxxi 12, and lxix 20, where *ṣrry* is parallel to vs. 21, *libbî,* "my heart." Note the poetic sequence A+B+C // Á+B́+Ć:

'āšᵉšāh mikka'as 'ēnî
'ātᵉqāh bᵉkālā ṣrry

The semantic relationship between "to grow old" and "to shrivel" is present in synonymous *yāšan,* "to dry up, grow old," as is clear from UT, 56:33, *yṯnm,* "dried raisins," and UT, 1107:6, *mlbš trmnm k yṯn,* "When the garment of TRMNM wears out."

9. *the sound of my weeping.* The seemingly tautologous phrase *qōl bikyî,* which is a hapax legomenon, does fall in with Canaanite phraseology, as, e.g., in UT, Krt:120–122, *lqr ṯigt ibrh lql nhqt ḥmrh,* "for the

noise of the neighing of his stallion, for the sound of the braying of his donkey."

10. *has heard . . . has accepted.* The imperfect form *yiqqaḥ*, parallel to perfect *šāma'*, has occasioned translation difficulties. Thus RSV translates curiously, "The Lord has heard my supplication; the Lord accepts my prayer." The dissonance disappears with the recognition that in ancient Canaanite poetry the prefixed tense (*yiqqaḥ*) was the normal form for expressing the past narrative. Cf. Ps iv 4.

11. The sense of this verse is uncertain.

let them return. The return to Sheol motif is found in Job i 21, xxx 23, xxxiv 15; Eccles iii 20–21, v 14, xii 7.

be humbled in Perdition. With due reservation, relating *rega'* to *rāgā'*, "to destroy, annihilate," treated at Ps xxx 6. That *rega'* (vocalization uncertain) is a name for the underworld appears highly probable from Num xvi 21; Ps lxxiii 19; and Job xxi 13. For the thought, cf. Ps ix 18, "Let the wicked return to Sheol," and Ps xxxi 18, "Let the wicked be humiliated, hurled into Sheol."

PSALM 7

(vii 1–18)

1 *Shiggayon of David which he sang to Yahweh to the words of Kush the Benjaminite.*

2 O Yahweh, my God, in you have I trusted,
save me from all my pursuers.
3 Rescue me lest he tear me apart [2]*
like a lion
Rending my neck with none to rescue me.
4 O Yahweh, my God, if I have committed an indignity, [3]
if there is guilt on my hands,
5 If I have repaid my ally with treachery, [4]
troubled his heart with idle talk:
6 Let the foe pursue and overtake me, [5]
Let him trample my vitals into the nether world,
Let him cause my liver to dwell in the mud. *Selah*
7 Arise, O Yahweh, in your wrath, [6]
rise up against the arrogance of my adversaries;
Bestir yourself, O my God,
a judgment appoint!
8 Let the congregation of peoples surround you, [7]
and over it preside, O Exalted One!
Let Yahweh judge the nations!
9 Judge me, O Yahweh, according to my justice, [8]
and according to my integrity, O Most High.
10 Avenge the treachery of the wicked, [9]
and reassure the just man,
Since the searcher of mind and heart
is God the Just.
11 My Suzerain is the Most High God, [10]
the Savior of the upright of heart.

* Verse numbers in RSV.

12 God is a righteous ruler, [11]
and El is a vindicator at all times.
13 O that the Victor would again [12]
sharpen his sword
draw and aim his bow!
14 O that he would prepare his lethal weapons, [13]
make his arrows into flaming shafts!
15 Look, he conceives malice, [14]
is pregnant with mischief,
and gives birth to treachery.
16 He dug a pit but it pitted him, [15]
and he fell into the hole he made.
17 His mischief recoiled upon his head, [16]
and upon his skull his malice redounded.
18 I will thank Yahweh as befits his justice, [17]
and will sing the name of Yahweh Most High.

Notes

vii. An individual lament in which the psalmist prays for deliverance from his enemies, especially from a colleague who has betrayed him.

1. *Shiggayon.* The meaning of this technical term is obscure. Both LXX and Vulg. simply translate it *psalmus,* "a psalm," but some modern scholars relate it to the root denoting "to go astray, err," and define it as "dithyramb."

3. *Rescue me . . . rescue me.* This stichometric division, which differs from that of BH^{3}, has been suggested by D. N. Freedman. It has the marked advantage of creating an inclusion in vs. 3, which now begins with *w^{e}haṣṣīlēnī* and terminates with *maṣṣīl.*

lest he tear me apart. I.e., by slander and calumny. In Ps xxxv 15–16, the slanderers of the psalmist are compared to ravening wolves. The disconcerting shift from plural "my pursuers," to singular *yiṭrōp* is a characteristic of impassioned language commented upon at Ps v 10, where pertinent parallels are listed.

like a lion. A fine example of enjambment with *k^{e}'aryeh* linking together the two halves of the verse. Cf. Pss xxv 19, xxviii 8, xxxii 5, lxix 13, lxxiv 20, cxxix 4.

my neck. This is one of the senses of *npš* in Ugaritic which merely confirms the conclusion set forth by L. Dürr in 1926 and today accepted by the lexicons of Zorell (ZLH) and of L. Koehler and W. Baumgartner (abbr. KB), the *Lexicon in Veteris Testamenti Libros* (Leiden, 1951; Grand Rapids, Michigan, 1953). The present example is not among those usually listed; cf. NOTE on Ps xxii 21.

none to rescue me. The principle of the double-duty suffix permits *maṣṣīl* to share that of *haṣṣīlēnī* and of *napšī*. Cf. NOTE on Ps iii 4.

4. *committed an indignity.* That the substantive *zō't,* "indignity, insult," whose vocalization is problematical and whose etymology is not immediately evident (some connection with *ṣō'āh,* "excrement, filth, spittle," is not unlikely), must be admitted into the Hebrew lexicon follows from its balance here with *'āwel,* "guilt," and from these texts: (a) Ps xliv 18, "Every indignity (*zō't*) has come upon us, but we have not forgotten you"; (b) Ps lxxiv 18, "Remember the insult (*zō't*) of the foe who scoffs [*ḥērēp*], O Yahweh, and of the impious people that reviles [*ni'ᵃṣū*] your name"—here the association of *zō't* with *ḥērēp* and *ni'ᵃṣū* is convincing; (c) Zeph ii 10, "Indignity (*zō't*) shall be theirs instead of their majesty, because they scoffed (*ḥērᵉpū*) and spun tales about the people of Yahweh of Hosts"—note again the affiliation of *zō't* with *ḥārap,* and the contrast between *zō't* and *gā'ōn,* "exaltation, majesty"; (d) Job ii 11, "Now when Job's three friends heard of all the evil, the indignity that came upon him" (*kol hārā'āh hazzō't habbā'āh 'ālāyw*)—here *zō't* is a synonym of *rā'āh,* while its predicate *habbā'āh* recalls the construction of Ps xliv 18.

This analysis of *zō't* uncovers the chiastic arrangement of vss. 4–5, with *zō't,* "indignity, insult," matched chiastically with *rēqīm,* "idle talk," and *'āwel,* "guilt," paired with *rā',* "evil, treachery."

5. *repaid my ally.* Reading (for MT *šōlᵉmī*) *šᵉlūmī,* qal passive participle from *šālam,* "to make a covenant," found in Job xxii 21, *hasken nā' 'immō ūšᵉlām,* "Come to terms with him and make a covenant." The proposal to emend qal *šᵉlām* to hiphil *hašlēm* does not impose itself, though in Job v 23 one does find the hophal: *kī 'im 'abnē haśśādeh bᵉrītekā wᵉḥayyat haśśādeh hošlᵉmāh lāk,* "For with the stones of the field will be your covenant, and the beasts of the field will be allied to you." In Isa xlii 19, however, there is a pual participle from this root, so the safest conclusion to draw from the evidence is that several conjugations of the denominative verb *šālam* were in use. The text reads *mī 'iwwēr kīmᵉšullām,* "Who is blind like the covenanted one?" On this text see E. J. Kissane, *The Book of Isaiah* (Dublin, 1943), II, p. 43, and p. 48, where Kissane terms his translation "covenanted one" doubtful. In view of usage in Psalms, the translation now appears less doubtful. On Ps xli 10; Jer xx 10, xxxviii 22; Obad vii, see W. F. Albright in BASOR 163 (1961), 52, where Gen xiv 18 is formally discussed; in Ps lv 21, the correct solution seems to lie in the reading *šᵉlūmāyw,* qal passive participle, for MT *šᵉlōmāyw;* "He stretched forth his hand against his

allies, he violated his covenant." Similarly in Ps lxix 23 where one may render, "May their table before them be a trap and even their allies a snare" (cf. Exod xxxiv 12). The association of "ally" and "sharing one's table" recurs in Ps xli 10. Jean Nougayrol in *Iraq* 25 (1963), 110, has remarked that for the Hittites in particular the word *sulummū* had the double value of "peace" and "treaty."

with treachery. This specification of generic *ra'*, "evil," is dictated by the context of covenant terminology. In vs. 10 *ra'* receives the same definition.

6. *pursue and overtake me*. Understanding *napšī* as the interposed object of the two verbs *yiraddōp* (unusual vocalization on the part of MT) and *yaśśēg*. A similar type of enjambment was noted above in connection with vs. 3.

the nether world. For *'ereṣ*, "nether world," see NOTE on Ps xviii 8.

cause my liver to dwell. Translating literally the hiphil jussive *yaškēn*, and reading *kebēdī*, "my liver," for MT *kebōdī*, "my glory." The same Masoretic confusion between *kābēd*, "liver," and *kābōd*, "glory," can be seen in Ps xvi 9 and Gen xlix 6.

in the mud. For *'āpār*, "mud," as another name for the infernal regions, see NOTE on Ps xxii 16. The parallelism between *'ereṣ* and *'āpār* is commented on at Ps xxii 30.

7. *Arise, O Yahweh*. *qūmāh yahweh* begins an inclusion or "envelope figure" which ends with vs. 8, *lammārōm šūbāh*, "preside, O Exalted One."

arrogance of my adversaries. In other words, their presumption that Yahweh will not come to the defense of the psalmist.

O my God. MT *'ēlay*, often repunctualized singular *'ēlī*, may turn out to be correct with the admission that *'ēlīm* is a *plurale majestatis*, as in Phoenician and probably in Ugaritic; e.g., Phoen. *rb khnm 'lm nrgl*, "the chief priest of the god Nergal." Other examples may be found in Friedrich, PPG, § 306; Z. S. Harris, *A Grammar of the Phoenician Language* (New Haven, 1936), p. 77; and C. F. Jean and J. Hoftijzer, *Dictionnaire des inscriptions sémitiques de l'ouest*, I–II (Leiden, 1960), p. 13, line 45. In view of this usage, there should be less hesitation in accepting *ilm* as a plural of majesty in UT, 2 Aqht:v:20.29, where *ilm* refers to *kṯr wḫss*, a god with a double-barreled name but nonetheless one god. Gordon, UT, 13.18, is being overcautious when demurring to admit that *ilm* is plural in form but singular in meaning. Incidentally, this inquiry further points up the necessity of studying Hebrew grammar within the larger framework of Northwest Semitic.

Another interesting occurrence of this plural of majesty is in the mouth of pagans in Ps cxxix 8, *welō' 'āmerū hā'ōberīm birkat yhwh 'alēkem*, "And those passing by will not say, 'the blessing of Yahweh your God!'" Job xxxi 23, *paḥad 'ēlay 'ēd 'ēl*, possibly to be rendered "The fear of my God is the supreme distress," calls for further study.

a judgment appoint. Following the three imperatives *qūmāh, hinnāśē'*, and *'ūrāh,* perfect *ṣiwwītā* is almost certainly a precative perfect, described at Ps iii 8. Gunkel, *Die Psalmen,* p. 26, proposed the emendation to imperative *ṣawwēh,* "entbiete Gericht," but his literary tastes were evidently different from those of the psalmist, who would have found four successive imperatives a bit tiresome. The precative perfect occurs frequently in the Psalter precisely because the psalmists desired stylistic variation.

8. *congregation of peoples*. The theme of God surrounded by the congregation of peoples has been discussed by Patton, CPBP, p. 24, where pertinent passages are cited.

over it preside. The frequent repointing of MT *šūbāh* to *šēbāh,* from *yšb,* may prove unnecessary with the knowledge that the interchange between *primae waw* and *mediae waw* verbs was, owing to poetic exigencies, more common than heretofore allowed. Thus in Isa xxx 15, *bᵉšūbāh wānaḥat* means "by sitting still and resting," as suggested by the association of these ideas in UT, 49:III:18, *aṯbn ank wanḫn,* "I myself shall sit down and rest." See Dahood, CBQ 20 (1958), 41–42, and Walter Baumgartner, ZAW 70 (1958), 140. In Ps xxiii 6, *wᵉšabtī bᵉbēt yhwh,* "And I shall dwell in the house of Yahweh," *wᵉšabtī* can be parsed either as deriving from *šwb,* "to sit," or as a syncopated form of *wᵉyāšabtī,* just as Ugar. *wld* is syncopated from *wa-yalādu*. The pairing with *šalwat kᵉsīlīm,* "the ease-taking of fools," makes it quite evident that *mᵉšūbat pᵉtāyīm* in Prov i 32 denotes "the idleness of the simple," from the root *šwb,* a by-form of *yšb*. Cf. Dahood, PNWSP, pp. 6 f. Notoriously difficult Ps xxxv 13 yields a measure of coherency on this hypothesis: *tᵉpillātī 'al ḥēqī tāšūb,* "My prayer rested upon my breast," i.e., my prayer was unceasing. For Ps lxxiv 11, one may propose, "Why do you keep (reading *tōšīb* for MT *tāšīb*) your left hand and your right hand in your bosom?"

The poetic exigency dictating the option for the by-form *šwb* as against *yšb* is the desired assonance between vss. 7–8, *qūmah yhwh, 'ūrāh 'ēlay,* and *lammārōm šūbāh,* three imperatives from *mediae waw* verbs accompanied by divine names in the vocative case.

O Exalted One. Perhaps one should vocalize *lᵉmārōm* for MT *lammārōm,* and parse the *lᵉ* as the vocative *lamedh* followed by the divine epithet *mārōm,* literally "heights," which came to be a designation of Yahweh, just as Ugar. *ǵr,* "mountain," is one of Baal's appellations (W. F. Albright in *Festschrift Alfred Bertholet* [Tübingen, 1950], pp. 3 ff.) and Heb. *ṣūr* "mountain," a designation of Yahweh. On this hypothesis, the divine appellative *mārōm* balances *yhwh* and *'ēlay* in vs. 7, while imperative *šūbāh* matches imperatives *qūmāh* and *'ūrāh*. Moreover, *lᵉmārōm šūbāh,* vocative plus imperative, forms a chiastic *inclusio* with vs. 7, *qūmāh yhwh,* imperative plus vocative.

Other instances of *mārōm,* "Exalted One," are found in Pss x 5, lvi 3, and thanks to the parallelism very clearly, in lxxv 6, *'al tārīmū lammārōm qarnᵉkem tᵉdabbᵉrū bᵉṣū'r* (MT *bᵉṣawwā'r*) *'ātāq* "Raise not your horn against the Exalted One, nor speak arrogantly against the Mountain." F. Zorell, *Psalterium ex Hebraeo Latinum,* 2d ed. (Romae, 1939), p. 185, n. d., makes this interesting comment: *"Vox* marom *nonnunquam, fortasse hic quoque, caelum et Altissimum connotat"* ["The word *mārōm* sometimes, perhaps also here, connotes 'heaven' and 'the Most High' "]. See also Ps xcii 9, *wᵉ'attāh mārōm lᵉ'ōlām yhwh,* rendered by LXX, "You are the Most High (*hýpsistos*) forever, O Lord." Cf. Isa xxxviii 14 and Jer xxxi 12 for other occurrences.

9. *Most High.* Vocalizing *'ēlī* (vocalization based on personal name *'ēlī,* "Eli," which is the apocopated form of *yᵉḥaw'ēlī* of the Samaria Ostraca) for the purported preposition of MT *'ālāy.* This pointing and interpretation sets up a perfect balance with *yhwh,* as in Pss xiii 6, xvi 5–6, xxxii 5; I Sam ii 10; and Lam iii 61, *šāma'tā ḥerpātām yhwh kol maḥšᵉbōtām 'ēlī* (MT *'ālāy*), "Hear their insults, O Yahweh, all their plottings, O Most High." Cf. UT, 126:III:5–8, *larṣ mṭr b'l wlšd mṭr 'ly n'm larṣ mṭr b'l wlšd mṭr 'ly,* "Upon the earth Baal rained, and upon the field rained the Most High; sweet to the earth was the rain of Baal, and to the field the rain of the Most High." The Canaanite poet pairs the titles *b'l* and *'ly,* whereas the Yahwistic poet balances *yhwh* and *'ēlī.* Cf. M. Dahood, "The Divine Name 'ELĪ in the Psalms," TS 14 (1953), 452–57; Pope, *Wörterbuch der Mythologie,* p. 255. See also the pat examples in Pss lxxxvi 13 and cvi 7.

Just as assonance was operative in vss. 7–8, so here rhyme may have been a factor since *'ēlī* rhymes with *ṣidqī.*

10. *Avenge the treachery.* Parsing *yigmor-nā'* as energic jussive continuing the imperative *šopṭēnī* of vs. 9; cf. Joüon, GHB, § 113m, who registers under this heading Pss xvii 8, liv 3, lix 2, lxiv 2, cxl 2, etc. Michel, TSP, § 25.208–16, p. 168, gives substantially the same listing. For Ugaritic practice, consult NOTE on Ps x 15. On *gāmar,* "to avenge," see M. Dahood, "The Root GMR in the Psalms," TS 14 (1953), 595–97; M. Tsevat, *A Study of the Language of the Biblical Psalms* (Philadelphia, 1955), p. 80, n. 34; Driver, CML, p. 81, n. 7, and Dahood in *Biblica* 45 (1964), 400.

mind and heart. Literally "heart and kidneys." The antiquity of the phrase is documented in UT, 1001:3, *klyth wlbh,* though in reverse order.

11. *My Suzerain.* For MT *māginnī* one should perhaps read *mᵉgānī,* from *māgān* (Punic *māgōn*); consult NOTE on Ps iii 4.

the Most High God. Explaining the composite divine name *'al 'elōhīm* as containing *'al,* the by-form of *'ēlī,* discussed above, and which occurs in II Sam xxiii 1, as noted by Henri Cazelles in *Mélanges André Robert* (Paris, 1957), pp. 138 f., who analyzes *'al* as an abbreviation of *'elyōn.* Cf. Ps lxviii 30, *hēkāleka 'al yerūšālaim lekā yōbīlū melākīm šay,* "Your temple, Most High, is Jerusalem; to you will the kings bring gifts," and possibly vs. 35, *tenū 'ōz lē'lōhīm 'al yiśrā'ēl,* "Give glory to God the Most High of Israel." See H. S. Nyberg, ARW 35 (1938), 329–87. Compare Ps xviii 42, *'al yahweh,* "Most High Yahweh," and the Ugaritic personal name *yrm'l* in UT, 2106:4.

the Savior. mōšīa' is a divine title that recurs in Pss xvii 7 and xviii 42.

12. *El is a vindicator.* The accumulation of ancient divine titles in these verses suggest that *'ēl* here as in Ps x 11 retains its archaic Canaanite value as the name of the head of the pantheon.

13. *the Victor.* Commonly labeled corrupt, consonantal *'m l' yšb* yields to satisfactory explanation when vocalized *'im lē' yāšūb,* and when *lē'* is derived from the very frequent Ugaritic-Phoenician root *l'y,* "to be strong, to prevail." The root is also well known from Akk. *lē'ū,* "to be strong," and its presence in Hebrew was proposed many decades ago by those scholars who saw it in the Hebrew feminine name *lē'āh, "domina."* The stative vocalization *lē'āh* supports the pointing *lē'* for the masculine form. For recent discussions of Northwest Semitic occurrences of this root, see A. M. Honeyman, PEQ (1961), 151–52, and Maurice Sznycer, *Semitica* 13 (1963), 21–30.

Other instances of optative *'im,* balancing precative *lū* in the next verse, are in Pss lxxxi 9, xcv 7, cxxxix 19.

would again. Referring to primeval times when God destroyed his foes. A similar prayer is articulated in Isa li 9, "Awake, awake, put on strength, O arm of Yahweh! Awake as in days of old, as in generations long gone! Wasn't it you who cut Rahab to pieces, who pierced the dragon?"

sharpen his sword. Compare *ḥarbō yilṭōš* with Job xvi 9, *ṣārī yilṭōš,* "He (Yahweh) sharpens his (third-person singular suffix *-ī;* cf. NOTE on Ps ii 6) blade," and with UT, 137:32, *ḥrb lṭšt,* "the sharpened sword." Note the *yqtl-qtl* sequence in the verbs *yilṭōš* and *dārak,* and cf. NOTE on Ps viii 7.

14. *O that he would prepare.* Reading *lū hēkīn* for MT *lō hēkīn.* The alternation between *qtl* (*hēkīn*) and *yqtl* (*yip'āl*), as in the previous verse, might be noted; the precative particle *lū* would balance optative *'im.*

his lethal weapons. Assuming the suffix of parallel *ḥiṣṣāyw* on the principle of the double-duty suffix examined in the NOTE on Ps iii 4. Cf. especially Ps xviii 15 where *ḥiṣṣāyw,* "his arrows," balances *berāqīm,* "his shafts." In a surprising number of texts where the divine appellative *lē',* "the Victor," is purportedly found, the context is one of life and death. This is seen most clearly in I Sam ii 3 and Hab i 12, but cf. also

Pss xxii 30, xxvii 13, lxxxv 7, and Job xiii 15, *hēn yiqṭᵉlēnī lē'* (MT *lō'*) *'ᵃyaḥēl 'ak dᵉrākāy 'el pānāyw 'ōkīᵃḥ,* "Even if the Victor should slay me, still will I hope; indeed, will I defend my conduct before his face." By noticing the divine title *lē'*, one finds the heretofore lacking antecedent to the pronominal suffix of *pānāyw*.

make his arrows. Compare *ḥiṣṣāyw . . . yip'al* with UT, 2 Aqht: VI:24, *tn lkṯr wḫss yb'l qšt l'nt,* "Give them to the Skillful and Cunning One that he might make a bow for Anath."

16. *it pitted him.* The wordplay on *yippōl* and *yip'al* in the second verse permits one to surmise that the first colon also indulges in paronomasia in the verb *yaḥpᵉrēhū,* from *ḥāpar* I, "to be ashamed," or from *ḥāpar* II, "to dig a pit." One notices a similar pun in Luke xvi 3, "To dig (*ḥāpar* II) I am not able, to beg I am ashamed (*ḥāpar* I)." Hence *yaḥpᵉrēhū* is parsed as hiphil denominative from *ḥāpar,* "to dig," with *bōr,* "pit," its subject. The pit is likewise personified in Ps xxxv 8, "May the pit come upon him unawares," while a cognate pun appears in Prov xi 9, *bᵉpūh* (MT *bᵉpeh*) *ḥānēp yšḥt rē'ēhū,* "By watching a godless man his friend is corrupted/pitted." The verbal root *šḥt* (vocalizing pual *yᵉšūḥat*) suggests both "to corrupt" and "to pit," a denominative verb from *šaḥat,* "pit." See Dahood, PNWSP, pp. 21 f.

17. *upon his head . . . skull.* The pairing of *rō'š* and *qodqōd* is found in similar-sounding UT, 127:55–57, *yṯbr ḥrn rišk 'ṯtrt šm b'l qdqdk,* "May Horon smash your head, Athtart, the name of Baal, your skull." Cf. Gevirtz, *Patterns in the Early Poetry of Israel,* pp. 7 f.

18. *I will thank.* The psalmist promises to give formal thanks for deliverance from his foes.

Yahweh Most High. A reminiscence of vs. 9, *'ēlī,* "O Most High," and vs. 11, *'al 'ᵉlōhīm,* "the Most High God."

PSALM 8

(viii 1–10)

1 *For the director; upon the gittith. A psalm of David.*

2 O Yahweh our Lord,
how glorious is your name through all the earth!
I will adore your majesty
above the heavens,
With the lips of striplings and sucklings. [2]*
3 You built a fortress for your habitation,
having silenced your adversaries,
the foe and the avenger.
4 When I see your heavens, [3]
the work of your fingers,
The moon and the stars which you created:
5 What is man that you should think of him, [4]
or the son of man that you should care for him?
6 Yet you have made him a little less than the gods, [5]
with honor and glory you crowned him.
7 You gave him dominion over the works of your hands, [6]
put all things at his feet.
8 Small and large cattle—all of them, [7]
yes, even the beasts of the steppe.
9 The birds of heaven, and the fishes in the sea, [8]
whatever crosses the routes of the seas.
10 O Yahweh our Lord, [9]
how glorious is your name through all the earth!

* Verse numbers in RSV.

Notes

viii. A hymn celebrating God's infinite majesty (vss. 2–5) and the dignity and power to which God has raised man (vss. 6–10).

1. *the gittith.* The precise force of this word, found also in the headings of Pss lxxxi and lxxxiv, is unknown.

2. *I will adore.* Reading for MT *'ašer tᵉnāh* with no consonantal changes, *'ašārᵉtannāh,* the imperfect *modus energicus* of piel *šērēt,* "to serve, worship, adore," a very frequent root in Hebrew which some scholars (e.g., Aistleitner, Driver) would identify in UT, Krt:77, *šrd b'l bdbḥk,* "Worship Baal with your sacrifice." Phonetically, the equation offers no difficulty since the Hebrew form can be explained through the dissimilation of sonant *d* to mute *t;* compare Heb. *šāpat,* "to place," with Ugar. *ṯpd,* "to place"; Heb. *šēt,* "foundation," with Ugar, *išd,* "leg."

The high incidence of energic forms in Ugaritic (UT §§ 9.11; 13.38) suggests a breakthrough in this area of Hebrew morphology and syntax. Being unknown to the Masoretes, these energic forms must now be extricated from the Masoretic thicket. Cf. my preliminary remarks (the subject merits a monographic study) in PNWSP, pp 3 f., and the favorable comments of Louis Hartman in CBQ 26 (1964), 106. Among the texts cited there are Judg v 26, *tišlāḥannāh,* as read by Freedman in ZAW 72 (1960), 102; Job xvii 16, *tᵉrēdannāh,* xxxix 23, *tāronnāh;* Prov i 20 and viii 3, *tāronnāh;* and Lam i 13, *yᵉrēdannāh.* One may add Gen iii 17, *tō'kālannāh,* a reading proposed by D. N. Freedman in ZAW 64 (1952), 191. New instances include Pss ii 8, xx 4, xxxix 7, xlv 16 (twice), lxv 13; Num xxiii 19, 20; Obad xiii; Job vii 14, xxxv 13; Prov v 3, xii 25. On Isa xxvii 11, *tiššᵉbārannāh,* see G. R. Driver in JTS 41 (1940), 163. His assertion that Isa xlix 15 contains the clearest example of the energic form of the imperfect tense is invalidated, however, by the observation that *'iššāh* and *mᵉraḥēm* (MT *mēraḥēm*) are two different persons, and consequently MT *tiškaḥnāh* is correctly pointed as the third-person feminine plural. Hence Isa xlix 15 should be rendered "Can a woman forget her sucking infant, or one pregnant the child in her womb? Even though these should forget (*'ēlleh tiškaḥnāh*), I will not forget you"; cf. *Biblica* 44 (1963), 204–5. On the energic form in Ps i 23, see H. Bauer and P. Leander, *Historische Grammatik der hebräischen Sprache* (Halle, 1922), p. 338r, s.

With the lips. Literally "with the mouth." The syntax of *mippī* resembles that of Ps xxviii 7, *miššīrī 'ahōdennū,* "So with my song I shall praise him."

of striplings and sucklings. Before the majesty of God the psalmist can but babble like an infant. This exegesis sharply differs from the interpretation proposed by Claus Schedl in FuF 38 (1964), 183–85, who would identify the *yōn^eqīm* with the divine beings mentioned in UT, 52:23–24, *ilm n'mm . . . ynqm bap zd aṯrt,* "the gracious gods . . . who suck the nipples of Asherah's breasts." Henri Cazelles in *Parole de Dieu et Sacerdoce,* eds. E. Fischer and L. Bouyer (Tournai, 1962), pp. 79–91, seeks to identify the infants with the angelic powers and the stars, but this hypothesis seems equally unnecessary.

3. *You built a fortress.* The lexicons (BDB, GB, ZLH) recognize from its collocation with *yissadtā* that *'ōz* must mean something like "fortress" or "stronghold," but commentators have not been clear as how to fit this meaning into the over-all context. A consistent metaphor emerges, however, when *'ōz,* "fortress," is recognized as a poetic name for heaven, which is mentioned in vs. 2. The clearest example of this metaphorical usage is, thanks to the parallelism, Ps lxxviii 26, *yassa' qādīm baššāmayim way^enahēg b^e'uzzō tēmān,* "He let loose the east wind from heaven, and led forth the south wind from his fortress." The verbs *yassa'* and *y^enahēg,* and the substantives *qādīm* and *tēmān,* being perfectly balanced, it follows that *šāmayim* and *'uzzō* must be parallel. Cf. Ps cl 1, *hal^elū 'ēl b^eqodšō hal^elūhū bīr^eqī^a' 'uzzō,* "Praise God in his sanctuary, praise him in his vaulted fortress." In other terms, the hendiadys *r^eqī^a' 'uzzō* parallels Gen i 14, 15, 17, *r^eqī^a' haššāmayim,* "the vault of heaven." Other texts where *'ōz* denotes "fortress, stronghold," though not metaphorically "heaven," include Pss lxii 8, cviii 14; Exod xv 2; Isa xii 2, xvii 9, xxvi 1; Jer li 53; Amos iii 11, v 9; Prov xxi 22. With the phrase *yissadtā 'ōz* compare Amos ix 6, *habbōneh baššāmayim ma'^alōtāw wa'^aguddātō 'al 'ereṣ y^esādāh,* "Who builds his upper chambers in the heavens, and founds his vault upon the earth." A perfect analogy to *'ōz,* "strength, fortress," lies in *g^ebūrāh,* "power, force," but also "fortress (of heaven)," as proposed at Ps xx 7. In Ps xxxi 22 heaven is termed a "fortified city" (*'īr māṣōr*); cf. NOTE there.

for your habitation. Reading *l^emā'ōn* for MT *l^ema'an,* with pronominal suffix forthcoming from preceding *hōd^ekā* and following *ṣōr^erekā,* on the principle of the double-duty suffix treated in the NOTE on Ps iii 4. In Ps lxviii 6, *m^e'ōn qodšō* is the name of God's heavenly habitation, whereas in Deut xxvi 15 *mā'ōn* is synonymous with *šāmayim:* "Look down from your holy habitation, from heaven (*mimm^e'ōn qodš^ekā min haššāmayim*), and bless your people Israel." See NOTE on Ps xxvi 8; for the root *'wn* in Deut xxxiii 28, see Freedman, IEJ 13 (1963), 125–26.

having silenced your adversaries. For the syntax of *l^ehašbīt,* an infinitive construct describing attendant circumstances, see GK, § 114o. Cf. especially Pss lxiii 3, lxxviii 18, ciii 20, civ 14–15, cxi 6. The logical nexus between erecting a dwelling and the subduing of rivals is probably to be sought in Canaanite mythology. According to one motif, a sovereign god must have a worthy dwelling which can be constructed only after he has vanquished his adversaries. Thus UT, 68, describes the combat between Baal and the sea-god Yamm; once Baal vanquishes Yamm, he receives permission from El to build a palace for himself. UT, 51, describes the construction of this palace in considerable detail. If Baal were to remain without a palace, he would be subject to constant insults at the hands of the gods; see Gaster, *Thespis*, 1961, p. 179. Similar reasoning seems to underlie David's anxiety to build a temple for Yahweh; cf. Ps cxxxii 5. A reflex of this motif is articulated in Ps lxxxix 11–12, "You have crushed Rahab like one who is slain, with your strong arm you scattered your foes. The heavens are yours and the earth is also yours; the world and its fullness you have founded (*y^{e}sadtām*)." Having disposed of his foes Rahab, Leviathan, et al., Yahweh set about fashioning and arranging heaven and earth.

There may be some overtones present in *hašbīt,* which is related to the verbs *šābam* and *šābaḥ,* "to muzzle, silence," discussed in the NOTE on Ps xlvi 10.

the foe and the avenger. This phrase stands grammatically in apposition with plural "adversaries." Cf. Ps xvii 7, "Muzzle your assailants with your right hand." In Canaanite myth, the principal foes of Baal are Yamm and Mot, while in biblical mythopoeic language the rivals of Yahweh are Yamm and Tannin in Ps lxxiv 13, Rahab in Ps lxxxix 11, and Rahab, Tannin, Yamm, and Tehom—four in number—in Isa li 9–10.

6. *the gods.* I.e., the members of the heavenly court of Yahweh; cf. NOTE on Ps i 5 and see Pss lxxxii 1, lxxxvi 8, lxxxix 6, 8.

you crowned him. The construing of *ʿāṭar* with a double accusative is found in Ps. v 13, lxv 12, ciii 4 and in a Phoenician inscription from Piraeus, *lʿṭr ʾyt šmʿbʿl . . . ʿṭrt ḥrṣ,* "to crown SMʿBʿL . . . with a crown of gold"; cf. Cooke, TNSI, p. 96. For accusative of means preceding the verb, see NOTE on Ps v 10.

7. *You gave him dominion.* The balance of imperfect *tamšīlēhū* with perfect *šattāh,* as often in Ugaritic, should be noted; see NOTE on Ps iv 4.

put all things. Cf. Phoenician Azitawaddu, I:16, *wʾnk ʾztwd štnm tḥt pʿmy,* "But I, Azitawaddu, put them under my feet."

at his feet. Or "under his feet." Compare *taḥat raglāyw* with UT, 1 Aqht:115–16, *tqln tḥt pʿnh,* "(The eagles) fall at his feet." Gunkel, *Die Psalmen,* p. 27, more correctly renders, *"alles legtest du ihm zu Füssen."*

8. *Small and large cattle.* Reading (for MT *ṣōneh*) *ṣōnāh,* with an archaic accusative ending, *ṣōnāh* being the direct object of *šattāh;* I am indebted to D. N. Freedman for this observation. The phrase seems to be an example of merismus, denoting all domestic cattle as in UT, 51:VI:40–43, *ṭbḫ alpm ap ṣin šql ṭrm wmria ilm ʿglm dt šnt imr qmṣ llim,* "He slaughtered large and small cattle; he felled bulls and fatted

rams, one year old calves, lambs, [?], kids." The opening phrase *alpm ap ṣin* is a generic expression which includes the animals that are later specified in the verse. In El Amarna 263:12, *ṣūnu,* "sheep and goats [used as a collective]," is a West-Semitic gloss for Akk. *ṣēnu;* CAD 16 (Ṣ), p. 248b. On the merism in Job xviii 20, which closely resembles that in UT, 'nt:II:7–8, see Dahood in BCCT, p. 63.

beasts of the steppe. bhmt, a word rarely attested in other Semitic languages, appears in an unpublished text from Ras Shamra. The text reads: *ibn yḫlq bhmt,* "Our foe will destroy the cattle"; cf., provisionally, UT, Glossary, No. 450a, p. 371.

9. *The birds of heaven.* The dangers attendant upon textual emendation can be illustrated here by citing Briggs, CECBP, I, p. 67, who deleted *šāmayim,* "heaven," as unnecessary and making the verse too long. His reasoning has been seriously undermined by UT, 52:62–63, *'ṣr šmm wdg bym,* "the birds of heaven and the fish of the sea," which is the equivalent of biblical *ṣippōr šāmayim ūd^{e}gē hayyām.* One may remark in passing that Ugar. *dg bym,* parallel to the construct chain *'ṣr šmm,* may likewise be a construct chain of the type found in Isa ix 2, *śimḥat baqqāṣīr,* "harvest joy"; Ps xvii 9, *'ōy^{e}bay b^{e}nepeš,* "my mortal foes"; or Pss ix 10, x 1, *'ittōt baṣṣārāh,* "times of trouble."

PSALM 9

(ix 1–21)

1 *For the director; according to Muth Labben. A psalm of David.*

2 I will thank you, O Yahweh, with all my heart,
I will declare your wonderful deeds.
3 I will rejoice and exult in you, [2]*
and sing hymns to your name, Most High,
4 When my foes turn back, [3]
toppled and destroyed by your fury.
5 Oh that you would defend my right and my cause, [4]
sit upon the throne, O righteous Judge!
6 Rebuke the nations, destroy the wicked, [5]
blot out their name forever and ever.
7 The foes—may they be destroyed, [6]
a heap of ruins forever;
Root out their gods,
may their memory perish.
8 Behold Yahweh who has reigned from eternity, [7]
has established his throne for judgment.
9 It is he who governs the world with justice, [8]
judges the peoples with equity.
10 Yahweh is a stronghold for the oppressed, [9]
a stronghold in times of trouble.
11 Let those who cherish your name trust in you, [10]
for you do not abandon
those who care for you, O Yahweh.
12 Sings hymns to Yahweh, the King of Zion, [11]
publish his deeds among the peoples.
13 For he cares for those who mourn, [12]
their lament he remembers;
He does not forget the cry of the afflicted.

* Verse numbers in RSV.

14 Have pity on me, O Yahweh, [13]
see my afflictions brought on by my Enemy;
Raise me up from the gates of Death,
15 That I may recount all your praises [14]
from the gates of Daughter Zion,
That I may rejoice in your victory.
16 May the nations be mired in the pit they made, [15]
in the net they hid may their feet get caught.
17 May Yahweh be known by the judgment he passes; [16]
by the work of his hands
let the wicked man be snared. *Higgaion. Selah*
18 Let the wicked return to Sheol, [17]
perish the nations that ignore God!
19 For not forever shall the needy be forgotten, [18]
nor the hope of the afflicted eternally perish.
20 Arise, O Yahweh, lest men should boast, [19]
let the nations be judged before you.
21 Put, O Yahweh, a snaffle on them, [20]
let the nations know that they are but men. *Selah*

Notes

ix. Psalms ix–x originally formed a single alphabetical poem in which every second, third, or fourth verse began with a successive letter of the Hebrew alphabet. M. Löhr once proposed that the letters of the alphabet possessed magical significance, but the discovery at Ras Shamra of several tablets inscribed with just the alphabet confutes the theory of Löhr. The acrostic arrangement served rather as an aid to the memory of the learner and provided a framework, like the sonnet, within which the poet could work.

The dispute whether Ps ix is a pure lament or a lament introduced by verses which properly belong to a hymn of thanksgiving is very simply resolved, it would seem, by parsing, with Buttenwieser, the verbs in vss. 5–7 as precative perfects. In this analysis the poem can be seen to be a lament throughout. The opening verses become a promise to thank Yahweh on condition that he put the psalmist's enemies to flight. Once the nature of the verbs in vss. 5–7 is correctly appreciated, the long-standing grammatical and logical difficulties are quickly resolved.

1. *Muth Labben.* The meaning of this technical term is unknown.

2. *I will thank you.* Contrary to the opinion of many textual critics, the pronominal suffix after *'ōdeh* is strictly not required; the principle of the double-duty suffix permits that of *niplᵉ'ōtekā,* "your wonderful deeds," to supply for *'ōdeh.* Cf. NOTE on Ps iii 4.

3. *exult in you.* Yahweh, the Most High, will be the source of the poet's happiness. In the clause *'eśmᵉḥāh wᵉ'e'elᵉṣāh bāk,* the preposition *b* expresses the same relationship as *min* in UT, 1015:10–11, *w um tšmḫ mab,* "And may my mother draw her happiness from my father."

4. *When my foes turn back.* This is the plain sense of *bᵉšūb 'ōyᵉbay 'āḥōr,* as rightly seen by *Juxta Hebraeos, "cum ceciderint inimici mei retrorsum"* ["when my enemies fall backwards"]. To render this temporal clause with the *Psalterium Novum* as *"Quia cesserunt inimici mei retrorsum"* ["because my enemies withdrew"], or with Kraus, *"Denn meine Feinde wandten sich um"* ["because my enemies turned back"], would suppose the reading *kī šābū* or something similar, but not *bᵉšūb.*

by your fury. This sense of *pānīm* is discussed in the NOTE on Ps xxi 10.

5. *Oh that you would defend.* Parsing *kī 'āśītā* as emphatic *kī* followed by the precative perfect; for this construction, see NOTE on Ps iii 8. The most pertinent parallel is Ps xxxix 10, *kī 'attāh 'āśītā,* "Oh that you yourself would act!" Buttenwieser, PCTNT, pp. 428 f., was the first, I believe, to have recognized the mood of *'āśītā,* though he overlooked the similar formula in Ps xxxix 10.

sit upon the throne. Parsing *yāšabtā* as precative perfect; cf. preceding NOTE. The rare construction *yāšabtā lᵉkissē'* compares with UT, 49: I:30–31, *yṯb lkḥṯ aliyn b'l,* "He sits upon the seat of Victor Baal," and with 127:22–24, *yṯb krt l'dh yṯb lksi mlk lnḫt lkḥṯ drkt,* "Kirta sits upon his seat, he sits upon his royal throne, upon the peaceful bench of his authority." One should observe in this second Ugaritic text the use of the triple-duty suffix, where the suffix of *'dh,* "his seat," in the first colon also modifies the parallel phrases *lksi mlk* and *lkḥṯ drkt.* The use of a double-duty suffix was commented upon in the NOTE on vs. 2.

6. *Rebuke . . . destroy . . . blot out.* With Buttenwieser, understanding all three verbs as precative perfects. It will now be seen that these verbs correspond to the imperatives and jussives in vss. 20–21.

7. *The foes. 'ōyēb* is a collective singular, as is clear from its plural verb *tammū;* see GK, § 145c. The verse is chiastically arranged: initial *hā'ōyēb tammū* balances final *'ābad zikrām,* while the middle cola *ḥᵒrābōt lāneṣah* and *'ārīm nātaštā* are paired.

Root out their gods. Again the verb is precative perfect, as in preceding verses. *'ārīm* is related to the root appearing in Ugaritic as *ǵyr,* "to protect"; hence *'ārīm* literally denotes "protectors." That this is a name for pagan divinities may be gathered from the clear parallelism in Mic v 13, *wᵉnātaštī 'ᵃšērekā miqqirbekā wᵉhišmadtī 'ārekā,* "And I will root out your Asherim and will destroy your gods." The orthographic and phonic coincidence of *'ārīm,* "cities," and *'ārīm,* "gods," forms the basis of the pun in Jer ii 28, *kī mispar 'ārekā hāyū 'ᵉlōhekā yᵉhūdāh,* "For your gods, O Judah, were the number of your cities/gods." The same pun occurs in Jer xix 15. In the psalm the double sense of *'ārīm* is also intended, since both pagan gods, represented by idols, and cities could be turned into a heap of ruins.

Other texts preserving the root *'yr,* "to protect," include Deut xxxii 11; I Sam xxviii 16; Isa xiv 21, xxxiii 8; Pss lxxviii 38, cxxxix 20; Job viii 6; Dan iv 10, 20. The Syriac word for "Angel," *'īrā,* is most suitably derived from this root. Formal discussions of Ugar. *ǵyr* are H. L. Ginsberg, BASOR 95 (1944), 28, n. 14; H. N. Richardson, JBL 66 (1947), 322; Samuel E. Loewenstamm, *Tarbiṣ* 28 (1958 f.), 248 f.; Dahood, *Biblica* 43 (1962), 226; O. Rössler, ZA 20 (1961), 164 f.; John Gray, *I & II Kings, A Commentary* (London, 1964), p. 222.

8. *Behold Yahweh.* On the basis of Ugar. *hm,* "look, behold!," Patton, CPBP, p. 37, has correctly identified the same interjection here. Other instances are Pss xxiii 4, xxvii 2, xxxviii 11, xliii 3, xlviii 6 (M. Dahood in CBQ 16 [1954], 16), lix 16, lxii 10, cvii 24; Deut xxxiii 3, 17 (F. M. Cross, Jr., and D. N. Freedman in JBL 67 [1948], 195); Isa xxiv 14, xxxv 2 (M. Dahood *apud* J. T. Milik in *Biblica* 38 [1957], 252, n. 1); xliv 9. A convenient listing of Ugaritic examples can be found in Aistleitner, WuS, p. 90.

has reigned from eternity. Retaining the MT pointing *yēšēb* as the past narrative, parallel to perfect *kōnēn,* as in Ugaritic, and interpreting *l* in *lᵉ'ōlām* as "from." For the balance of *yqtl* with *qtl* verbal forms, cf. NOTE on Ps iv 4 and especially vii 14, where *hēkīn* (same root as our *kōnēn*) is paired with *yip'al.* There is a clear counterpart to *lᵉ'ōlām,* "from eternity," in Ps xxix 10, *wayyēšeb yhwh melek lᵉ'ōlām,* "And Yahweh has sat enthroned, the king from eternity," as rightly recognized by Kirst in FuF 32 (1958), 216, n. 46, where a number of biblical texts with *l,* "from," are listed. Cf. Pss xlv 3, lxxviii 69, and cxix 152, *qedem yāda'tī-m 'ēdōtekā kī lᵉ'ōlām yᵉsadtām,* "Of old I knew your commandments since you established them from eternity."

'ōlām should be understood in the sense of "primeval time [*Vorzeit, Urzeit*]," as in Pss lxxvii 6, xcii 9, xciii 2; Isa li 9, etc.; cf. Edward Lipiński in *Biblica* 44 (1963), 435 f., with full bibliography. The reference to God's victory over the foes of primordial times is a motif that recurs in Pss xxix 10, xcii 9–10, xciii 2.

9. *with justice . . . with equity.* For the balance between the roots in *ṣedeq* and *mēšārīm,* cf. UT, Krt:12–13, *aṯt ṣdqh lypq mtrḫt yšrh,* "His legitimate wife he truly found, his lawful spouse," and Phoenician

Yehawmilk, 6–7, *kmlk ṣdq wmlk yšr lpn 'l gbl qdšm,* "For he is a legitimate king and a lawful king through the favor of the holy gods of Byblos."

10. *times of trouble.* For the parsing of *'ittōt baṣṣārāh,* see NOTE on Ps viii 9.

11. *cherish your name.* This particular nuance of *yāda'* has been registered in the NOTE on Ps i 6.

who care for you. I.e., in contrast to those of vs. 18, *šᵉkēḥē 'ᵉlōhīm,* "those who ignore God." This sense of *dāraš* is well treated in BDB, p. 205b.

12. *King of Zion.* For the pregnant sense of *yōšēb,* see NOTE on Ps ii 4. Cf. Ps cxxxv 21, *šōkēn yᵉrūšālāim,* "the Resident of Jerusalem," another of Yahweh's titles.

13. *he cares for.* See NOTE on vs. 11.

those who mourn. Reading *dammīm* (for MT *dāmīm,* "blood") qal participle of *dāmam,* "to weep, mourn," studied at Ps iv 5. The sequence "mourn . . . lament . . . cry" is unexceptionable.

their lament. Reading for MT *nota accusativi* plus suffix *'ōtām* with no consonantal changes, *'awwōtām,* piel infinitive construct followed by pronominal suffix, from *'āwāh,* "to lament," Ar. *ta'awwaha,* "to sigh, lament," the root underlying Pss x 17 and xxxviii 10, *ta'ᵃwāh,* as first noted by Jacob Barth, *Etymologische Studien zum semitischen inbesondere zum hebräischen Lexicon* (Leipzig, 1893), pp. 29 ff. There are other occurrences in Ps cvi 14; Num xi 34, and Job xxxiii 20. Cf. GB, p. 868a, and Zorell, ZLH, p. 886a.

14. *my Enemy.* The mention of the "gates of Death" in the second colon is sufficent warrant for interpreting plural *śōnᵉ'ay* as a *plurale majestatis,* a reference to the psalmist's archenemy. See NOTE on Ps xviii 4 where plural *'ōyᵉbay,* "my Foe," is a poetic name for Death.

Raise me up. Balancing imperatives *ḥonᵉnēnī* and *rᵉ'ēh,* the participle *mᵉrōmᵉmī* apparently has the force of an imperative. The same is true in Ps xvii 14, where *mᵉmītām* (MT *mimᵉtīm*) is paired with imperative *ḥallᵉqēm* (MT *ḥelqām*).

the gates of Death. The domain of the dead was pictured as a vast city with gates ruled over by king Death. Job xxiv 12 speaks of *'īr mētīm* (MT *mᵉtīm*), "the city of the dead," while Jer xv 7 mentions *ša'ᵃrē hā'āreṣ,* "the gates of the nether world." The poet aims to contrast the gates of Death with the gates of Daughter Zion in the following verse.

15. *That I may recount . . . rejoice.* Though usually described as cohortatives, *'ᵃsappᵉrāh* and *'āgīlāh* are more accurately parsed as subjunctive forms ending in *-āh,* as in Arabic and Ugaritic. See Joüon, GHB, § 116b, and NOTE on Ps xxxix 5. The lack of copula before *'āgīlāh* is further indication that it is subjunctive; cf. Pss xxii 23, xxxix 5, lxi 5.

from the gates. Evidently intended to contrast with *miššaʿarē māwet,* the *b* of *bešaʿarē* is better taken as "from," as suggested by D. N. Freedman. Compare Prov i 21, *berōʾš ḥōmīyyōt* (MT *hōmīyyōt*) *tiqrāʾ,* "From the top of the walls she cries out."

Daughter Zion. Hebraic for Jerusalem. The alternative rendition "Daughter of Zion" becomes less probable in view of such Canaanite expressions as *btlt ʿnt,* "the virgin Anath," and *rḥm ʿnt,* "the lass Anath."

your victory. Namely the victory you will grant me over Death. The imagery reflects the myth describing the battle and ultimate victory of Baal over Mot.

16. *be mired . . . get caught.* Interpreting *ṭābeʿū* and *nilkedāh* as precative perfects; see NOTE to vs. 5.

17. *be known . . . be snared. nōdaʿ* and *nōqēš* are precative perfects; cf. preceding NOTE.

18. *return to Sheol.* I.e., let them perish; see NOTE on Ps vi 11. The classic text expressing the theme of the return to the earth (with connotations of the nether world) is Gen iii 19, *ʿad šūbekā ʾel hāʾadāmāh,* where the same verb is employed as in the present verse. According to Ps cxxxix 15, man was created *betaḥtīyyōt ʾāreṣ,* "in the lowest regions of the nether world," so one may properly speak of the "return to Sheol."

perish the nations. Reading *kālū gōyim* for MT *kol gōyim,* a mispunctualization doubtless due to *scriptio defectiva,* and analyzing *kālū* as precative perfect in balance with jussive *yāšūbū.* This pointing provides the dynamism that has long been felt to be lacking in the second colon; thus F. Baethgen, *Die Psalmen,* 3d ed. (Göttingen, 1904), p. 25, wrote "The text does not seem to be undamaged. A metrical foot is missing" [*"Der Text nicht unversehrt zu sein scheint. Es fehlt ein Versfuss"*]. The proposed reading shows the verse to be complete and perfectly balanced.

19. *nor the hope.* The force of the negative *lōʾ* carries over from the first stich to the second. The use of double-duty negatives (as well as double-duty suffixes, prepositions, conjunctions, etc.) characterizes Canaanite poetic style. Cf. UT, ʿnt:IV:49–50, *lib ypʿ lbʿl ṣrt lrkb ʿrpt,* "No foe has risen against Baal, no adversary against the Mounter of the Clouds," and 76:II:4–5, *in bʿl bbhth*[*t*] *il hd bqrb hklh,* "Baal is not in his mansion, nor El Hadad in the midst of his palace." In the latter text, *in* serves for both cola. To the list of double-duty negatives given by Joüon, GHB, § 160q, add Pss xxxi 9, l 8, and Prov xxxi 4.

20. *Arise, O Yahweh.* Energic imperative *qūmāh* has the specific sense "arise for judgment," as is clear from the parallelism with *yiššāpeṭū,* and from usage in Ps lxxvi 10, *beqūm lammišpāṭ ʾelōhīm,* "When God arises for judgment"; Zeph iii 8, *leyōm qūmī leʿad,* "when I arise from the throne" (for this translation see M. Dahood in *Sacra Pagina,* eds.

J. Coppens et al. [Paris-Gembloux, 1959], I, p. 277), and Job xxxi 14. It thus appears that imperative *qūmāh* semantically and structurally balances precative perfect *kī 'āśītā mišpāṭī wᵉdīnī,* "Oh that you would defend my right and my cause," in vs. 5, to form an *inclusio.*

lest men should boast. 'al, "lest," occurs in Pss xix 14, xxxv 24, cxix 122, cxli 3–4, and UT, 51:VIII:15–18, *al tqrb lbn ilm mt al y'dbkm kimr bph,* "Do not approach divine Mot lest he put you into his mouth like a lamb." The shade of meaning attributed to *yā'ōz* comports with the meaning "glory, arrogance" that this root sometimes carries. Cf. Ps lii 9, "And he trusted in his mass of wealth, he boasted (*yā'ōz*) of his lust."

21. *a snaffle on them.* The syntactical similarity of *šītāh yhwh mōrāh lāhem* to Ps cxli 3, *šītāh yhwh šomrāh lᵉpī,* "Put, O Yahweh, a muzzle on my mouth," suggests that here *mōrāh* denotes something like "snaffle, muzzle." The association of "arrogance" (*yā'ōz*) with "snaffle" is equivalently found in Ps xxxii 9, "With muzzle and straps must his petulance be curbed." A passable etymology for *mōrāh* is proffered by *yārāh,* "to guide, instruct," just as *mōsēr,* "band, bonds," derives from *ysr,* "to instruct, admonish," and not from *'sr,* "to bind," as customarily stated by the lexicons. For the theme of muzzling the foe, see NOTE on Ps xvii 7.

PSALM 10

(x 1–18)

1 Why, O Yahweh, do you stand afar off,
and hide yourself in times of trouble?
2 In the breast of the wicked simmers affliction,
he pantingly pursues the plans he laid.
3 For the wicked boasts of his desire,
and the despoiler worships his appetite.
4 The wicked contemns Yahweh:
"Since the Lofty One will not avenge his anger,
God will not upset his plans,
And his wealth will last for all time."
5 O Exalted One, your decrees are far from him,
with all his being he sniffs at them.
6 He says to himself, "I will not stumble,
forever happy without misfortune."
7 His mouth is full of cursing and deceit and violence,
under his tongue are mischief and iniquity.
8 He sits in ambush in open villages,
in secret places he murders the innocent;
His eyes spy on the unfortunate.
9 He lurks in secret, like a lion in his lair,
he lurks to seize the afflicted;
He seizes the afflicted to drag him away.
10 Into his net the oppressed man tumbles,
while the unfortunate fall into his pit.
11 He says to himself, "El forgets,
he turns away his face, he never looks."
12 Arise, O Yahweh God, lift up your hand!
Forget not the afflicted!
13 Must the wicked man contemn God forever?
saying to himself, "You will not requite."
14 See for yourself the misery, and the sorrow behold,
since you give them from your own hand!

To you entrusts himself the unfortunate, the fatherless,
you be his helper!
15 Break the arm of the wicked,
and requite his malice!
Can't you find his wickedness?
16 Yahweh is the eternal and everlasting king,
let the heathen perish from his earth!
17 Hear, O Yahweh, the lament of the poor,
direct your attention, give close heed.
18 If you defend the fatherless and the oppressed,
no more shall the arrogant
frighten men from the earth.

NOTES

x. A prayer for divine intervention against the wicked.

1. *stand afar off*. The phrase *ta'*^{a}*mōd b*^{e}*rāḥōq* being hapax legomenon, some commentators would emend *b*^{e}*rāḥōq* to *mērāḥōq;* this emendation is made suspect with the knowledge that *b* in Ugaritic-Phoenician frequently denotes "from." In Ugaritic poetry, in fact, there is no preposition *min,* "from," so this idea is expressed by *b* and *l.* The existence of *min* in Hebrew did not, however, completely supplant *b* denoting "from." Compare Ps vi 8, *'āš*^{e}*šāh mikka'as 'ēnī,* with Ps xxxi 10, *'āš*^{e}*šāh b*^{e}*ka'as 'ēnī,* and see N. H. Sarna, "The Interchange of the Prepositions Beth and Min in Biblical Hebrew," JBL 78 (1959), 310–16.

times of trouble. 'ittōt baṣṣārāh is discussed in the NOTE on Ps ix 10.

2. *In the breast.* On *ga'*^{a}*wāh,* "midst," see NOTE to Ps xlvi 4.

simmers affliction. Namely, thoughts of how to afflict others, just as *'āmāl,* "trouble," also signifies "trouble done to others."

pantingly pursues. Reading (for MT *yittāp*^{e}*śū*) *yittāpāšū,* an infixed -*t*- form of **nāpaš,* "to pant after," Ar. *nāpasa,* "to aspire after something, desire." A similar semantic development can be noticed in *nāšam,* "to pant," from *n*^{e}*šāmāh,* "breath." In Nah iii 18b one should read the piel privative of the root *npš: nipp*^{e}*šū 'amm*^{e}*kā 'al hehārīm w*^{e}*'ēn m*^{e}*qabbēṣ,* "Your people expire upon the mountains with none to gather them." For other examples of the infixed -*t*- conjugation, see NOTE on vs. 11; the ending of *yittāpāšū* is to be explained as the old indicative ending of the imperfect in singular -*u,* which the Masoretes have taken for the plural ending. In view of the survival of archaic verbal endings with the perfect third-person masculine singular, listed in the NOTE on Ps iv 7, there is no reason to doubt the preservation of some indicative endings with imperfect forms. Cf. Pss xiii 5, xxxii 9, lxxii 5; Job xxxvii 3.

plans he laid. Reading *ḥāšab* for MT *ḥāš^{e}bū,* attaching final *waw* to following word as the conjunction.

3. *his desire.* Parsing *ta'^{a}wat* as feminine absolute ending in *-t,* discussed in the NOTE on Ps xxvii 4. The suffix of parallel *napšō* serves likewise to determine *ta'^{a}wat;* cf. NOTE on Ps iii 4. For the thought, cf. Ps lii 9, *yā'ōz b^{e}hawwātō,* "He boasted of his lust." By placing the caesura after *ta'^{a}wat,* we arrive at three synonymous three-beat cola.

worships his appetite. Literally "bends his knee," a denominative verb from *berek,* "knee," attested in Ugaritic in the purely physical sense; see A. Jirku in FuF 32 (1958), 212. Other biblical occurrences are Gen xxxii 27; Pss xxvi 12 and xlix 19, *kī napšō b^{e}ḥayyāyw y^{e}bārek,* "Though he worshiped his appetite while he lived."

4. *The wicked contemns Yahweh.* Joining the final two words of vs. 3 to vs. 4 and reading *ni'ēṣ yhwh rāšā';* cf. vs. 13, *ni'ēṣ rāšā' '^{e}lōhīm.*

Since the Lofty One. Reading *kī gābō^{a}h* for MT *k^{e}gōbah.* The *kī* introduces the reasoning of the wicked as expressed by the poet. Preceded by the divine name *yhwh* and followed by *'^{e}lōhīm* and the divine epithet *mārōm,* "Exalted One," *gābō^{a}h* is most suitably explained as a divine appellative. It is chosen to stress the remoteness of God from human vicissitudes as conceived by the wicked man. As a divine title, the adjective *gābō^{a}h* recurs in Ps cxxxviii 6 and Job xxii 12, and as a plural of excellence in Eccles v 7. On the last passage, see Zorell, ZLH, p. 137b. The former two claim a word of comment. In Ps cxxxviii 6, *kī rām yhwh w^{e}šāpāl yir'eh w^{e}gābō^{a}h mimmērḥāqī* (MT *mimmērḥāq y^{e}yēdā'*) *yēdā',* "Though Yahweh is the Exalted One, he sees what is lowly; though he is the Lofty One, he knows from afar off," adversative *kī* serves for both cola while difficult *y^{e}yēdā'* is eliminated by attaching initial *yod* to the preceding noun as an archaic genitive ending. Notice the presence in this verse of the roots *gbh* and *rḥq,* both of which are found in the opening verses here. In Job xxii 12 one should read *h^{a}lō' '^{e}lōhīm gābō^{a}h* (MT *gōbah*) *šāmāyim w^{e}rō'eh rō'š kōkābīm kī rāmū,* "Isn't God the Lofty One of heaven who sees the tops of the stars though they are high?"

avenge his anger. Though God's ire might be aroused by his behavior, the wicked is convinced that God will take no action to vindicate his law.

upset his plans. Reading *'^{e}lōhīm m^{e}kalle m^{e}zimmōtāyw* for MT *'^{e}lōhīm kol m^{e}zimmōtāyw* and explaining *m^{e}kalle* as piel participle (a participle is desired with *'ēn*) from *kālāh,* "to be at an end." The most relevant parallel is Hos xi 6, *'^{a}kalle-m* (!) *mō'^{a}ṣōtēhem,* "I will upset their counsels"; cf. further Josh xviii 7, *w^{e}'ēn m^{e}kalle-m* (MT *maklīm*) *dābār bā'āreṣ,* "And there was no one disturbing anything in the land." Another instance of defective spelling involving *kālāh* is Ps cxxxv 5, *kī '^{a}nī yāda'tī kī gādōl yhwh wa'^{a}dōnēnū m^{e}kalle* (*mikkol*) *'^{e}lōhīm,* "Indeed I know that Yahweh is great and that our Lord made an end of the gods." My translation tries to make clear that the wicked man does not deny the existence of God but only his intervention in human affairs.

And his wealth. Consonantal *drkw* is defective spelling for *d^{e}rākāyw;* for *derek,* "power, dominion, wealth," see NOTE on Ps i 1 and compare the semantic range of *ḥayil,* "strength, efficiency, wealth." The parallelism in Prov xxxi 3 is instructive: *'al tittēn lannāšīm ḥēlekā ūd^{e}rākekā lam^{e}ḥōt m^{e}lākīn,* "Give not your resources to women nor your wealth in the full measure of kings."

will last. This sense of *yāḥīlū* occurs in a similar context in Job xx 21, *'al kēn lō' yāḥīl ṭūbō,* "And so his prosperity will not last."

5. *O Exalted One.* Synonymous with the divine title *gābō^{a}h* in vs. 4. On *mārōm* as a divine epithet, see NOTE on Ps vii 8.

with all his being. Literally "with all his heart or innards"; this signification of *ṣrr* is treated in NOTE on Ps vi 8. Semantically, the phrase here is the equivalent of Ps ix 2, *b^{e}kol libbī,* "with all my heart." It should be noticed that the following clause in this psalm contains the phrase *b^{e}libbō,* a balance that likewise emerges by the transposition of *kl ṣrry* in Ps lxix 20 to the next verse: *ḥerpāh šāb^{e}rāh libbī w^{e}'inn^{e}šāh kol ṣwrry,* "Insults have broken my heart and sickened all my being."

he sniffs at them. Suggesting his action is in contempt of the decrees of the Exalted One who is too far removed from earth to be interested in its affairs.

6. *forever happy.* Reading (for MT relative *'^{a}šer*) the adjective *'āšēr* that is found in the proper name Asher, "happy one." Also possible is the pointing *'ōšer* (Gen xxx 13), "happiness."

7. *full of cursing.* Cf. UT, 1001:2, *alt in ly,* "I have no curse." That this is the most probable meaning of *alt* (Virolleaud, *Palais royal d'Ugarit,* II, p. 3, leaves it untranslated) follows from recognizing that the text is in the nature of an incantation. Substantive *'lt* also occurs in the Phoenician incantation of Arslan Tash; Donner and Röllig, KAI, II, p. 45.

8. *on the unfortunate.* The precise meaning of consonantal *ḥlkh* is uncertain.

9. *to drag him away.* Consonantal *bmškw* may also signify "in his bag," as argued by Robert Gordis in JQR 48 (1947), 116–17.

10. *Into his net.* Attaching the final phrase of vs. 9, *b^{e}rištō,* to vs. 10; it creates a fine balance to *ba'^{a}ṣūmāyw* and produces a verse of two 3-beat cola.

into his pit. To explain *ba'^{a}ṣūmāyw* (if this is the correct pointing), it is necessary to postulate a root *'ṣm,* "to dig," a supposition that finds surprising confirmation in UT, 75:I:23–25, *kry amt 'pr 'ẓm yd ugrm,* "Dig the earth with your arm, burrow in the field with your hand."

Though this version is far from certain, the parallelism with *kry,* "to dig," permits a measure of confidence in the interpretation of *'ẓm.*

11. *El forgets.* Here *'ēl* appears to be the personal name of the deity; in Ugaritic texts *'ilu* is the name of the head of the pantheon. See Ps xvii 6.

he turns away his face. The frequency of the infixed *-t-* conjugation in Ugaritic and its occasional incidence in Phoenician and Moabite indicate that this conjugation was not as obsolete in biblical Hebrew as the standard grammars would suggest. The traditional view has found recent expression in Garbini, *Il Semitico di Nord-Ovest,* p. 130, who asserts that the reflexive theme with infixed *-t-* had long since vanished in Hebrew of the first millennium B.C. But the fact is that both LXX and Vulg. very frequently reproduce *histīr pānāyw* by *apéstrepsen to prósopon autoú* and *avertit faciem suam,* respectively. Such is their understanding of *histīr* in the present verse, which should accordingly be derived from *sūr,* "to turn away." See Dahood in *Orientalia* 32 (1963), 498; ZAW 74 (1962), 207–9; PNWSP, pp. 45 f., 54. For the parallelism between *histīr* and *šākaḥ,* cf. Ps xliv 25, where LXX translates *tastīr* by *apostrépseis,* and cii 3, where the opposite of *'al tastēr pānekā mimmennī* is *haṭṭēh 'ēlay 'ozneka,* "Turn your ear to me." Also relevant are Isa l 6, *pānay lō' histartī mikkᵉlimmōt wārōq,* "I did not turn away my face from ignominy and spittle"; LXX *ouk apéstrapsa,* "I turned not"; Vulg. *non averti;* the synonymity with vs. 5, *'āḥōr lō' nᵉsūgōtī,* "I did not turn backward"; and vs. 6, *gᵉwī nātattī lᵉmakkīm,* "I gave my back to the smiters." All add up to a strong case for deriving *histartī* from *sūr.*

12. *Arise, O Yahweh God.* Many critics—most recently Kraus, *Psalmen,* I, pp. 76 f.—delete *'ēl* in the divine title *yhwh 'ēl,* but this deletion is ruled out by the observation that this composite name represents the original form of the Tetragrammaton which may be rendered, "El brings into being." The authenticity of the full form *yhwh 'ēl* is vouched for by the stereotyped name *yahweh 'ēl,* which is separated into its components in the parallel cola of Pss xviii 3 and xxix 3, and by improved readings and stichic divisions in Pss xxxi 6–7, *pādītāh 'ōtī yahweh 'ēl 'ᵉmet śānē'tī haššōmᵉrīm hablē šaw',* "Ransom me, O Yahweh El; truly I hate those who keep worthless idols," and xxxix 13, *šim'āh tᵉpillātī yahweh wᵉšaw'ātī ha'ᵃzīnāh 'ēl* (MT *'el*) *dim'ātī 'al teḥᵉraš,* "Hear my prayer, O Yahweh, and give ear to my cry, O El; be not deaf to my tears." For a discussion of the original full form of the Tetragrammaton, cf. D. N. Freedman, "The Name of the God of Moses," JBL 79 (1960), 151–56, especially p. 156; Cross, HTR 55 (1962), 225–59, especially pp. 250 ff.

13. *contemn God forever.* Reading (for MT *'al meh*) *'ōlāmāh,* the substantive *'ōlām* followed by the *he-temporale,* as in UT, 1 Aqht:154

(=161), *p'lmh,* "and to eternity"; UT, § 11.1; Georg Beer and Rudolf Meyer, *Hebräische Grammatik* (Berlin, 1952), I, p. 120. This parsing confirms the authenticity of vs. 11, *lāneṣaḥ,* which Briggs and others would delete as a gloss. Another instance of *he-temporale* with *'ōlām* is in Job xiii 14, which I have examined in BCCT, pp. 58 f. Cf. Ps lxxiv 10, *yenā'ēṣ 'ōyēb šimekā lāneṣaḥ,* "Shall the foe contemn your name forever?"

14. *See for yourself.* Parsing *rā'ītāh* as precative perfect; the same form, with the *scriptio plena* of the final *-āh,* recurs in Ps xxxv 22; Lam iii 59, 60. The particle *kī* is emphatic, emphasizing the pronoun *'attāh,* which in turn reinforces the subject of *rā'ītāh.* Cf. NOTE on Ps iii 8 for precative perfect, and NOTE below on vs. 17. Other instances of this emphatic construction occur in Pss iii 8, xxxix 10, lvi 9, lxi 6.

since you give them. This version of *lātēt* is highly doubtful; literally, one would render "by giving from your own hand." Cf. Karatepe, III:4, *ltty,* "by giving to him."

from your own hand. As so often in Ugaritic-Hebrew, *b* denotes "from"; see NOTE on Ps ii 4.

entrusts himself. Literally "puts himself upon you." This being the only example of the construction *'āzab 'al,* one may challenge the usual derivation from *'zb,* "to abandon," and propound an etymology from *'zb* II, "to put, place," Ugar. *'db.* With verbs of placing, the preposition *'al* is natural and frequent. For other biblical texts employing *'zb* II, see NOTE on Ps xxxvii 33. Since the object of *ya'azōb* is reflexive "himself," it need not formally be expressed; good parallels to this usage are forthcoming from UT, Krt:156, *yadm,* "He rouges himself," and 'nt:IV:86, *trḥṣ,* "She washes herself." Cf. Ps lv 23, *hašlēk 'al yhwh yehobekā,* "Cast yourself upon Yahweh that he might provide for you."

the fatherless. Stands in apposition to "the unfortunate."

you be his helper. The fact that this psalm is a prayer and that the following verse contains the imperative *šebōr* and vs. 16 the precative perfect *'ābedū* make it almost certain that *hāyītā* is a precative perfect like *rā'ītāh* in vs. 14. In other words, *'attāh hāyītā 'ōzēr* is the equivalent of Ps xxx 11, *yhwh heyēh 'ōzēr lī,* "Yahweh, be my helper!"

15. *Break the arm.* With *šebōr zerōa' rāšā',* compare the request made to Baal in UT, 1 Aqht:108, *b'l yṯbr diy hmt,* "May Baal break their wings."

requite his malice. See NOTES on vss. 4 and 13. Other texts employing *dāraš* with the collateral idea of requiting include Gen ix 5; Deut xviii 19; Ezek xxiii 6, the balance with *riš'ō* permitting *ra'* to dispense with pronominal suffix; cf. NOTE on Ps iii 4. The sequence imperative-jussive (*šebōr-tidrōš*), a stylistic practice widely recognized by Hebrew grammarians (Joüon, GHB, § 113m; C. Brockelmann, *Hebräische Syntax* (Neukirchen, 1956), § 135c) deserves comment in light of Ugaritic usage, where it has received less recognition by specialists. Thus UT, 51:VIII:7–9, *wrd bthpṯt arṣ tspr byrdm arṣ,* awkwardly rendered by C. H. Gordon, *Ugaritic Literature* (Rome, 1949), p. 37, "And go down into the nether-reaches of the earth, so that ye will be counted among those who go down into the earth," has been rightly analyzed by Goetze in *Studia Orientalia Ioanni Pedersen . . . dicata,* p. 117, n. 8, who showed that *tspr,* parallel to imperative *rd,* meant "be numbered." Cf. also 51:VIII:26–27, *lp'n mt hbr wql tštḥwy wkbd hwt,* "At the feet of Mot bow down and fall; prostrate and honor him." Here jussive *tštḥwy* functions as an imperative. Cf. also Pss xvii 8, xxxii 7, xliii 1; Deut xxxii 1. The Ugaritic-Hebrew agreement in the usage of the imperative-jussive sequence bears on the question of the linguistic classification of Ugaritic.

Can't you find his wickedness? Or affirmatively, "Surely you can find, etc.," since *bal* can carry both positive and negative connotations, as is evident from Ugaritic usage; UT, §§ 9.18; 11.10, and NOTE on Ps xlix 13.

16. *the eternal and everlasting king.* Literally "the king of eternity and everlasting." *melek 'ōlām wā'ed* is understood as a construct chain in which the genitive is the composite noun *'ōlām wā'ed,* synonymous with Ugar. *dr.dr* and Heb. *dōr dōr* and *dōr wādōr*. Other examples of composite nouns are discussed in the Introduction and in the NOTE on Ps v 5. Cf. Pss xxi 5, xlviii 15, li 10, and especially xlv 7, *'elōhē-m* (enclitic *mem;* MT *'elōhīm*) *'ōlām wā'ed,* "the eternal and everlasting God," the equivalent of Isa xl 28, *'elōhē 'ōlām.*

The expression *melek 'ōlām wā'ed* resembles UT, 68:10, *tqḥ mlk 'lmk,* "You will receive your eternal kingship," and, even more closely, UT, 2008:9, *nmry mlk 'lm,* "Nimriya, eternal king."

perish from his earth. Israel Eitan in AJSL 46 (1929), 25, correctly recognized here, on the strength of Arabic usage, the optative perfect in *'ābedū.* His observation has been confirmed by Ugaritic practice and by the large number of examples which have been subsequently identified in the Psalter; cf. NOTES on Ps iii 8 and above on vs. 14.

17. *Hear, O Yahweh.* Understanding *šāma'tā* as optative perfect; see NOTE on previous verse, gloss on *"perish from his earth."*

the lament of the poor. Cf. NOTE on Ps ix 13. Being the object of *šāma'tā, ta'awāh* must be something audible, just as Ps xl 2, *qawwōh qiwwītī yhwh* must mean "Constantly I invoked Yahweh," since his reaction is described in the words, "And he stooped to me and heard my cry (*šaw'ātī*)."

direct your attention. The balance with *'oznekā* indicates that in consonantal *lbm* an enclitic *mem* is present and that the principle of the double-duty suffix is operative, so that *lbm* may be rendered "your attention." Other examples are found in Pss v 10, xii 8; Isa xxxiii 2 and Mic vii 19, discussed by me in CBQ 20 (1958), 45–46, and in Ps cix 13; Job v 5, xv 29, xxxvi 15; Obad i 13; Zeph ii 8. I am unable to accept the explanation of some of these passages (e.g., Mic vii 19) propounded by Raphael Weiss, "On Ligatures in the Hebrew Bible (*m=nw*)," JBL 72 (1963), 188–94. The present readings derive from poetic principles rather than from assumptions of scribal ineptitude.

18. *If you defend.* Literally *lišpōṭ* means "by defending." Cf. Ps viii 3 and Job xxxiv 3, *wᵉḥēk yiṭʻam le'ᵉkōl,* "And the palate tastes by eating."

the arrogant. Relating *ʻōd* to the root *ʻādad,* Ugar. *ĝdd,* studied at Ps xxxii 9; cf. Isa lii 1, *kī lō' yōsīp yābō' bāk ʻōd ʻārēl wᵉṭāmē',* "No more shall there come to you one arrogant, uncircumcised, or unclean."

PSALM 11

(xi 1–7)

1 *For the director. Of David.*

In Yahweh do I seek refuge.
How can you lie in wait for my life,
and pursue me like a bird?
2 For look, the wicked are bracing their bow,
placing their arrows upon the string,
To shoot from ambush the upright of heart.
3 When foundations are being torn down,
what is the Just One doing?
4 Yahweh—in the temple is his holy seat,
Yahweh—in the heavens is his throne.
His eyes inspect,
His pupils assay the sons of men.
5 Yahweh is the Just One
who will indeed assay the wicked;
So that he who loves injustice
hates his own life.
6 Let him send upon the wicked
bellows, fire, and sulphur,
With scorching wind their lot.
7 For the Just One is Yahweh,
who loves just actions;
Our face shall gaze upon the Upright One.

NOTES

xi. A song of trust. Since Yahweh is the Just One, the psalmist is confident that justice will ultimately prevail. This type of psalm may have developed from the laments, in which expressions of confidence are a common feature.

1. *lie in wait.* As in Akkadian-Ugaritic, biblical *'āmar* often means "to see, watch for"; cf. NOTE on Ps iii 3 and *Biblica* 44 (1963), 295 f. There is an analogous semantic range in *šūr,* "to behold, lie in wait."

pursue me like a bird. With no change of the strictly consonantal text, reading *nidhōr k^emō ṣippōr* for MT *nūdū harkem ṣippōr.* Parsing *nidhōr* as niphal infinitive absolute from *dāhar,* "to pursue, chase in war or hunting." In Nah iii 2, *sūs dōhēr* is rendered by LXX *híppou diókontos,* "pursuing horse." The object suffix after *nidhōr* must be mentally supplied from that of *napšī* on the strength of the double-duty suffix. For the simile, see Lam iii 52, *ṣōd ṣādūnī kaṣṣippōr 'ōy^ebay ḥinnām,* "My stealthy foes hunted me down like a bird." For fowling scenes, consult *The Ancient Near East in Pictures,* ed. James B. Pritchard (Princeton, 1954), Figs. 185, 189.

2. *their bow.* By reason of its balance with suffixed *ḥiṣṣām, qešet* receives a suffix on the strength of the principle of double-duty suffix treated at Ps iii 4; cf. Brekelmans in *Jaarbericht . . . Ex Oriente Lux* 17 (1963), 203.

To shoot from ambush. Like *b,* "from," longer *b^emō* can also bear this meaning. With *līrōt b^emō 'ōpel* compare Ps lxiv 5, *līrōt bammistārīm tām,* "to shoot from concealed positions at the innocent" (courtesy Raphael Serra). For an artistic representation of this practice, see Michael Avi-Yonah and Emil G. Kraeling, *Our Living Bible* (London, 1962), p. 180.

3. *When foundations. šātōt* is the plural of *šēt,* which appears in Ugaritic as *išd,* "leg," with prothetic aleph, as noted by UT, Glossary, No. 394, pp. 367 f. On the interchange of *t* and *d* in the Northwest Semitic dialects, compare Heb. *šāpat,* "to place," with Ugar. *ṯpd,* "to place"; Heb. *šārat,* "to serve," but Ugar. *šrd,* "to serve, honor" (cf. NOTE on Ps viii 2). The fact that Ugar. *išd* contains a prothetic aleph increases the probability that the plural Phoenician form *'štt,* usually defined as "pillars," or "pillared hall," has been correctly interpreted; cf. Harris, *A Grammar of Phoenician,* p. 83, and Donner and Röllig, KAI, II, p. 55.

the Just One. The sense of this much-canvassed verse becomes pellucid once *ṣaddīq* is recognized as a divine appellative which recurs in Pss xxxi 19 and lxxv 11. The complaint of the poet is not unlike the reasoning of the practical atheist in Ps x 4–5, who was convinced that God in his heavens was too far removed to intervene in behalf of justice.

4. *his holy seat.* Ps xlvii 9, *kissē' qodšō,* "his holy throne," suggests that the psalmist has here employed the poetic device known as the breakup of stereotyped phrases into their two components, placing one in the first colon and the other in the second half verse, with the result

that the two halves become still more tightly interlocked. The practice is Canaanite in origin, as may be inferred from UT, 2 Aqht:v:10–11, *hlk kṯr ky'n wy'n tdrq ḫss,* "The gait of Kothar indeed he eyes, and he eyes the tread of Khasis." The composite name *kṯr wḫss* is separated into its components, which are set in different halves of the verse. For the numerous biblical instances of this practice, consult Melamed, "Break-up of Stereotype Phrases," *Studies in the Bible* (Scripta Hierosolymitana, VIII, pp. 115–53. The recognition of this poetic usage uncovers the perfect parallelism subsisting in 4a, with *qodšō,* "his holy seat," balancing *kisᵉ'ō,* "his throne." Pss xxii 4 and cxiv 2 employ *qādōš* in the sense of "holy seat."

His pupils assay. One must agree with Ginsberg, LKK, p. 39, when commenting upon Ugar. *'p'pm,* that "It is time the practice of rendering the Hebrew *'ap'appayim* by 'eyelids' was discontinued; see Ps. 11:4, for example." The metallurgical connotation of *bāḥan* is evident in the metallurgical passage of Jer vi 27–30. For example, Jer vi 27, *wᵉtēda' ūbāḥantā 'et darkām,* "And you shall know and assay their worth" (cf. NOTE on Ps x 5, on *derek,* "value, wealth").

5. *the Just One.* The doubts expressed in vss. 3–4 give way to thoughts of trust in divine justice.

hates his own life. Parsing *śānᵉ'āh* as an archaic Canaanite *qatala* form of the third-person singular masculine verb; other examples are found in Pss iv 7, xvi 6, xviii 35, lxxxix 8; Isa xl 2; Eccles vii 27 (cf. xii 8).

6. *bellows, fire, and sulphur.* Consonantal *pḥym* allows several explanations, but in collocation with *'ēš* and *goprīt,* and in balance with *rūᵃḥ zil'āpōt,* "scorching wind," an association with Prov xxvi 21 appears the most reasonable: *pāḥēm* (MT *peḥām*) *lᵉgᵉḥālīm wᵉ'ēṣīm lᵉ'ēš wᵉ'īš midwānīm lᵉḥarḥar rīb,* "Bellows for hot coals, and logs for fire, and a quarrelsome man for kindling strife." Here *pāḥēm* is a contracted Northern dual from *pwḥ,* "to blow," and is morphologically akin to Jer vi 29, *mappūḥēm* (MT *mappāᵃḥ mē'eštām*), "bellows," a contracted dual as in Ugaritic-Phoenician and in some biblical passages, e.g., Job xxiv 11.

their lot. Literally "the portion of their cup"; cf. Ps xvi 5; Isa li 17. A painted vase from Ras Shamra depicts El with a cup in his hand; see Schaeffer, AfO 20 (1963), 211, Fig. 30.

7. *the Just One.* See NOTE on vs. 3.

who loves just actions. The word order *ṣᵉdāqōt 'āhēb* may be of significance for the exegesis of disputed Ps xcix 4, *wᵉ'ōz melek mišpāṭ 'āhēb 'attāh kōnantā mēšārīm,* "The strongest king, the lover of justice, you established equity."

Our face shall gaze upon. Translation of *yāšār yeḥᵉzū pānēmō* is doubtful. This version assumes that the pronominal suffix *-ēmō* of *pānēmō* refers to the first-person plural as in *lāmō* in Ps xxviii 8 (see NOTE there). The version proposed here is a statement of belief in the beatific vision in the afterlife; cf. NOTE on Ps xvii 15.

the Upright One. A divine appellative corresponding to *ṣaddīq* of vss. 3, 5, 7. In other words, we have in this verse the breakup of the stereotyped phrase (as in vs. 4) found in Deut xxxii 4, *'ēl 'emūnāh we'ēn 'āwel ṣaddīq weyāšār hū'*, "A God of faithfulness and without iniquity, the Just and Upright One is he." The vision of God mentioned here is doubtless that of Pss xvi 11, xvii 15, xli 13, xlix 16, lxxiii 26, which suggest a belief in an afterlife in the presence of Yahweh. If perfect justice is not attained in this life, it will be in the next; this seems to be the ultimate motive for the psalmist's confidence.

PSALM 12

(xii 1–9)

1 *For the director; upon "the eighth." A psalm of David.*

2 Help, O Yahweh, for the devoted man has ceased,
faithful men have disappeared from the sons of men!
3 Falsehood they speak, each with his neighbor, [2]*
with pernicious lips and a double mind they speak.
4 May Yahweh cut off all pernicious lips, [3]
every tongue that speaks distortions,
5 Those who boast, "By our tongue we are powerful, [4]
our weapon is our lips,
Who shall master us?"
6 "For the sobs of the poor, [5]
the groans of the needy,
Will I now arise," says Yahweh,
"I will give my help to him who longs for it."
7 The promises of Yahweh [6]
are promises unalloyed,
silver purged in a crucible,
of clay refined seven times.
8 You, O Yahweh, have protected us, [7]
you have guarded us from everlasting, O Eternal One.
9 On every side the wicked prowl, [8]
digging pits for the sons of men.

* Verse numbers in RSV.

Notes

xii. Prayer for deliverance from personal enemies; a lament.

1. *the eighth.* See Note on Ps vi 1.

2. *faithful men.* Abstract *'emūnīm,* "fidelity," acquires a concrete meaning from its pairing with concrete *ḥāsīd,* precisely as in Ps xxxi 24; cf. discussion of this poetic practice in the Note on Ps v 8.

have disappeared. The balance in Ps lxxvii 9 between *'āpēs* and *gāmar* suggests that *kī passū* has undergone the aphaeresis of initial *aleph.* The loss of *aleph* after a vowel is occasionally attested in Ugaritic; e.g., *pštbm* for *pištbm* and *ytmr* for *yitmr;* UT, § 9.33.

3. *with.* Though not preceded by a preposition, consonantal *śpt* receives one in translation by reason of its parallelism with *belēb,* on the principle of the double-duty preposition examined at Ps xxxiii 7.

pernicious lips. Reading (for MT *śepat*) *śāpōt,* the plural of *śāpāh,* as in Ugaritic; see UT, § 8.12. In Hebrew one also finds the plural *qešātōt,* "bows," as well as the Canaanite form *qāšōt* in Ps cxli 9 and I Sam ii 4. Deriving *ḥalāqōt* from *ḥlq* II, Ugar. *ḫlq,* "to perish"; compare Ps v 10, "With their tongue they bring death." Though the root *ḥlq* I, "to be smooth," is likewise predicated of lips and speech, the general stress of the psalm is upon the poisonous effects of slander upon a community.

a double mind. Literally "a double heart."

4. *every tongue. kol* of the first colon seems to modify *lāšōn* in the second as well.

speaks distortions. Vocalizing *gedīlōt* for MT *gedōlōt* and deriving it from *gādal,* "to spin, weave," from which stems *gedīlīm,* "twisted threads, tassels." Cf. Ps xli 10, *higdīl 'ālay 'āqōb,* "He spun slanderous tales about me." There are illuminating analogies in Ps xxxi 21, *rukse 'īš,* "the slanderings of men," where the root is *rks,* "to bind, join together," and in Ps l 19, *taṣmīd mirmāh,* "You weave deceit." Ugar. *šrg,* "to lie," in Arabic denotes "to plait, tress [*saraja*]." For relevant remarks on the semantic relationship between "to weave, twist" and "to lie" see D. R. Hillers, *Treaty-Curses and Old Testament Prophets* (Rome, 1964), p. 73, n. 81. It may be observed that Felix Perles, *Analekten zur Textkritik des Alten Testaments* (München, 1895), II, p. 47, proposed the emendation *daggālūt* which signifies "lies" in Aramaic; the above explication obviates the need for emendation. Cf. *Biblica* 45 (1964), 397.

5. *we are powerful.* Explaining *nagbīr* as a denominative verb from *geber,* "man, hero," just as Ps xx 8, *nazkīr,* "we are strong," derives from *zākār,* "male." See *Biblica* 45 (1964), 396.

our weapon. Relating *'ittēnū* (MT *'ittānū*) or *'ētēnū* to the substantive *'ēt* that denotes a cutting instrument of iron, usually translated "plowshares," in I Sam xiii 20, 21; Isa ii 4 ‖ Mic iv 3. Cf. also Isa xxx 8; and for II Kings vi 5, see Gray, *I & II Kings,* p. 460.

6. *sobs of the poor.* That *šōd ʿaniyīm* does not signify "oppression of the poor" or "violence done the poor" follows from these considerations. First, its balance with *'enaqat 'ebyōnīm* suggests that *ʿaniyīm* is a subjective rather than an objective genitive. Second, in Mal ii 13, *'anāqāh* is parallel to *dimʿāh,* "tears," and *bekī,* "weeping"; hence *šōd* should denote something similar. Finally, UT, 125:34 seems to attest to such a root: *al tšt bšdm mmh,* "Let her not dry up (root *nšt*) her waters by sobbing," which seems to be synonymous with 125:26–28, *al tkl bn qr ʿnk my* (!) *rišk udmʿt,* "Do not exhaust, my son, your eye with flowing, the water of your head with tears." Ginsberg, LKK, p. 26, has tentatively proposed a similar rendition of line 34, "Let not her waters be dried up with grief (*šdm*)."

I will give. This nuance of *šīt* is commented upon at Ps xxi 7.

my help. Explaining the *b* of *beyēšaʿ* as an emphasizing particle, fulfilling here the function of the possessive suffix; cf. discussion at Ps xxix 4.

7. *promises of Yahweh.* This signification of *'imarōt,* sufficiently attested, is chosen here by reason of the translation adopted in vs. 6b.

purged in a crucible. Reading (for MT *baʿalīl lā'āreṣ*) *beʿelī lā'āreṣ,* omitting the final *lamedh,* an instance of dittography. Equating the substantive *ʿelī* with that found in Job xxx 17, *laylāh ʿaṣāmay niqqar mēʿelī* (MT *mēʿālay*), "At night my bones are hotter than a caldron"; and xxx 30, *ʿōrī šāḥar mēʿelī* (MT *mēʿālay*) *weʿaṣmī ḥārāh minnī ḥōreb,* "My skin is blacker than a caldron, and my bones are hotter than a scorching wind." Though an uncertain phrase precludes the perfect understanding of Prov xxvii 22, the parallelism seems sufficient to establish the sense of *ʿelī: 'im tiktōš 'et hā'ewīl bammaktēš betōk hārīpōt baʿelī lō' tāsūr mēʿālāyw 'iwwālātō,* "Though you should pound a fool in a mortar, among grits in a crucible, his folly will not leave him." The balance with *maktēš,* "mortar," is a solid indication of the meaning of *ʿelī.* Cf. further Prov xvi 27; Ar. *ġala, inġala,* "to boil, simmer," provides a satisfactory etymology. Heb *ʿōlāh,* "whole burnt offering," is apparently related, as proposed by Fritz Hommel, *Die Altisraelitische Überlieferung* (München, 1897), p. 279.

of clay refined. Taking *l* in *lā'āreṣ* in the frequent Ugaritic-Hebrew sense "from." For *'ereṣ,* "clay," see J. L. Kelso, *The Ceramic Vocabulary of the Old Testament* (New Haven, 1948), p. 39. This too is the meaning of *'ereṣ* in Lam ii 21, *šākebū lā'āreṣ ḥūṣōt naʿar wezāqēn,* "In the mud of the streets lie the young and the old," which is to say that *'ereṣ ḥūṣōt,* often emended, is the equivalent of *ṭīṭ ḥūṣōt* (Ps xviii 43; Zech ix 3, etc.), "mud of the streets." One may remark further that *ṭīṭ,* "mud, mire," likewise denotes "potter's clay" in Isa xli 25 and "brick-clay" in Nah iii 14.

8. *have protected us*. The reading *tišmᵉrēm* becomes capable of an explanation in light of the poetic principle of balancing a pronominal suffix (in this case found in *tiṣṣᵉrennū*) with an enclitic *mem;* cf. NOTE on Ps x 17.

you have guarded us from everlasting. The poet offers a reason why Yahweh should continue to watch over the just. The psalmists often appeal to Yahweh's former mercies as motive for his intercession in the present straits.

O Eternal One. Interpreting *zū lᵉʿōlām* not as an epithet or appellative but as a divine name. Thus while it signifies "The One of Eternity" (cf. NOTE on Ps xxiv 7), it can nevertheless be understood as vocative (courtesy D. N. Freedman). Of course, it would make an excellent parallel to vocative *yahweh*.

9. *digging pits*. The translation is problematical. Reading (for MT *kᵉrūm zullūt*) infinitive absolute *kārō mᵉzālōt*. The verb *kārāh*, "to dig," is well known, but the verb *mzl*, evidently related to *nzl*, "to fall," is hypothetical. Cf. UT, Krt:99–100, *ʿwr mzl ymzl*, a disputed clause, but which in view of Matt xv 14 might be rendered, "The blind man falls into the ditch." In Qumran Hodayot, 11.5, the phrase *mzl śpty* may possibly mean "the flow of my lips," from *mzl*, "to fall." See *Gregorianum* 43 (1962), 78.

PSALM 13

(xiii 1–6)

1 *For the director. A psalm of David.*

2 How long, O Yahweh? Will you eternally forget me?
How long will you turn your face from me?
3 How long must I place doubts in my soul, [2]*
creating grief in my heart?
How long must my Foe rejoice over me?
4 Look at me, answer me, O Yahweh, my God! [3]
Enlighten my eyes, avert the sleep of death!
5 Lest my Foe should boast, "I overcame him!" [4]
Lest my Adversary should exult when I stumble.
6 But I will trust in your kindness; [5]
let my heart rejoice in your saving help.
Then shall I sing to Yahweh, [6]
since the Most High is a benefactor.

* Verse numbers in RSV.

NOTES

xiii. The lament of a man on the verge of death. Temporarily abandoned by God, the psalmist begins to harbor doubts about the goodness of Yahweh. His confidence prevails, however, and he promises to praise Yahweh for the deliverance from death which he feels God will grant him.

2. *eternally forget me.* "Eternally" may have a twofold meaning here. Should God continually ignore the prayer of the psalmist, the psalmist would pass on to Sheol, forever cut off from God's remembrance and love; cf. Ps lxxxviii 6.

turn your face from me. Deriving *tastīr* from *sūr* (LXX *apostrépseis*); consult NOTE on Ps x 11.

3. *doubts in my soul.* The disputed substantive *'ēṣōt* can passably be

derived from Ar. *naǵaḍa,* "to shake, totter," which scholars generally agree is found in UT, 68:17–18, *nhr ʿz lymk ltnǵṣn pnth lydlp tmnh,* "River is strong, he does not fall; his joints do not wobble, his frame does not collapse." The substantive probably recurs in Ps cvi 43, *peʿāmīm rabbōt yaṣṣīlēm wehēmmāh yamrū baʿaṣātām wayyāmōkkū baʿawōnām,* "Many times he delivered them, but they rebelled in their doubt and were brought low through their malevolence." What should be remarked here is the collocation of *ʿaṣātām* and *yāmōkkū;* if our derivation from *nǵṣ* is sound, then we have here the two roots which are collocated in UT, 68:17, *lymk ltnǵṣn.* The semantic nexus between "to shake, totter" and "doubt" is present in I Sam xxv 31, *pūqāh,* "anguish of conscience," from *pūq,* "to reel, totter." Cf. Luke xxiv 38, "Why are you disturbed, and why do doubts arise in your minds?".

creating grief. Reading (for MT *yōmām*) *yōmēm,* qal participle from **ymm,* a by-form of Ugar. *ybm,* which probably denotes "to create, beget." Thus the goddess Anath is called both *ybmt limm* and *ymmt limm;* UT, § 5.33. For this meaning of *ybm-ymm,* see W. F. Albright *apud* Millar Burrows in BASOR 77 (1940), 7 f. This hypothesis bids fair to bring sense out of Ps lxviii 18, *ʾādōn yābam* (MT *ʾadōnāy bām*) *sīnay baqqōdeš,* "The Lord created Sinai as his sanctuary." Cf. Exod xv 17 and Ps lxxviii 54. Cf. UT, 2 Aqht:VI:41, *wblb tqny,* "But in her heart she creates."

my Foe. I.e., Death. In Canaanite mythology the chief enemy of Baal, the god of life and fertility, was Mot, the god of death and sterility. Much of this imagery has passed over into the religious vocabulary of the psalmists; cf. NOTE on Ps xviii 4.

rejoice over me. The phrase *yārūm ʾōyebī ʿālāy* is evidently meant to counterbalance vs. 5, *ṣāray yāgīlū.* Just as *śāmēaḥ* denotes both "to rejoice" and "to be high" (cf. Jonas C. Greenfield, HUCA 30 [1959], 141–51), so *rūm* can also denote "to rejoice" as well as "to be high." The clearest biblical example, because *yārūmū* is balanced by *yāgīlū,* is Ps lxxxix 17, as noted by L. Kopf in VT 9 (1959), 249. This version sharpens the contrast between the sorrow of the psalmist and the *Schadenfreude* of his enemy, Death.

4. *Look at me.* I.e., instead of turning your face from me. The balance with *ʿanēnī* permits one to understand the suffix as attaching to both imperatives. In fact, the energic ending of *habbīṭāh* may be intended as the metrical surrogate for the suffix, just as the energic ending in Hab ii 17 is meant to balance the pronominal suffix of the first colon: *kī ḥamas lebānōn yekassekkā wešōd behēmōt yeḥītan,* "The violence of Lebanon will cover you and the ravaging of the Great Ridge will terrify you." The parallelism between a pronominal suffix and an energic ending is analogous to that between a pronominal suffix and an enclitic *mem,* discussed in the NOTES on Pss x 17 and xii 8.

Enlighten my eyes. As in vs. 2, a twofold meaning may be intended. First, the phrase means "to restore to health" (cf. Ps xxxviii 11), and secondly, it may denote "to grant immortality," since "to see the light" is idiomatic for "to enjoy immortality," as noted at Ps xxxvi 9–10. The parallelism with "avert the sleep of death," which likewise may bear a double sense, sustains this interpretation.

avert the sleep of death. This is a request for both restoration to health and the gift of immortality. Reading *panne 'īšōn hammāwet* for MT *pen 'īšan hammāwet.* Parsing *pannē* as piel imperative of *pānāh,* "to turn aside," as in Zeph iii 15, *hēsīr yhwh m^e^šapp^e^ṭayik* (MT *mišpāṭayik*) *pinnāh 'ōy^e^bēk,* "Yahweh has removed your smiters, has turned aside your foe." See BDB, p. 815b. Thus the two imperatives *hā'īrāh* and *pannē* perfectly balance the two imperatives of the first colon, *habbīṭāh* (energic like *hā'īrāh*) and *'^a^nēnī.* The root of substantive *'īšōn* is *yšn,* "to sleep," and the phrase *'īšōn hammāwet* is conceptually equivalent to Prov xx 20, *'īšūn ḥōšek,* "the sleep of darkness." Since *ḥōšek* here equals Sheol or Death, the equivalence of the two phrases is evident. See Dahood, PNWSP, pp. 14 f.

The phrase *'īšōn hammāwet* should be compared to the parallelism between *qbr* and *šnt* in UT, 1 Aqht:150–51, *hm t'pn 'l qbr bny tšḫtann bšnth,* "If they should fly over the grave of my son, if they should disturb him in his sleep"; cf. Driver, CML, p. 63, n. 5.

5. *Lest.* The force of *pen,* "lest," in the first colon extends to the second half verse; hence the translation "Lest my Adversary."

my Foe. As in vs. 3, Death is signified.

I overcame him. Proposals to emend *y^e^koltīū* to *yākoltī lō* (e.g., Kraus, *Psalmen*) may safely be shelved in view of the syntax of synonymous *l'y,* "to overcome, prevail over," in UT, Krt:33, *šnt tluan,* "sleep overcomes him." The fact that *l'y* governs a direct accusative object is a strong argument in support of the MT pointing *y^e^koltīū.*

my Adversary. Plurale majestatis ṣāray is another name for the psalmist's archrival, Mot. Consult the discussion of the plural of majesty *'ōy^e^bay,* "my Foe," in the NOTE on Ps xviii 4. There are but three actors in the psalm, making a dramatic picture of the psalmist caught between Yahweh and Mot.

should exult. The verb *yāgīlū* suggests several analyses. It may be a plural form corresponding to the plural form (though singular in meaning) of the subject *ṣāray;* at Ps xlvi 5 it is noted that the plural of excellence *'^e^lōhīm* is occasionally accompanied by a plural verb. One may also parse *yāgīlū* as the Canaanite singular form, an archaic usage remarked at Pss x 2, xxxii 9, lxxii 5 and Job xxxvii 3.

when I stumble. The verb *'emmōṭ* is freighted with connotations; here it connotes stumbling into the jaws of Death. In fact, in Ps lxvi 9 *mōṭ* may well be a poetic name for the underworld: *haššām napšēnū baḥayyīm welōʼ nātan lammōṭ raglēnū,* "Who has kept us among the living and has not put our foot in the Quagmire." Cf. Ps cxxi 3.

6. *the Most High.* For MT *ʻālāy,* perhaps one should read *ʻēlī,* the divine appellative studied at Ps vii 9. It might be observed that LXX reads, "And I shall hymn the name of the Lord, the Most High," an addition which scholars describe as a reminiscence of Ps vii 18.

is a benefactor. Or, "has dealt bountifully." Note the beneficence of *ʻly* in UT, 126:III:7–8, *nʻm larṣ mṭr bʻ[l] wlšd mṭr ʻly,* "Sweet to the earth is the rain of Baal, and to the field the rain of the Most High (*ʻly*)."

PSALM 14

(xiv 1–7)

1 *For the director. Of David.*

The fool says in his heart:
"There is no God."
They perform corrupt, abominable deeds;
there is no one who does good.
2 From heaven Yahweh looks down,
upon the sons of men,
To see if there be one who ponders,
one who searches for God.
3 Each one is stubborn,
together they are depraved;
There is no one who does good,
no, not a single one.
4 Don't they know, all the evildoers,
that they who devour his people,
Devour the grain of Yahweh
they did not harvest.
5 See how they have formed a cabal,
but God is in the assembly of the just.
6 The council of the poor will humiliate it,
for Yahweh is its refuge.
7 O that out of Zion would come the salvation of Israel!
with Yahweh restoring the fortunes of his people.
Then let Jacob rejoice and Israel be happy.

NOTES

xiv. Though commonly classified as a lament, this psalm has many points of contact with Wisdom Literature and could, with equal validity, be put in the category of Wisdom psalms.

This psalm is very similar to Ps liii, though both were evidently transmitted through different channels and finally incorporated into different books of the Psalter. There are several striking textual variations in the two poems, but to emend one on the basis of the other would be temerarious; they may simply reflect Northern (Ps liii) and Southern (Ps xiv) traditions.

3. *Each one.* Cf. Gen xvi 12; Job xxiv 24; Eccles x 3; UT, 2 Aqht:vi:38, *mt kl amt,* "The death of every man will I die," and Phoenician Kilamuwa, i:6, *wkl šlḥ yd,* "And every man stretched forth his hand."

is stubborn. Deriving *sār,* not from *sūr,* "to turn aside," but from *sārar,* "to be stubborn, rebellious"; note the adjective *sar,* "stubborn, sullen," in I Kings xx 43, xxi 4, and Jer vi 28.

4. *his people.* Apparently identical in meaning with vs. 7, *'ammō,* "his people," *'ammī* may be parsed as bearing the third-person suffix *-y,* studied in the Note on Ps ii 6.

the grain of Yahweh. Well attested in Hebrew (BDB, p. 537a), *leḥem,* "grain," likewise bears this connotation in Ugaritic, though the glossaries of Gordon, Driver, and Aistleitner are not cognizant of this meaning. See Ginsberg, LKK, p. 47, on UT, 126:iii:14, where *lḥm* is parallel to *yn,* "wine," and *šmn,* "oil," precisely as in Ps civ 15.

For the imagery, see Num xiv 9, "Have no fear then of the people of the land, for they are grain for us (*laḥmēnū*)," and St. Ignatius of Antioch, *Epistle to the Romans,* 4, I, "Grain of God am I, ground by the teeth of wild beasts."

the grain . . . they did not harvest. The lack of relative pronoun with relative clauses is rather frequent in Psalms and Job; see Note on Ps xxxv 15. For *qārā',* "to collect, harvest," see S. Speir in VT 3 (1953), 307, with references to earlier studies; Ps cxlvii 9, *nōtēn libehēmāh laḥmāh libnē 'ōrēb 'ašer yiqrā'ū,* "Who gives to the cattle their grain, to the crows that which they gather," should be added to his examples. For the usage in Prov xxvii 16, see Zorell, ZLH, p. 734b.

5. *See how.* For El Amarna *šumma,* "behold!", see W. L. Moran in JCS 7 (1953), 78–80, and Dahood in *Biblica* 38 (1957), 306–9. New examples are in Ps lxvi 6; Judg v 11; I Sam iv 4, vii 6 (courtesy Raphael Serra). E. Zolli, *Il Salterio* (Milano, 1951), p. 24, renders *šām* by *Ecco là* but provides no explanatory note.

formed a cabal. The persons described here recall those depicted in Ps ii 1–2. Since traditional "they feared a fear" is not feasible in the context (cf. Briggs, CECBP, I, p. 107), one must seek another root in *pāḥedū paḥad.* Ugar. *pḫd,* "flock"; Palmyrene *paḥdā,* "family, clan, tribe" (W. F. Albright, *From the Stone Age to Christianity,* 2d ed. [Anchor Books, 1957], p. 248, n. 71), and the balance with *dōr,* "assembly," are the basis for the present version. The precise nuance "cabal" (which may have to be modified) is inferred from Ps lxiv 2, *paḥad 'ōyēb,* which equals *sōd mᵉrēʿīm,* "council of wicked men," and *rigšat pōʿᵃlē 'āwen,* "concourse of evildoers." On the basis of Ps xci 5 and Song of Sol iii 8, *paḥad* may also be rendered "pack."

assembly of the just. On Ugaritic-Hebrew *dōr,* "family, assembly," see Frank J. Neuberg in JNES 9 (1950), 216. Cf. Pss xlix 20, *dōr, 'ᵃbōtāyw,* "the assembly of his fathers," and cxii 2, *dōr yᵉšārīm,* "the assembly of the upright." Compare Ps cxi 1, *sōd yᵉšārīm,* "the council of the upright," which suggests that Pss cxi and cxii come from the same poet (courtesy E. Vogt). In other words, *dōr ṣaddīq* is synonymous with Ps i 6, *derek ṣaddīqīm,* an indication that both psalms belong to the same literary genre, namely, Wisdom Literature.

6. *The council of the poor.* On *ʿēṣāh,* "council," see second NOTE on Ps i 1.

will humiliate it. Namely, the cabal of unbelievers. Vocalizing *tōbīšō* for MT *tābīšū.* The pronominal suffix *ō* of *tōbīšō* refers back to *paḥad;* for this unusual suffix with the imperfect, see Hos viii 3, *yirdᵉpō;* Exod xxii 29, *tittᵉnō;* and GK, § 60d. Admittedly *ad hoc,* this solution will be dispensed with when a better solution is proposed for this enigmatic verse.

Yahweh is its refuge. To be compared with Ps i 6, "But Yahweh shall safekeep the assembly of the just."

7. *restoring the fortunes.* For the various shades of meaning of *šūb šᵉbūt,* see most recently Henri Cazelles, "L'expression hébraïque *šūb šᵉbūt* viendrait-elle de l'accadien d'Assarhaddon?" in GLECS 9 (1961), 57–60. There is a good treatment in Zorell, ZLH, p. 826a.

PSALM 15

(xv 1–5)

1 *A psalm of David.*

Yahweh, who shall be a guest in your tent?
Who shall dwell upon your holy mountain?
2 He who walks with integrity and practices justice,
and speaks the truth from his heart.
3 He who does not trip over his tongue,
who does no wrong to his fellowman,
and casts no slur on his neighbor.
4 The despicable man is rejected from his presence,
but those who fear Yahweh he feasts.
He swore to do no wrong and did not waver.
5 His money he does not lend at interest,
nor accept compensation from the hungry.
Who does these things will never stumble.

Notes

xv. A liturgy specifying the moral qualities required for admission to the temple. It may also be classified as a Wisdom psalm.

1. *in your tent.* The presence of *'ōhel* and *yiškōn* in the same verse echoes the Canaanite balance of *ahlm,* "tents," with *mšknt,* "tabernacles," in UT, 128:III:18–19. Contrast Ps v 5, "No evil man can be your guest."

2. *from his heart. b* in *bilᵉbābō* denotes "from," as so frequently in Ugaritic and Hebrew. Cf. Ps lx 8, *'ᵉlōhīm dibber bᵉqodšō,* "God spoke from his sanctuary"; Ps xcix 7, *bᵉ'ammūd 'ānān yᵉdabbēr 'ᵃlēhem,* correctly rendered by CCD, "From the pillar of cloud he spoke to them." Further examples are discussed by Sarna in JBL 78 (1959), 310–16, and by Dahood in *Biblica* 44 (1963), 300 f. As a matter of fact, Driver, CML, p. 59b, renders UT, 1 Aqht:34–35, *tbky pġt bm lb tdm' bm kbd,* "Pughat wept from (her) heart, she sobbed from

(her) liver," though he does offer the alternate possibility of "in her heart," etc.

3. *trip over his tongue.* This problematic version of *rāgal ʿal lᵉšōnō* considers the following elements. There is a pronounced penchant in Ugaritic and Hebrew to form denominative verbs from names of parts of the body; in Ugaritic, at least nine examples have been recognized. See Dahood, *Biblica* 43 (1962), 364, to which *tqtnṣn,* "to crouch," from *qnṣ,* "shin," should be added; and *Biblica* 44 (1963), 204 f. See also W. F. Albright, "The Beth Shemesh Tablet in Alphabetic Cuneiform," BASOR 173 (1964), 52, where *ḥtq* is parsed as a denominative infixed *-t-* form of *ḥq,* "bosom." Also, the image has good parallels in Pss xxxix 2, "I will heed my steps lest I stumble over my tongue," and lxxiii 9, "They set their mouth against the heavens, and their tongue struts upon the earth." As Johannes Hempel points out in IDB, III, p. 954a, some humorous formulations are used in the pedagogic psalms to impress the young man on how he might keep his way pure.

4. *is rejected.* Vocalizing as perfect niphal *nimʾas,* rather than MT niphal participle *nimʾās.* After the niphal participle *nibzeh,* a finite verb is desiderated.

from his presence. As in vs. 2, the *b* of *bᵉʿēnayw* denotes "from." There are two other convincing examples of this phrase: Prov i 17, *kī ḥinnām mᵉzōrāh hārāšet bᵉʿēnē kol baʿal kānāp,* "For stealthily is the net spread out, out of the sight of every winged creature," and Prov xx 8, *melek yōšēb ʿal kissēʾ dīn mᵉzāreh bᵉʿēnāyw kol rāʿ,* "A king seated on the throne of judgment scatters from his presence every evil man." Just as no evil man can be a guest in Yahweh's tent (vs. 1, Pss v 5, xxiv 3), so the hospitality of the godly man does not extend to the wicked. See Ps ci 7, "No man who utters lies shall continue in my presence."

he feasts. For this meaning of *yᵉkabbēd,* see NOTE on Ps l 23.

He swore to do no wrong. The construction *nišbaʿ lᵉhāraʿ* becomes comprehensible in light of Isa liv 9, *nišbaʿtī mēʿᵃbōr,* "I swore off becoming angry." In other terms, *l* expresses the idea of separation, "from," as so often in Ugaritic and Hebrew; UT, § 10.1. See my article, "Note on Psalm 15, 4 (14, 4)," CBQ 16 (1954), 302.

5. *lend at interest.* The prohibition of interest looks more to charitable loans made to the poor (Exod xxii 25; Lev xxv 35–37) to relieve distress than to purely business transactions. GB and BDB are correct against KB and ZLH in subsuming *nešek,* "interest," under *nāšak,* "to bite," since both "to bite" and "interest" are written *nṯk* in Ugaritic; see Virolleaud, *Palais royal d'Ugarit,* II, p. 212, and Aistleitner, WuS, No. 1875, p. 217.

compensation. The balance with *nešek,* "interest," suggests this meaning of *šōḥad,* a nuance found in Prov vi 35 where *šōḥad* is paired with *kōper,* "gift." Consult BDB, p. 1005a, and R. B. Y. Scott's translation (The Anchor Bible, vol. 18), p. 62, "He will not look at any compensation (*šōḥad*)/, Nor be mollified though you make him many gifts (*kōper*)."

from. This meaning of *'al* was discussed in NOTE on Ps iv 7. The psalmist is thus seen to employ three different prepositions to express the various nuances of "from": *b* in vss. 2 and 4, *l* in vs. 4, and *'al* in vs. 5.

the hungry. For this sense of *nāqī,* see Amos iv 6, *niqyōn šinnayim,* traditionally rendered "cleanness of teeth" (RSV), but more correctly translated "hungry mouths" by J. B. Phillips, *Four Prophets: Amos, Hosea, First Isaiah, Micah. A Modern Translation from the Hebrew* (London, 1963), pp. xii, 12.

The customary understanding of this verse, "and does not take a bribe against the innocent" (RSV), raises the question as to why specification should be made with respect to the innocent. All bribetaking was illegal, and no distinction should be made between taking bribes from the guilty or the innocent.

will never stumble. I.e., will never encounter misfortune; cf. Ps xxx 7.

PSALM 16
(xvi 1–11)

1 A *miktam of David.*

Preserve me, O El,
for I have sought refuge in you.
2 I said, "O Yahweh, you are my Lord,
there is none above you."
3 As for the holy ones who were in the land,
and the mighty ones in whom was all my delight:
4 May their travail-pains be multiplied,
prolong their lust.
I surely will not pour libations to them from my hands,
nor will I raise their names to my lips.
5 O Yahweh, you have portioned out my cup of smooth wine,
you yourself have cast my lot.
6 The lines have fallen for me in pleasant places,
and the Most High has traced out my property.
7 I will praise Yahweh who counsels me,
and whose heart instructs me
during the watches of the night.
8 I keep Yahweh continually before me,
indeed, from his right hand I will never swerve.
9 And so my heart rejoices,
my liver leaps with joy,
and my body dwells at ease,
10 Since you will not put me in Sheol,
nor allow your devoted one to see the Pit.
11 You will make me know the path of life eternal,
filling me with happiness before you,
with pleasures at your right hand forever.

NOTES

xvi. This profession of faith was composed by a Canaanite convert to Yahwism. Verse 2 contains the *professio fidei,* vss. 3–4 are the abjuration of the false Canaanite gods he once served, while vss. 5–11 enumerate the joys and blessings which issue from this newly found faith in Yahweh. Verses 10–11 are a statement of the poet's belief in immortality, a doctrine well known among the Canaanites. His union with Yahweh will be eternal.

The language and style are peculiarly Phoenician, and there are three instances of the characteristic Phoenician *scriptio defectiva.*

1. *miktam of David.* Probably an inscription on a stone slab, LXX *stēlographía;* so H. L. Ginsberg in *Louis Ginzberg Jubilee Volume,* English Section, (New York, 1945), pp. 169 f. The eighteenth-century etymology of J. D. Michaelis, who connected *miktām* with *ketem,* "gold," and understood the inscription as gold-lettered, remains possible. In a Greek inscription studied by B. Lifshitz in ZDPV 76 (1960), 160, the word *psyche,* "stela" (Heb. *nepeš*), was painted red, while the cuneiform signs of the name of Darius I in the Behistun Inscription were overlaid with lead to prevent erosion and to assist legibility. Cf. Job xix 23 and Kurt Galling, WO 2, 1 (1954), 3–6.

O El. The poet uses the ancient Canaanite and patriarchal designation of the chief deity.

2. *I said.* Consonantal *'mrt* is Phoenician orthography for *'āmartī;* see vs. 5 *mnt* and vs. 6 *nḥlt.* Cf. GK, § 44i, and see now Isa xlvii 10, *'mrt,* which is read fully in 1QIs[a], *'mrty.*

O Yahweh. The *lamedh* of *lyhwh* is *vocativum,* which is quite frequent with divine names in Ugaritic; e.g., UT, 51:v:121, *šm' laliyn b'l,* "Listen, O Victor Baal." Cf. NOTE on Ps iii 9. There is a similar vocative in Ps cxl 7, *'āmartī lyhwh 'ēlī 'attāh ha'azīnāh yhwh qōl taḥnūnāy,* "I said, 'O Yahweh, you are my God; hear O Yahweh, my plea for mercy.'" Here *lyhwh* is balanced by vocative *yhwh* in the second colon.

none above you. I.e., you are peerless. This ancient formula sounds like the Canaanite profession of faith found in UT, 51:VI:43–44 (= 'nt:v:40–41), *mlkn aliy[n] b'l ṯpṭn win d'lnh,* "Our king is Victor Baal, our ruler; there is none above him."

3. *the holy ones. qedōšīm* is the name of the Canaanite deities; e.g., the Yeḥawmilk Inscription from Byblos calls the gods *mpḥrt qdšm,* "the assembly of holy ones." For Ugaritic usage see Marvin H. Pope, *El in the Ugaritic Texts* (VTS, II; Leiden, 1955), p. 13, and for Northwest Semitic and biblical citations, Luke Dequeker, "Les *Qedošim* du

Ps. LXXXIX à la lumière des croyances sémitiques," in *Ephemerides Theologicae Lovanienses* 39 (1963), 469–84.

In the land. Refers to the land of Canaan.

the mighty ones. This is another name for Phoenician gods. For the Phoenician parallelism between *qdšm* and *'dr*, as here, see T. H. Gaster in JQR 37 (1947–48), 292.

in whom was all my delight. The construct *'addîrê* depends upon the genitive phrase *kol ḥepṣī bām;* see GK, § 130d. Related, though not identical, is UT, 52:65, *ybn ašld,* "O sons whom I bore," where *bn* is construct before the finite verb. Cf. UT, § 8.16, p. 56, and W. F. Albright in BASOR 82 (1941), 47.

4. *their travail-pains.* This curse harks back to Gen iii 16 and employs essentially the same terms: *harbāh 'arbeh 'iṣṣ*^{e}*bōnēk w*^{e}*hērōnēk,* "I will greatly increase your travail-pains and your lust."

prolong their lust. Though lacking a suffix, *māhār* (initial *mem* may be an enclitic to be attached to preceding word) shares that of parallel *'aṣṣ*^{e}*bōtām.* Parsing *'aḥēr* as piel imperative, and deriving *māhār* (joining final *waw* to next word) from *hrr,* "to lust," parallel to *ḥmd,* "to desire," in UT, 75:I:38–39, *b'l ḥmdm yḥmdm bn dgn yhrrm,* "Baal greatly desires them, Dagan's son lusts after them." The fact that Baal is the subject of *yhrr* points up the appositeness of the psalmist's choice of words to curse the gods he once worshiped. The correct derivation of *hērōn* in Gen iii 16 originates from Chaim Rabin, *Studies in the Bible* (Scripta Hierosolymitana, VIII), p. 391. For another possible occurrence of *hrr,* in association with *ḥmd,* see Ps lxviii 17 and Dahood, *Biblica* 45 (1964), 404.

There may be an allusion in this curse to the Astarte plaques representing a naked female goddess of fertility that are found in considerable numbers in Palestinian sites of the Late Bronze Age and the Early Iron Age.

I surely will not pour. The *waw* detached from *mhrw* and prefixed to *bl* may serve an emphasizing function; cf. NOTE on Ps iv 7.

libations to them. The value of the suffix of *niskēhem* is datival; see NOTE on Ps xx 3. The real sense of the balancing clauses is, "I will neither worship nor swear by false gods"; these two ideas are juxtaposed in Ps xxiv 4.

from my hands. Consonantal *mdm* should perhaps be pointed *middēm,* the preposition *min* followed by the Northern contracted dual for "hands," and should be compared with such Ugaritic expressions as UT, 68:13, *bd b'l km nšr,* "From the hands of Baal like an eagle," or 1008:19–20, *w bd bnh 'd 'lm,* "Nor from the hands of his sons forever." Other examples of contracted or Northern duals appear in Jer vi 29; Job xvii 2, xxi 16, xxiv 10; Prov xxvi 21; see NOTE on

Ps xvii 4, where the same balance between "hands" and "lips" is found. See also Dahood, *Biblica* 43 (1962), 298. The lack of the pronominal suffix with *middēm,* "my hands," may be explained either on the principle of the double-duty suffix, parallel *śᵉpātāy* being furnished with one, or by the frequently attested practice of omitting the suffix with names of parts of the body. For example UT, 1 Aqht:I:34–35, *tbky pġt bm lb tdmʻ bm kbd,* "Pughat weeps in her heart, she cries in her liver." Further examples have been collected by Michael C. Astour in RHR 164 (1963), 6, n. 4.

raise their names. This is the metaphor of drinking a chalice.

5. *you have portioned out.* Vocalizing consonantal *mnt* as *mānītā,* another instance of Phoenician *scriptio defectiva,* which also characterizes the Book of Ecclesiastes. On I Sam i 4, *mānōt,* "portions of a sacrifice," cf. Gaster, *Thespis,* 1961, p. 338.

my cup of smooth wine. Literally "my smooth (wine) and my cup," a case of hendiadys. Relating *ḥelqī* to *ḥālaq,* to be "smooth"; cf. UT, 1084:1–3, *yn ṭb . . . yn d l ṭb . . . yn ḫlq,* "sweet wine . . . wine that is not sweet . . . smooth wine." The smooth wine symbolizes a tranquil and happy existence as opposed to the cup of fury that Jerusalem received from the hand of Yahweh (Isa li 17) or the bowl with bitter dregs that the wicked must imbibe (Ps lxxv 9). In the twenty-third-twenty-fourth campaigns at Ras Shamra (1960–61) a pitcher with a reddish-brown painting that shows the seated god El with a goblet in his right hand was unearthed. There can be little doubt that the personage represented is El, since texts found hard by contain a description of El the banquet-giver. He is said to invite his seventy children to eat and drink. Virolleaud, who does not give the original text, renders, "*Mangez, ô dieux, et buvez, buvez encore.*" See Virolleaud, CRAIBL, 1962 (appeared 1963), 110 f., and for a reproduction of the painted pitcher, C. F. A. Schaeffer, AfO 20 (1963), 211, Fig. 30.

you yourself have cast my lot. If the pointing *tōmīk* is correct, the root is *ymk,* a by-form of *mkk,* "to sink, fall." The verb *yāmak* would seem to underlie the strange form in Prov v 5, *raglehā yōrᵉdōt māwet šᵉʼōl ṣᵉʻādehā yitmōkū.* "Her feet go down to Death, her steps sink into Sheol." *yitmōkū* is parsed as an infixed *-t-* conjugation of *ymk;* cf. Ugaritic infixed *-t-* conjugation *itrṯ* from *yrṯ.* In other words *tōmīk,* "you make fall," creates a fine balance to vs. 6 *nāpᵉlū.* With the brace *mkk-ymk,* compare *ḥmm-yḥm.*

6. *and the Most High.* As in Ugaritic, the conjunction *ʼap,* "also," has lost its emphatic quality and simply denotes "and"; consult NOTE on Ps xviii 49. Reading the divine appellative *ʻēlī,* studied in the NOTE on Ps vii 19, for MT *ʻālāy.* This reading creates an *inclusio* which encloses vss. 5–6; vs. 5 begins with *yhwh* and vs. 6 closes with *ʻēlī.*

has traced out. Parsing *šāpᵉrāh* as third-person singular masculine preterite with archaic verbal ending, as in Ps iv 7 and elsewhere. Relating the verb to *šābar,* "to measure," to Ar. *šabara,* "to measure," a verb which apparently occurs in Job xxxviii 10, *wā'ešbōr 'ālāyw ḥuqqī wā'āśīm* b^e*rīaḥ ūd*^{e}*lātāyim,* "And I traced out its limits, and set bars and two doors." This explanation of the Job passage, set forth by Gaster in *Thespis,* (New York, 1950, not, however, in the 1961 edition), p. 456, has been proffered again by A. Guillaume in *Promise and Fulfilment,* S. H. Hooke Anniversary Volume (Edinburgh, 1963), p. 123. The nonphonemic interchange of labials *b* and *p* (cf. Dahood, PNWSP, pp. 10, 32 f., 43) has recently been documented in the Ugaritic personal name *yp'l* where one would expect *yb'l,* UT, 2027:4, and in an unpublished tablet in which *ypky* (=*ybky*) is paired with *ydm',* "he weeps."

For the motif of the Most High determining boundaries, see Deut xxxii 8, b^e*hanḥēl 'elyōn gōyīm* b^e*haprīdō* b^e*nē 'ādām,* "When the Most High gave the nations their patrimony, when he separated the sons of men."

my property. On *naḥ*^{a}*lat,* see NOTE on Ps ii 8. The spelling again is defective, without the final *-y,* as in vs. 2, *'mrt.* Or it may be feminine absolute of Phoenician form, sharing the suffix of *lī.*

7. *whose heart.* Literally "his kidneys"; the suffix of *kilyōtay* is third-person masculine, as in Phoenician; cf. NOTE on Ps ii 6. Cf. Ps xxxiii 11, *maḥš*^{e}*bōt libbō,* "The thoughts of his (God's) heart." The similarity of the phrase *yiss*^{e}*rūnī kilyōtay* with UT, 127:26, *ywsrnn ggnh,* "His inward parts instruct him," has been commented upon by Ginsberg, LKK, p. 48.

watches of the night. For this meaning of plural *lēlōt,* see Pss xcii 3, cxxxiv 1.

8. Compare *mīmīnī bal 'emmōṭ* with Pss xvii 4 and xxi 8, b^e*ḥesed 'elyōn bal yimmōṭ,* "From the love of the Most High he will not swerve." The balance of "before me" with "right hand" equivalently recurs in Ps xxxviii 18 and Job xviii 12, y^e*hī rā'ēb 'ōnō* $w^{e'}$*ēd nākōn* l^e*ṣal'ō,* "Let the Hungry One be the one to meet him, with Death stationed at his side."

from his right hand. The suffix of *mīmīnī* is third-person masculine, as in vs 7.

9. *my heart . . . my liver.* Cf. UT, 75:I:12–13, *il yẓḥq bm lb wygmḏ bm kbd,* "El laughs in his heart and chuckles in his liver."

rejoices . . . leaps with joy. The parallelism of *śāmē*^{a}*ḥ* and *gīl* is recorded in UT, 125:14–15, *bḥyk abn nšmḫ blmtk ngln,* "In your life eternal, our father, we rejoice, in your immortality we leap with joy."

10. *you will not put me.* Deriving *ta'*^{a}*zōb* from *'zb* II, Ugar. *'db,* "to put," which occurs in parallelism with *ntn,* as here, in UT, 2 Aqht:v:26–28, *bd dnil ytnn qšt lbrkh y'db qṣ't,* "Into the hands of Daniel he puts the bow, upon his knees he places the arrows." See

M. Dahood, "The Root *'zb* II in Job," in JBL 78 (1959), 303–9. The synonymous use of *'āzab* II and *nātan* can be seen in Gen xxxix 4, 6; Neh ix 27, 28; and possibly in Ps x 14. Full treatment of vs. 10 can be found in JBL 78 (1959), 308, n. 16.

The psalmist firmly believes that he will be granted the same privilege accorded Enoch and Elijah; he is convinced that God will assume him to himself, without suffering the pains of death. This sentiment is also expressed in Pss xlix 16 and lxxiii 24.

11. *the path of life eternal.* Within the context of vss. 10–11, *ḥayyīm* denotes "eternal life," precisely as in UT, 2 Aqht:VI:27–29, *irš ḥym watnk blmt wašlḥk ašsprk 'm b'l šnt 'm bn il tspr yrḫm,* "Ask for eternal life and I will give it to you, immortality and I will bestow it upon you. I will make you number years with Baal, with the gods you will number months." The balance with *blmt,* "immortality," clearly points to the denotation of *ḥym.* Cf. Prov xii 28, *beʾōraḥ ṣedāqāh ḥayyīm wederek netībāh 'al māwet,* "In the path of virtue is eternal life, and the treading of her way is immortality." Consult Dahood, *Biblica* 41 (1960), 176–81, and Scott (The Anchor Bible, vol. 18), pp. 91 f.

filling me with happiness. Vocalizing piel infinitive absolute *śabbēa'* instead of MT *śeba';* a verbal element is required to keep the sentence in motion. Cf. NOTE on Ps xlix 4. It may or may not be significant that the dis legomenon plural *śemāḥōt* occurs in highly Phoenicianizing contexts; see NOTE on Ps xlv 16. Syntactically, *śemāḥōt* is an accusative of material-with-which.

before you. Compare *'et pānekā* with Phoen. *'t pn mlqrt,* "in the presence of Melqarth"; see A. Dupont-Sommer, *Semitica* 3 (1950), 44; and M. Lidzbarski, *Kanaanäische Inschriften* (Giessen, 1907), 52.8. Cf. Ps cxl 14.

with pleasures at your right hand. ne'īmōt, like *śemāḥōt,* is also an accusative of material-with-which, like UT, 'nt:II:40–41, *ṭl šmm tskh rbb nskh kbkbm,* "With dew the heavens anoint her, with spray the stars anoint her." The same construction occurs in Ps civ 15, *weyayin yeśammaḥ lebab 'enōš,* "With wine he gladdens the heart of man."

The theme of being feted at the right hand of God has literary antecedents in UT, 51:V:107–10, *št alp qdmh mra wtk pnh t'db ksu wyṯṯb lymn aliyn b'l,* "An ox is set before him, a fatted one directly in front of him. A throne is placed and he is seated to the right of Victor Baal."

PSALM 17

(xvii 1–15)

1 *A prayer of David.*

Hear, O Yahweh, my plea for vindication;
attend to my cry,
Give ear to my prayer.
Destroy deceitful lips!
2 Let my justice shine before you,
may your eyes gaze upon my integrity.
3 Examine my heart, probe me at night,
test me with fire,
You will find no idolatry in me.
4 My mouth has not transgressed
against the works of your hands,
To the command from your lips have I hewed.
5 My legs held firmly to the rugged paths,
from your tracks my feet never swerved.
6 I call upon you—
O that you would answer me, O El!
Turn your ear to me,
listen to my words.
7 Fell those who revile you, O Savior,
with your right hand muzzle your assailants!
8 Guard me as the pupil in your eye,
hide me in the shadow of your wings,
9 From the fury of the wicked who would rend me,
of my deadly foes who encircle me.
10 They are clogged with their blubber,
with their mouth they speak arrogance itself.
11 My legs tottered, they surrounded me,
they fixed their eyes
To pitch me into the very Land of Perdition,

12 Like a lion that is avid for prey,
like a young lion that lurks in ambush.
13 Arise, O Yahweh, confront his fury,
bring him low;
Rescue my life from the wicked who wars on you.
14 Slay them with your hand, O Yahweh,
slay them from the earth,
Make them perish from among the living!
But as for your treasured ones—
fill their belly,
May their children enjoy abundance,
and leave their wealth to their offspring.
15 At my vindication
I will gaze upon your face;
At the resurrection
I will be saturated with your being.

Notes

xvii. Though this psalm is generally classed as an individual lament, a clearer understanding of the psalms of innocence, especially v, xxvi, and cxxxix, shows that it too belongs to this *Gattung*. The poet has been falsely accused of worshiping idols and asks for vindication.

1. *my plea for vindication.* Apparently the direct object of *šimʿāh,* and hence something audible, and parallel to *rinnātī* and *tᵉpillātī, ṣedeq* must mean something like this, as recognized by Zorell, ZLH, p. 683b, for this passage and for Ps iv 2; cf. also Ps l 6 and Job xxxiii 32. The first-person suffix is forthcoming from those of the parallel nouns on the strength of the principle discussed at Ps iii 4 and which operates in vss. 2, 3, 4, 7, and 8 of this poem.

Destroy deceitful lips. This phrase strikes the theme of the psalm; the poet has been falsely accused. Cf. Pss xii 4, lv 10.

Reading (for MT *bᵉlōʾ*) *ballēʾ*, piel imperative of *blʾ*, "to wear out, destroy," a by-form of *bālāh,* that is preserved in the Ugaritic substantive *nblʾt,* "flame," and in Jer xxxviii 12, *bᵉlōʾē hassᵉḥābōt,* "tattered rags," which appears in vs. 11 as *bᵉlōyē hassᵉḥābōt.* Clearly, then, *blʾ* is a by-form of *blh.* Cf. Job xxx 28, *qōdēr hālaktī bᵉlūʾ* (MT *bᵉlōʾ*) *ḥammāh,* "I went about blackened, seared by the sun."

2. *shine before you.* Since the verse speaks of visual activity, *yēṣēʾ* makes better sense when taken in the Ugaritic-Arabic sense "to be clean, to shine." This nuance is rather frequent in Hebrew, as ad-

mitted by a number of scholars; cf. Pss xxxvii 6, lxv 9, lxxiii 7; Isa xiii 10; Hos vi 3; Job xxviii 1. For bibliography, see Dahood in *Sacra Pagina,* I, p. 274, n. 3, and PNWSP, p. 52, n. 3. Especially relevant are Ps xxxvii 6, "And he will make your justice shine like the sun, and your cause like the noonday," and Isa lxii 1, "Until her vindication shine like the sun, and her salvation glow like a torch"; see Ginsberg, LKK, p. 45, and S. Esh in VT 4 (1954), 305 ff.

before you. For this meaning of *millᵉpānekā,* see I Kings viii 54. The practice of heaping up prepositions is typically Phoenician; cf. Friedrich, PPG, § 253. Other biblical instances are in Deut iv 32; Isa xxxvii 26; Sirach xv 14, and, above all, in Ecclesiastes; see H. Cazelles in GLECS 8 (1958), 21.

my integrity. Its balance with *mišpāṭī,* "my justice," permits *mēšārīm* to dispense with a formal suffix; cf. NOTE on vs. 1 and note the parallelism of *ḥᵃsīdāyw,* "his devoted ones," and *'ᵉmūnīm,* "his faithful ones," in Ps xxxi 24.

3. *Examine my heart.* Parsing *bāḥantā* as precative perfect following the imperatives of vs. 1 and the jussives of vs. 2; see NOTE on Ps iii 8. Less probable is the assumption that *bāḥantā* is a conditional verb without the morphologic indicator *'im;* so RSV, "If thou triest my heart." See Michel, TSP, § 30.28, p. 191.

Examine . . . test. The verbs *bāḥan* and *ṣārap,* likewise found in parallelism in Ps xxvi 2, a psalm of innocence, are sound indications that Ps xvii belongs to this category. Compare the equivalent series of verbs in Ps cxxxix 1.

probe me at night. Its closeness to suffixed *libbī* permits *pāqadtā* to forgo the accusative suffix. As in Ps lxv 10, *pāqadtā* is a precative perfect; cf. NOTE on Ps iii 8.

idolatry in me. With the Vrs., vocalizing *zimmātī* for MT *zammōtī;* for this specification of meaning see NOTE on Ps xxvi 10. The psalmist has been accused of worshiping idols and asks God himself to examine the accusation; he is convinced of his innocence and of his vindication, if not in this life, in the afterlife. See NOTE on vs. 15.

The suffix of *zimmātī* has a local sense, much like Ps lix 4, *lō' pišʿī wᵉlō' ḥaṭṭā'tī yhwh,* "There is no guilt nor sin in me, O Yahweh."

4. *My mouth has not transgressed.* In contrast to the arrogance of his enemies described in vs. 10, the psalmist meekly accepted without murmur the workings of divine providence.

against. lᵉ has this force in Pss xli 6, 8, lxxv 6; Exod xix 4; Hos v 1 (in LXX rendition); UT, 'nt:IV:48, *mnm ib yp' lb'l,* "What foe has risen up against Baal?" and Phoenician Karatepe, III:16, *wyp'l lš'r zr wšt šm 'ly,* "And (if) he should do damage to this gate, or set his own name upon it." Donner and Röllig, KAI, II, p. 37, failing to grasp this nuance of *l,* propose a translation that appears unsatisfactory, *"Macht aber ein anderes (fremdes) Tor* und setzt seinen Namen darauf." In other words, the phrase *yp'l l* becomes intelligible upon comparison with its Hebrew equivalent in Exod xix 4, *'ᵃšer 'āśītī lᵉmiṣrāyim,* "What I did against Egypt."

the works of your hands. Identifying *pᵉ'ullōt 'ādēm* (MT *'ādām*) with FELIOTH IADEM in a Punic-Latin inscription from Leptis Magna in Tripolitania, republished in Donner and Röllig, KAI, I, p. 32, No. 178, and studied in II, p. 165. Explaining *'ādēm* as the contracted Northern dual of *'ad,* "hand," a by-form of *yad;* see NOTE on Ps xvi 4. Substantive *'ad,* "hand," occurs in the Ugaritic bound form *šb'id,* "seven times," in Ar. *'idun,* "time"; cf. Gen xliii 34 and Dan i 20, where *yādōt* signifies "times." Hence, the discussion of A. M. Honeyman in VT 11 (1961), 349, in which the author denies the existence of Ar. *'idun,* is wide of the mark. See G. R. Driver in PEQ 87 (1955), 93, on Elephantine Aram. *ṣb'ydyn,* "twice-dyed." Another convincing instance of this vocable materializes in Ps lxviii 19, *lāqaḥtā mattānōt bᵉ'ādēm* (MT *bā'ādām*), "You received gifts from their hands." Gaster, *Thespis,* 1950, p. 458, approached a correct solution when he wrote that *"bā'ādām* is a false interpretation of original BDM-*miyyādām,* as in Ugaritic." Cf. Ps cv 14.

The interchange between *primae yod* and *primae aleph* nouns and verbs is well documented; e.g., Ps xxi 3, *'ᵃrešet,* "request," but Ps lxi 6, *yᵉrešet* (MT *yᵉruššat*); UT, Krt:96, *yḥd,* but the parallel passage in line 184 reads *aḥd.* Further examples are given in W. F. Albright, JAOS 71 (1951), 262, n. 7, and D. W. Young, "Notes on the Root NTN in Biblical Hebrew," in VT 10 (1960), 457–59.

The protestation that he never sinned in speech against the works of God must be interpreted in the light of such statements as Ps xxviii 5, "Because they do not consider the works of Yahweh (*pᵉ'ullōt yhwh*)," and Ps lxxvii 13, "And I will meditate on all your work."

As in Ps xvi 4 where *middēm* balances *śᵉpātāy,* so *'ādēm,* without suffix, balances suffixed *śᵉpātekā,* a phenomenon noted at vs. 1, while the balance between *pī* and *śᵉpātekā* recalls UT, 77:45–47, *bpy sprhn bšpty mnthn,* "In my mouth is their story, on my lips their tale."

5. *My legs.* The parallelism with *pᵉ'āmay* here, with *libbō* in Ps xxxvii 31, with *raglay* in Pss xl 3 and lxxiii 2, with *'ᵃṣāmay* in Hab iii 16, with *'ēnay* in Job xxxi 7, all names of parts of the body, indicates that *'ᵃšūray* refers to a part of the body. In UT, 8:7–10, *aṯr aṯrm* is followed by *išdym,* "two legs."

held firmly. MT *tāmōk,* an infinitive absolute, can be justified in light of the widespread use of the infinitive absolute to express past time in Ugaritic, Phoenician, and Hebrew; cf. NOTE on *ḥārōq* in Ps xxxv 16.

rugged paths. Literally "paths of ruggedness." LXX translated *hodoùs sklērás,* "rugged ways." MT *pārīṣ* may be correct though the pointing *pereṣ* is also possible.

from your tracks. In *b^ema'g^elōtekā, b* denotes "from"; cf. NOTE on Ps ii 4, and compare Ps xvi 8, *mīmīnī bal 'emmōṭ,* "From his right hand I will not swerve," and xxi 8, *b^eḥesed 'elyōn bal yimmōṭ,* "From the love of the Most High he will not swerve."

It is surprising that the massive evidence for *b,* "from," in Ugaritic, Phoenician, and Hebrew should be lost on A. van den Branden, who in *Oriens Antiquus* 3 (1964), 256, is still explaining *b* in such Phoenician expressions as *bgbl šd nrnk, "provenant de la région de la plaine de Narnaka"* (the translation is his), as a dissimilation of *min.*

6. *O that.* On emphatic *kī,* see NOTE on Ps iii 8, and cf. Ps lxxxvi 7.

O El. Cf. NOTE on Ps x 11.

7. *Fell those who revile you.* Vocalizing *happīlāh* for MT *haplēh* and parsing the form as hiphil energic imperative; in vs. 13 there are three energic imperatives. Reading *ḥōs^edekā,* from *ḥsd* II, "to revile, contemn," for MT *ḥ^asādekā.* A good parallel is Ps lii 3, *ḥesed 'ēl,* "the contempt of God." A slightly different parsing is proposed, though from the same root, of *ḥsd,* in Ps lii 3 by C. Schedl in BZ 5 (1961), 259 f.

O Savior. See Pss vii 11, xviii 42.

muzzle your assailants. Reading (for MT *ḥōsīm*) *ḥ^asōm,* qal imperative of *ḥāsam,* "to muzzle" (Deut xxv 4; Ezek xxxix 11), a root preserved in Ps xxxix 2, *maḥsōm,* "muzzle." The theme of muzzling the foe is found in Akkadian, Ugaritic, and Hebrew literatures (e.g., Pss ix 21, lxviii 23; Job vii 12); cf. S. E. Loewenstamm in IEJ 9 (1959), 260 f.; M. Dahood in JBL 80 (1961), 270 f. In UT, 'nt:III:37–38, *ištbm,* "I muzzled," is balanced by *mḫšt,* "I smote," a brace that is not unlike the pairing of "fell" and "muzzle" in the present verse.

If MT *ḥōsīm* is the correct reading, then it would be the only example of *ḥāsāh* used absolutely.

The suffix of *ḥōs^edekā* entitles matching *mitqōm^emīm* to a suffix on the principle remarked in the NOTES on vs. 1 and Ps iii 4. The first of the two *mems* in consonantal *mmtqwmmym* may be an enclitic to be attached to preceding *ḥ^asōm* (cf. NOTE on Ps xxix 6), or it may be dittographic.

8. *Guard me.* Referring to the metaphor of an eagle protecting its young ones; cf. Deut xxxii 10b–11a, *yiṣṣ^eren^ehū k^e'īšōn 'ēnō k^enešer yā'īr qinnō,* "He watched him like the pupil of his eye, like an eagle he protected (Ugar. *ǵyr*) his nest."

pupil in your eye. 'īšōn bat 'āyin (MT) is generally translated "the pupil, the daughter of your eye" (AT), but the phrase in Deut xxxii 10, *'īšōn 'ēnō,* allows one to propose that MT *bat* be pointed *bēt,* "within, between," found in Ezek xli 9; Job viii 17; Prov viii 2. In Lam ii 18, for MT *bat 'ēnekā* read *bat^a'īnekā,* piel infinitive construct like Ugar. *tdmm,* *tbrrt, tidm* (UT, § 8.48), and rendering the clause, "Do not desist from your weeping."

shadow of your wings. The motif of the eagle with outstretched wings is studied at Ps xviii 11.

9. *From the fury.* This sense of *pānīm* is discussed in NOTE on Ps xxi 10.

rend me. Occurring in the metaphor of wolves pursuing their victim, *šaddūnī,* explicitly predicated of a wolf in Jer v 6, naturally lends itself to this translation.

my deadly foes. For the syntax of *'ōyebay benepeš,* see NOTE on Ps viii 9, and for the thought compare Ps xxxviii 20, *'ōyebay ḥayyīm,* "my mortal foes," with a pronominal suffix interposed between the *regens* and the genitive, analogous to the preposition, or to the enclitic *mem,* intervening between the *regens* and the genitive.

who encircle me. The language of the chase is evident here; cf. Pss xxii 17, xl 13–14.

10. *They are clogged.* Reading qal passive *sūgārū* (pausal) for MT *sāgerū.* The thesis of F. Böttcher, *Ausführliches Lehrbuch der hebräischen Sprache* (Leipzig, 1868), II, §§ 903–7, that very many MT puals, of which the piel is nowhere attested, are to be pointed as qal passives, has been confirmed by the frequency of this form in the El Amarna Letters, Ugaritic (UT, § 9.31), and its sporadic appearance in Phoenician. For example, compare Gen vi 4, *wyldw lhm hmh* with UT, 2 Aqht:II:14, *k yld bn ly,* "For a son has been born to me." It becomes evident that MT *yāledū* should be pointed as qal passive *yūledū* and the clause translated, "And these were born to them." Wherever the consonantal text allowed it, the Masoretes pointed the passive qal as niphal or pual, under the influence of postbiblical Hebrew, where passive qal does not exist. Since the phenomenon is widely accepted, there is no point in multiplying examples from the Bible. In the Psalter clear instances are recorded in iii 7, xlix 15, lxxiii 2, cv 27, cvi 17, cix 2, 15. A recent discussion appears in Dahood, PNWSP, p. 8, in connection with Prov ii 22b.

with their blubber. ḥelbāmō is an accusative of material-with-which preceding its verb, a stylistic trait remarked at Ps v 10.

In biblical idiom fatness sometimes connotes arrogance; cf. Deut xxxii 15; Jer v 28, and especially Ps lxxiii 7–8.

with their mouth. Accusative of means preceding verb, as very frequently in Psalms; see NOTE on Ps v 10.

they speak arrogance itself. In the phrase *dibberū begē'ūt,* the *be* serves an intensifying function; cf. discussion at Ps xxix 4 and the similar expression in Ps lxxiii 8, *wīdabberū berā',* "And they speak malice itself." Other relevant texts are Ps l 19, *pīkā šālaḥtā berā'āh,* "With your mouth you forge evil itself," and Jer xxix 9, *kī bešeqer hēm nibbe'īm,*

"It's a lie that they are preaching to you in my name!" (John Bright, *Jeremiah* [The Anchor Bible, vol. 21; New York, 1965], p. 205), but in xiv 14, *šeqer hann^{e}bî'îm nibb^e'îm.*

The arrogance of the psalmist's accusers stands in opposition to the humility of the poet who in vs. 4 maintains that he never spoke arrogantly against the designs of providence.

11. *My legs tottered.* Dividing consonants to read *'^{a}šūray nō'ātāh.* On *'^{a}šuray,* see NOTE on vs. 5; *nō'ātāh* is tentatively parsed as the feminine dual participle from *nw',* "to tremble, totter." The extensive use of the dual in Ugaritic, even with adjectives (UT, § 8.72), leads one to suppose that Hebrew employed the dual more widely than is customarily admitted. The plural feminine participle *nā'ōt* occurs in I Sam i 13; a new instance of the root *nw'* was identified in Isa ix 18 by W. L. Moran in CBQ 12 (1950), 153–54.

The description resembles Ps xxxv 15, "When I stumbled, they gathered with glee," where the imagery is also that of the chase.

they surrounded me. The language of the hunt is suggested; cf. vs. 9.

To pitch me. The accusative suffix of *lîn^{e}ṭôt* must be supplied from *s^{e}bābūnî* according to the practice noticed at vs. 1. For the use of *nāṭāh* in connection with the nether regions, cf. Job xv 29, *w^{e}lo' yiṭṭeh lā'āreṣ minlō-m* (MT *minlām*), "Nor his possessions reach the nether world" (Pope, The Anchor Bible, vol. 15).

very Land of Perdition. This is one of the thirty-odd names for the underworld in the Bible. Deriving *dimyōnō* from *dāmāh,* "to cease, destroy" ("Land of Cessation" is also a viable translation); the pronominal suffix may be explained as a mild emphatic like the article. Cf. BASOR 163 (1961), 47, where Albright in his treatment of *mātu ša îmērēšu,* "the Land of the Asses," cites the insistence of P. Haupt on the fact, supported by Ethiopic and other parallels, that the pronominal suffix gives the *nomen regens* determinate meaning, as though it had a definite article. Haupt would invariably quote the seventh-century B.C. Assyrian expression *nēšu ša ṣērišu,* "the desert lion."

13. *confront his fury.* Cf. NOTE on vs. 9.

bring him low. The staccato style of this verse closely resembles that of vs. 3.

who wars on you. The position of consonantal *ḥrbk* at the end of its clause, while the verb it putatively modifies stands at the beginning, indicates that it is not an accusative of means, as traditionally explained, but rather stands in apposition to the immediately preceding *rāšā'.* Hence it is vocalized as pausal participle *ḥōr^{e}bekā.*

The unexpected shift from the plural in vss. 9–12 to the singular in vs. 13 is characteristic of imprecatory speech, as noted at Ps v 10.

14. *Slay them.* Vocalizing consonantal *mmtm* as *m^{e}mîtām,* a par-

ticiple employed as an imperative, a usage remarked in Ps ix 14. Cf. vs. 7, "With your right hand muzzle your assailants."

Make them perish. Reading (for MT *ḥelqām*) *ḥallᵉqēm,* piel imperative of *ḥālaq,* "to perish, die," studied at Ps v 10 and in *Biblica* 45 (1964), 408. The parallelism of the roots *mwt* and *ḥlq* in this verse is of a piece with UT, 49:I:13–14, *kmt aliyn bʻl kḫlq zbl bʻl arṣ,* "For Victor Baal has died, the Prince Lord of Earth has perished." Zolli, *Il Salterio,* p. 28, correctly saw that the verb here is related to Akk. *ḫalāqu,* "to perish," and accordingly rendered, *"Falli perire acciochè non vivano."*

from among the living. Since *bᵉḥayyīm* apparently balances *mēḥeled, bᵉ* must mean "from," as in vs. 5; for the pairing of *min* and *bᵉ,* see NOTE on Ps xx 7, and for the thought, Ps xxi 11.

your treasured ones. Vocalizing consonantal *ṣpynk* as plural *ṣᵉpīnekā;* compare Ps lxxxiii 4, *wᵉyityaʻᵃṣū ʻal ṣᵉpūnekā,* "And they consult together against your treasured ones." *Scriptio defectiva* in the *Vorlage* may account for the unsuccessful efforts of MT in the present passage as well as in vs. 7, *ḥᵃsōm,* and vs. 14a, *mᵉmītām.*

their wealth. To the several texts in which *yeter* bears this connotation might be added Hab ii 8, *kī ʼattāh šallōtā gōyīm rabbīm yᵉšollūkā kol yeter ʻammīm,* rendered by RSV, "Because you have plundered many nations, all the remnant of the peoples shall plunder you," but which probably means, "Because you have plundered affluent [the meaning of *rabbīm* in Ps xxxvii 16; Job xxxv 9; Eccles x 6; Isa liii 12] nations, the peoples will strip you of all your wealth."

15. *At my vindication.* In other words, at the final judgment when I shall be vindicated. The parallel with "at the resurrection" proves that the psalmist is dealing with the final judgment, as in Ps i 5.

Stylistically, *ṣedeq* forms an inclusion begun in vs. 2, *ṣedeq.* See NOTES on Pss iv 2–4, iv 7–8, xviii 31–33.

gaze upon your face. Implying, in the afterlife. The beatific vision, the face to face meeting with God, is clearly intended, as in Pss xi 7, xvi 11, xxi 7, xxvii 4, 13, xxxvi 10, xli 13, xlii 3, lxiii 3.

Note the inclusion formed by *ʼeḥᵉzeh pānekā* with vs. 2, *ʻēnekā teḥᵉzenāh mēšārīm.* Just as God gazed upon the rectitude of the psalmist in this life, so will the psalmist gaze upon the face of God in the future life.

At the resurrection. This seems to be the plain sense of *bᵉhāqīṣ* when one compares it with the eschatological passages Isa xxvi 19, "But your dead will live, their bodies will rise. Arise (*hāqīṣu*) and sing, O you who dwell in the slime!" and Dan xii 2, "And many of those who sleep in the land of slime will arise (*yāqīṣū*), some to everlasting life, and others to everlasting reproach and contempt."

saturated with. See NOTES on Pss xxxiv 9 and xlii 3.

your being. tᵉmūnāh describes the "form" or "figure" of God as he appeared to Moses. Num xii 8 states that Moses alone was permitted to behold the *t^emūnāh* of Yahweh, but the psalmist is confident that he will receive this privilege after the final judgment. In Pss xvi 10–11, xlix 16, lxxiii 23–24 the psalmists express their conviction that they will be accorded the grace of assumption that was bestowed upon Enoch and Elijah.

Just precisely what is meant by the *t^emūnāh* cannot be firmly established, but its parallelism with *pānekā* indicates that "being" is a warranted translation; LXX rendered it *tēn dóksan sou,* "your glory."

In UT, 68:17–18, one reads *ltnġṣn pnth lydlp tmnh,* "His joints (Heb. *pinnāh*) do not bend, his frame does not collapse." The balance in our verse between *pānekā* and *t^emūnātekā* makes it possible that Ugar. *pnt* is a feminine plural of *pn,* "face," even though the normal Ugaritic plural form is *pnm.* The presence in Phoenician of feminine *pnt* in the prepositional phrase *lpnt,* "before," while probably formed on the analogy of other prepositions in *-t,* shows that the possibility of identifying Ugar. *pnm* and *pnt* should not be ruled out. At any rate, the existence of *tmn* in Ugaritic bespeaks the antiquity of the substantive; its occurrence in Ps xvii comports well with the archaic language throughout the psalm and suggests that the Israelite belief in the beatific vision was very ancient indeed.

PSALM 18

(xviii 1–51)

1 *For the director. Of David, the servant of Yahweh, who sang to Yahweh the words of this song, when Yahweh rescued him from the grasp of all his enemies and from the hand of Sheol. He said:*

2 I love you, Yahweh, my strength.
3 Yahweh is my rock and my fortress; [2]*
my deliverer is my God,
My mountain where I take refuge;
my shield and my horn of salvation,
My stronghold, worthy of praise.
4 I called Yahweh, [3]
and was saved from my Foe.
5 The breakers of Death encompassed me, [4]
the torrents of Belial overwhelmed me.
6 The cords of Sheol surrounded me, [5]
the traps of Death confronted me.
7 In my anguish I called Yahweh, [6]
and to my God I cried for help;
My voice was heard in his palace,
my cry reached his ears.
8 The nether world reeled and rocked, [7]
the foundations of the mountains shuddered;
They reeled when his anger blazed.
9 Smoke rose from his nostrils, [8]
and fire from his mouth devoured;
Coals flamed forth from him.
10 He spread apart the heavens and came down, [9]
a storm cloud under his feet.
11 He mounted the Cherub and flew, [10]
and soared on wings outstretched.

* Verse numbers in RSV.

12 He set darkness about him [11]
with the rain cloud his pavilion.
13 From his light clouds scudded before him, [12]
hailstones and flashes of fire.
14 Yahweh thundered from the heavens, [13]
and the Most High gave forth his voice.
15 He forged his arrows and scattered them, [14]
he multiplied his shafts and dispersed them.
16 The fountainheads of the sea were exposed, [15]
and the world's foundations were laid bare,
At your roar, O Yahweh,
at the blast from your nostrils.
17 He reached down from high and snatched me, [16]
he drew me from the waters deep.
18 He rescued me from my powerful Foe, [17]
and from my Enemy though stronger than I.
19 He went before me on the day of my death, [18]
and Yahweh became my staff.
20 He brought me out of the broad domain, [19]
liberated me because he loved me.
21 Yahweh rewarded me because I was just, [20]
because my hands were innocent he repaid me.
22 For I have kept the ways of Yahweh, [21]
and have not been guilty, O my God.
23 For all his judgments are before me, [22]
his laws I have never put aside.
24 I have always been candid with him, [23]
and have taken care not to offend him.
25 And Yahweh repaid me because I was just, [24]
because my hands were innocent in his eyes.
26 With the faithful you are faithful, [25]
with the candid you are candid;
27 With the sincere you are sincere, [26]
but with the cunning you are crafty.
28 Indeed you are the Strong One [27]
who saves the poor;
But you humble the eyes that are proud.
29 You shine for me; [28]
my lamp is Yahweh,
My God illumines my darkness.

30 For through you I run well-sinewed, [29]
and with my God I can scale any wall.
31 God, his dominion is complete, [30]
the command of Yahweh is well tested
The Suzerain is he to all who trust in him.
32 For who is God beside Yahweh? [31]
Who is the mountain but our God?
33 The God who girded me with strength, [32]
and the Bestower whose dominion is complete.
34 Who made my feet like hinds, [33]
and brought me to stand upon his heights.
35 Who trained my hands for battle, [34]
lowered the miraculous bow into my arms.
36 And you gave me your shield of victory, [35]
with your right hand you sustained me,
And by your triumph you made me great.
37 You have given me long-striding legs, [36]
and my ankles did not give way.
38 I pursued my foes and overtook them, [37]
I turned not back till they were annihilated.
39 I smote them so that they could not rise, [38]
they fell at my feet.
40 You girded me with strength for battle, [39]
you felled my assailants beneath me.
41 You gave me the neck of my foes, [40]
and my enemies I exterminated.
42 They implored, but the Savior was not there, [41]
the Most High Yahweh,
but he did not answer them.
43 I pulverized them like dust in the square, [42]
like the mud in the streets I trampled them.
44 You delivered me from the shafts of people, [43]
protected me from the venom of nations.
45 An alien people must serve me, [44]
as soon as they hear, they obey me;
Foreigners cringe before me.
46 Foreigners shrivel up, [45]
and their hearts are seized with anguish.
47 May Yahweh live! [46]
Praised be my Mountain!
And exalted the God of my triumph!

48 The God who gave me victory, [47]
and made nations subject to me.
49 Who delivered me from my Foe, [48]
exalted me above my assailants
rescued me from calumniators.
50 And so shall I praise you among the nations, [49]
celebrate your name in song, O Yahweh.
51 Who made his king famous through victories, [50]
showed kindness to his anointed,
to David and his offspring forever.

NOTES

xviii. A royal song of thanksgiving, which appears with a number of orthographic and grammatical variants in II Sam xxii. In both places it is attributed to David and there is no internal evidence militating against such an attribution. Its many archaic features will be registered in the following notes.

The hymn divides into two parts. In the first, after an introductory stanza of praise to God (vss. 2–4), the royal poet describes his mortal peril (5–7), and then depicts, in language with many similarities to Canaanite mythology, God's intervention in the form of a theophany (8–20). He closes the first part with an acknowledgment of God's justice (21–31). In the second half, the psalmist praises God for having trained him for war, supplied him with a miraculous bow (32–35), given him victory over his military and political enemies (36–44), and invested him with dominion over foreign peoples (44–46). The final five verses are a hymn of thanksgiving which recapitulates his motives for thanking God.

1. *from the hand of Sheol.* It could hardly be considered radical to point MT *šā'ūl* "Saul," as *š^{e}'ōl,* "Sheol," since the poet's delivery from Sheol forms the subject matter of vss. 4–7. In fact, rescue from the grasp of all his enemies and from the hand of Sheol fairly summarizes the contents of the entire poem. An unpublished psalm in Akkadian found at Ras Shamra begins with the words, "Since the day you delivered me from the mouth of Death."

3. *Yahweh . . . my God.* The readings *yhwh . . . 'ēlī* are probably correct. II Sam xxii 3 reads *'^{e}lōhē* for *'ēl* and some modern critics would emend it to *gō'^{a}lī,* but the lection *'ēl* is to be preferred since the poet was probably employing the technique of separating composite divine

titles into their components, placing one in the first colon and the other in the second. The ancient title *yhwh 'ēl,* which was probably the original, non-apocopated form of the Tetragrammaton, occurs in Pss x 12, xxxi 7, and xxxix 13.

My mountain. *ṣūrī* answers to Ugar. *ǵr,* "mountain," one of Baal's appellatives. See Albright, "Baal-Zephon," in *Festschrift Alfred Bertholet,* pp. 1–4.

My stronghold. With *miśgabbī,* compare the Mari personal name *Sagbi-Addu,* "my stronghold is Addu"; see George Dossin, *Archives royales de Mari* (Paris, 1952), V, 1:12 and p. 24.

worthy of praise. Attaching *m^ehullāl* of vs. 4 to the end of vs. 3, as proposed by F. M. Cross, Jr., and D. N. Freedman, JBL 72 (1953), 15–34, especially p. 22 (see Selected Bibliography). All other instances of pual participle *m^ehullāl* find it modifying God.

4. *from my Foe.* Plural *'ōy^ebay* appears to be a *plurale excellentiae* describing Death, the adversary par excellence. Death receives this label, again in plural form in Pss xxx 2, xli 3, but in the singular in Pss vii 6, xiii 3, xxxi 9, lxi 4. Analogously, in Ps ix 14, plural *śōn^e'ay,* "my Enemy," refers to Death. In this connection, consult the remarks of W. F. Albright, "The Beth-Shemesh Tablet in Alphabetic Cuneiform," BASOR 173 (1964), 52. By the same token, one can account for the apparently anomalous, and hence often emended form, in Job xix 11, *wayyaḥš^ebēnī lō k^eṣārāyw,* "And he counts me his archadversary."

5. *The breakers of Death.* II Sam xxii 5 reads *mišb^erē māwet,* "the breakers of Death," and this is usually adopted as the preferred reading.

torrents of Belial. For possible etymologies of *b^eliyya'al,* see Cross and Freedman, in JBL 72 (1953), 22, n. 6, and D. Winton Thomas in *Biblical and Patristic Studies in Memory of Robert Pierce Casey,* eds. J. N. Birdsall and R. W. Thomson (Freiburg, 1963), pp. 11–19, who derives the name from *bl',* "to swallow," hence the "Swallower." This appears to be the preferable etymology in view of the prominence in Canaanite myth of the motif of the engorging capacity of the nether world. The theme very frequently occurs in the Bible as well. In fact, the wordplay in Prov xxiii 2 is based on the two roots *bl'* and *b'l: w^eśamtā śakkīn bil'ekā* (MT *b^elō'ekā*) *'im ba'al nepeš 'attāh,* "And put a knife to your throat if you are a man of big appetite/throat." Contrary to the standard word-analysis, the substantive in consonantal *bl'k* is not *l'* but rather *bl',* a substantive denoting "throat," from the root *bl'* "to swallow." What has been overlooked is that the preposition *b* is sometimes omitted before words beginning with *b,* in both Ugaritic and Hebrew. There is also a wordplay upon *bl',* "throat," and *nepeš* which denotes both "appetite" and "throat."

7. *My voice was heard.* The parallelism is much better maintained if

for MT *yišma'* we read qal passive *yušma'* or niphal *yiššāmē*ᵃ*'*. The subject of the first half verse is thus *qōlī,* "my voice," which makes an ideal balance to *šaw'ātī,* "my cry."

in his palace. Explaining the preposition of *mēhēkālō* as *min* with a locative meaning. On Gen ii 8, *miqqedem,* "in the East," see Speiser, The Anchor Bible, vol. 1, p. 16. Other convincing examples of this locative usage are in II Sam v 13, xiii 34; II Chron xv 8; Prov xx 4 (I am indebted to Raphael Serra for these texts) and Ps lxviii 27. *hēkāl* refers to God's palace in heaven as in Pss xi 4, xxix 9. Though ultimately of Sumerian origin, *hēkāl,* which is common in Ugaritic, was borrowed by the Israelites from the Canaanites; this is also true of the other names for habitations. See S. E. Loewenstamm in IEJ 12 (1962), 163, and Werner Schmidt in ZAW 75 (1963), 91 f. Compare UT, 76: II:5, *il hd bqrb hklh,* "El Hadd is (not) inside his palace."

reached his ears. Contrast Ps xxii 2, *raḥōq-m šaw'ātī,* "dismissing my plea." On the possible conflate nature of *l*ᵉ*pānāyw tābō' b*ᵉ*'oznāyw,* see Cross and Freedman, JBL 72 (1953), 23.

8. *The nether world reeled.* The balance with "the foundations of the mountains," which are set in the nether world, suggests this version of *'ereṣ*. Cf. Isa xiv 9, "Sheol beneath is astir to greet your coming." Other texts which place the foundations of the mountains in the underworld include Deut xxxii 22; Isa xxiv 18; Jer xxxi 37; Mic vi 2; Jon ii 7.

Though seven decades have passed since Gunkel in his *Schöpfung und Chaos in Urzeit und Endzeit,* p. 18, n. 1, observed that in Exod xv 12; Isa xiv 12; and Eccles iii 21 *'ereṣ* denoted "nether world," and though at least a dozen scholars have since corroborated Gunkel's insight by new examples from Akkadian, Aramaic, Ugaritic, and biblical literature (not to mention Greek parallels), this philological datum seems to have made little impact upon translators of the Bible. Hence a listing of biblical passages employing this term may not be out of order: Gen ii 6; Exod xv 12; I Sam xxviii 11–13; Isa xxvi 19, xxix 4, xliv 23; Jer xv 7, xvii 13; Jon ii 7; Pss vii 6, xviii 8, xxii 30, xli 3, lxi 3, 10, lxxi 20, xcv 4, cvi 17, cxli 7, cxliii 3, cxlvii 6, cxlviii 7; Job x 21, xii 8, xv 29; Prov xxv 3; Sirach li 9. A selected bibliography includes Christoph Barth, *Die Errettung vom Tode* (Zürich, 1947), p. 83; Dahood, PNWSP, p. 52, with partial bibliography. For the Ugaritic texts, cf. Driver, CML, p. 135; Gordon's UT Glossary inexplicably fails to list this meaning of *arṣ*.

foundations . . . shuddered. Cf. El Amarna, 147:14–15, "Who gives forth his voice from heaven like Haddu, and all the mountains quake at his voice," and UT, 51:VII:31–35 (badly damaged), "His holy voice shakes the earth . . . the mountains quake, aquiver are . . . the east and the west, the ridges of the earth rock."

9. *from his nostrils.* As frequently in Ugaritic-Phoenician-Hebrew, *b* denotes "from"; also in vss. 14 and 16.

fire . . . devoured. 'ēš . . . tō'kēl equals UT, 51:vi:24–25, *tikl išt.*

10. *He spread apart.* For this meaning of *wayyēṭ,* see Cross and Freedman, JBL 72 (1953), 24, n. 23.

a storm cloud. 'ărāpēl now appears in an unpublished text from Ras Shamra as *ǵrpl,* which reveals the nature of the initial consonant. Some of the false etymologies may now be eliminated from the Hebrew lexicons.

11. *He mounted the Cherub.* Compare Ps lxviii 5, *rōkēb ba'ᵃrābōt* and Ugaritic *rkb 'rpt.* On *rākab,* "to mount," see Robert De Langhe, "Bible et Littérature Ugaritique," in *L'Ancien Testament et l'Orient* (Orientalia et Biblica Lovaniensia 1, 1957), pp. 65–87, especially pp. 85 f.; Gray, *The Legacy of Canaan,* p. 23, n. 8; W. L. Moran in *Biblica* 43 (1962), 323 f., who takes exception to the definition of *rkb* proposed by Sigmund Mowinckel, "Drive and/or Ride in OT," in VT 12 (1962), 278–99. Ezek xxviii 14, *kᵉrūb mimšaḥ,* "Cherub outstretched," indicates that the plural reading of the versions is not necessarily preferable to the singular.

soared. On the rather frequent Ugaritic root *d'y,* "to fly, soar," see Dahood, *Biblica* 45 (1964), 401. II Sam xxii 11 incorrectly reads *wayyērā'* for *wayyēde';* the orthographic confusion between *daleth* and *resh* prompts the emendation of Ps xl 13, *lir'ōt* to *lidō't.*

on wings outstretched. Reading *kanᵉpē rewaḥ* (also in Ps civ 3), literally "the wings of broadness," for MT *kanᵉpē rūᵃḥ,* "the wings of the wind." The Masoretes make the same mistake in vs. 43, where they read *'al pᵉnē rūᵃḥ,* which is meaningless in the context, for *'al pᵉnē rewaḥ,* "upon the square," which is parallel to *ḥūṣōt,* "streets." The root is Ar. *rawiḥa,* "to be wide, ample," a root that is found in biblical *rewaḥ,* "space, interval" (Gen xxxii 17; Esther iv 14); in Arabic-Ugaritic *rāḥat,* "palm of the hand"; and in Mishnaic-Hebrew *rewaḥ,* "wide space." In Job xli 8, the Masoretes again confuse *rewaḥ* with *rūᵃḥ;* see Marvin Pope, The Anchor Bible, vol. 15, p. 284.

The image of God flying upon the Cherub of extended wings is related to the widely mistranslated and misinterpreted phrase of Ezek xxviii 14, *kᵉrūb mimšaḥ hassōkēk,* "The overshadowing Cherub of wings outstretched." Vulg. preserves the correct sense, *Cherub extentus* (Exod xxv 20), the version adopted by É. Dhorme in *La Bible de la Pléiade,* II, pp. 543 f. Hence we must distinguish between *mšḥ,* "to anoint," and *mšḥ,* "to measure, extend," Aramaic-Akkadian *mašāḫu.* The latter root occurs in UT, 76:ii:22–23, *qrn dbatk b'l ymšḥ b'l ymšḥ hm b'p,* "Your powerful wings will Baal stretch out, Baal will stretch them out for flight." On *qrn,* "wings," see Dahood, "Ugaritic Lexicography," in *Mélanges Eugène Tisserant,* I, p. 95. Among Ugaritic specialists, R. De Langhe, *Les Textes de Ras-Shamra-Ugarit* (Paris,

Gembloux, 1945), II, p. 217, recognized that *ymšḥ* denoted *il mesurera.* The recent discussion of Kutsch, *Salbung als Rechtsakt,* p. 8, misses the point of the Ugaritic strophe, and consequently is forced to describe Ezek xxviii 14, *kᵉrūb mimšaḥ,* as *ganz unklar* (p. 53, n. 205a).

In Hab iii 3–4, Yahweh is pictured as an eagle flying from the south whose extended wings fill the heavens: "His majesty covered the heavens, and his brilliance filled the earth. His shining was like the sun, two wings were at his sides (*qarnayim miyyādō lō*)."

The motif of the divine bird of great wing-span is richly documented in Canaanite and biblical literature. Thus in UT, 125:8–9, Baal is termed *ḥlm adr ḥl rḥb mknpt,* "glorious phoenix, phoenix wide of wings." Albright gives full treatment of this passage in *Festschrift Alfred Bertholet,* pp. 2 ff. UT, 9:4, mentions a deity, *b'l knp,* while Exod xix 4 reads, *wā'eśśā' 'etkem 'al kanᵉpē nᵉšārīm,* "And I bore you on the wings of eagles" (cf. UT, 1 Aqht:118, *knp nšrm*). Deut xxxii 11 compares God to an eagle that "spreads out its wings" (*yiprōś kᵉnāpāyw*). Related metaphors of God occur in Pss xvii 8, xxxvi 8, lvii 2, lxi 5, xci 4.

Stylistically, *kᵉrūb . . . kanᵉpē rewaḥ* is a case of a stereotyped phrase being separated into its components, i.e., the original phrase was *kᵉrūb kanᵉpē rewaḥ* and is semantically identical with Ezek xxviii 14, *kᵉrūb mimšaḥ,* correctly rendered by Jerome, *Cherub extentus.*

12. *He set darkness.* The verse is highly problematical; I follow the reading and analysis of Cross and Freedman, JBL 72 (1953), p. 25.

13. *scudded before him.* The imagery is not particularly clear, but it may be related to that of Job xxxvii 11, *'ap bārī* (MT *bᵉrī*) *yaṭrīḥ 'āb yāpīṣ 'ūnān* (MT *'ᵃnan*) *'ōrō,* "His sun dispels the clouds, his light scatters the cloud-mass." For a full grammatical explanation of this text, see Dahood, *Biblica* 45 (1964), 412.

14. *Yahweh thundered.* The verb *rā'am* now appears in unpublished Ugaritic personal names *yrǵm il* and *yrǵm b'l;* UT, Glossary, No. 1159a, p. 415.

from the heavens. This is another instance of *b,* "from"; II Sam. xxii 14 reads, less originally, *miššāmayim.* From this expression it may be argued that El Amarna 147:13, *ša iddin rigmašu ina šame kima addi,* is preferably rendered, "Who gives his voice from the heavens like Adad." In Akkadian *ina* often denotes "from." The immediate effect of Baal's thunder being the quaking of the earth, the stress seems to be on the outward effects of the thunder from the skies.

the Most High. Placing *yhwh* in the first colon and *'elyōn* in the second is another instance of the breakup of composite divine titles to create tighter unity in the verse. A similar literary expedient can be seen in UT, 2 Aqht:v:10–11, where the compound name *kṯr wḫss* is split in poetic parallelism: *hlk kṯr ky'n wy'n tdrq ḫss,* "The gait of

Kothar indeed he sees, and he sees the tread of Hasis." The third colon, *bārād wᵉgaḥᵃlē 'ēš* seems to be dittographic of vs. 13b.

15. *He forged his arrows.* Ugar. *šlḥ,* "to forge, hammer," suggests that in Hebrew a distinction should be set up between *šlḥ,* "to send," and *šlḥ,* "to forge." Cf. UT, 51:26–27, *yṣq ksp yšlḥ ḫrṣ,* "He poured silver, hammered out gold." Biblical instances in Pss l 19 (see NOTE), cx 2, *maṭṭēh 'uzzᵉkā yišlaḥ yhwh-m ṣiyyōn,* "Yahweh of Zion has forged your victorious mace," and cxliv 6, *šᵉlaḥ ḥiṣṣekā ūtᵉhummēm,* "Forge your arrows and disperse them." In Roman mythology, Jupiter gave Venus to Vulcan (Canaanite Kothar) for the service he had rendered in forging thunderbolts. The biblical poet ascribes to Yahweh the attributes of the artisan-god Kothar; see NOTE on vs. 35. Cf. Ps vii 14, "O that he would create the weapons of death, make his arrows into flaming shafts."

Many exegetes have related the pronominal suffixes of *yᵉpīṣēm* and *yᵉhummēm* to the enemies of the psalmist, but these do not make their appearance till vs. 18. B. Duhm, *Die Psalmen* (Freiburg i. B., 1899), p. 54, is surely right in maintaining, in view of Ps cxliv 6, that the suffixes refer to the arrows and lightning. My proposed etymology of *yišlaḥ* bears out his observation and further uncovers a progression of thought from the forging of arrows to the shooting of arrows.

he multiplied his shafts. Namely, his bolts of lightning. Pointing MT *rab* as *ribbā,* another instance of defective spelling in this poem. The form is piel from *rābāh,* "to be or become many." Defective spelling may likewise account for the Masoretic misunderstanding in Deut xxxiii 7, *yādāyw rabbe lō* (MT *rāb lō*), "Increase (piel imperative of *rbh*) his forces for him." For the thought, cf. Judg ix 29, *rabbeh ṣᵉbā'ᵃkā,* "Increase your host." Cf. UT, 2 Aqht:v:12–13, *hl yšrb' qṣ't,* which would signify, "Behold, he multiplies arrows," if *rb',* "four," is the root of the verb *šrb';* scholars differ in their interpretation. No suffix is required with *bᵉrāqīm,* "his shafts," by reason of its parallelism with *ḥiṣṣāyw,* "his arrows"; cf. NOTE on Ps iii 4. Of especial relevancy is the double-duty suffix illustrated by Ps lxxvii 19, *qōl ra'amᵉkā baggalgal hē'īrū bᵉrāqīm tēbēl,* "The peal of your thunder came from the vault of heaven, your shafts of lightning lit up the world," and the balance in Ps cxxxv 7 between *bᵉrāqīm,* "his shafts," and *'ōṣᵉrōtāyw,* "his treasuries."

16. *fountainheads of the sea.* Reading *'ᵃpīqē-m yam,* with enclitic *mem.* The *mem* was preserved, though not understood as such; hence the erroneous word division *'ᵃpīqē mayim.* II Sam xxii correctly grasped the sense of the phrase, but the grammatically embarrassing *mem* was edited out of the text. Another instance of enclitic *mem* being deleted from the text can be seen in Isa xxx 20 where MT reads *mayim lāḥaṣ* but where 1QIsᵃ offers *my lḥṣ.* It would appear that the correct reading

is *mēy-m laḥaṣ,* "waters of oppression," a construct chain with an interposed enclitic *mem.* On Isa xxxvii 25, *ye'ōrē-m ṣūr,* "mountain streams," see P. J. Calderone in *Biblica* 42 (1961), 428. Cf. UT, 2 Aqht: VI:48 = ʻnt:v:15, *apq thmtm,* "the fountainheads of the two deeps."

the world's foundations. UT, 51:I:41, *msdt arṣ* compares with biblical *mōsedōt tēbēl.*

were laid bare. I.e., the penetrating shafts of light from heaven reached the bottom of the ocean. Job xxxvi 30, which has been misinterpreted through failure to recognize the privative force of the piel conjugation, will be seen to express a kindred idea: *hēn pāraś ʻālāyw 'ōrō wešoršē hayyām kissāh,* "If Aliy spreads his light, he exposes the roots of the sea."

At your roar. The suggestion of H. G. May in JBL 74 (1955), 17, n. 32, that here and in Isa l 2; Nah i 4; and Ps civ 7, *gʻr* (*gʻrh*) signifies "roar," is supported not only by Aram. *gʻr,* "to shout, cry out," but also by Ugar. *gʻr,* which denotes both "to roar" and "to rebuke." The former sense occurs in UT, 56:23, *k ygʻr* [*śśw*], "If the horse roars," and the latter in UT, 137:24, *bhm ygʻr bʻl,* "Baal rebukes them."

17. *the waters deep.* I.e., the waters of the nether world; the psalmist has been rescued from death. See May, "Some Cosmic Connotations of Mayim Rabbim, 'Many Waters'," JBL 74 (1955), 9–21, especially p. 20.

18. *my powerful Foe.* Namely, Mot or Death, the chief enemy of Baal in Canaanite mythology. In UT, 49:VI:18, he is specifically stated to be strong: *mt ʻz,* "Mot is strong." To balance plural *śāne'ay,* I am reading, with the Vrs., plural *'ōyebay,* and explaining both forms as *pluralia excellentiae;* in vs. 49, the form is plural *'ōyebay.*

A more delicate problem touches on the vocalization of *ʻz:* Is it the adjective *ʻāz* or the noun *ʻōz?* If the correct reading is *'ōyebay ʻōz,* we have a construct chain with an interposed possessive suffix, a topic lately treated by Gevirtz, *Patterns in the Early Poetry of Israel,* p. 80. To those already discussed by GK (§§ 128d, 131r), Gevirtz adds a few new examples. Further examples are forthcoming from the Psalter, and this is the principal reason for believing that *'ōyebay ʻōz* is the preferred reading. Consider Pss xxxv 16, *lōʻegay* (MT *laʻagē*) *māʻōg,* "my encircling mockers"; xxxv 19, *'ōyebay šeqer,* "my deceitful foes," and *śōne'ay ḥinnām,* "my stealthy enemies"; xxxviii 20, *'ōyebay ḥayyīm,* "my mortal foes"; cx 4, *malkī ṣedeq,* "his legitimate king"; and cxvi 1, *qōlī taḥanūnāy,* "my plea for mercy."

from my Enemy. Cf. preceding NOTE. The plural verb *'āmeṣū* with the plural of majesty is similar to the occasional use of a plural verb with the plural of majesty *'elōhīm.*

19. *He went before me.* Textual critics have as a rule failed to note that II Sam xxii 19 contains the orthographic variant *yqdmny* against Ps xviii *yqdmwny.* I am vocalizing piel singular *yeqaddemēnī,* with God

the subject; for the meaning "to go before," see Ps lxviii 26. The image is that of a shepherd going before his flock.

day of my death. Implying, when I was overpowered by my Enemy and engulfed by deep waters. In Job xviii 12, *'ēd,* parallel to *rā'ēb,* "the Hungry One," denotes "Death."

my staff. The image of the shepherd continues with the figurative use of *miš'ān,* "a shepherd's staff." See especially Ps xxiii 4.

20. *He brought me out.* The construction *yōṣī' l^e* recurs in Ps lxvi 12, *wattōṣī'ēnū lār^ewāyāh,* "after you had brought us out of abundance." Cf. Ps lxviii 21, *lammāwet tōṣā'ōt,* "the escape from death"; W. F. Albright in HUCA 23 (1950), 26 (see Selected Bibliography); Buttenwieser, PCTNT, p. 257.

the broad domain. merḥāb is a poetic name for the nether world, as in Ps xxxi 9 and possibly in cxviii 5; the observation is that of Evasio de Marcellis (unpublished). Since vs. 17 speaks of being rescued *from* the rushing waters, vs. 18 of being saved *from* the powerful foe, vs. 19 of the imminence of death, it seems very probable that the preposition of *yōṣī'ēnī lammerḥāb* denotes "from." Hence *merḥāb* must have a pejorative sense.

The theme concerning the vastness of the nether world makes an early appearance in UT, 49:I:33–37, "And Athtar the terrible replied: 'I cannot rule in the heart of Zaphon.' Athtar the terrible came down from the throne of Baal, and became king in the vast underworld, all of it." Scholars have invariably taken *barṣ il klh* to refer to the earth, but this interpretation overlooks the consideration that this was Baal's domain. Being unable to fill Baal's throne, Athtar was obviously unfit to supplant Baal as the ruler of the visible earth and had to be content with governing the dead. The phraseology of Job xxxviii 18 points to the same motif: *hitbōnantā 'ad raḥ^abē 'āreṣ haggēd 'im yāda'tā kullāh,* "Have you comprehended the vast reaches of the nether world? Speak out if you are familiar with all of it." From its enumeration among the other names for the lower realms in vss. 16–18, namely, *yam, t^ehōm, māwet* and *ṣalmāwet,* it becomes reasonably certain that *'ereṣ* here signifies "nether world." Other references to the vastness of the lower regions include Ps xxxvi 7, *t^ehōm rabbāh,* and Ps xcv 4, *meḥq^erē 'āreṣ,* "the inaccessible parts of the nether world." The motif is also Mesopotamian, as in the phrase *ina irat erṣetim rapaštim,* "on the bosom of the vast nether world"; cf. CAD, IV (E), p. 310b. On *'ereṣ,* "nether world," cf. Barth, *Die Errettung vom Tode,* p. 83 and *passim.*

22. *O my God.* The construction *rāša'tī min* being elsewhere unattested, one may propose attaching the *mem* as enclitic to *rāša'tī* and parsing *'^elōhay* as vocative.

24. *candid with him.* The fact that II Sam xxii reads *tāmīm lō* where the psalm has *tāmīm 'immō* suggests that *'immō* has a local sense,

"toward him," a usage amply illustrated by Ugaritic, where *'m* more often denotes "toward" than "with." Cf. UT, § 10.14. English idiom, however, prefers "with him."

not to offend him. me'ᵃwōnī can scarcely signify "from my iniquity," since throughout these verses the poet protests his innocence before God. The suffix of *'immō,* "toward him," hints that the suffix of *'ᵃwōnī* is likewise that of the third person, as in vs. 33, a morpheme discussed in the NOTE on Ps ii 6. The suffix is objective, "offense against him"; cf. Ps xxvi 3, *ba'ᵃmittekā,* "in fidelity to you."

27. *you are crafty.* The background to such a statement is possibly to be sought in the Canaanite tradition which attributed to the artisan-god *kṯr wḫss* the qualities of craft and cunning. Note that in vs. 35 Yahweh is pictured as the artisan-God who forges the weapons of the psalmist.

28. *you are the Strong One.* Dividing the verse into a 2+2+3 beat to form a couplet with vs. 29, which also scans into 2+2+3. This metric division isolates the adjective *'am* employed as a divine epithet, "the Strong One." To account for the biblical data, one must assume the existence of a root *'mm,* "to be strong, wise," cognate with *'mq,* "to be strong, wise." The verbs *pārar* and *pāraq,* both denoting "to break," offer a good analogy. The following texts come into consideration, and though not all the examples are fully convincing, a rather full listing may have some heuristic value: (a) Deut xxxiii 3, where *'ammīm* is often considered a substitute for an original *'ēlīm,* "gods" —most recently noted by I. L. Seeligmann in VT 14 (1964), 80; (b) Deut xxxiii 21, *ṣidqat yhwh 'āśāh ūmišpāṭāyw 'am* (MT *'im*) *yiśrā'ēl,* "Yahweh has executed his justice and the Strong One of Israel his commands"; (c) I Sam xvii 42, *kī hāyāh na'ar wᵉ'admōnī 'am* (MT *'im*) *yᵉpēh mar'eh,* "For he was youthful and ruddy, strong [and] of attractive appearance"; (d) Ps xlvii 2, *kol ha'ammīm tiqᵉ'ū kap hārī'ū lē'lōhīm bᵉqōl rinnāh,* "All you strong ones clap your hands, acclaim, you gods, with shouts of joy"; (e) Ps xlvii 10, *'am 'ᵉlōhē 'abrāhām,* "The God of Abraham is the Strong One"; (f) Ps lxii 9, *biṭᵉḥu bō bᵉkol 'ēt 'am,* "Trust in him, at all times the Strong One"; (g) Ps lxxvii 16, *gā'altā bīzᵉrōᵃ' 'ammekā bᵉnē ya'ᵃqōb wᵉyōsēp,* "You redeemed with your powerful arm (cf. Ps lxxxix 11) the sons of Jacob and Joseph," a neat example of enjambment; (h) Ps lxxxix 20, *šiwwītī 'ezer* (MT *'ēzer*) *'al gibbōr hᵃrīmōtī bāḥūr mē'ām,* "I preferred a lad to a warrior, I exalted a youth above a strong man"—the balance with *gibbōr* marks the meaning of *'am;* (i) Ps xcix 1, *yhwh mālak yirgᵉzū 'ammīm yōšēb kᵉrūbīm tānūṭ hā'āreṣ,* "Yahweh has become king, let the gods tremble; he is seated upon the cherubim, let the earth quake" —here the emendation of *'ammīm* to *šāmayim,* lately propounded by Lipiński in *Biblica* 44 (1963), 437, n. 2, is no longer impressive;

(j) Ps xcix 2, *yhwh b^eṣiyyōn gādōl hū' w^erām 'al kol ha'ammīm,* "Yahweh is too great for Zion, and higher is he than all the strong ones"—as in Deut xxxiii 3, *'ammīm* is regarded as a deliberate substitution for *'ēlīm;* (k) Ezek xxviii 3, *hinnēh ḥākām 'attāh middānī'ēl kol sātūm lō' 'ām^emūkā,* "Look, you are wiser than Daniel and no secret is too deep for you"; (l) Job xii 2, *'omnām kī 'attem 'ām w^e'imm^ekā tāmūt ḥokmāh,* "You no doubt are the Strong/Wise One and with you will wisdom die." Notice in these last two texts the association of *'am* with wisdom, and in the Job passage the theological wordplay of *'am* with the preposition *'im,* as in Pss xviii 27–28 and xlvii 10, where the pun devolves upon the senses "strong" and "people." Cf. also Isa ii 6 (cf. Targ.); Ezek xxxi 8 and Job xx 11, and the wordplay in Deut xxxii 21.

Though no undoubted examples of this root have materialized in Ugaritic, there are several possible occurrences—UT, 51:IV:41–42; 1 Aqht:I:27–28, and the theophoric element in such proper names as *'mrpi, ykn'm, yrb'm, ṯb'm, 'mlbu,* etc.

who saves the poor. A relative sentence without the relative pronoun, a poetic usage attested in Ugaritic 1 Aqht:220–21, *yd mḫṣt a[qh]t ǵzr tmḫṣ alpm ib,* "The hand that smote Aqhat the hero will smite thousands of foes," and in Phoen. *bt 'b' 'l tb',* "The house I enter you shall not enter"; Donner and Röllig, KAI, II, p. 45. Biblical usage is more frequent than the grammars would suggest; to examples usually listed the following may be added from the Psalter: xxxv 15, l 8, lii 3, lxxi 18, lxxiv 18.

eyes that are proud. Metonymy for "the proud." The proposed emendations of *'ēnayim rāmōt* appear unnecessary. Grammatically, we have a dual noun modified by a morphologically plural adjective. Hebrew apparently did not preserve a dual form of the adjective as Ugaritic did in such phrases as *špthm mtqtm,* "their lips are sweet," or *ṯt aṯtm adrtm,* "two noble wives."

29. *You shine for me.* Referring to Yahweh, not the goddess *špš* who is termed *nrt ilm,* "the lamp of the gods," in the Ras Shamra tablets, nor the Moon-god Yariḫ who in UT, 77:38–39 is besought: *wyrḫ yark,* "And may the Moon-god shine for you." Cf. Isa lx 19–20. The dative suffix required with *tā'īr* is to be supplied from *nērī,* "my lamp"; metrical considerations may have prompted the elliptical usage. Note the syntax and style of Ps cxxxix 12, *gam ḥōšek lō' yaḥšīk mimmekā w^elāylāh kayyōm yā'īr kaḥ^ašekā kā'ōrāh,* "Darkness is not too dark for you and the night shines for you like the day; as the darkness, so the light." Here the suffix of *mimmekā* functions also for *yā'īr.*

my lamp is Yahweh. Compare II Sam xxii, *kī 'attāh nērī yhwh,* "Indeed you are my lamp, O Yahweh." In Canaanite mythology the goddess Shapsh is termed *nrt ilm,* "the divine lamp."

30. *I run well-sinewed.* The hapax legomenon *g*ᵉ*dūd* (preferably pointed as passive participle *gādūd*) looks like a reduplicated form of *gīd,* "sinew, tendon," found also in UT, 2 Aqht:vi:21, *adr gdm brumm,* "Cut tendons from buffaloes." The reduplicated form *hāgīg* from *hāgāh* was discussed in the Note on Ps v 2. Needless to say, this explanation nicely squares with the second colon, "I can scale any wall."

31. *his dominion is complete.* Suggesting that he is therefore able to invest others with strength. On Ugar. *drkt* and its biblical correspondent *derek,* see Notes on Pss i 1 and x 5.

command of Yahweh. For this nuance of *'imrāh,* see Ps cv 19, etc., as well as in Phoenician Haddad of Zincirli, lines 26, 29, 32, *'l 'mrth,* "according to his command." See Cooke, TNSI, pp. 162 f.; Jean and Hoftijzer, *Dictionnaire . . . ,* p. 18.

The Suzerain. On *māgān* (MT *māgēn*), cf. Note on Ps iii 4. The Suzerain was obliged to protect the vassals bound to him by treaty-oaths.

33. *who girded me.* Cross and Freedman, JBL 72 (1953), 30, n. 73, find the article of *ham*ᵉ*'azzērēnī* suspicious, but the abundant attestation of this construction in Hebrew (GK, §§ 116 f., 128i) and in Phoenician (Cooke, TNSI, p. 22) should put the reading above suspicion. Isa ix 12 merits a word of comment: *w*ᵉ*hā'ām lō' šāb 'ad hammakkēhū,* "But the people did not return to him who smote them." 1QIsᵃ reads *hmkhw,* with the *he* above the line. The scribe's reverence for the sacred text evidently induced him to insert the *he* after his classical Hebrew instincts had led him to omit it.

and the Bestower. D. N. Freedman suggests reading *yōtēn* for MT *yittēn,* a participle from *ytn,* the normal form of the verb "to give" in Ugaritic-Phoenician. That this by-form existed in biblical poetry may be inferred from the reading in II Sam xxii 41, *w*ᵉ*'ōy*ᵉ*bay tattāh,* which becomes grammatically explicable if we suppose the haplography of a *yod* or simply *scriptio defectiva, 'yb ytt,* which vocalized will read *'ōy*ᵉ*bay yātattāh.* See Cross and Freedman, JBL 72 (1953), 32, n. 91.

The participle *yōtēn,* serving as a divine epithet, is semantically akin to *māgān* (or *mōgen*), "the Benefactor, a title discussed at Ps iii 4. This reading and analysis are confirmed by vs. 48, where the divine names *hā'ēl* and *yōtēn,* which in the present verse are placed in the parallel cola, are equivalently joined in the phrase *hā'ēl hannōtēn,* "the God who gives."

whose dominion is complete. Identifying *darkī* with Ugar. *drkt,* "dominion, power," studied in the Notes on Pss i 1 and x 5, and parsing the suffix as third-person singular, as in Ps ii 6. There thus emerges an inclusion beginning in vs. 31, *hā'ēl tāmīm darkō,* and closing here with *tamīm darkī.* That a third-person suffix is desiderated here is clear from II Sam xxii 33, which reads *darkō,* another instance of the modernization of the text evident in a number of verses in the II Samuel recension.

34. *upon his heights.* The suffix of *bāmōtay* is third-person singular following plural noun, as in Hab iii 19, *'al bamōtay yadrīkēnī,* "Upon his heights he makes me tread." The correct vocalization is very likely *bāmōtēy.* The efforts of Cross and Freedman to restore *yam* to both these passages have been rightly criticized by Moran in *Biblica* 43 (1962), 327, n. 1. The expression "his heights" is of a piece with *harᵉrē 'ēl,* literally "the mountains of God," but really, "the towering mountains."

Other instances of third-person suffix *-y* after plural nouns are found in Pss xxxii 9, xlii 5, lxviii 34, 36, lxxviii 49, cxli 6, cxlvii 6, 20; Isa lix 3; Jer xvii 13; Job xli 2; Prov xxviii 23. Of unusual interest is Ps lxviii 34: *lārōkēb bēšamēy šᵉmē qedem hēn yittēn bᵉqōlō qōl 'ōz,* "For him who rides forth from his heavens, the heavens of old; behold he gives forth his voice, a voice of power." Stylistically, *šāmēy* balances *qōlō,* and *šᵉmē qedem* pairs with *qōl 'ōz.*

35. *Who . . . lowered.* II Sam xxii reads *niḥat,* the modernized form of *niḥᵃtāh.* Here explaining *niḥᵃtāh* as preserving the *qatala* form of ancient Canaanite, discussed in the NOTE on Ps iv 7. The theme of lowering celestial weapons into the arms of terrestrial warriors finds early expression in UT, 68:11, where the artisan-god Kothar is said to bring down two clubs for Baal to rout Yamm: *kṯr ynḥt ṣmdm,* "Kothar lowers the two clubs." The motif reappears in Deut xxxiii 27 as revocalized by Dahood, PNWSP, pp. 45 f.: *mᵉ'annēh* (MT *mᵉ'ōnāh*) *'ᵉlōhē qedem ūmuttaḥēt* (MT *mittaḥat*) *zᵉrō'ōt 'ōlām,* "The God of Old is a conqueror, and one who lowers his arms the Eternal." A piel participle of the infixed *-t-* conjugation underlies consonantal *mtḥt* from *mntḥt.* There is a fleeting allusion to the theme in Isa xxx 30, *naḥat zᵉrō'ō,* "the lowering of his arm." Cf. also Ps xxxviii 3.

the miraculous bow. Deriving *nᵉḥūšāh* from *nḥš,* "to practice divination, to charm, enchant." The point of the Aqhat legend, it will be recalled, is that the mortal Aqhat came into possession of a miraculous bow designed by the artisan-god Kothar for the hunt-goddess Anath. For full discussion, see Gaster, *Thespis,* 1961, pp. 340 f. The present phrase, then, must be distinguished from homonymous Job xx 24, *qešet nᵉḥūšāh,* "a bronze bow," a phrase itself much contested.

36. *with your right hand . . . by your triumph.* Cf. vs. 51, "who made his king famous through victories." Just as Yahweh is the subject of *tittēn* in the first colon, so canons of Hebrew style would suggest that he remain subject of the verbs *tis'adēnī* and *tarbēnī* in the second half verse. This becomes possible when *yᵉmīnᵉkā* and *'anwātᵉkā* are parsed as accusatives of means. An especially close parallel, using the verb *sā'ad,* is Ps civ 15, *wᵉleḥem lᵉbab 'ᵉnōš yis'ad,* "And with bread

he sustains the heart of man." Note that both accusatives of means in Ps civ 15 precede their respective verbs, a stylistic trait of the psalmists remarked in the NOTE on Ps v 10.

your triumph. The victory really belongs to Yahweh, who has clothed the psalmist with strength and supplied him with weapons. Apparently synonymous with *yiš'ekā,* "your victory," of the first colon, *'anwāt^{e}kā* is most suitably derived from *'nw,* "to conquer," a root notably clarified by Phoenician Karatepe I:18, *w'n 'nk 'rṣt 'zt,* "And I conquered powerful lands." Other biblical occurrences are in Pss lx 7, lxxxix 23, cxviii 21; Num xxiv 24; Deut xxxiii 27 (see NOTE on vs. 35 above), and Eccles x 19. Discussions of this root are offered by R. T. O'Callaghan in *Orientalia* 18 (1949), 186; W. L. Moran in *Biblica* 42 (1961), 239, and, for pre-Phoenician treatment, Buttenwieser, PCTNT, p. 252.

37. *long-striding legs.* Literally "You made wide my steps beneath me."

39. *fell at my feet.* Comparing UT, 1 Aqht:115–16, *tqln tḥt p'nh,* "(The eagles) fell at his feet," with *yipp^{e}lū taḥat raglāy.*

40. *beneath me.* Where MT has *taḥtāy,* II Sam xxii 40 reads *taḥtēnī* (to be pointed *taḥtānī*), a significant variant that has gone unrecorded in the apparatus of Kittel; the same situation obtains in vss. 37 and 48. In view of the two series of prepositions preserved in ancient Canaanite, such as Ugar. *b* and *bn; b'd* and *b'dn; l* and *ln; 'm* and *'mn,* while Phoenician Kilamuwa I:14 registers the phrase *yšb tḥtn,* "who shall sit in my place," one may consider the form in II Samuel as original and Ps xviii *taḥtāy* a modernized reading. Cf. Tsevat, *A Study of the Language of the Biblical Psalms,* p. 109, n. 237, and F. M. Cross, Jr., *Studies in Ancient Yahwistic Poetry* (Baltimore, 1950), p. 311. The unique form *taḥtennāh* in Gen ii 21 becomes morphologically explicable on the basis of the preposition *tḥtn* followed by the feminine suffix *-āh.* Hence I have vocalized as *taḥtānāh.* For Amorite *taḫtun,* "beneath," see I. J. Gelb in *Rendiconti Lincei* 13 (1958), 164; I have discussed the longer form of *b'd* in Ps cxxxix 11 in *Biblica* 44 (1963), 302 f.

41. *the neck of my foes.* Literally "You have given me the foes as to the neck." The parallelism of *'ōy^{e}bay* and *m^{e}śan^{e}'ay* appears in UT, 51:VII:35–36, *ib b'l* ‖ *šnu hd.* Customarily interpreted as denoting the flight of enemies (so GB, p. 621a; Kraus, *Psalmen,* I, p. 137), these words evoke rather the image of the victor placing his foot on the neck of the vanquished, as represented on reliefs and described in literary texts. For example, Josh x 24, "And Joshua summoned all the men of Israel, and said to the chiefs of the men of war who had gone with him, 'Come near, put your feet upon the necks of these kings.'" Cf. Exod xxiii 27 and Isa li 23.

I exterminated. The emphatic position of *'aṣmītēm,* Ugar. *ṣmt,* at the end of the verse suggests that the *mem* is enclitic, serving for emphasis, and that "my enemies" is the direct object of *'aṣmīt* rather than a *casus pendens.* II Sam xxii transposes the *waw* from *meśane'ay* to the verb *weaṣmītēm;* if this is the original reading, as seems probable, we have an example of the *waw emphaticum* which, like emphatic *kī,* often effects the postposition of the verb. See NOTE on Ps iv 5. Cf. UT, 68:9, *tṣmt ṣrtk,* "You will exterminate your adversary."

42. *the Savior.* Its balance with *'al yhwh* marks *mōšīa'* as a divine appellative. In Ps vii 11 this appellative stands in apposition with the composite divine title *'al 'elōhīm,* "the Most High God," whereas in Ps xvii 7 it occurs alone.

was not there. Just as *yēš* means "to be [concretely] present," so *'ēn,* its contrary, sometimes denotes "he is not present"; cf. Pss x 4 and xiv 1, and the very pertinent remarks of W. F. Albright in BASOR 94 (1944), 31, n. 12, on Ugar. *iṯ,* "he is present."

the Most High Yahweh. 'al yhwh is a composite divine title like *'al 'elōhīm* in Ps vii 11. The redactor of II Sam xxii did not understand the meaning of *'al* which he altered to the preposition *'el.* On *'al,* "the Most High," see NOTE to Ps vii 11. Also to be noted is the use of *yešawwe'ū* with both halves of the verse, a practice that falls in with double-duty suffixes, prepositions, interrogatives, etc.

43. *in the square.* Vocalizing *rewaḥ* for MT *rūaḥ;* consult NOTE on vs. 11. The emendation to *reḥōb,* "square," is unnecessary.

I trampled them. With II Sam xxii, reading *'adīqēm* for MT *'arīqēm,* a confusion between *resh* and *daleth* remarked at vs. 11.

44. *the shafts of people.* Reading (for MT *rībē*) *rabbē,* related to *rbb,* "to shoot arrows"; consult NOTE on Ps iii 7. Royal Psalm lxxxix 51 expresses a similar sentiment, where the parallelism with *ḥērepū* in vs. 52, "whom your foes, O Lord, insulted," is illuminating: *śe'ētī beḥēqī kol rabbē-m* (MT *rabbīm*) *'ammīm,* "(Remember) his bearing in his bosom all the shafts of peoples."

After having described his deliverance from Death and from his military rivals, the poet relates his rescue from slanderers.

protected me. Reading, with II Sam xxii and Targum, *tišmerēnī* for MT *teśīmenī.* Cf. Ps lxiii 11, "But the king shall rejoice in God; everyone who swears by him shall sing praises, for the mouth of liars shall be closed."

from the venom. Relating *rō'š* to the substantive denoting "venom," rather than to the homonym signifying "head." Prepositional *l* often denotes "from," in Hebrew and Ugaritic; UT, § 10.11. Venomous remarks and calumnies are intended. On the use of poisonous arrows, see Deut xxxii 24; Job vi 4; and Ps lxiv 4, *dārekū ḥiṣṣām dābār mār,* "They tipped their arrow with a poisonous substance." This metaphor occurs in a context describing the activity of calumniators.

46. *their hearts.* Reading *weyaḥregū-m* (enclitic *mem*) *misgerōtēhem,*

and relating the substantive to Hos xiii 18, *s*ᵉ*gōr libbām,* "the enclosure of their heart," i.e., pericardium, and Mic vii 17, *yirg*ᵉ*zū-m* (enclitic *mem*) *misg*ᵉ*rōtēhem 'el yhwh '*ᵉ*lōhēnū yipḥādū w*ᵉ*yīr*ᵉ*'ū mimmekkā,* "May their hearts tremble before Yahweh our God; may they quake and be afraid of you."

seized with anguish. Associating *yaḥr*ᵉ*gū* with Aram. *ḥarg*ᵉ*tā',* "anguish." For example, Targum reads at Deut xxxii 25, *ḥargat mōtā',* "the dread of death."

47. *May Yahweh live.* Adopting the explication of Heinrich Ewald, *Ausführliches Lehrbuch der hebräischen Sprache,* 6th ed. (Leipzig, 1855), § 223, p. 501, who describes *ḥay yhwh* as an archaic formula of precative type. His analysis is supported by the ancient formula recorded in UT, 76:II:20, *ḥwt aḫt,* "May you live, O my sister." In this salutation the precative perfect *ḥwt* is addressed by Baal to the goddess Anath.

my Mountain. The association of the two roots found in *ṣūrī* and *yārūm* hints that these same roots may be associated in Ps lxxv 6, *'al tārīmū lammārōm qarn*ᵉ*kem t*ᵉ*dabb*ᵉ*rū baṣṣū'r* (MT *b*ᵉ*ṣawwā'r*) *'attīq* (MT *'ātāq*), "Do not raise up your horn against the Exalted One [on *mārōm,* see Zorell, *Psalterium ex Hebraeo Latinum,* p. 185] nor speak against the Ancient Mountain."

exalted the God. Parallel to the passive participle *bārūk, yārūm* is preferably parsed as a passive participle from the root *yrm,* a by-form of *rwm.* Hence *yrm* should be classed with *ṭwb+yṭb, kwn+ykn, qyṣ+yqṣ,* etc.; cf. P. Boccaccio in *Orientalia* 32 (1963), 498. The root *yrm* also appears in Ps xxvii 6, *w*ᵉ*'attāh yārūm rō'šī,* "And now my head is raised"; Ps lxi 3, *b*ᵉ*ṣūr yārūm mimmennī tanḥēnī,* "Onto a lofty mountain you led me from it (the edge of Sheol)." Cf. also Isa lii 13 and Dan xi 12. This same root may be present in the recently published Ugaritic personal names *yrmb'l,* "exalted by Baal" (UT, 2121:3), and *yrm'l,* "exalted by the Exalted One" (UT, 2106:4), which is the conceptual equivalent of II Sam xxiii 1, *n*ᵉ*'ūm haggeber hūqam 'āl,* "utterance of the man raised up by the Most High." The name "Jeremiah" may well derive from the root *yrm.*

48. *made nations subject.* Literally "made nations bend their back beneath me." Cross and Freedman, JBL 72 (1953), 34, n. 109, adopt the reading *mōrīd* of the ben Chayyim edition, but the ample attestation of *dbr,* "to turn the back, render supine," especially in archaic texts, argues for the MT lection. See Gaster, *Thespis,* 1950, p. 457, whose analysis can be supported by the observation that the penchant to form denominative verbs from names of parts of the body was more pervasive than heretofore realized. Ugaritic offers nine examples of such verbal formations, and two new ones have recently turned up in Hebrew; see *Biblica* 44 (1963), 204 f.

49. *my Foe . . . my assailants.* II Sam xxii reads *w*ᵉ while Ps xviii

has *'ap*. The sense is the same, though *'ap* is doubtless the original reading. The attenuation of the meaning of *'ap* is already attested in Late Bronze Age as appears from UT, 124:12, *ṭbḫ alpm ap ṣin*, "He butchered oxen and sheep." Gordon's comment in UT, § 11.10 that "*ap* is little more than a conjunction joining nouns" is sustained by the present verse and the variant in II Sam xxii.

my Foe. I.e., Death. The form is *plurale excellentiae;* cf. NOTE on vs. 4.

my assailants. I.e., the military opponents of the king.

calumniators. On *ḥāmās*, "falsehood, calumny," cf. Ps xxvii 12, *y*^{e}*pē*^{a}*ḥ ḥāmās*, parallel to *'ēdē šeqer*, "lying witnesses."

It will thus be seen that vs. 49, in listing the three classes of enemies, summarizes the contents of the poem before proceeding to the doxology of the final two verses.

51. *through victories*. Parsing *y*^{e}*šū'ōt* as accusative of means; cf. NOTE on vs. 36.

PSALM 19

(xix 1–15)

1 *For the director; a psalm of David.*

2 The heavens are proclaiming the glory of God,
and the sky manifests the work of his hands.
3 Day unto day pours forth speech, [2]*
and night unto night unfolds knowledge.
4 Without speech and without words, [3]
without their voice being heard.
5 Through all the earth their call went forth, [4]
and their words to the edge of the world.
6 To the sun he gave a tent; [5]
Then like a bridegroom it goes forth from its bower,
rejoicing like a warrior to run its course.
7 From the edge of the heavens is its going forth, [6]
and its return is to their edge,
Never turning aside from its pavilion.
8 The law of Yahweh is perfect, [7]
refreshing my soul;
The decree of Yahweh is stable,
giving my mind wisdom.
9 The precepts of Yahweh are direct, [8]
rejoicing my heart;
The command of Yahweh is radiant,
enlightening my eyes.
10 The edict of Yahweh is pure, [9]
enduring forever.
The judgments of Yahweh are truth,
all of them are just.
11 More desirable than gold, [10]
and much fine gold.
And sweeter than honey,
honey from the comb.

* Verse numbers in RSV.

12 Indeed your servant is enlightened by them; [11]
in observing them there is great reward.
13 Who can understand errors? [12]
From my aberrations cleanse me.
14 Above all, keep your servant from the presumptuous ones, [13]
lest they rule over me.
Then shall I be blameless
and innocent of the great crime.
15 May the words of my mouth [14]
be according to your desire,
And the thoughts of my heart
according to your will,
O Yahweh, my Mountain, and my Redeemer.

Notes

xix. The psalm clearly divides into two distinct but related parts. The first seven verses are probably an adaptation to Yahwistic purposes of an ancient Canaanite hymn to the sun. Verses 8–15 are a didactic poem describing the excellence of the Law, often in terms which properly describe the sun. If the use of the double-duty suffixes is a safe criterion, the author of both parts of the psalm was the same poet. Compare vs. 6, *'ōraḥ* with vs. 8, *nepeš*.

2. *The heavens are proclaiming*. The chiastic arrangement should be noted: A+B+C // Ć+B́+Á. To reproduce the chiasmus in English would result in ambiguity in the second half verse. There is a similar chiasmus involving related categories in UT, 'nt:III:21–22:

tant šmm 'm arṣ "The meeting of the heavens with the nether world,
thmt 'mn kbkbm of the deeps with the stars."

3. *pours forth speech*. The interesting root *nb'*, which has been the object of a recent study by F. Vattioni in *Annali dell'Istituto Universitario Orientale di Napoli* 13 (1963), 279–86, is now attested in the Ugaritic personal name *nb'n,* which reveals the nature of the third consonant.

4. *their voice*. The antecedent of *qōlām* is "day" and "night" in vs. 3, while the antecedent of *qawwām,* "their call," in vs. 5 is "heavens" and "sky" in vs. 2. This analysis brings out the chiastic arrangement of vss. 2–5, with vss. 3 and 4 balancing vss. 2 and 5.

5. *their call.* The antecedent of "their" is "heavens" and "sky" in vs. 2. Though Jacob Barth in his *Etymologische Studien* (Leipzig, 1893), pp.

29 ff., demonstrated this meaning of *qawwām,* the definition has not gained entry into the Hebrew lexicons published since. A review of the evidence is thus in order: (a) Ps xl 2, *qawwōh qiwwītī yhwh wayyēṭ 'ēlay wayyišma' šaw'ātī,* "I loudly called to Yahweh, and he paid heed to me and heard my cry"—obviously, the action expressed by *qiwwītī* is synonymous with *šaw'ātī,* "my cry," and therefore cannot be "hope" as in the standard versions; (b) Ps lii 11, *wa'aqawwēh šimekā kī ṭōb neged ḥasīdekā,* "And before your devoted ones I shall proclaim how sweet is your name"; (c) Job xvii 13, *'im 'aqawweh še'ōl bētī,* "When I call Sheol my home," which is a restatement of vs. 14, *laššaḥat qārā'tī 'ābī 'āttāh,* "When I address the Pit, 'You are my father'." See also Job xxxi 14, and NOTE on Ps xxxvii 9.

The root should be equated with *qāwāh* II, "to collect." The semantic bond between "call" and "collect" is well illustrated by *qōl,* "voice," which is cognate with *qāhal,* "to gather," as shown by W. F. Albright in VTS, IV (1957), 256, and by *qārā',* "to call," but which denotes "to gather" in the Arabic fifth form and in Ps cxlvii 9 and Prov xxvii 16; see Zorell, ZLH, p. 734b.

Hence my earlier attempt in CBQ 19 (1957), 148, to equate *qawwām* with Ugar. *g,* "voice," and Manfred Weippert's emendation of *qawwām* to *qrm* in ZAW 74 (1961), 99, can now be correctly labeled exercises in misplaced ingenuity.

6. *To the sun he gave.* The subject is God. For the construction *śām l,* "to give to," cf. I Sam viii 5–6; II Sam xxiii 5; Isa xlii 12, 15; and compare Aramaic Nerab II, *śmny šm ṭb,* "He gave me a good name."

a tent. There is an indirect reference to the habitation of the sun in the astrological text in UT, 1162:2–4, *'rbt špš ṯġrh ršp,* "The sun-goddess set, her doorkeeper being Resheph."

Then like a bridegroom. Detaching *bāhem* from preceding words and joining it to the following clause. This conclusion arises from the observation that *laššemeš śām 'ōhel* is metrically intended to balance vs. 7, *'ēn nistār mēḥēmātō,* with which it forms an *inclusio.* For the meaning of *bāhem,* "then, thereupon," see Isa xlviii 14 and Job xxii 21. Its components seem to be *bā,* "from, after," and *hem,* "these," hence, "after these, then." There is a possible occurrence in UT, 137:24, *bhm yg'r b'l,* "Then Baal shouts."

it goes forth from its bower. Compare Judg v 31, *keṣē't haššemeš bīgebūrātō,* "like the going forth of the sun from his (Yahweh's) fortress." See NOTE on Ps xx 7 for *gebūrāh,* "fortress."

its course. No pronominal suffix needed with *'ōraḥ* since parallel *ḥuppātō* has it: cf. NOTE on Ps iii 4. In vs. 8, suffixless *nepeš* is paired with suffixed *pty,* in vs. 9, *lēb* receives its suffix from *'ēnāy,* and in vs. 15 *rāṣōn* shares the suffix of *pānekā.*

7. *its return is to their edge.* *tᵉqūpāh* is cognate with Ugar. *nqpt,* "year."

Never turning aside. The daily course of the sun is straight and direct. *nistār* is here analyzed as niphal participle of the infixed *-t-* conjugation of *sūr,* "to turn aside"; see NOTE on Ps x 11, and for the thought, cf. Eccles i 5, "The sun rises and the sun sets, and hastens to the place where it rose."

from its pavilion. Vocalizing *ḥēmātō* for MT *ḥammātō* and identifying vocable with Arabic-Ugaritic *ḫmt,* "tent, pavilion, arbor." Stylistically, *ḥēmātō* balances vs. 6a, *'ōhel,* "tent," and with it forms an *inclusio.* Ugar. *ḫmt,* "tent, pavilion," lends support to the proposal set forth in 1929 by Edward Robertson ("Isaiah XXVII 2–6," ZAW 6 [1929], 200), who maintained that Isa xxvii 4, *ḥēmāh 'ēn lī* means "Shelter I have none," a natural complaint of a watchman of a vineyard. The basis of his etymology was Ar. *ḫaymatu.*

8. *my mind.* Forming part of the series which includes *nepeš,* "soul," *lēb,* "heart," and *'ēnāy,* "eyes," *pty* can scarcely signify "simple." A connection with the disputed vocable *pōt* in Isa iii 17, parallel to *qodqōd,* "head," and often equated with Akk. *pūtu,* "forehead, face," more adequately meets the demands of synonymous parallelism. A connection with Ugar. *ph,* "to see," is a definite possibility. One should parse the *y* of consonantal *pty* as the pronominal suffix which also serves for parallel *nepeš* of the preceding line; cf. NOTE on Ps iii 4.

9. *rejoicing my heart.* Scholars have compared El Amarna, 142:7–10, "When I heard the words on the tablet of the king, my lord, my heart rejoiced and my eyes became very radiant." The suffix of *lēb* is forthcoming from parallel *'ēnāy,* "my eyes"; cf. NOTE on Ps iii 4.

is radiant. One should notice that *bārāh* is predicated of the sun in UT, 1005:2–4, *km špš dbrt,* "like the sun that is pure"; cf. Song of Sol vi 10, *bārāh kaḥammāh,* "radiant as the sun." In Job xxxvii 11, *bār* is the name of the sun itself: *'ap bārī yaṭrīᵃḥ 'āb yāpīṣ 'ānān 'ōrō,* "And his shining one dispels the mist, and his sun scatters the clouds." The balance with *'ōrō,* "his sun," indicates that *bārī* (MT *bᵉrī*) is a substantive followed by third-person suffix *-y;* cf. NOTE on Ps ii 6.

enlightening my eyes. The root idea of *mᵉ'īrāh* is often predicated of the sun. Reading *'ēnāy* and attaching final *mem* to next word. The suffix of *'ēnāy* also modifies balancing *lēb* in the preceding line.

10. *The edict of Yahweh.* Being synonymously parallel to preceding *miṣwāh,* "command," and to following *mišpāṭīm,* "judgments," *yir'at yhwh,* "the fear of Yahweh," can hardly be right. What is more, *yhwh* in the parallel phrases is a subjective genitive, whereas in the traditional versions it must be understood as an objective genitive, if *yir'āh* denotes "fear." Hence I have detached the *mem* from *'ēnāyim* to read *'ēnāy,* "my eyes," and joined it to the following word to read *mir'at yhwh.*

In Ugaritic and Aramaic, *mr'* I signifies "to command"; see UT, No. 1543, p. 437; Aistleitner, WuS, No. 194, pp. 194 f.

are truth. This literal rendition of the Hebrew is more muscular than, say, RSV, "The ordinances of the Lord are true." Cf. Ps xxxiii 4, "Every work of his is truth itself."

12. *your servant.* The close rapports between Ugaritic and Hebrew, which some scholars fail to appreciate or tend to minimize, can be illustrated in Ugaritic correspondence and in the Bible by the frequent use of *'bd* as a polite substitution for the personal pronoun when an inferior is writing to or addressing a suzerain or superior. Thus UT, 95:17–18, *rgm ṯṯb l 'bdk,* "Send back word to your servant," really means "Send back word to me." Cf. UT, § 6.15, and for a rather full listing of biblical occurrences, BDB, p. 714a. Examples in the Psalter include xix 14, xxvii 9, xxxvii 27, lxix 18, cix 28, cxliii 2.

is enlightened. Instead of rendering it "is warned" with most moderns, the *La Bible de la Pléiade* (ed. É. Dhorme), II, p. 927, retains the root meaning of *zhr,* "éclairer," on the basis of Dan xii 3. The consideration that *zhr* may also be predicated of the sun supports the *Pléiade* translation; to describe the Law, the psalmist, it has been noted, chose terms that are properly predicable of the sun. In Ugaritic *ḏhrt* signifies "vision, illumination," but cf. NOTE on Ps xlii 9.

great reward. Contrast CCD, "very diligent," a translation difficult to sustain in view of the didactic nature of the second part of the psalm; hence *'ēqeb* should be understood as in Prov xxii 4.

13. *From my aberrations.* The niphal participle *nistārōt* probably stems from the infixed *-t-* conjugation of *sūr,* "to turn aside"; see NOTE on vs. 7. The parallel most frequently cited in defense of the customary translation "hidden sins" is Ps xc 8, *'alūmēnū,* usually translated "our hidden sins," but one should point out that the Targum understood the word as "sins of our youth," which is probably correct.

14. *Above all.* The second *gam* (see vs. 12) aims at a climactic effect, since the sin to be avoided above all others is the "great sin" of idolatry.

your servant. Cf. first NOTE on vs. 12.

the presumptuous ones. In the present context, the frequent plural adjective *zēdīm* concretely means "idols or false gods," i.e., those who presume to be God. It derives from *zy/wd,* "to act presumptuously," and enjoys a fine analogue in Ps xl 5, *rehābīm,* "arrogant ones, false gods," from *rhb,* "to act arrogantly."

lest. On *'al,* "lest," as in Ugaritic, see NOTE on Ps ix 20; a most relevant parallel is Ps cxix 122.

they rule over me. With *yimšelū bī,* compare Ps cxxxix 24, *ūre'ēh 'im dārak* (MT *derek*) *'ōṣeb bī,* "And see if an idol ever held sway over me."

Then shall I be blameless. MT *'ēytām* supposes the root *ytm,* a by-form of *tmm;* the reading may easily be defended since biliteral roots often appear in variant weak stems of similar meaning, such as *ṭwb* and *yṭb.* Cf. NOTE on Ps xviii 47. T. Noeldeke, *Beiträge zur semitischen Sprachwissenschaft* (Strassburg, 1904), p. 39, correctly postulated the by-form *yśm,* "to place," to explain the verbs written *wyyśm* in Gen xxiv 33, l 26.

the great crime. I.e., idolatry. In this context *peša' rāb* is a synonym of *ḥᵃṭā'āh gᵉdōlāh* (Gen xx 9; Exod xxxii 21, 30, 31; II Kings xvii 21), "the great sin," which really means "idolatry." See NOTE on Ps xxv 11. Akkadian texts from Ras Shamra use the term *ḫiṭṭu rābū,* "the great sin," to describe "adultery"; since for the Israelites "idolatry" and "adultery" were collateral terms, the expression "great sin" signified for them "idolatry." See W. L. Moran, "The Scandal of the 'Great Sin' at Ugarit," JNES 18 (1959), 280–81.

15. *according to.* For this usage of *lᵉ,* see BDB, p. 516a; and for the synonymy of *lᵉ* and *kᵉ,* "according to," compare Ps cxix 154, *lᵉ'imrātᵉkā ḥayyēnī,* "According to your promise restore me to life," with vs. 58, *ḥonnēnī kᵉ'imrātekā,* "Have pity on me according to your promise."

your desire. The principle of the double-duty suffix permits suffixless *rāṣōn* to share that of its counterpart *pānekā,* "your will." Other instances of this poetic practice have been noted at vss. 6, 8, and 9, and in the general *locus* at Ps iii 4. In Ps v 13, *rāṣōn,* "your favor," shares the suffix of vs. 12, *šᵉmekā,* "your name."

your will. Several studies since 1940 have shown that *pānīm* sometimes denotes "intent, purpose, will." In interpreting UT, 67:I:14–15, *pnh š npš lbit thw,* "His will is that a sheep should arouse the appetite of a lioness," W. F. Albright in BASOR 83 (1941), 41, n. 22, cited Heb. *pānīm* and Akk. *pānu,* "intent, purpose, will." Patton, CPBP, pp. 24 f., followed with observations in a similar vein, and in 1947 A. R. Johnson published an article, "Aspects of the Use of the Term *pānīm* in the Old Testament," *Festschrift Otto Eissfeldt* (Halle, 1947), pp. 155–59, where he cited II Chron xxxii 2, *ūpānāyw lᵉmilḥāmāh,* "And his intention was war." Speiser, *Genesis* (The Anchor Bible, vol. 1), p. LXVIII, correctly shows that in Gen x 9, *lipnē yhwh* denotes "by the will of Yahweh"; cf. also Gen xvii 18, xxvii 7, xliii 33. This may be the intended nuance in Phoenician Yeḥimilk, 6–7, *kmlk ṣdq wmlk yšr lpn 'l gbl q[dšm],* "For he is the legitimate and lawful king by the will of the holy gods of Byblos."

In the present passage, the parallelism with *rāṣōn* greatly facilitates the interpretation of *pānekā.*

PSALM 20
(xx 1–10)

1 *For the director; a psalm of David.*

2 May Yahweh grant you triumph
in time of siege,
The Name of Jacob's God
be your bulwark.
3 May he send you help from his sanctuary, [2]*
from Zion sustain you.
4 May he remember all your gifts,
and consider your burnt offerings generous. *Selah* [3]
5 May he give you what you strive for, [4]
and every plan of yours accomplish.
6 That we might exult in your victory, [5]
and in the Name of our God
hold high the banners;
May Yahweh accomplish all your petitions.
7 Now I know [6]
that Yahweh has given his anointed victory,
Has granted him triumph
from his sacred heaven,
And from his fortress
has given victory with his right hand.
8 Some through chariots, [7]
and others through horses,
But we through the Name of our God are strong.
9 They slumped and fell, [8]
while we stood erect and reassured.
10 Yahweh has given the king victory, [9]
granted him triumph
when we called.

* Verse numbers in RSV.

Notes

xx. A prayer of the congregation for the king setting out for battle (vss. 2–6), and the answer to the prayer announced by a priest or prophet (7–10).

2. *grant you triumph.* Relating the verb *ya'ᵃnᵉkā* to *'nw,* "to conquer, triumph," studied in Note on Ps xviii 36; see Notes below on vss. 7 and 10.

in time of siege. The prevalence of military language throughout the psalm indicates that generic *bᵉyōm ṣārāh,* "in time of distress," should be given a more specific nuance in translation. A similar situation obtains in Ps xxxvii 39, where, because of its collocation with *mā'ūzzām,* "their fortress," *bᵉ'ēt ṣārāh* is properly rendered "in time of siege." Cf. Nah i 7–8, *ṭōb yhwh lᵉmā'ōz bᵉyōm ṣārāh wᵉyōdēᵃ' ḥōsē bō (ū)bᵉšeṭep 'ōbēr,* "In time of siege Yahweh is better than a fortress, and he cares for those who in him seek refuge from the onrushing flood."

The Name of Jacob's God. Cf. especially Exod xxiii 21, "Give heed to him [my angel] and hearken to his voice; . . . for my Name is in him." The Name of Yahweh is a personification which has roots in Canaanite theology since, for example, Athtart is identified in UT, 127:56, as *'ṯtrt šm b'l,* "Athtart the Name of Baal." It is accordingly risky to use the presence of this term as a criterion for the dating of this psalm, as Kraus attempts to do.

be your bulwark. The psalmist may have employed the verb *yᵉśaggebᵉkā* to elicit the thought of a *miśgāb,* "retreat, bulwark," thus continuing the metaphor of the first half verse.

3. *send you help.* The text literally reads "may he send your help," but the pronominal suffix not infrequently has a dative meaning; see Joüon, GHB, § 129h. Cf. UT, 51:v:89, *bšrtk yblt,* "I bring you good tidings," literally "I bring your good tidings"; see Notes on Pss ii 8 and xvi 4.

from his sanctuary. Attaching the *waw* of *wmṣyn* to the preceding word to read *qodšō* for MT *qōdeš.* That the sanctuary on Mount Zion was a source of power is also stated in Ps lxxvii 14 if we give to *darkekā* its Ugaritic sense of "power, dominion": *'ᵉlōhīm baqqōdeš darkekā mī 'ēl gādōl kē'lōhīm,* "O God, your power is in the sanctuary; what god is great as God?"

4. *your gifts.* The antiquity of the term *minḥāh* is documented in Ugaritic, where it occurs in the masculine form *mnḥ* with the signification "gift, tribute." Compare UT, 137:37–38, *ybl argmnk kilm* [. . .] *ybl wbn qdš mnḥyk,* "He will bring you tribute [for syntax, see Note

on vs. 3] as a god, . . . the sons of holiness will also bring you gifts," with Zeph iii 10, *yōbīlūn minḥātī,* "They will bring me a gift."

consider . . . generous. Vocalizing *y^e^daššannāh,* an energic form, for MT *y^e^dašš^e^neh.* The high incidence of energic forms in Ugaritic (UT, § 9.11) permits the Hebrew grammarian to explain as such a good number of apparently anomalous forms; cf. NOTE on Ps viii 2. On the declarative use of the piel, "declare or consider generous," see GK, § 52g.

5. *what you strive for.* Literally "according to your heart."

6. *hold high the banners.* I.e., as a sign of victory, if the parallelism is not misleading. A doubtful translation of consonantal *ndgl,* here vocalized as piel *n^e^daggēl* and parsed as a denominative verb from *degel,* "banner." Cf. Ps lx 6, *nātattāh llīrē'ekā nēs l^e^hitnōsēs mipp^e^nē qōšeṭ,* "Give a banner to those who fear you that they might rally in the face of the archers." A full treatment of banners and their uses in the Qumran texts may be found in Yigael Yadin, *The Scroll of the War of the Sons of Light against the Sons of Darkness,* trs. Batya and Chaim Rabin (Oxford, 1962), pp. 38–64.

7. *Now I know.* A priest or prophet has received word that the king has scored a military triumph and announces to the congregation that the king's prayers and theirs have been answered.

The *yqtl* verbs that follow in vss. 7–10 (except *nazkīr* in vs. 8) all express past time, as normally in Ugaritic; cf. NOTE on Ps iv 4. The preterite verbs in vs. 9 and the balance between preterite (*qtl*) *hōšī'āh* and the *yqtl* form *ya'^a^nennū* in vs. 10 thus become intelligible.

Has granted him triumph. In the present context, where it is preceded and followed by verbs of victory, *ya'^a^nēhū* is manifestly to be derived from *'nw,* "to conquer, triumph," discussed in the NOTES on vs. 2 and Ps xviii 36. For the parallelism with the root *yš',* cf. Pss xviii 36 and lx 7, *hōšī'āh y^e^min^e^kā wa'^a^nēnū,* "Give us victory with your right hand and grant us triumph."

from his fortress. g^e^būrōt is a poetic name for heaven, as is clear from its balance with *mišš^e^mē qodšō.* Thus the preposition *b* in *bīg^e^būrōt,* parallel to *min,* denotes "from"; other instances of like parallelism are found in Pss xvii 14, xxxi 21, xxxiii 19, cxlviii 1; Job v 21, vii 14; cf. Sarna in JBL 78 (1959), 310–16.

The plural pointing of MT is retained on the ground that names for fortifications, like names for dwellings, are sometimes plural in form though singular in meaning. The singular form is attested in Judg v 31, *w^e^'ōh^a^bāyw k^e^ṣē't haššemeš bīg^e^būrātō,* "But those who love him will be like the going forth of the sun from his fortress," and Ps lxvi 7, *mōšēl bīg^e^būrātō 'ōlām 'ēynāyw baggōyim tiṣpenāh,* "He rules from his eternal fortress, his eyes keep watch upon the nations."

Ps lxxviii 26 is instructive in that it matches the two ideas of "heaven" and "fortress": *yassa' qādīm baššāmāyim way^enahēg b^e'uzzō tēmān,* "He let loose the east wind from heaven, and led forth the south wind from his fortress" (cf. Pss cxxxv 7, cl 1; Job xxvi 14). The word for "fortress" in this passage, *'ōz,* neatly illustrates the semantic nexus between "to be strong" and "fortress" that is also found in the vocable *g^ebūrāh,* "fortress," from *gābar,* "to be strong." In the NOTE on Ps viii 3 one will find a full discussion of *'ōz,* "fortress."

Finally, the suffix of *qodšō* supplies for suffixless *g^ebūrōt* on the principle treated in the NOTE on Ps iii 4.

has given victory. Pointing as hiphil *yōšī^a'* for MT *yeša'* and for the synonymy of the roots *yš'* and *'nw;* cf. Ps lx 7 cited above. Besides creating a fine balanced sentence with two three-beat cola, the proposed reading does away with the congested construct chain of MT, *bīg^ebūrōt yēša' y^emīnō,* which has lent itself to many various translations.

with his right hand. y^emīnō is an accusative of means as in Pss lx 7, *hōšī'āh y^emīn^ekā wa'^anēnū,* "Give us victory with your right hand and grant us triumph," and cxxxviii 7, *w^etōšī'ēnī y^emīn^ekā,* "And you will give me victory with your right hand." Cf. NOTE on Ps v 10 for discussion of accusative of means.

8. *we . . . are strong.* The priest associates himself with the assembly of worshipers. Parsing *nazkīr* as a denominative verb from *zākār,* "male," just as Ps xii 5, *nagbīr,* "we are powerful," is a denominative verb from *geber,* "man." Ugar. *da-ka-rum,* "man," occurs in the still (December 1964) unpublished quadrilingual vocabulary discovered at Ras Shamra in 1958. The Vulgate and Syriac understood *nazkīr* in this manner. Cf. Exod xxxiv 19 and Nah ii 6, *yizk^erū* (MT *yizkōr*) *'addīrāyw yikkāš^elū bah^alīkōtām,* "His captains are strong, they hurtle in their march" (courtesy W. Beuken).

Name of our God. Omitting *yhwh* as secondary, since it seriously disrupts the meter.

10. *has given . . . victory.* Syntactically, *hōšī'āh* is identical with vs. 7, *hōšī^a'* but morphologically differs in its preservation of the archaic ending of the third-person singular perfect masculine, an archaism recorded in NOTE to Ps iv 7; I am indebted to D. N. Freedman for this suggestion.

granted him triumph. Pointing *ya'^anennū,* instead of MT *ya'^anēnū;* for this meaning of the verb, see NOTES on vss. 2 and 7. Notice the balance with *hōšī'āh,* as in vs. 7, and the inclusion with vs. 2, *ya'^an^ekā,* "May (Yahweh) grant you triumph."

The balance with preterite *hōšī'āh* shows that the *yqtl* form expresses past time, as in Ugaritic; cf. NOTE on Ps iv 7.

PSALM 21

(xxi 1–14)

1 *For the director; a psalm of David.*

2 O Yahweh, in your triumph the king rejoices,
and in your victory how greatly he exults!
3 His heart's desire you gave him, [2]*
and the request of his lips did not withhold. *Selah*
4 But you set before him the blessings of prosperity, [3]
put upon his head a crown of gold.
5 Life eternal he asked of you, [4]
you gave it to him;
Length of days, eternity, and everlasting.
6 Great is his glory through your victory, [5]
splendor and majesty you set upon him.
7 Indeed you will give him blessings forever, [6]
you will make him gaze with happiness upon your face.
8 Indeed the king trusts in Yahweh, [7]
and from the love of the Most High will never swerve.
9 Your left hand overtook all your foes, [8]
your right hand overtook those who hate you.
10 You put them as into a blazing furnace, [9]
at the time of your fury, O Yahweh!
In his wrath he engorged them,
and his fire devoured them.
11 Their race you made perish from the earth, [10]
and their children from the sons of men.
12 For they plotted a revolt against you, [11]
devised malice, but could not succeed.
13 But you made them all shoulder, [12]
with your bowstrings you aimed at their faces.
14 Rejoice, O Yahweh, in your triumph, [13]
we shall sing and praise your vigor.

*** Verse numbers in RSV.**

NOTES

xxi. A psalm of thanksgiving for the royal victory prayed for in the preceding psalm. Through the vigorous intervention of Yahweh, who fought at the side of the king, a resounding victory was won.

The psalm is composed of two parts. Verses 3–8 enumerate the blessings that Yahweh has bestowed upon the king; for these the people register their thanks. Verses 9–13 describe the battle that resulted in the victory and occasioned the composition of the present work. Verses 2 and 14 are refrains which form an *inclusio.*

Contrary to the prevailing exegesis (Gunkel, Briggs, Mowinckel, Kraus), the subject of vss. 9–13 is not the king but Yahweh, precisely as in Ps cx 5–6; see critical NOTES below. Artur Weiser, *Die Psalmen* (ATD; 5th ed., Göttingen, 1959), p. 145, has also correctly seen that vss. 9–13 describe a *Kriegsgott,* but failing to understand that the imperfect forms in Ugaritic and in archaic Hebrew poetry are used to describe past narrative action, he translated the verbs of vss. 9–13 as future and consequently categorized these verses (erroneously, it seems) as *Vertrauensgebet.*

2. *in your triumph.* These words strike the keynote of the psalm. The king's victory was really achieved by divine intervention and hence must be attributed to Yahweh. This nuance of *'ōz* is present in I Sam ii 10; Pss xxix 11, lxviii 29, and lxxxix 18; cf. W. F. Albright in HUCA 23 (1950), p. 31. Its parallelism with *yešū'ātekā,* "your victory," points to the same conclusion.

rejoices . . . exults. The frequent pairing of *yiśmaḥ-yāgīl* is documented in UT, 125:14–15, *bḥyk abn nšmḫ blmtk ngln,* "In your life eternal, O father of ours, we rejoice; in your immortality we exult." The attempt of Horace D. Hummel in his article, "Enclitic *MEM* in Early Northwest Semitic, Especially Hebrew," JBL 76 (1957), 99, to find an enclitic *mem* in this verse is not particularly felicitous.

in your victory. BDB, p. 447b, lists some fifteen passages where this is the denotation of *yesū'āh.*

3. *request of his lips.* The root of the hapax legomenon *'arešet* is frequently attested in Ugaritic, in both verbs and substantives; cf. C. Virolleaud in GLECS 8 (1957–60), 27, and J. Aistleitner, WuS, No. 423, p. 37. The root is further attested in still unpublished tablets from Ras Shamra. There is a by-form of the root in the noun *yerūšāh* in Ps lxi 6 and possibly in Job xvii 11, *mōrāšē lebābī,* "the desires of my heart."

4. *you set before him.* Parsing *teqaddemennū* as a denominative

verb from *qedem* "front," followed by a dative suffix; cf. Maurice Bogaert in *Biblica* 45 (1964), 235, n. 5. The parallelism of *tᵉqaddᵉmennū* with *tāšīt* recalls the collocation of these roots in UT, 'nt:IV:85, *št alp qdmh,* "Put an ox in front of him."

5. *Life eternal.* Since *ḥayyīm šā'al* is of a piece with UT, 2 Aqht: IV:27–28, *irš ḥym watnk blmt wašlḥk,* "Ask for life eternal and I will give it to you, immortality and I will bestow it upon you," it follows with considerable probability that *ḥayyīm* here, as well as in Prov xii 28, means "eternal life." The balance with *'ōrek yāmīm, 'ōlām,* and *'ād* points to the same conclusion. See NOTE on Ps xxvii 13 and M. Dahood in *Biblica* 41 (1960), 176–81; PNWSP, 19 f.

you gave it to him. The king was thought to receive the gift of immortality on the day of his coronation. In Ugaritic poetry, King Kirta was also considered to be immortal, but this in virtue of his being the son of El and Asherah; UT, 125:10–15. In Ps ii 7 the king is said to become the son of God through adoption on the day of his anointing as king.

Length of days. The phrase *'ōrek yāmīm* occurs in UT, 1018:20, *urk ym b'ly* as well as in Phoenician Karatepe III:5.

eternity, and everlasting. Synonyms in apposition with *'ōrek yāmīm* and *ḥayyīm,* rather than accusatives of time. For the association of the ideas of life and length of days, cf. UT, 76:II:20, *ḥwt aḫt wnark,* "May you live, O my sister, and prolong your days." On the reading *nark* (UT has *nar-*), see Andrée Herdner, *Corpus des tablettes en cunéiformes alphabétiques découvertes à Ras Shamra-Ugarit de 1929 à 1939* (Paris, 1963), p. 50, n. 4.

6. *splendor and majesty.* These two concepts are elucidated by the corresponding Akkadian idea of *melammu.* This Akkadian term denotes a characteristic attribute of the gods consisting of a dazzling aureole or nimbus which surrounds the divinity. The king as representative and likeness of the gods also has such an aura, which constitutes the divine legitimation of his royalty. This *melammu* is bestowed upon him when he becomes king; see A. L. Oppenheim, "Akkadian *pul(u)ḫ(t)u* and *melammu,*" JAOS 63 (1943), 31–34.

7. *you will give him.* With LXX, understanding the suffix of *tᵉšītēhū* as datival, as in vs. 4; see Bogaert in *Biblica* 45 (1964), 235 f. The definition of *šīt,* "to give," which the lexicons generally recognize only in Gen iv 25 and here (see BDB; GB), is important for the interpretation of the Ugaritic texts, where this sense seems to be rather frequent, though Virolleaud and others have missed this signification. Thus (a) UT, 2060:34–35, *aṯr iṯ bqṯ wštn ly,* "Find out what is available and give it to me" (see Gen iv 25 for the same construction); (b) 1171:1–4, *spr 'psm dt št uryn lmlk ugrt,* "A list of *'psm* which URYN gave to the king of Ugarit"; (c) 2065:14–17, *[i]rš 'my mnm irštk dḫsrt*

wank aštn l iḫy, "Ask me, whatever your request for what is lacking, and I will give it to my brother."

gaze . . . upon your face. Suggesting in the afterlife; see discussion in the NOTES on Pss xvi 10–11 and xvii 15. The verb *teḥaddēhū* is a Canaanism for *teḥazzēhū*. Dialectal forms in the Bible involving the interchange of *d* and *z* have been studied by Dahood in PNWSP, pp. 21, 31 f., 46. The Canaanite form *ḥdy* for *ḥzy* has been examined most recently in *Biblica* 45 (1964), 407 f., with bibliography. In the Psalter the dialectal form appears in the present passage, xxxiii 15, xlix 11, and cxxxix 16; on the last text, see Bonnard, *Le Psautier selon Jérémie,* p. 226.

The sentiment expressed here closely relates to Ps xvi 11, "You will make me know the path of life eternal, filling me with happiness before you, with pleasures at your right hand forever."

8. *from the love.* Ps xvi 8, *mīmīnī bal 'emmōṭ,* "From his right hand I will not swerve," suggests that in the clause, *beḥesed 'elyôn bal yimmōṭ,* the preposition *be* denotes "from"; the same construction is found in Ps xvii 5.

The love mentioned here is the covenantal love that binds the vassal king of Israel to Yahweh, his Suzerain. This may further be inferred from the mention of "trust in Yahweh"—covenant terminology—in the first colon. Compare the similar expression in Ps xviii 31, "The Suzerain is he to all who trust [*ḥōsīm*] in him." The present phrase uses the synonym *bōṭēaḥ*. On covenantal love, consult the suggestive study by W. L. Moran, "The Ancient Near Eastern Background of the Love of God in Deuteronomy," CBQ 25 (1963), 77–87.

9. *Your left hand.* I.e., the left hand of God. See NOTE below on Ps xxvi 10 for this meaning of *yādekā*.

overtook. The construction *timṣā' l* should be compared with UT, 49:v:4, *ymṣi larṣ,* "he reaches earth."

your foes . . . those who hate you. Referring to the foes of God, who are also foes of his king. For the same parallelism, UT, 51:VII:35–36, *ib b'l tiḫd y'rm šnu hd gpt ǵr,* "The foes of Baal seize the forests, those who hate Hadd the ridges of the mountain."

10. *as into a blazing furnace.* Just as a fiery furnace consumes everything put into it, so God is pictured as a blazing furnace devouring his enemies. This is merely a more graphic equivalent of *be'appō yeballe'ēm,* "In his wrath he engorged them."

at the time of your fury. For *pānīm,* "fury," see Pss xxxiv 17, *penē yhwh be'ōśē rā' lehakrīt mē'ereṣ zikrām,* "The fury of Yahweh is with the evildoers, to cut off from the earth all memory of them"; lxxx 17; Eccles viii 1; Lam iv 16; and possibly UT, 75:I:33, *wbhm pn b'l,* "And with them was the fury of Baal." The close connection with *'ap* of the following colon, and the similarity with the related literary genre of Ps cx 5, *'ᵃdōnay 'al yᵉmīnekā māḥaṣ bᵉyōm 'appō mᵉlākīm,* "The Lord at your right hand will smash kings when he rages," lend considerable weight to this interpretation of *pānīm.*

he engorged them. The sudden shift from the second to the third person in impassioned language is on a par with the disconcerting shift from the singular to the plural number commented upon in the NOTE on Ps v 10. The image is that of Isa xxv 8, *billa' hammāwet lāneṣaḥ,* "He [Yahweh] engorged Mot forever," and both go back to older Canaanite phraseology, as may be gathered from a perusal of such texts as UT, 67:I:6–7, *lyrt bnpš bn ilm mt,* "I have descended into the maw of divine Mot."

his fire. Balancing *'appō* with a suffix, *'ēš* need not be furnished with one on the principle of the double-duty suffix. For the metaphor, see Ps xviii 8 f. The chiastic order of the final two cola should not be overlooked.

11. *Their race.* Literally "their fruit."

their children. In the Phoenician Inscription of Yeḥawmilk, the figurative sense of *zera'* has been noted by Cooke, TNSI, p. 25, who also cites the present passage.

12. *a revolt against you.* Meaning against God and his king, as in Ps ii 2, "Why do kings of the earth take their stand, and the princes make common cause against Yahweh and against his anointed?"

13. *you made them all shoulder.* The hapax legomenon phrase *tᵉšītēmō šekem,* usually explained as "you put them to flight," seems to indicate that God will make the enemies supine so that the king might put his feet upon their necks as a sign of conquest. Cf. Josh x 24, "Come near, put your feet upon the necks of these kings." This is also the sense of Ps xviii 41, "You gave me the neck of my foes," which does not mean that the king's enemies fled, but that they were brought captive before the king, who put his foot on their neck. See further Ps xlvii 4, "He made nations prostrate beneath us." When the idiom is taken to mean that God put the enemies of the king to flight, it becomes rather difficult to see how he could have aimed his bow at their faces, as stated in the ostensibly synonymous colon; the parallelism of vss. 9–13 being synonymous, one may infer that the same obtains in the present verse.

with your bowstrings. In this sense *mētār* is a hapax legomenon. Still plausible is my proposal (*Biblica* 38 [1957], 65) to read in UT, 2 Aqht:VI:22–23, *mtrm* (*editio princeps mtb*[*m*]) *b'qbt ṯr,* "sinews from the hocks of a bull."

14. *Rejoice, O Yahweh.* Exegetically difficult *rūmāh* is synonymous with vs. 2, *yiśmaḥ.* In vs. 2 the king is said to rejoice in Yahweh's

victory, while here Yahweh himself is invited to celebrate his triumph. On *rūm,* "to rejoice," see NOTE on Ps xiii 3 and Moran in *Biblica* 42 (1961), 239 (on Ps lxxxix 17).

in your triumph. Cf. NOTE on vs. 2.

your vigor. I.e., your vigorous intervention on behalf of the king.

PSALM 22

(xxii 1–32)

1 *For the director; according to "The hind of the Dawn." A psalm of David.*

2 My God, why have you forsaken me?
dismissing my plea,
the roar of my words?
3 My God, I call out by day, [2]*
but you answer not;
And by night—no respite for me.
4 While you sit upon the holy throne, [3]
the Glory of Israel.
5 In you trusted our fathers, [4]
they trusted and you delivered them.
6 To you they cried and were delivered, [5]
in you they trusted and were not disappointed.
7 But I am a worm and not a man, [6]
the scorn of men
and the most despicable of the people.
8 All who see me make sport of me, [7]
they gape at me,
they wag their heads.
9 "He lived for Yahweh, [8]
let him deliver him;
Let him rescue him,
if he cares for him."
10 Yet you brought me forth from the womb, [9]
made me tranquil on my mother's breast.
11 Upon you was I cast from birth, [10]
from my mother's womb you are my God.
12 Stay not far from me, [11]
for the adversaries are near,
for there is none to help.

* Verse numbers in RSV.

13 Strong bulls surround me, [12]
wild bulls of Bashan encircle me.
14 They open their mouths against me, [13]
like a ravening and raging lion.
15 I am poured out like water, [14]
and all my bones are racked;
My heart has become like wax,
dripping out of my bosom.
16 My strength is dried up like a potsherd, [15]
my tongue sticks to my jaws,
And they put me upon the mud of Death.
17 For dogs have surrounded me, [16]
a pack of evildoers encircle me,
Piercing my hands and my feet.
18 I can number all my bones, [17]
they glare, they stare at me.
19 They divide my garments among them, [18]
and over my robe they cast lots.
20 But you, Yahweh, be not far away, [19]
O, my army, hasten to my help.
21 Rescue my neck from the sword, [20]
my face from the blade of the ax.
22 Save me from the lion's mouth, [21]
over the horns of wild oxen
make me triumph.
23 That I might proclaim your name to my brethren, [22]
in the midst of the congregation praise you.
24 You who fear Yahweh, praise him; [23]
all you race of Jacob, honor him;
Stand in awe of him,
all you race of Israel.
25 For he has not despised [24]
nor disdained the song of the afflicted;
He did not turn his face from him,
but when he cried, he listened to him.
26 One hundred times will I repeat to you [25]
my song of praise in the great congregation;
I will fulfill my vows
before them who fear him.

27 The poor will eat and be content, [26]
those who seek Yahweh will praise him.
May your heart live forever.
28 All the ends of the earth [27]
will remember and return to Yahweh;
And all the clans of the nations
will bow down before him.
29 For truly is Yahweh the king [28]
and the ruler over the nations.
30 Indeed to him shall bow down [29]
all those who sleep in the nether world;
Before him shall bend the knee,
all who have gone down to the mud.
For the Victor himself restores to life.
31 May my progeny serve him, [30]
tell of Yahweh forever.
32 May they begin to recount his generosity, [31]
to a people yet to be born that he has acted.

Notes

xxii. An individual lament; the poet complains of his sufferings in graphic terms and tries to move God to help him. Convinced of the forthcoming help, the psalmist makes a vow to praise God in the great assembly.

1. *The hind of the Dawn*. See NOTE on vs. 20.

2. *dismissing*. Parsing *rāḥōq* as the piel infinitive absolute, an alternate form of *rāḥēq* (GK, § 52o), which continues the action of the main verb. Appending the initial syllable of *mīšū‘ātī* as enclitic to *rāḥōq* and comparing the cognate construction in UT, 126:v:20–21, *my bilm ydy mrṣ gršm zbln,* "Which of the gods will cast out the sickness, exorcising the disease?" *gršm* is the infinitive absolute followed by enclitic *mem* and continuing the action of the synonymous main verb *ydy*.

my plea. Vocalizing *šaw‘ātī,* initial *mem* having been attached to the preceding word as enclitic. Cf. Ps cii 2, *w*^{e}*šaw‘ātī ’ēlekā tābō’*, "And let my plea come unto you."

roar of my words. Literally "words of my roaring."

4. *holy throne*. The unusual construction *qādōš yōšēb* becomes intelligible in view of Ps cxiv 2, *hay*^{e}*tāh y*^{e}*hūdāh l*^{e}*qodšō yiśrā’ēl*

mamšᵉlōtāyw, "Judah became his holy throne, Israel his kingdom," and Ps xi 4, discussed above. The adjective *qādōš,* "holy," becomes, by metonymy, the name of the throne itself. The use of an adjective for a noun is evident in Ugar. *rḥbt,* "a wide-brimmed jar," and in Canaanite Akk. *rabītu,* "a large drinking vessel"; see Jean Nougayrol, *Palais royal d'Ugarit,* III (Paris, 1955), p. 183.

the Glory of Israel. tᵉhillōt is derived, it would seem, from *hll,* "to shine," Ugar. *hll.* Cf. Jer xvii 14 and especially Hab iii 3, where *tᵉhillāh* is associated with *hōd,* "splendor," and *nōgah,* "light": *kissāh šāmayim hōdō ūtᵉhillātō mālᵉ'āh hā'āreṣ,* "His splendor covered the heavens, and his glory filled the earth." A good analogy is further provided by I Sam xv 29, *nēṣaḥ yiśrā'ēl,* "the Splendor of Israel," from *nāṣaḥ,* "to shine." For the divine appellative *kābōd,* "Glorious One," consult the NOTE on Ps iii 4.

7. *a worm.* The frequent metaphorical use of animal names in the Bible finds literary antecedents in the Ugaritic epics, where several instances have been noticed; e.g., *ẓby,* "gazelle," signifies a dignitary, just as in Isa xxiii 9. See Dahood, *Biblica* 40 (1959), 161 f., and NOTE on Ps ii 5.

most despicable of the people. The Ugaritic construction *'mq nšm,* "the strongest/wisest of men," shows that no morphological indicator is needed to express the superlative. Hence one may render Isa liii 3, *nibzeh wᵉḥādal 'īšīm,* "the most despicable and stupid of men," while difficult Ps xcix 4, *wᵉ'ōz melek mišpāṭ 'ōhēb,* may signify "the strongest king, the lover of justice." On *ḥādal,* "stupid," in Isa liii 3, see Philip J. Calderone in CBQ 24 (1962), 416–19.

9. *He lived.* Reading *gāl,* from *gyl,* "to live," for MT *gōl;* cf. NOTE on Ps ii 11.

if he cares. The subject is God, as rightly understood in Matt xxvii 43.

10. *you brought me forth.* The meaning and etymology of *gōḥī* are uncertain.

made me tranquil. Or, to preserve the participial force of *mabṭīḥī,* "my pacifier." In El Amarna, 147:56, the Canaanite verb *batiti* (= *batiḥtī*) is glossed by another Canaanite verb *nuḫti,* "I am at rest." See Dahood, PNWSP, p. 7, n. 1, and references given there.

11. *was I cast.* The precise imagery intended here is not clear; the sense seems rather evident, namely, "I was placed in your custody." Cf. Ps lv 23, *hašlēk 'al yhwh yᵉhabᵉkā,* "Cast yourself upon Yahweh that he might provide for you."

12. *the adversaries are near.* Since it is contrasted with concrete *'ōzēr,* and since the following verse concretely enumerates the foes of the psalmist, *ṣārāh* should logically be understood as an abstract form with a concrete meaning. The poetic practice of pairing an

abstract noun with one that is concrete has been examined at Ps v 8. Cf. Nah i 9, *lō' tāqūm pa'ᵃmayim ṣārāh,* "His adversaries will not rise up twice," balances vs. 8, *'ōyᵉbāyw yᵉraddēp ḥōšek,* "He will pursue his foes into Darkness." This is the same pairing recorded in UT, 68:9, *ht ibk tmḫṣ ht tṣmt ṣrtk,* "Now you will smite your Foe, now will you destroy your Adversary." The lack of vocalization precludes certainty, but there is reason to believe that both these forms are *pluralia majestatis* to be translated in the singular. Cf. further Ps liv 9, *kī mikkol ṣārāh hiṣṣīlanī ūbᵉ'ōyᵉbay rā'ātāh 'ēnī,* "For from all my adversaries he rescued me, my eye has gloated over my foes."

13. *Strong bulls.* They symbolize the formidable enemies; cf. Isa xxxiv 7.

wild bulls of Bashan. Bashan was a fertile region east of the Jordan, famous for its cattle and sheep; see Deut xxxii 14; Amos iv 1; Mic vii 14.

15. *dripping out of my bosom.* In the context, and fully in accord with biblical hyperbolic language, *bᵉtōk* is preferably taken as "out of"; cf. Ezek xxiv 11, *wᵉnittᵉkāh bᵉtōkāh ṭum'ātāh,* "And her impurity shall flow out of her midst."

16. *my tongue sticks.* With Hummel in JBL 76 (1957), 99, reading *lᵉšōnī-m dōbēq,* with enclitic *mem,* for MT *lᵉšōnī mudbāq,* the only attested instance of hophal from *dbq.*

they put me. tišpᵉtēnī is the third-person feminine collective with plural subject, as in Pss xvii 5, xliv 19, lxviii 3; Job xxxviii 17. See Albright in HUCA 23 (1950), p. 17. For the construction *šāpat lᵉ,* see Isa xxvi 12, *yhwh tišpōt šālōm lānū,* "O Yahweh, you will put peace upon us" (contrast RSV, "Thou wilt ordain peace for us"), and UT, 49:III:15, *p'nh lhdm yṯpd,* "He puts his feet upon the footstool."

the mud of Death. On *'āpār,* "Kot," see Gunkel, *Die Psalmen,* p. 128, and N. H. Ridderbos, "*'āpār* als Staub des Totenortes," *Oudetestamentische Studien* 5 (1948), 174–78. The phrase evokes the theme of Sheol as a place of mud and filth; Gaster, *Thespis,* 1961, pp. 203 f. In a number of passages *māwet* denotes the place of death, parallel to Sheol; cf. BDB, p. 560a, who cite Isa xxviii 15, 18; Ps vi 6, etc.

17. *pack of evildoers.* The imagery being that of the chase, *'ᵃdat,* "council, assembly," rather takes on the nuance "pack." In Ps lxxiv 2 *'ēdāh* signifies a "flock (of sheep)"; cf. Ps lxviii 31, *'ᵃdat 'abbīrīm,* "the herd of bulls." Gillis Gerleman, *Contributions to the Old Testament Terminology of the Chase* (Lund, 1946), p. 10, doubts that this verse refers to the chase, but the early (Aquila, Theodotion, Jerome) vocalization of MT *kᵉlābīm,* "dogs," as *kallābīm,* "hunters," makes serious inroads into his position.

Piercing my hands. Much-contested *k'ry* is here tentatively analyzed as an infinitive absolute from *kry,* "to dig," with the archaic ending *-i,* as in Gen xxx 8, xlix 11; Exod xv 6. See W. L. Moran in *The Bible and the Ancient Near East: Essays in Honor of William Foxwell Albright,* ed. G. E. Wright (New York, 1961), p. 62; J. M. Solá-Solé, *L'infinitif sémitique* (Paris, 1961), p. 185b. The *aleph* would be intrusive as, e.g., in Prov xxiv 7, *r'mwt* for *rmwt.*

20. *my army.* Ginsberg, LKK, p. 37, has related the hapax legomenon *'ᵉyālūtī* to UT, Krt:88, *ṣbuk ul mad,* "Your troops are a mighty army." In vs. 1, LXX, Targ., and Symm. read *'ᵉyālūt,* "help," for MT *'ayyelet,* "hind," and this reading may well be the correct one.

to my help. Or possibly, "to my war"; cf. NOTE on Ps xxxv 2.

21. *my neck from the sword.* On *nepeš,* "neck," see NOTE on Ps vii 3. Especially relevant parallels are Ps cv 18 and Job vii 15, *wattibḥar maḥᵃnaq napšī māwet-m 'aṣmōtay,* "And my neck preferred strangulation, my bones death." On the *mem* enclitic following *māwet,* see Nahum Sarna, JJS 6 (1955), 109 f.

my face. Since "my loneliness" (CCD) yields precious little sense in the context, the presumed parallelism with "neck" desiderating the name of a part of the body, *yᵉḥīdātī* (again balancing *napšī* in Ps xxxv 17) may be a dialectal form from Ugar. *ḥdy,* Heb. *ḥāzah,* "to see." The substantive would thus be cognate with *yaḥdāw,* "his face," in Ps iv 9 and Isa xl 5, as proposed in CBQ 20 (1958), 46–49. For dialectal *ḥdy* as a verbal form, see NOTE on Ps xxi 7.

from the blade of the ax. Since *mayyad keleb* "from the dog's paw," forms such a curious and unexampled parallel to *mēḥereb,* "from the sword," one may be permitted to submit, with due reserve, that consonantal *klb* is a by-form of *kēlappōt,* "ax," which occurs in Ps lxxiv 6. Both *kᵉlōb* and *kēlūp,* "ax," are found in Late Hebrew (see G. Dalman, *Aramäisch-Neuhebräisches Wörterbuch* [Frankfurt a. M., 1897], pp. 187–89), while Aramaic has *kūlbā',* "ax." Since the word for "ax" is an Akk. loanword, its labial was particularly subject to non-phonemic variation; it is well known that this class of words underwent considerable change in spelling and pronunciation. Recent examples from Ras Shamra include the loanwords *brd̲l* and *prd̲l,* "iron," and *spsg* and *sbsg,* "glaze." Of course, the interchange between *p* and *b* was not limited to loanwords; this is particularly clear from Ugaritic, where some fifteen pairs of non-phonemic variants have thus far been identified; e.g., *bky* and *pky; b'l* and *p'l; lbš* and *lpš; nbk* and *npk; šbḥ* and *špḥ; t̲bṭ* and *t̲pṭ;* Phoenician attests *nbš* for common Semitic *npš,* and *'lb* for *'lp.* Hebrew employs the variant roots *kbš* and *kpš; pzr* and *bzr; nšb* and *nšp; rbd* and *rpd.* Cf. Dahood, PNWSP, pp. 32 f.

With the phrase *yad kᵉlōb* (?), compare Ps lxiii 11, *yᵉdē ḥāreb,* "the edges of the sword." Not only does "ax" make a fine parallel to "sword," but in Ezek xxvi 9, *bᵉḥarbōtāyw* is rendered by LXX as "with his axes." The use of an ax as a weapon in the Bible appears from Judg ix 48, where Abimelech and his men cut brushwood to burn the fortress of Shechem. These axes probably served the double purpose of tool and weapon, since it is unlikely that an extra set of axes was carried solely for the purpose of cutting brush.

22. *wild oxen.* As in Job xxxix 9, *rēmīm* is simplified spelling for *re'ēmīm,* Ugar. *rumm.* The term is metaphorical for puissant adversaries; cf. NOTE on Ps ii 5. The Targum took it to refer to puissant kings. Cf. UT, 49:VI:18–19, *mt 'z b'l 'z ynghn krumm,* "Mot is powerful, Baal is powerful; they gore like wild oxen."

make me triumph. Balancing imperative *hōšī'ēnī* at the beginning of the verse, *'anītanī,* closing out the verse, should be parsed as precative perfect from *'ānāh,* "to conquer, triumph," studied in the NOTE on Ps xviii 36, while other cases of precative perfect have been listed in NOTE on Ps iii 8. Cf. especially Ps lx 7, *hōšī'āh yemīnekā wa'anēnū,* "With your right hand give victory and make us triumph."

23. *That I might proclaim.* Parsing *'asapperāh* as subjunctive; cf. NOTE on Ps ix 15.

25. *the song.* On Ugaritic-Hebrew *'ny,* "to sing an antiphonal song," see T. H. Gaster in JAOS 66 (1946), 56. Cf. also Ps cxxxii 1, "Remember David, O Yahweh, and all his psalmody (*'anūtō*)," and Ps cxlvii 7.

did not turn his face. For the expression *histīr pānāyw,* with the infixed *-t-* conjugation from *sūr,* see NOTE on Ps x 11. LXX reads *apéstrepsen,* and the CCD correctly renders "nor did he turn his face away," though no explanatory note is appended.

26. *One hundred times.* Pointing consonantal *m'tk* as *mī'ētīkā,* a piel denominative verb from *mē'āh,* "hundred," followed by a datival suffix, precisely as in Ugar. *aṯnyk,* "I shall repeat to you." Consult the article on non-accusative suffixes by Bogaert in *Biblica* 45 (1964), 220–47, especially p. 231.

27. *your heart.* The Vrs. were bothered by the suffix of *lebabekem,* but it evidently refers to the members of the congregation being addressed by the psalmist, who recounts his deliverance from his enemies through divine assistance.

28. *return to Yahweh.* Implying in Jerusalem. There may be an allusion here to the theme which made Jerusalem the navel of the earth, a motif discussed in connection with Ps xlviii 3. The book of A. J. Wensinck, *The Ideas of the Western Semites regarding the Navel of Earth* (Amsterdam, 1916), is unavailable to me. The mention of "all the ends of the earth" suggests that this motif may be present in Ps lix 14, *weyēde'ū kī 'elōhīm mōšēl beya'aqōb le'apsē hā'āreṣ,* "That they might know that God rules from Jacob to the ends of the earth." God's

governance of the world radiated from Israel, the navel of the earth.

before him. The usual emendation of second-person *l^epānekā* to third-person *l^epānāyw,* following some MSS and LXX, Syr. and *Juxta Hebraeos,* is sustained by its balance with third-person Yahweh but invalidated by the parallelism between the second person and the third person in vs. 26, "One hundred times will I repeat to *you* . . . before them who fear *him.*" This disconcerting shift of persons, which characterizes the prophetic style as observed by *La Bible de la Pléiade,* II, p. 800, in a note to Nah iii 9, is not unlike the unexpected change from the singular to the plural number remarked at Ps v 10. Cf. final two cola of Pss lxxiii 28 and cii 16.

29. *truly is Yahweh.* Parsing the *l* of *lyhwh* as *lamedh emphaticum,* a particle whose existence was recognized in Hebrew at the beginning of the century by Paul Haupt; he argued from Arabic and Akkadian analogues. The rich attestation of this particle in Northwest Semitic allows the Hebraist to move with greater assurance, since Ugaritic offers so many examples which closely parallel those that have been heretofore identified in the Bible. The most recent article on the subject is that of Jorge Mejía, *"El lamed enfático en nuevos textos del Antiguo Testamento,"* in *Estudios Biblicos* 22 (1963), 179–90, with bibliography. Cf. also Dahood, PNWSP, p. 8, n. 2, p. 72.

Examples of emphatic *lamedh* in the Psalter number Pss xxv 14, lxix 11, 23, lxxxv 10 (*Biblica* 37 [1956], 338–40), lxxxix 19 (twice), ci 5, cix 16, cx 3. As commentary on the present verse, the most relevant passage is Ps lxxxix 19, *kī lyhwh m^egānēnū* (MT *māginnēnū*) *w^elīqdōš yiśrā'ēl malkēnū,* "For truly Yahweh himself is our Suzerain, the Holy One of Israel is himself our King." Cf. Johnson, *Sacral Kingship in Israel,* p. 100, n. 31, on Ps lxxxix 19.

the king. The pairing with concrete *mōšēl,* "ruler," suggests that abstract *m^elūkāh* traces a semantic development much like that of Hebrew-Phoenician abstract *mmlkt,* "royalty, kingdom," which frequently denotes concretely, "king." On *mmlkt,* "king," see W. L. Moran in BCCT, pp. 7–20. Other texts with *m^elūkāh,* "king," include II Sam xii 26 (cf. vs. 30); I Kings i 46; Isa xxxiv 12; Jer x 7 (vocalizing *m^elūkōtām*); Ezek xvi 13.

30. *Indeed to him.* With many commentators, reading *'ak lō* for MT *'āk^elū.*

who sleep. Analyzing consonantal *dšny* into relative pronoun *dī,* as in Ugaritic and Aramaic, and *šēnē*<*y^ešēnē,* from *yāšēn,* "to sleep," with syncope of the initial syllable of *y^ešēnē.* Other instances of syncope are discussed in NOTE on Ps xxiii 6.

For the thought, note Dan xii 2, *y^ešēnē 'admat 'āpār,* "those who sleep in the land of mud," and Ps xiii 3, *pannē 'īšān hammāwet,* "Avert the sleep of death."

the nether world. The frequent pairing of *'ereṣ,* "nether world," and *'āpār,* "mud," finds a counterpart in UT, 76:II:24–25, *nṭ'n barṣ iby wb'pr qm aḫk,* "We have planted my foes in the nether world, and in the mud those who rose up against your brother." On *'ereṣ,* "nether world," cf. NOTE on Ps xviii 8.

the Victor himself. Reading (for MT *lō'*) *lē',* a stative participle like *gēr,* or Ugar. *ib,* "foe," from *l'y,* a root frequently attested in Ugaritic and Phoenician. The most suggestive use is in the divine appellative *'lyn b'l,* "the Victor Baal." See my comments in *Mélanges Eugène Tisserant,* I, p. 92. The following texts might be studied in the light of *l'y,* "to be strong, prevail": (a) I Sam ii 3, *kī 'ēl dē'ōt yhwh w*^{e}*lē'ōn tōkēn '*^{a}*līlōt* (MT *w*^{e}*lō' nitk*^{e}*nū '*^{a}*līlōt*), "For a God of knowledge is Yahweh, and the Victor is a weigher of actions"—the title *lē'ōn* seems to coincide morphologically with the adjective found in UT, 127:13–14, *š'tqt dm lan,* "Sha'taqat, be victorious!" The same form apparently being present in Hab i 12, *'*^{e}*lōhē qodšī lē'ōn māwet* (MT *'*^{e}*lōhay q*^{e}*dōšī lō' nāmūt*), "My holy God is the Victor over Death"; (b) Ps lxxv 7, *kī lē'* (MT *lō'*) *mimmōṣā' ūmimma'*^{a}*rāb w*^{e}*lē' mimmidbār hārīm,* "For he is the Victor from the East and from the West; he is the Victor from the desert to the mountains"; (c) Ps lxxxv 7, *hallē' 'attāh* (MT *h*^{a}*lō' 'attāh*) *tāšūb t*^{e}*ḥayyēnū,* "You are the Victor, you will again revive us"; (d) Job xiii 15, *hēn yiqṭ*^{e}*lēnī lē'* (MT *lō'*) *'*^{a}*yaḥēl 'ak d*^{e}*rākāy 'el pānāyw 'ōkī*^{a}*ḥ,* "If the Victor should slay me, I will yet hope; indeed, I will defend my conduct to his face." Cf. Pss xxvii 13, c 3; Mal ii 15. What should be noticed in many of these passages is the association of the divine title *lē'* or *lē'ōn* with questions of life and death.

31. *my progeny.* With Vrs., pointing *zar'ī* for MT *zera'.*

forever. That unreduplicated *dōr* can signify "eternity" follows from the clearer understanding of Pss xii 8, xxiv 6, lxxi 18.

32. *May they begin. yābō'ū* seems to serve an inchoative function like Ugaritic-Arabic *'aḫada, qāma,* etc.; cf. UT, § 13.52. Similar syntax is found in Gen xxxvii 35; Pss xlii 3, cix 28; Job xxix 8, xxxvii 14; see Dahood in BCCT, pp. 68 f.

generosity. For this connotation of *ṣ*^{e}*dāqāh,* well attested in Qumranic literature, see Zorell, ZLH, p. 648a, and NOTE on Ps v 9.

a people yet to be born. With *'am nōlād,* cf. Ps cii 19, *'am nibrā',* "a people yet to be created."

he has acted. Cf. Ps cxviii 24, *zeh hayyōm 'āśāh yhwh,* "This is the day Yahweh acted."

PSALM 23

(xxiii 1–6)

1 *A psalm of David.*

Yahweh is my shepherd,
I shall not lack.
2 In green meadows he will make me lie down;
Near tranquil waters will he guide me,
to refresh my being. [3]*
3 He will lead me into luxuriant pastures,
as befits his name.
4 Even though I should walk
in the midst of total darkness,
I shall fear no danger
since you are with me.
Your rod and your staff—
behold, they will lead me.
5 You prepare my table before me,
in front of my adversaries.
You generously anoint my head with oil,
my cup overflows.
6 Surely goodness and kindness will attend me,
all the days of my life;
And I shall dwell in the house of Yahweh
for days without end.

* Verse 3 in RSV begins with this line.

NOTES

xxiii. A psalm of trust or confidence; cf. NOTE on Ps xi. The psalmist is quietly confident that Yahweh is his shepherd, who will guide him through the vicissitudes of this life to the eternal bliss of Paradise. Verses 2–3 are a description of the Elysian Fields that closely resembles the one given in Ps xxxvi 9–10, while vss. 4–5 describe life upon earth under God's watchful protection. Verse 6a summarizes vss. 4–5 and 6b resumes the thought of vss. 2–3. Thus there is a chiastic arrangement of verses and thoughts.

1. *my shepherd.* Compare Ps xlix 15, where Mot is portrayed as the shepherd of Sheol.

I shall not lack. Implying neither in this life nor in the next. Note that in the description of the afterlife in Ps lxxiii 23–25 there occurs the question in vs. 25, *mī lī baššāmāyim weʻimmekā lō' ḥāpaṣtī bā'āreṣ,* "What shall I lack in heaven, and with you I have no interest in earth." On *mī,* "what," cf. Speiser, *Genesis* (The Anchor Bible, vol. 1), NOTE on xxxiii 8; Isa li 12; Mic i 5; Ruth iii 16.

The rare absolute use of *ḥāsēr,* "to lack" (Prov xiii 25; Neh ix 2), is now matched by Ugaritic usage in UT, 2065:14–17, *irš ʻmy mnm irštk dḫsrt wank aštn l iḫy,* "Request of me whatever may be your desideratum for what is lacking, and I shall give it to my brother."

2. *he will make me lie down.* Contrary to the usual versions, the *yqtl* verb forms in vss. 2–3 are rendered as future rather than as present tense.

Near tranquil waters. Water forms an essential element in the description of the Elysian Fields; cf. NOTE on Ps xxxvi 10.

The precise force of *ʻal* is notably clarified by Ugaritic practice in which *ʻl* sometimes denotes "near." For example, UT, 1 Aqht:152–53, *ylk qr mym dʻlk mḫṣ aqht ǵzr,* "Woe to you, O fountain of waters, since near you was struck down Aqhat the hero." The occasional emendation of *ʻal* to *'el* becomes dispensable; consult Pío Suárez, "Praepositio ʻal=coram in Litteratura Ugaritica et Hebraica-Biblica," in *Verbum Domini* 42 (1964), 71–80.

3. *He will lead me.* One may fairly describe *yanḥēnī* as a *terminus technicus* denoting "to lead into Paradise"; cf. NOTE on Ps v 9.

into luxuriant pastures. Semantically, *yanḥēnī bemaʻgelē ṣedeq* appears to be synonymous with vs. 2, *bīne'ōt deše' yarbīṣēnī,* and structurally, forms with it a chiasmus and an inclusion. Hence hapax legomenon *maʻgelē ṣedeq* equals *ne'ōt deše',* "green meadows," an inference borne out by comparison with Ps lxv 12–13, *ūmaʻgālekā yirʻapū dāšen yirʻapū ne'ōt midbār,* "And may your pastures drip with fatness, may the meadows in the wilderness drip." Here *maʻgālīm* is synonymous with *ne'ōt* and is rendered by LXX *ta pedía sou,* "your fields." The notion of "abundance" inherent in the root *ṣedeq* has been examined at Ps v 9. Particularly relevant is Joel ii 23, *kī nātan lākem 'et hammōreh līṣedāqāh,* "Indeed he gave you the early rain in abundance."

4. *in the midst.* LXX reads here *en mésō,* which is probably correct. Thus *gē'* is related to *ga'awāh,* "back, midst," found in Deut

xxxiii 26 and Job xli 7, as proposed in *Biblica* 45 (1964), 398 f., and in Pss x 2 and xlvi 4 (see NOTE there). It is also connected with Heb. *gēw* and Aram. *gawwā'*, "midst"; hence one may raise the question whether Phoen. *bgw*, "in the midst," is really an Aramaism, as virtually all philologians insist, or just a word common to the various Northwest Semitic dialects.

total darkness. Though often described as a rabbinic conceit, the vocalization of *ṣalmāwet* may prove to be correct, with *māwet* serving the function of a superlative. Composite nouns in Hebrew are more frequent than grammars allow, especially since they are clearly attested in the Ras Shamra tablets; see NOTES on Pss v 5 and xxxvi 5, and for *ṣalmāwet,* Thomas in JSS 7 (1962), 199 f.

behold. Identifying *hēmmāh* with the Ugaritic interjection *hm,* "behold," examined in the NOTE on Ps ix 8. Compare Ps xliii 3, "Send forth your light and your truth; behold, let them lead me (*hēmmāh yanḥūnī*)."

they will lead me. The consonantal cluster *ynḥmny* may well contain an internal "enclitic" *mem* which follows the root and precedes the pronominal suffix. Hence the verb is *nāḥāh,* "to lead," found in vs. 3 and in the cognate context of Ps xliii 3; see preceding paragraph. D. N. Freedman has called my attention to a similar occurrence of internal "enclitic" *mem* involving the same consonants (but a different root *nwḥ*) in Gen v 29. Cf. Phoen. *lhdd b'lmy,* "to Haddad his lord," which analyzes into *b'l* plus internal "enclitic" *mem* followed by pronominal suffix *-y.* Cf. Dahood, *Gregorianum* 43 (1962), 66, for other biblical examples.

5. *You prepare my table.* Ugar. *ṯlḥn,* "table," is a glaring example of the impact of the Ras Shamra tablets upon Hebrew phonetics and etymology, as well as upon biblical exegesis. Hebrew lexicons have been associating *šulḥān* with Ar. *salaḫa,* "to strip off the hide," while commentators (e.g., Briggs, CECBP, I, p. 202), on the basis of the Arabic etymology, describe *šulḥān* as "a mat or piece of leather spread on ground." The *Lexicon* of Koehler and Baumgartner (1953) continued to list this false Arabic etymology, but in their *Supplementum ad Lexicon in Veteris Testamenti Libros* (Leiden, 1958), p. 190, one finds this correction: "Ugar. *ṯlḥn* (connexum c. Arab. *slḫ* excludit)." The false etymology has not, however, been completely exorcised from biblical commentaries. Thus one reads in Edgar Jones, *Proverbs and Ecclesiastes* (London, 1961), p. 104 (on Prov ix 2), "The word for TABLE refers to some material, leather or straw, spread out on the ground." Shades of Arabic *slḫ!* In translation, *šulḥān* is entitled to a suffix by virtue of its balance with suffixed *rō'šī* and *kōsī.*

in front of my adversaries. A petty ruler of the fourteenth century

B.C. addressed the following request to the Pharaoh: "May he give gifts to his servants while our enemies look on" (El Amarna, 100: 33–35).

my cup overflows. The presence of *šulḥan* and *kōsī* in the same verse recalls UT, 51:III:14–16, *štt p*[. . .] *bṯlḥny bks ištynh,* where suffixed *ṯlḥny,* "my table," is paired with *ks,* "my cup"; in the biblical verse the situation is reversed.

6. *goodness and kindness.* The metaphor may be an adaptation of the motif of two attendants accompanying a god or a dignitary; cf. Pss xxv 21, xxxvii 37, xliii 3, lxxxix 15; Hab iii 5. In Canaanite myth, the gods are often accompanied by two messengers; cf. Ginsberg, "Baal's Two Messengers," BASOR 95 (1944), 25–30. See Geo Widengren, "Early Hebrew Myths and Their Interpretation," in *Myth, Ritual, and Kingship,* ed. S. H. Hooke (Oxford, 1958), pp. 149–203, especially p. 163; Gaster, *Thespis,* 1961, pp. 157 f.

I shall dwell. Two equally probable explanations are possible for MT *wešabtī* in light of Northwest Semitic philology. First, it may be a contracted form of *weyāšabtī,* just as Ugar. *wld* (*walādu*) is contracted from *wa* and the infinitive absolute *yalādu,* according to the analysis of Ginsberg, LKK, p. 40. See the favorable comments on Ginsberg's analysis by W. Baumgartner in JBL 67 (1948), 405; A. D. Singer in JPOS 21 (1948), 104; W. F. Albright in JBL 69 (1950), 387. Other instances of syncopation are in Isa i 27 (again with *yāšab*), xxxvii 27; Jer xii 13.

The second possibility is that *wešabtī* stems from *šwb,* "to sit, dwell," a by-form of *yāšab,* discussed in the NOTE on Ps vii 8. See UT, Glossary, No. 1177, p. 416. J. Giblet's allegation in *Supplément au Dictionnaire de la Bible,* Fascicule 38 (Paris, 1963), col. 640, that I defend the emendation of Isa xxx 15 *šūbāh* to *šebet* simply does not accord with the facts. In CBQ 20 (1958), 41–43, I defended the reading *šūbāh* but derived it from *yšb,* "to sit," not from *šwb,* "to turn back," and rendered it "sitting still." Today I would continue to translate it "sitting still" but would prefer a derivation from the by-form *šwb,* "to sit," as morphologically more feasible. The three parallel substantives in Isa xxx 15 clearly show that *šūbāh* does not mean "conversion."

in the house of Yahweh. Note that the Tetragrammaton occurs but at the beginning of the psalm and at the very end; this suggests that this poem, like Ps xxix, may be an adaptation of an older non-Israelite composition.

Like *hēkāl,* "palace," which in a number of passages refers to God's celestial habitation (cf. NOTE on Ps xxix 10), *bēt* here, in Pss xxvii 4, xxxi 3, xxxvi 9, and Isa vi 4, signifies the heavenly dwelling of Yahweh. After a peaceful life under the guidance and protection of

Yahweh, the psalmist looks forward to eternal happiness in God's celestial abode. Cf. especially Ps xxvii 4.

for days without end. Literally "for length of days." Cf. Ps xxi 5 where *'ōrek yāmīm* is the parallel synonym of *ḥayyīm,* "life eternal," and UT, 1018:20–22, *wurk ym b'ly lpn amn w l pn il mṣrm,* "And length of days for my lord in the presence of Amon and in the presence of the gods of Egypt." The phrase *'rk ymm* likewise occurs in Phoenician Karatepe, III:5, a further indication of how closely the Northwest Semitic dialects are related.

PSALM 24

(xxiv 1–10)

1 A *psalm of David.*

The earth is Yahweh's and its fullness,
the world and those who dwell therein.
2 For he based it upon the seas,
established it upon the ocean currents.
3 Who shall ascend the mountain of Yahweh?
And who shall stand in his holy place?
4 The clean of hands and pure of heart;
who has not raised his mind to an idol,
nor sworn by a fraud.
5 He shall receive blessings from Yahweh,
and generous treatment from his saving God.
6 The One of Eternity seek,
O you who search for the Presence of Jacob. *Selah*
7 Lift up your heads, O gates!
and be lifted up, O gates of the Eternal!
For the King of Glory is coming!
8 Who, then, is the King of Glory?
Yahweh strong and mighty,
Yahweh mighty in battle.
9 Lift up your heads, O gates!
Lift them up, O gates of the Eternal!
for the King of Glory is coming.
10 Who, then, is the King of Glory?
Yahweh of hosts,
He is the King of Glory. *Selah*

NOTES

xxiv. A psalm composed for the liturgy, probably used in connection with a procession of the ark. The dialogue structure of the poem suggests that it was sung by alternating choirs; cf. II Sam vi 12 ff.

2. *he based it*. I.e., the pillars upon which the earth rests have been sunk into the subterranean ocean; cf. Job xxxviii 6; I Sam ii 8.

the ocean currents. This meaning of *nᵉhārōt* ‖ *yammīm* has been amply illustrated on the basis of UT, 68:12 ff., where *ym* is parallel to *nhr*, by Johnson, *Sacral Kingship in Ancient Israel*, p. 58, n. 3, and p. 101, and by Schmidt, *Königtum Gottes in Ugarit und Israel*, p. 29. Other instances of this meaning occur in Pss xlvi 5, lxxxix 26; Isa xliv 27; Jon ii 4.

4. *pure of heart*. With *bar lēbāb*, compare UT, 1005:2–4, *km špš d brt kmt br ṣtqšlm*, "Like the sun that is pure, so is Ṣidqi-Šalim pure." The biblical writer uses *bar* in a moral sense, while the Canaanite scribe intends it in a legal connotation.

his mind. The standard emendation of *napšī* to *napšō* becomes bootless once the existence of third-person suffix *-y* is recognized, as in Phoenician; cf. NOTE on Ps ii 6. The phrase "to raise one's mind," like *sursum corda*, means "to worship, adore." Cf. NOTE on Ps xvi 4.

to an idol. The evidence that *šāw'*, "emptiness, vanity," is also a term for "idol" is impressive. Thus Ps xxvi 4, *mᵉtē šāw'* are "idol worshipers," while Ps xxxi 7, *hablē šāw'* is correctly translated by *Bible de Jérusalem* (Paris, 1956), p. 680, *"idoles vaines."* Ps cxix 37, *ha'ᵃbēr 'ēnay mērᵉ'ōt šāw'*, "Prevent my eyes from looking at an idol," while Jon ii 9, *hablē šāw'* is understood by many exegetes to signify "vain idols." With our sentiment, cf. Jer v 7, *wayyiššābᵉ'ū bᵉlō' 'ᵉlōhīm*, "And they swore by no-gods." See also Isa i 13; Jer xviii 15; Ezek xviii 5; Job xxxi 5.

by a fraud. Abstract *mirmāh*, "deceit," concretely refers to an idol, i.e., "a fraud." Cf. NOTE on Ps v 7. The same sequence of the ideas "to worship" and "to take an oath" is found in Ps xvi 4.

5. *generous treatment*. For this sense of *ṣᵉdāqāh*, see Zorell, ZLH, p. 684a, who writes, "From the benevolent justice of God flow generous gifts that are given to the just" [*"ex benevola iustitia Dei fluunt larga dona quae iustis dantur"*]. He then cites a list of nouns with which *ṣᵉdāqāh* is found in parallelism; cf. Isa xxxiii 5, xlv 8, xlviii 18; Ps lxxii 3; etc. See NOTE on Ps xxiii 3.

6. *The One of Eternity*. *zeh dōr* is the equivalent of *'l d 'lm*, "El,

the One of Eternity," found in the Sinai Inscription and studied by Cross, in HTR 55 (1962), 225–59, especially p. 238 f. A very instructive parallel is Ps lxxv 10, *wa'anī 'agaddēl* (MT *'aggīd l*) *'ōlām 'azammerāh lē'lōhē ya'aqōb,* "But I shall tell out the greatness of the Eternal One, sing to the God of Jacob." As in the present verse, there is mention of the Eternal and of the God of Jacob. On the divine appellative *'ōlām,* see Cross and Freedman, JBL 67 (1948), 201 f.; Dahood, PNWSP, p. 45, n. 4, with bibliography.

On *zeh,* "the one of," cf. Judg v 5, *zeh sīnay,* "the One of Sinai," and Moran, "The Hebrew Language in Its Northwest Semitic Background," in *The Bible and the Ancient Near East,* p. 61. D. N. Freedman has called my attention to two new examples of this usage in Ps lxxv 8.

That *dōr* alone (as against *dōr wādōr*) can signify "eternity" is the conclusion to which Pss xii 8, xxii 31, and lxxi 18 point.

seek. Vocalizing qal imperative *direšū* for MT *dōrešāw.*

the Presence of Jacob. Reading (for MT *pānekā ya'aqōb*) *penē-kī ya'aqōb,* with *kī* parsed as emphatic *kī* set in the middle of a construct chain, much like enclitic *mi,* later merely *m.* This analysis accords with the conclusion reached in various recent studies that biblical poets were prone to interpose emphatic particles between the *regens* and the genitive. See NOTE on Ps xviii 18. The LXX reading supports this reconstruction: "who seek the face of the God of Jacob."

"The Presence of Jacob" seems to be a divine appellative based on Exod xxxiii 14. On the signification of *pānīm,* "Presence," see Albright, *From the Stone Age to Christianity,* p. 298, who compares the late Canaanite (Carthaginian) idea that Tinnit was the "presence (power) of Baal." Cf. G. von Rad, *Theologie des Alten Testaments* (München, 1962), p. 298, and see NOTES below on Pss xlii 12 and xliii 5.

7. *Lift up your heads.* An idiom denoting "to rejoice, be of good hope," found in UT, 126:III:12–16, *nšu riš ḥrṯm lẓr 'db dgn kly lḥm bdnhm kly yn bḥmthm kly šmn bq*[*bthm?*], "The plowmen lift up their heads, upwards the planters of wheat. For spent was the grain from their jars, spent the wine from their bottles, spent the oil from their vats (?)." This is a description of the reaction of the farmers to the coming of the first rains after the long summer drought. Cf. Luke xxi 28. Also important for the exegesis of the phrase is Zech ix 9, *gīlī me'ōd bat ṣiyyōn . . . hinnēh malkēk yābō' lāk,* "Rejoice greatly, O daughter Zion . . . behold your king is coming to you."

and be lifted up. Stylistically noteworthy is the fact that two different conjugations of *nāśā'* are employed in the same verse. The same phenomenon may be noticed in Ps xxix 5, *šōbēr* and *yešabbēr,* and in Ps xxxviii 3, piel *niḥatū* and qal *wattinḥat.*

gates of the Eternal. On the divine appellative *'ōlām,* see NOTE on vs. 6. The relationship between the king of a city and its gates is highlighted by one of the king's titles which has come to light in UT, 1007, where some of the titles of King Niqmepa', the son of Niqmad, king of Ugarit, are listed; his titles include (lines 4–8), *b'l ṣdq skn bt mlk ṯǵr [m]lk bny,* "Legitimate lord, governor of the palace, king of the gate (metonymy for city?), builder king." The personified gates welcome home the conquering hero.

8. *Who, then.* In the interrogative phrase *mī zeh,* the pronoun *zeh* is attached enclitically, almost as an adverb to impart directness and force; cf. BDB, p. 261a, 4. Another example occurs in Ps xxv 12, not listed by BDB.

strong and mighty. In the classic description of the God of Eternity in Isa xl 28–31, the attributes of power and strength stand forth. These are also the qualities that are prominent in Deut xxxiii 27, as translated and interpreted by Dahood, PNWSP, p. 45.

PSALM 25

(xxv 1–22)

1 *Of David.*

To you, O Yahweh, I raise my mind.
2 My God, in you do I trust,
let me not be humiliated;
Let not my foes gloat over me.
3 None who invoke you aloud will be humiliated;
humiliated will be the faithless through idle talk.
4 Your ways, O Yahweh, make me know,
teach me your paths.
5 Make me walk faithful to you and teach me,
for you are the God who will save me.
It is you I invoke all the day long.
6 Remember, Yahweh, how ancient are
your compassion and your kindness.
7 The sins of my youth and my transgressions
remember not!
According to your kindness remember me,
in keeping with your goodness, Yahweh.
8 Good and upright is Yahweh,
and so he shows sinners his way.
9 He guides the humble in his justice,
and teaches the poor his way.
10 All the paths of Yahweh are kindness and truth,
for those who keep his covenant stipulations.
11 For your name's sake, O Lord,
forgive my iniquity,
great though it be.
12 Who, then, is the man who fears Yahweh?
him will he show the path he must choose.

13 His soul shall dwell at ease,
and his progeny will inherit the land.
14 The friendship of Yahweh is for those who fear him,
and his covenant he truly reveals to them.
15 My eyes are ever toward Yahweh,
for he will lead my feet out of the net.
16 Turn to me and have pity on me,
for alone and oppressed am I.
17 Anguish cramps my heart,
of my distress relieve me.
18 See my affliction and my trouble,
and take away all my sins.
19 See how numerous are my foes,
my treacherous enemies who hate me.
20 Preserve my life and rescue me;
let me not be humiliated since I trust in you.
21 Let integrity and uprightness safeguard me,
when I invoke you.
22 Ransom Israel, O God,
from all its anguish.

Notes

xxv. An individual lament in acrostic form, each successive verse beginning with another letter of the Hebrew alphabet.

2. *gloat over me.* Cooke, TNSI, p. 136, has compared Punic *k' 'lṣ' 'lty,* "For she exulted over me," with biblical *ya'al^{e}ṣū lī.*

3. *who invoke you aloud.* After Jacob Barth's discovery of the root *qāwāh,* "to call, invoke" (cf. Note on Ps xix 5), it should not be considered bold to propose that the six instances of the qal plural participle *qōwīm* be assigned to this root and not to *qwh,* "to wait for," whose finite form is witnessed only in the piel conjugation. This proposal does not slight the fact that there are several qal participles, such as *dōbēr, bārūk, šōḥēr* (Prov xi 27), and *šōqēr* (Prov xvii 4), whose finite forms are employed exclusively in other conjugations, but merely maintains that the texts in question can equally well (if not better) be explained from *qāwāh,* "to call." To be sure, the verbal forms of *qāwāh* uncovered by Barth (in Pss xl 2, lii 11) are pointed piel, but this doubtless is the result of their being identified by the Masoretes with *qiwwāh,* "to wait for." On this hypothesis, apparently otiose *gam* is made to work; its ancient Canaanite meaning comes to the fore, as

in a number of other passages discussed in *Biblica* 45 (1964), 399. A similar situation obtains in Judg v 4, where the double occurrence of *gam* has yet to be accounted for: *gam šāmayim nāṭāpū gam ʿābīm nāṭᵉpū māyim,* "With a loud voice the heavens dropped, with a loud voice the clouds dropped water," evidently the same theme that is expressed in Ps lxxxv 13, *gam yhwh yittēn haṭṭōb wᵉʾarṣēnū tittēn yᵉbūlāh,* "With a loud voice Yahweh gives his rain, and our land gives its produce."

the faithless through idle talk. The psalmist is embittered over friends who have betrayed him through malicious gossip. Both terms—*hobbōgᵉdīm rēqām*—have covenant associations. Thus in Hos vi 7; Mal ii 11; Ps lxxviii 57, *bāgad* means "to prove faithless to covenant stipulations," while in Ps vii 5, *rēqām* is used in connection with *šᵉlūmī,* "my covenant colleague."

5. *faithful to you.* Literally "in fidelity to you." From vs. 7 we learn that in his youth the psalmist had been guilty of certain sins and transgressions, while in vs. 11 the poet confesses that Yahweh had pardoned his "great iniquity." From other sources (cf. NOTE on vs. 11) we know that the "great sin" was idolatry; hence the poet's prayer for grace to remain faithful to Yahweh.

This too is the nuance borne by *baʾᵃmittekā* in Pss xxvi 3 and lxxxvi 11. This latter text is particularly illuminating since Ps lxxxvi belongs to the same literary genre as the present composition and employs *baʾᵃmittekā* in the context of a profession of faith in Yahweh and a repudiation of the pagan deities. Verse 8 of Ps lxxxvi reads, "There is none like you among the gods; O Yahweh, there is nothing like your works," and vs. 10 continues, "For you are great and the one who works wonders, you alone are God." Verse 11 reads, *hōrēnī yahweh darkekā ʾᵃhallēk baʾᵃmittekā,* "Teach me, O Yahweh, your way, that I might walk faithful to you." RSV recognizes this connotation in Ps xxvi 3, *wᵉhithallaktī baʾᵃmittekā,* "And I walk in faithfulness to thee," but overlooks this nuance in the other two texts.

It is you. The prominent position of the *nota accusativi ʾōtᵉkā* at the head of its clause confirms the exegesis of *baʾᵃmittekā* set forth in preceding NOTE. It is Yahweh that the poet invokes, not some other god whom he invoked in his youth.

I invoke. Pointing as qal *qāwītī;* see NOTE on vs. 3. Cf. Ps xxii 3, *ʾeqrāʾ yōmām,* "I call out by day."

6. *how ancient are.* An example of enjambment; see NOTES on vs. 19 and on Ps vii 3.

7. *sins of my youth.* Among them idolatry, as proposed in NOTE on vs. 5. Note that the Targum understood Ps xc 8, *ʿᵃlūmēnū,* normally rendered "our secret sins," as "sins of our youth."

remember me. According to some (e.g., Gunkel), the independent pronoun *'attāh* in the clause *kᵉḥasdᵉkā zᵉkōr lī 'attāh* serves to emphasize the suffix of *ḥasdᵉkā,* while others (e.g., Briggs) find it pointing to the subject in *zᵉkōr*. If the former analysis is accepted, we have fine syntactic analogues in Ugar. *šmk at,* "your own name" (UT, § 6.14), Phoenician Yeḥawmilk, 12, *šm 'nk yḥwmlk,* "My own name is Yeḥawmilk" (Donner and Röllig, KAI, II, p. 15), and Karatepe, II:5, *wbymty 'nk,* "and in my own days." This usage points up the close linguistic relationships between these three dialects of Northwest Semitic.

8. *he shows sinners*. There is an autobiographical touch here, since the poet had been guilty of various sins (cf. vss. 5, 7, 11) but through the kindness of Yahweh had returned to his service.

his way. The suffix of vs. 9 *darkō* apparently does triple duty: for *mišpāṭ* in vs. 9 and for *derek* in vs. 8. A similar usage is UT, 127:22–24, *yṯb krt l'dh yṯb lksi mlk lnḫt lkḥṯ drkt,* "Kirta sits upon his seat, he sits upon his royal throne, upon the peaceful bench of his authority." The determining suffix of *'dh,* "his seat," serves for the two succeeding cola. On double-duty suffixes, see NOTE on Ps iii 4.

9. *in his justice*. The lack of a suffix with *mišpāṭ,* which balances *darkō,* was possibly prompted by the poet's desire not to make the first colon longer than the second. By employing the double-duty suffix (really triple-duty; cf. preceding NOTE), the psalmist was able to maintain eight syllables in each half verse.

10. *his covenant stipulations*. An example of hendiadys.

11. *forgive my iniquity*. Parsing *wᵉ* of *wᵉsālaḥta* as *waw emphaticum,* a topic treated at Ps iv 5, where the particle precedes imperative *dommū,* rather than as a *waw consecutivum* with the perfect carrying on the jussive implicit in the previous verse (Briggs, CECBP). In view of the rather extensive use of the *waw emphaticum,* a subsumption under this heading seems indicated. Perfect *sālaḥtā* is precative, a subject discussed at Ps iii 8. *Juxta Hebraeos* rendered it correctly by imperative *propitiare* and a number of modern commentators (e.g., Baethgen, Gunkel) have recognized the imperative force of *sālaḥtā*.

great though it be. This phrase echoes the theme of "the great sin" commented upon at Ps xix 14. Since for the Israelites the "great sin" was idolatry, it is not far-fetched to submit that the sin alluded to by the psalmist in vss. 5, 7, 8, 18, was that of idolatry. See NOTE on vs. 5.

12. *Who, then*. On the phrase *mī zeh,* see NOTE on Ps xxiv 8.

13. *His soul shall dwell at ease*. This, the KJ of *napšō bᵉṭōb tālīn,* which has been variously rendered, receives confirmation from a Ugaritic text which collocates the same ideas as those of the present verse: UT, 2 Aqht:II:13–15, *wtnḫ birty npš kyld bn ly km aḫy wšrš km aryy,* "And my soul shall be at ease in my breast, for a son is born to me like my brethren's, a scion like my kindred's."

will inherit the land. The central concern of the Legend of King Keret is the continuation of his dynasty; hence the term *yrṯ,* "heir," occurs a number of times in this text.

14. *friendship of Yahweh.* Gunkel's observation (*Die Psalmen,* p. 108) that *sōd* here bears the connotation "friendship" is supported by remarking that it stands parallel to *bᵉrīt,* "covenant." That these two notions were associated comes out clearly in the three occurrences of the expression *'dy' wṭbt',* "the treaty and the friendship," in the Aramaic treaty texts of Sefire. See W. L. Moran, "A Note on the Treaty Terminology of the Sefire Stelas," JNES 22 (1963), 173–76. In the Akkadian expression *ṭubtu ù šulummū,* "friendship and peace," the peace is that effected by treaty, as noted by Moran, *ibid.,* p. 174.

he truly reveals to them. Parsing *lᵉ* of *lᵉhōdī'ām* as *lamedh emphaticum,* a particle discussed in the NOTE on Ps xxii 29, while *hōdī'ām* is the preterite hiphil of *yd'.* See NOTE on vs. 11 for the emphatic *waw.* The postposition of the verb may be due to the emphasizing nature of the particle, like emphatic *kī,* which often effects the postposition of the verb in Ugaritic and Hebrew, as remarked at Ps xlix 16. Other attestations of postposition with emphatic *lamedh* are found in Pss xxxi 3, cix 16; Isa xxxviii 20; Hab iii 6–7; on the last text see W. F. Albright in *Studies in Old Testament Prophecy,* ed. H. H. Rowley (see Selected Bibliography), p. 15, n. u, with bibliography. Ugaritic examples number UT, 51:v:66, *šbt dqnk ltsrk,* "The grayness of your beard has truly instructed you," and Krt:12, *aṯt ṣdqh lypq,* "His legitimate wife he truly found."

16. *alone and oppressed.* Relating *yāḥīd* to Ugar. *yḥd,* "a person without kith or kin"; see UT, Glossary, No. 1087.

17. *Anguish cramps my heart.* An uncertain version. The most attractive solution is to parse *hirḥībū* as *hiphil privativum,* like *hōrīš,* "to dispossess," the hiphil privative of *yāraš,* "to possess," See G. Bergsträsser, *Hebräische Grammatik,* (Leipzig, 1929), II Teil, § 19g. Unexplained *yaršīᵃ'* in I Sam xiv 47 makes excellent sense on this hypothesis: "he removed evil," the idea expressed by King Azitawaddu in Karatepe, I:9, *wtrq 'nk hr' 'š kn b'rṣ,* "And I removed the evil that was in the land."

The close relationship of Ugaritic to Hebrew is further evident from the fact that Ugaritic also employed the causative privative in UT, Krt:24–25, *wbtmhn špḥ yitbd wbpḫyrh yrṯ,* "And in its entirety his family perished, and in its totality dispossessed." An unpublished incantatory tablet from Ras Shamra, reported on by C. Virolleaud in GLECS 10 (1964), 5–6, contains the phrase *šmrr nḥš 'qšr,* which is apparently synonymous with the expression *ydy ḥmt,* "He expelled the poison," that occurs later in the incantation. Hence *šmrr* must be a shaphel privative denoting "Remove the venom," a denominative from *mrr* in the specific sense of "venom" that is found in Ps lxiv 4 and Job xx 14.

my distress. The root of *m*ᵉ*ṣûqōtay* appears in UT, 1012:27, *w hn ibm šṣq ly,* "And look, my foes are pressing me." The psalmist's distress is probably caused by remorse stemming from his sin of idolatry.

19. *how numerous.* Cf. NOTE on vs. 6.

my treacherous enemies. Balancing *'ōy*ᵉ*bay, śin'at ḥāmās* is another example of an abstract noun acquiring a concrete meaning by virtue of its parallelism with a concrete noun. Cf. NOTE on Ps v 8 and compare Prov viii 13.

21. *integrity and uprightness.* Personified as two messengers sent by God to accompany and protect the psalmist. This is also the metaphor in Pss xxxvii 37, xliii 3, "Send forth your light and your truth—behold, let them lead me," and lxii 8, *ḥesed we'*ᵉ*met mūnū* (MT *man*) *yinṣ*ᵉ*rūhū,* "Kindness and truth have been appointed to safeguard him." Cf. NOTE on Ps xxiii 6.

This interpretation of *tōm wāyōšer* makes it difficult to maintain that "integrity and uprightness" are intrinsic virtues of the poet who confesses himself guilty of serious sin in vss. 4, 7, 8, 11. *The Oxford Annotated Bible,* eds. H. G. May and B. M. Metzger (Oxford, 1962), describes vs. 21 as a protestation of innocence, and Kraus, *Psalmen,* I, p. 209, argues from the phrase that the psalmist has been falsely accused, but these interpretations ill comport with the contents of the poem.

when I invoke you. Pointing as qal rather than piel with MT. This definition of *qāwītī* is supported by the related image in Ps xliii 3, where the messengers are sent upon the explicit request of the suppliant. Hence *qāwītī* more likely expresses a vocal action calling for help rather than silent expectation. See NOTE above on vs. 3.

22. *from all its anguish.* The possibility remains that here and in vs. 17 *ṣārōt* is a case of abstract for concrete noun and hence to be rendered "adversaries." One more properly ransoms from an adversary than from "anguish"; consult NOTE on Ps xxii 12.

PSALM 26

(xxvi 1–12)

1 *Of David.*

Judge me, O Yahweh!
On my word, I have walked in my integrity,
and in Yahweh have I trusted;
I have not wavered!
2 Examine me, O Yahweh, and try me,
testing my heart and my mind.
3 Indeed your love has ever been before my eyes,
and I have walked faithful to you.
4 I have not sat with idol-worshipers,
nor entered the home of the benighted.
5 I have hated the company of evildoers,
and with the wicked never sat down.
6 I have washed my hands in innocence,
that I might march around your altar, O Yahweh,
7 Proclaiming aloud your praise,
and rehearsing all your wonders.
8 O Yahweh, I love to live in your house,
the home where your glory dwells.
9 Snatch me not away with sinners,
nor my life with men of idols,
10 In whose left hand are idols,
and whose right hand is full of bribes.
11 But as for me, I have walked in my integrity,
ransom me and show me your mercy.
12 My foot has stood firm among the upright,
in the congregations I have adored Yahweh.

Notes

xxvi. A psalm of innocence. Accused of idol-worship, the psalmist responds with a plea for judgment (vss. 1–2), a protestation of innocence (3–7), a prayer to Yahweh (8–10), and a reaffirmation of his innocence (11–12).

1. *Judge me, O Yahweh.* The Psalmist intrepidly asks for a clear-cut decision, convinced as he is of his innocence. Hence it is somewhat inexact to categorize vss. 1–3 as a cry for vindication (e.g., *The Oxford Annotated Bible*) since it is difficult to see in what respect vindication was needed. As Briggs (CECBP, I, p. 231) has noted, "The context shows that the Psalmist was assured of his integrity, and all that was needed was divine recognition and acceptance in worship."

On my word. Parsing *kī* as an emphatic particle rather than an adverb introducing the cause.

I have not wavered. The staccato translation attempts to reflect the staccato style of the original.

2. *testing . . .* Consonantal *ṣrwph* may well represent the infinitive absolute *ṣārōp,* followed by adverbial *-h,* (vocalized *ṣārōpāh*) a construction attested in UT, 125:29, *yqrb trẓẓh,* "He approaches on the run"; see Ginsberg, LKK, p. 40. Other possible instances in UT, 128:III:7, *'dt ilm ṯlṯh,* "the council of the gods in its threefoldness," 'nt:II:19, *wl šb't tmtḫṣh,* "But she is not sated with smiting"; contrast, however, J. Aistleitner, *Untersuchungen zur Grammatik des Ugaritischen* (Berlin, 1954), p. 71. Cf. further UT, 1029:8–9, *ṯlṯ alp ṣpr dt aḫd ḥrṯh,* "Three oxen of ṢPR that are skilled in plowing," and Krt:205–6, *ṯnh kspm atn,* "Twice over in silver will I give."

my heart and my mind. Found here; in Ps vii 10; Jer xi 20, xvii 10, and xx 12, *kilyōtay wᵉlibbī* is now documented in UT, 1001:3, *klyth wlbh.* The Canaanite documentation of the phrase is enormously significant in that it necessitates the revaluation of a method long in use among biblical scholars, namely, the attempt to date the Psalms on the basis of similar phraseology. Thus Bonnard, *Le Psautier selon Jérémie,* p. 39, would find in the psalmist's use of this phrase a dependence upon Jeremiah, but the safest conclusion to draw is that both were heirs to an earlier Canaanite tradition long resident in Palestine. Similarly, in the work of Buttenwieser, PCTNT, the dates assigned to many of the Psalms are based on the similarity of language and metaphor subsisting between the Psalmists and Second Isaiah. The Ras Shamra finds, however, call into question the validity of this procedure.

3. *faithful to you.* With RSV, parsing the pronominal suffix of

ba'^a^mittekā as objective, not subjective; see NOTES on Pss xviii 24 and xxv 5, and see Ps lxxxvi 11.

4. *idol-worshipers.* Literally "men of the idol." For the phrase *m^e^tē šāw'*, see discussion under Ps xxiv 4.

home of the benighted. "Enter the home of" seems to be the apt equivalent of the hapax legomenon construction *'ābō' 'im.* In Ugaritic the more frequent sense of *'m* is "to, toward," with verbs of motion; UT, § 10.14. *na'^a^lāmīm* is parsed as niphal participle of *'ālam,* "to conceal, to be dark, ignorant"; compare Job xlii 3, *ma'līm 'ēṣāh,* "he who obscures counsel."

6. *I have washed my hands in innocence.* In other words, I have kept myself free of sin, as the parallelism in Ps lxxiii 13 makes clear: "All in vain have I kept my heart clean and washed my hands in innocence." More specifically, the innocence meant here is innocence of the sin of idolatry, if the cognate expression of Ps xxiv 4 is exegetically relevant: "The clean of hands (*n^e^qī kappayim*) and the pure of heart, who has not raised his mind to an idol."

Contrary to the prevailing view, *'erḥaṣ* expresses past time.

that I might march. Parsing *'^a^sōb^e^bāh* as subjunctive; cf. NOTES to Pss ix 15 and xxxix 5.

7. *your praise.* Paired with suffixed *nipl^e^'ōtekā, tōdāh* shares its double-duty suffix; see NOTE on Ps iii 4.

8. *I love to live in your house.* Reading *'āhabtī-m* (enclitic *mem*) *'ūn bēteka̅,* with *'ūn* parsed as infinitive construct, and *bēteka* as accusative object with verbs of dwelling; see GK, § 117bb. Or *bēteka̅* may stand for *b^e^bēteka̅* since with *bayit* the preposition *b^e^* is often elided in Hebrew and in Ugaritic; see UT, §§ 10.4; 11.8.

Though the lexicons usually list only one instance of the verb *'ūn,* "to live, dwell" (Isa xiii 22), K. Budde, *Der Segen Moses* (Tübingen, 1922), pp. 16–17, uncovered another instance in Deut xxxiii 28 that has found wide acceptance; cf. most recently Freedman in IEJ 13 (1963), 125–26. Its detection in Ps xci 9 may contribute to the resolution of a long-standing problem: *kī 'attāh yhwh maḥsī 'elyōn śamtā-m 'ūnekā,* "For you, O Yahweh, are my refuge; you, Most High, have granted me to dwell with you." For the construction of *'ūnekā,* cf. Pss v 5, *y^e^gūr^e^kā,* and xciv 20, *y^e^ḥobr^e^kā.*

The Levite Psalmist reminds Yahweh how much he treasures living in the temple in order to receive from him a judgment of not guilty; lacking such an acquittal, the Psalmist runs the risk of being banned from the temple.

the home. This more precise definition of *māqōm,* "place," results from comparison with Pss xxxvii 10, cxxxii 5; Mic i 3; Job vii 10, xviii 21, xx 9; and Gen xviii 33. On the last text, cf. Speiser, *Genesis* (The Anchor Bible, vol. 1), pp. 133 f.

your glory dwells. Schmidt in ZAW 75 (1963), 91 f., and Loewenstamm in IEJ 12 (1962), 163, have shown that *miškān* is a Canaanite loanword in the cultic language of Jerusalem.

9. *with sinners*. Polytheists are meant.

men of idols. *'anšē dāmīm* is a synonym of vs. 4, *m^e^tē šāw'*; on *dāmīm*, "images, idols," from *dāmāh*, "to be like," see NOTE on Ps v 7. The same phrase occurs in Ps cxxxix 19, which is also a psalm of innocence.

10. *In whose left hand*. Analyzing consonantal *ydyhm* into singular *yad* followed by the archaic genitive ending *-y* and the determining prononinal suffix *hem*. This follows from its pairing with singular *y^e^mīnām*, "their right hand."

Since *zimmāh* and *šōḥad* are two different and distinct things, *y^e^dīhem* and *y^e^mīnām* should refer to different hands. Melamed in *Studies in the Bible* (Scripta Hierosolymitana, VIII), pp. 145 f., has shown that in Judg iii 21, v 26, and II Sam xx 9–10 (long noted by Kimchi) *yad* specifically denotes "left hand." He could have added historical perspective to his arguments by appealing to Ugaritic, where similar usage obtains in several passages. For example, UT, 76:II:6–7, *qšthn aḫd bydh wqṣ'th bm ymnh*, "His bow he took in his left hand and his arrows in his right hand." Once it is appreciated that *yd* here refers to the left hand, the dispute whether *qṣ't* denotes "bow" or "arrows" is resolved in favor of the latter. Other examples of this conditioned meaning of *yd* are found in UT, Krt:66–67; 125:41.47. New biblical instances can be seen in Pss cxxxviii 7 and cxxxix 10. Melamed further proved that in Ps xci 7, *ṣad*, parallel to *yāmīn*, means "left side," and was able to cite the Targum, Rashi, and Ibn Ezra in support of his view.

are idols. Though it is usually difficult to give a precise translation of the fluid substantive *zimmāh*, the mention of "men of idols" in the previous verse notably relieves the uncertainty. What is more, the frequent use of *zimmāh* as a metaphor of idolatry of people under the figures of harlotry and adultery (Jer xiii 27; Ezek xvi 27, xxiii 21, etc.) points to the same definition. Its balance with concrete *šōḥad*, "bribes," permits abstract *zimmāh*, "idolatry," to assume a concrete signification in keeping with the practice examined in NOTE on Ps v 8. See NOTE on Ps xvii 3, *bal timṣā' zimmātī*, "You will find no idolatry in me."

11. *ransom me*. I.e., from the hands of those accusing me of idol-worship.

12. *has stood firm*. This sense of *'āmad* also appears in Ps xxx 8 and is confirmed by the observation that *'ām^e^dāh* forms an inclusion with vs. 1, *lō' 'em'ād*, "I have not wavered." At no time did the

Psalmist deviate from the path of Yahwism to walk in the way of idolatry.

among the upright. Explaining *mîšōr* as an abstract noun with a concrete meaning because it is in tandem with concrete "congregations," a phenomenon studied at Ps v 8. I am indebted to D. N. Freedman for this explanation.

in the congregations. Since *maqh*ᵉ*lîm* is a hapax legomenon, whereas *q*ᵉ*hēlîm* is twice attested, it is possible (but no more) that MT *b*ᵉ*maqhēlîm* should be divided to read *b*ᵉ*mō* (with *scriptio defectiva bm*) *q*ᵉ*hālîm;* thus emerges the prepositional sequence *b*ᵉ . . . *b*ᵉ*mō,* a sequence characteristic of the Keret legend. For example, UT, Krt: 66–67, *b . . . bm;* 101–2, *l . . . lm;* 103–5, *k . . . km.*

I have adored Yahweh. This forms an inclusion with vs. 1, "In Yahweh have I trusted." The mention of *raglî,* "my foot," in the first colon makes it possible to explain *'*ᵃ*bārēk* as a denominative verb from *berek,* "knee"; cf. NOTE on Ps x 3. The balance between *qtl* (*'ām*ᵉ*dāh*) and *yqtl* (*'*ᵃ*bārēk*) should be noted; cf. NOTE on Ps viii 7.

PSALM 27

(xxvii 1–14)

1 *Of David.*

Yahweh is my light and my salvation,
whom should I fear?
Yahweh is the stronghold of my life,
of whom should I be afraid?
2 When wicked men besiege me,
to devour my flesh;
My adversaries and my foes,
Lo! they stumble and fall.
3 Though an army encamp against me,
my heart will not fear;
Though troops should assail me,
even then will I be confident.
4 One thing I have asked a hundred times,
this, O Yahweh, do I seek:
To dwell in Yahweh's house
all the days of my life,
Gazing upon the loveliness of Yahweh,
awaking each dawn in his temple.
5 Indeed he will treasure me in his abode,
after the evil day;
He will shelter me in his sheltering tent,
will set me high upon his mountain.
6 And now my head is raised
above my foes on every side;
And so I will sacrifice in his tent
sacrifices with ovations;
I will sing and make music to Yahweh.

7 Hear, O Yahweh, my voice;
when I call
Have pity on me and answer me.
8 Come, said my heart, seek his face;
your face, O Yahweh, will I seek.
9 Turn not your face from me,
repel not in anger your servant,
Be my helper!
Do not reject me nor abandon me,
O God who can save me.
10 Though my father and my mother abandon me,
yet Yahweh will receive me.
11 Show me, O Yahweh, your way,
and lead me on an even path
because of my enemies.
12 Do not put me into the throat of my adversaries,
for false witnesses have testified against me,
as well as malicious testifiers.
13 In the Victor do I trust,
to behold the beauty of Yahweh
in the land of life eternal.
14 Wait for Yahweh!
be strong and let your heart be stout,
And wait for Yahweh!

NOTES

xxvii. A psalm of confidence; cf. NOTE on Ps xi. The psalmist is confident of Yahweh's protection in this life and is also convinced that he will gaze upon the loveliness of Yahweh in the next.

2. *to devour my flesh.* Metaphorical for "to reduce one to the last extremity," as in Isa ix 19, xlix 26; Jer li 57; Zech xi 9; Eccles iv 5 and, equivalently, in Phoenician Kilamuwa, 6–7, *km'š 'klt zqn w[km]'š 'klt yd,* "As though I were eating my beard, and as though I were eating my hand." Cf. CBQ 22 (1960), 404–6.

My adversaries and my foes. Note the unusual parallelism with the two subjects *ṣāray* *w*^{e}*'ōy*^{e}*bay* standing in the first colon while the two predicates *kāš*^{e}*lū* *w*^{e}*nāpālū* are placed in the second. Both subjects may be understood to go with both verbs. Cf. NOTE on Ps xxxv 23.

Lo! they stumble. Ambiguous *hēmmāh* may be either the independent pronoun or, more probably, the interjection occurring in Ugaritic as *hm,* examined in the Note on Ps ix 8.

3. *an army*. Like Heb. *maḥ*^{a}*neh,* Phoen. *mḥnt* denotes both "camp" and "army"; see Jean and Hoftijzer, *Dictionnaire . . . ,* p. 147.

Though troops. Since Hebrew idiom nowhere else attests "war rising up against me," *milḥāmāh* is preferably taken as referring to the participants in war. The parallelism with "army" corroborates this inference.

even then. b^{e}*zō't* is an adverbial expression related to adverbial *zeh* discussed at Ps xxiv 8. Cf. Lev xxvi 27 and Ps xli 12, *b*^{e}*zō't yāda'tī kī ḥāpaṣtā bī,* "Then shall I know that you love me."

4. This verse is a prayer for eternal bliss with Yahweh in heaven.

a hundred times. Reading (for MT *mē'ēt*) *mē'āt* or *m*^{e}*'at,* as in Eccles viii 12, *'*^{a}*šer ḥōṭē' 'ōśeh rā' m*^{e}*'at ūma'*^{a}*rīk lō,* "Because the sinner commits evil a hundred times and lives a long life." The feminine absolute ending in *-t* is normal in Ugaritic-Phoenician and is not unknown in Hebrew; e.g., Pss lviii 5, *ḥ*^{a}*mat,* "poison," lviii 9, *'ēšet,* "wife," and cxxxii 4, *š*^{e}*nat,* "sleep." Cf. GK, § 80, and Robert Gordis in *Biblica* 41 (1960), 398.

On prayers repeated a hundred times, see Note on Ps xxii 26.

To dwell. Construct infinitive *šibtī* stands in apposition with the accusatives *'aḥat* and *'ōtāh,* while the subsequent infinitives *laḥ*^{a}*zōt* and *l*^{e}*baqqēr* are circumstantial; cf. Note on Ps viii 3 and GK, § 114o.

Yahweh's house. The heavenly habitation of Yahweh is meant here, as in Ps xxiii 6, in the Note to which the evidence is cited.

Gazing. laḥ^{a}*zōt* is a circumstantial infinitive construct modifying *šibtī;* see Note above on *to dwell.*

The psalmist prays to receive the beatific vision in the next life. In Pss xi 7, xvii 15, xxi 7, and lxiii 3, *ḥāzāh* is the verb used to describe the act of beholding God face to face. See Note on Ps xvii 15, and Note below on vs. 13.

the loveliness of Yahweh. In UT, Krt:145, *n'm* is used to express the loveliness of the Canaanite goddess Anath: *dk n'm 'nt n'mh,* "whose loveliness is like the loveliness of Anath."

Here the poet refers to the beauty of Yahweh that he is sure he will behold in the future life. In vs. 13 the substantive *ṭūb* is used to describe the beauty of Yahweh, whereas here the poet employs *nō'am.*

awaking each dawn. The much-disputed *baqqēr* can satisfactorily be explained as a denominative verb from *bōqer,* "morning, dawn," just as *šiḥar,* "to seek diligently," may originally have meant "to arise at dawn." Ar. *bakkara* signifies "to arise very early in the morning."

For the thought, compare Ps xxx 6, "For death is in his anger, life eternal in his favor; in the evening one falls asleep in tears, but at dawn there are shouts of joy."

in his temple. hēkālō refers to the celestial temple of Yahweh; consult NOTE on Ps xxix 9.

5. *he will treasure me.* The mention of *ṣūr,* "mountain," in vs. 5b suggests that the verb *yiṣpᵉnēnī* may contain an allusion to Mount Zaphon (Ugar. *ǵr ṣpn*), the sacred mountain where the gods dwell in Canaanite mythology.

in his abode. The suffix of *sukkōh* resembles that of Byblian Phoenician *-h,* while in Ps xviii 12 (=II Sam xxii 12) and Job xxxvi 29 *sukkāh* refers to the celestial abode of Yahweh.

after the evil day. Understanding *bᵉ* of *bᵉyōm* as "from, after." "The evil day" (literally "the day of evil") means the day of death, as in Ps xlix 6.

sheltering tent. A case of hendiadys; literally "the shelter of his tent." The allusion is to God's dwelling in heaven; cf. Ps lxi 5 and the reference to the tent of the sun in Ps xix 5.

upon his mountain. No suffix is needed with *ṣūr* since parallel *'ohᵒlō* is provided with one; see NOTE on Ps iii 4.

6. *my head is raised.* Suggesting a sign of triumph. The psalmist's faith will overcome all the tribulations brought on by his foes.

Explaining *yārūm* as passive participle from the root *yrm,* studied in the NOTE on Ps xviii 47, where the balance with passive participle *bārūk* appears decisive.

7. *my voice.* Considerable discussion has centered about the stichic division of the verse, but meter indicates that *qōlī* terminates the first three-beat colon and *'eqrā'* begins the second three-beat colon.

when I call. 'eqrā' begins a conditional sentence lacking the morphological indicator *'im* or *kī.* This analysis will explain the presence of the *waw* of apodosis in *wᵉḥonnēnī* that is lacking in some MSS and which many critics would delete.

Have pity on me. Consult previous NOTE.

8. *Come, said my heart.* Reading qal imperative *lēk* from *hālak* for MT *lᵉkā;* cf. Ps xlv 15, where *lāk* should be read *lēk,* "Come!" and Ps cv 11, where grammatically dissonant *lᵉkā* should be pointed as qal imperative plural *lᵉkū,* "Come!"

seek his face. Reading imperative singular *baqqēš* for MT plural *baqqᵉšū* and attaching the final *waw* of consonantal *bqšw* to *pny* as *waw emphaticum,* a particle treated in the NOTE on Ps iv 5.

pānāy, "his face," is parsed as containing the third-person suffix *-y,* discussed in the NOTE on Ps ii 6. Particularly relevant is Job xli 2, *ūmī hū' lᵉpānay yityaṣṣāb,* "And who then can stand before his face?" Here the usual emendation to *lᵉpānāyw* can safely be discarded.

For the thought, see Ps cv 4, *baqqᵉšū pānāyw tāmīd,* "Seek his face always," and El Amarna, 165:5–7, "The beautiful face of the king, my lord, do I perpetually seek."

9. *Turn not your face. tastīr* belongs to the infixed *-t-* conjugation of *sūr,* "to turn aside," as correctly rendered by LXX *apostrépses* and Vulg. *avertas.* Cf. the balance of *sūr* with *nāṭāh* in Ps cii 3, and NOTE on Ps x 11.

your servant. In epistolary style, a polite substitution for "me"; cf. UT, § 6.15, and NOTE on Ps xix 12.

Be my helper. The preceding and following negative jussives (imperatives) favor the grammatical description of *hāyītā* as a precative perfect. Association with jussives or imperatives is the clue for detecting a precative perfect. Cf. Ps x 14, *'attāh hāyītā 'ōzēr,* "You be his helper," and NOTE on Ps iii 8.

Abstract *'ezrātī,* "my help," should be understood concretely, in keeping with the practice noted at Ps v 8.

10. *my father . . . my mother.* One encounters cognate expressions in a letter of King Abdiḫeba of Jerusalem to the pharaoh: El Amarna, 286:9–13, "Look, it was not my father nor my mother who put me in this place. The mighty hand of the king has brought me into the house of my father." Cf. further the curious expression in Ps xxii 11.

will receive me. A similar nuance of *'āsap* appears in UT, Krt:18–19, *mḫmšt yitsp ršp,* "A fifth part Resheph took to himself!"

12. *into the throat.* On *nepeš,* "throat, neck," see NOTE on Ps vii 3. The poet likens his false accusers to a monster that swallows its victims in its massive maw. The prominence in Ugaritic poetry of the theme of the gorge of Death, *npš mt,* suggests that more demythologized instances of this motif occur in biblical poetry than heretofore realized. Consult NOTES on Pss xxxv 25 and xli 3, and *Biblica* 44 (1963), 104 f.

malicious testifiers. Reading plural *wīpēḥē* for MT *wīpēaḥ.* Ugar. *ypḥ,* "witness, testifier," shows that Heb. *yāpēaḥ* does not derive from *npḥ* or *pwḥ;* were this the case, the Ugaritic substantive would be written *ypḫ,* with the velar fricative, since the Ugaritic correspondents of Heb. *npḥ* and *pwḥ* are *npḫ* (attested) and *pwḫ* (unattested). G. S. Colin in GLECS 7 (1955), 86, proposes Ar. *pwḥ,* "to divulge, proclaim," as a possible etymon of Heb. *ypḥ.* Full study of the vocable is given by S. E. Loewenstamm in *Leshonenu* 26 (1962 f.), 205–8. The present phrase is the semantic equivalent of Ps xxxv 11, *'ēdē ḥāmās,* "malicious witnesses."

The significance of the divine appellative *lē'* in this verse comes out clearly with the observation that Yahweh is the Victor over Death, and is called *lē'ōn māwet,* "The Victor over Death" in Hab i 12. For further associations of this appellative with questions of life and death, cf. NOTES on Ps vii 13–14.

13. *the Victor.* Reading *lelē'* for unexplained MT *lūlē';* the construction *he'emīn le,* "to believe or trust in a person," is well attested. Cf. Deut

ix 23 and BDB, p. 53a. The divine appellative *lē'* has been studied in the NOTE on Ps vii 13.

to behold. Referring to the afterlife; cf. NOTE on vs. 4.

the beauty of Yahweh. ṭūb is synonymous with vs. 4, *nō'am,* "loveliness." Other instances of *ṭūb,* "beauty," recur in Exod xxxiii 19 (of Yahweh himself); Hos x 11; and Zech ix 17. As in Ps xvii 15, where the falsely accused poet finds solace in the thought of eternal happiness in Yahweh's presence, so here the psalmist is sustained by the conviction that his will be the beatific vision in the land of life.

land of life eternal. Though the lexicons generally list only Dan xii 2 as distinctly using *ḥayyīm* to denote eternal life (e.g., BDB, p. 313a), the fact that it denotes precisely this in a text of the Late Bronze Age throws a different light on the problem. The text is UT, 2 Aqht:VI:27–28, *irš ḥym watnk blmt wašlḥk,* "Ask for life eternal and I will give it to you, immortality and I will bestow it upon you." The equivalent balance between *ḥayyīm* and *'al-māwet,* "immortality," in Prov xii 28 has been discussed in *Biblica* 41 (1960), 176–81; see NOTE on Ps xxxvi 10. Cf. NOTE on Ps xxi 5.

PSALM 28

(xxviii 1–9)

1 *Of David.*

To you, O Yahweh, I call,
  my Rock, be not silent toward me;
For should you heed me not,
  I would become like those who have descended the Pit.
2 Hear my plea for mercy
  when I cry to you,
When I lift up my hands
  toward your sacred shrine.
3 Do not rank me with the wicked,
  nor with the evildoers;
Who talk peace with their neighbors,
  with treachery in their heart.
4 Repay them as their actions merit,
  as befits their treacherous deeds;
For the work of their hands repay them,
  give them what they deserve.
5 Because they have no regard
  for the deeds of Yahweh,
  nor for the work of his hands;
He will tear them down,
  and never rebuild them.
6 Praised be Yahweh!
For he has heard my plea for mercy.
7 Yahweh is my strong shield,
  in him my heart has trusted;
I have been rejuvenated,
  and my heart leaps for joy,
So with my song I shall praise him.

8 Yahweh is our stronghold and our refuge,
the Savior of his anointed is he.
9 Give your people victory,
and bless your patrimony;
Shepherd them and carry them forever!

NOTES

xxviii. A psalm consisting of two distinct but related parts. Verses 1–5 give expression to a personal lament pleading for deliverance from imminent death, while vss. 6–9 are a hymn of thanksgiving for the recovery from the near-mortal illness. The well-founded assumption that he who prays in this psalm is the king best explains the presence of vss. 8–9, often described as a liturgical addition adapting an individual prayer to congregational use.

1. *become like those who have descended the Pit.* The phrase *nimšaltī 'im yōrᵉdē bōr* should be compared with Ps lxxxviii 5, *neḥšabtī 'im yōrᵉdē bōr;* Jer xvii 13, *yᵉsūray bā'āreṣ yikkātēbū,* "Those who turn from him shall be inscribed in the nether world"; and UT, 51: VIII:8–9, *tspr byrdm arṣ,* "Be numbered among those who have descended into the nether world." An unpublished Ras Shamra tablet relates that after a drinking bout, the god El became so ill that his voice was like that of those who have gone down to the realm of the dead; cf. Virolleaud in CRAIBL, 1962 (appeared 1963), 113.

2. *When I lift up my hands.* Cf. UT, Krt:75–76, *ša ydk šmm,* "Lift up your hands toward heaven."

3. *Do not rank me.* Upon comparing the present phrase *timšᵉkēnī 'im* with Hos vii 5, *māšak yādō 'et lōṣᵉṣīm,* "He associated with scoffers," as rendered by W. F. Albright (unpublished), one may favor the proposed version over the customary translation, "Take me not off with the wicked" (RSV). In other words, *māšak 'im* is the equivalent of *māšak 'et.* Buttenwieser, PCTNT, p. 829, has arrived at a similar understanding of the phrase, though for different but, in my opinion, erroneous reasons.

with treachery in their heart. A comparable situation is recounted in UT, 2 Aqht:VI:41, where the goddess Anath speaks cajoling words to Aqhat while trying to circumvent him: [g] *m tṣḥq 'nt wblh tqny,* "Anath laughs aloud while in her heart she schemes." For details, see H. L. Ginsberg in BASOR 98 (1945), 22.

5. *no regard for the deeds of Yahweh.* The moral obligation of revering the works of Yahweh comes out in the "negative confession" of Ps xvii 4, "My mouth did not sin against the works of your hands."

7. *my strong shield.* A case of hendiadys; literal reading would be "my strength (*'uzzī*) and my shield (*māginnī*)."

I have been rejuvenated. Parsing *ne'ezartī* as a niphal denominative verb from *'zr* II, Ugar. *ǵzr,* "lad, warrior," a root of rather frequent biblical occurrence, as pointed out by H. L. Ginsberg in JBL 57 (1938), 211, who, though sensing that the present passage contained this root, did not follow up his sound instinct. See NOTE on Ps xxii 20, and cf. Syr. *'allēm,* "to renew one's youth," a denominative from *'alīmā,* "youth." Some of the ancient versions discerned that the theme of rejuvenation was being expressed by the psalmist; e.g., the Syriac reads, "My flesh has flowered"; see H. Schmidt, *Die Psalmen* (see Selected Bibliography), p. 51. Of course, the motif of rejuvenation is not unknown in biblical poetry; cf. Ps ciii 5; Isa xl 31; Job xix 26, xxxiii 25.

So with my song. The construction *ūmiššīrī* resembles that in Ps viii 2, *mippī 'ōlelīm,* "with the mouth of babes."

This analysis entails a re-examination of the syntax in Ps cxxxvii 3b, *šīrū lānū miššīr ṣiyyōn,* where Hummel in JBL 76 (1957), 105, would find an enclitic *mem: šīrū lānū-m šīr ṣiyyōn,* "Sing us Zion's song." In view of *miššīrī 'ahōdennū,* one can defend the Masoretic consonantal division and render Ps cxxxvii 3b, "Sing for us with a song of Zion."

8. *our stronghold and our refuge.* The collocation with another military term strongly suggests that *'ōz* signifies "stronghold," as proposed in NOTE on Ps. viii 3. A highly relevant text, since it reflects a similar *Wortfeld,* is Isa xxvi 1, *'īr 'ōz lānū* (MT *'oz lānū*) *yešū'āh yāšīt ḥōmōt wāḥēl,* "A fortress-city is ours, the walls and bulwark provide safety." Cf. Franz Delitzsch, *Das Buch Jesaia,* 4th ed. (Leipzig, 1889), p. 298.

Besides denoting "for him" and "for them," *lāmō* also denotes "for us." This is the inescapable conclusion to which the following texts (in most of which *lāmō* is emended to *lānū*) point: Pss xliv 11, lxiv 6, lxxx 7; Isa xxvi 16, xliv 7, liii 8 ("for the crime of his people he was smitten by us"); Job xxii 17. By the same token, Ps lxxxix 18, *'uzzāmō* should not be emended to *'uzzēnū* with the Syriac. This is not to say, however, that *lāmō,* "for us," is of the same morphological origin as the homograph *lāmō,* "for him" or "for them." That is another problem, which need not detain us here.

The phrase *yhwh 'ōz lāmō ūmā'ōz,* employing enjambment, is the semantic equivalent of Ps xlvi 2, *'elōhīm lānū maḥaseh wā'ōz,* "God is our shelter and stronghold."

the Savior. Explaining *yešū'ōt* as an abstract plural with the concrete meaning "Savior," as in Pss xlii 6, 12, xliii 5. One may also define it as a *plurale majestatis* since it is predicated of God.

his anointed. I.e., the king; hence a pre-Exilic date for the Psalm.

9. *carry them forever.* The verb *nāśā'* is predicated of divinity in UT, 62:14–15, *tšu aliyn b'l lktp 'nt ktšth,* "She (the sun-goddess) lifts up Victor Baal, upon the shoulders of Anath she places him."

PSALM 29

(xxix 1–11)

1 A *psalm of David.*

Give Yahweh, O gods,
give Yahweh glory and praise, [2]*
Give Yahweh the glory due his name!
2 Bow down to Yahweh
when the Holy One appears.
3 The voice of Yahweh
is upon the waters,
The God of glory
rolls the thunder;
Yahweh is upon the mighty waters.
4 The voice of Yahweh
is strength itself,
The voice of Yahweh
is very splendor.
5 The voice of Yahweh
shivers the cedars,
And Yahweh
shivers the cedars of Lebanon;
7 The voice of Yahweh
cleaves with shafts of fire.
6 He makes Lebanon skip like a calf,
and Sirion like a young wild ox.
8 The voice of Yahweh
convulses the steppe,
Yahweh convulses
the steppe of Kadesh.
9 The voice of Yahweh
makes the hinds writhe,

* Verse number in RSV.

And strips the forests bare;
While in his temple—all of it,
a vision of the Glorious One.
10 Yahweh has sat enthroned
from the flood,
And Yahweh has sat enthroned,
the king from eternity.
11 Yahweh will give his people victory,
Yahweh will bless his people with peace.

Notes

xxix. A hymn in which the sons of God are invited to acclaim the sovereignty of Yahweh, who manifests his power in a storm. The recognition that this psalm is a Yahwistic adaptation of an older Canaanite hymn to the storm-god Baal is due to H. L. Ginsberg, "A Phoenician Hymn in the Psalter," in *Atti del XIX Congresso Internazionale degli Orientalisti* (Roma, 1935), pp. 472–76. Ginsberg's observations of thirty years ago have been corroborated by the subsequent discovery of tablets at Ras Shamra and by progress in the interpretation of these texts. Virtually every word in the psalm can now be duplicated in older Canaanite texts.

Certain hymnodic patterns, derived from earlier uses, have survived in biblical literary practice. Thus we find in this psalm the repetitive parallelism which characterizes the Ugaritic epics. This form of verse structure (type ABC:ABD:[ABE]) occurs throughout the poem. For example, vs. 1, *hābū layhwh bᵉnē 'ēlīm* (ABC), *hābū layhwh kābōd wā'ōz* (ABD), *hābu lyhwh kᵉbōd šᵉmō* (ABE). This compares with UT, 49:II:28–30, *klb arḫ l'glh* (ABC), *klb ṯat limrh* (ABD) *km lb 'nt aṯr b'l* (ABE). See F. M. Cross, Jr., "Notes on a Canaanite Psalm in the Old Testament," BASOR 117 (1950), 19–21.

1. *O gods.* In Canaanite mythology the *bn ilm,* "the sons of El," (e.g., UT, 51:III:14) are the minor gods who form part of the pantheon of which El is the head. In the Old Testament the term was demythologized and came to refer to the angels or spiritual beings who are members of Yahweh's court and do his bidding; cf. Pss lxxxix 7, ciii 20, cxlviii 1 ff.; I Kings xxii 19; Isa vi 2 ff.; Job i 6, ii 1.

The phrase *bᵉnē 'ēlīm* recurs in Ps lxxxix 7 and in Deut xxxii 8, where we should read with the Vrs. *lᵉmispar bᵉnē 'ēl(īm),* "According to the number of *bᵉnē 'ēl(īm),*" as against MT *bᵉnē yiśrā'ēl.* There has been some dispute as to what is meant here by *bᵉnē 'ēl(im)*, but Albright's contention that it simply means "stars" (*From the Stone Age to Christianity*, p. 296) is confirmed by the parallelism of *bn il* with *pḫr kkbm* in UT, 76:I:3–4. Though the immediate context is completely damaged, one can safely infer that the balance of "the sons of El" with "the assembly of the stars" is the same as that in Job xxxviii 7, "When the morning stars sang together and the sons of God (*bᵉnē 'ᵉlōhīm*) shouted with joy." A Punic inscription discovered on July 8, 1964, at Santa Severa, the ancient Etruscan city of Pyrgi, contains the phrase *šnt km hkkbm 'l*, "(May) its years (be) like the stars of El." Note the article and the enclitic *mem* (discussed under vs. 6 below) in the construct chain, *hkkbm 'l*. This should help solve the dispute concerning the syntax of Phoenician Karatepe I:1, *hbrk b'l*, "the one blessed by Baal": the enclitic *mem* in Phoenician is recorded in such phrases as *rb khnm 'lm nrgl*, "the chief of the priests of the god Nergal"; Donner and Röllig, KAI, II, p. 72.

2. *Bow down*. Ugar. *tšthwy*, whose root is *ḥwy*, proves that biblical *hištaḥᵃwū* is the hishtaphal conjugation of *ḥwy* and does not stem from *šḥw*, as found in the lexicons antedating Koehler and Baumgartner (1953), who give the correct derivation on the basis of Ugaritic.

the Holy One. Abstract *qōdeš* is a divine title like *kābōd*, "glory, the Glorious One," treated under vs. 9. In UT, 125:10–11, King Kirta is described as *krt bnm il špḥ lṭpn wqdš*, "Kirta the son of El, the offspring of Lutpan and Holiness." Here "Holiness" is the title of Asherah, the wife of El. The form is abstract *qudšu*, since if it were an adjective one would expect feminine *qdšt*, as in the personal name *bn qdšt*. In UT, 137:21, *bn qdš*, synonymously parallel to *ilm*, "gods," is probably to be rendered "the sons of Holiness (Asherah)."

appears. In UT, Krt:155, *hdrt*, "theophany," is synonymous with *ḥlm*, "dream, vision"; cf. Cross, BASOR 117 (1950), 19–21.

3. *voice of Yahweh*. Referring to the thunder. Cf. UT, 1 Aqht:46, *ṭbn ql b'l*, "the rain with Baal's voice," and 51:v:70, *wtn qlh b'rpt*, "And he gave forth his voice from the clouds."

upon the waters. The Mediterranean is probably meant, since in its present form the poem describes a storm moving in from the west. In the original composition the phrase *'al hammāyim* may have signified "against the waters," a reference to Baal's use of thunder against the chaotic waters.

rolls the thunder. It has been proposed that the clause *'ēl hakkābōd hir'īm* be deleted since the poem is concerned with Yahweh's thunder rather than with that of El (Briggs, Gunkel), but the two unpublished Ugaritic personal names, cited at Ps xviii 14, *yrǵm b'l* and *yrǵm il*, show that thunder was predicated of El as well as of Baal. The genuineness of the clause is further confirmed by the observation that the verse employs the stylistic device known as the breakup of stereotyped divine names. In the present instance, the compound title *yhwh 'ēl,* which was the original form of the Tetragrammaton (see NOTE on Ps x 12), is separated into its two components, *yhwh* being placed in the first colon and *'ēl* in the second, to form a tightly knit line. On the breakup of stereotyped phrases, see NOTE on Ps xi 4.

the mighty waters. On the cosmic connotations of *mayim rabbīm,* see May, "Some Cosmic Connotations of Mayim Rabbim, 'Many Waters'," JBL 74 (1955), 9–21, especially p. 20.

4. *is strength itself . . . is very splendor.* The *b* of *bakkōᵃḥ* and *behādār* is an emphasizing particle, a kind of exponential strengthening of the substantive. It can be identified in Pss xvii 10, xxxiii 4, xxxix 7, l 19, li 8, lv 19, lxxiii 8; Isa xxvi 4; Jer xxix 9; Ezek xvi 13; Prov xxxi 13. Since its correct understanding bears upon the correct interpretation of Phoenician and Punic texts, Ps lv 19 deserves a word of comment: *pᵉdēh* (MT *pādāh*) *bᵉšālōm napšī-m qᵉrab* (MT *napšī miqqᵃrab*) *lī kī bᵉrabbīm hāyū 'immādī,* "Ransom me unharmed; wage war on my behalf for very many are against me." That *bᵉrabbīm* expresses the superlative emerges from a comparison with Ps lvi 3, *kī rabbīm lōḥᵃmīm lī mārōm,* "For many are battling against me, O Exalted One." Herein lies the solution to much-disputed *brbm* in Karatepe, III:9–11, *wbrbm yl[d] wbrbm y'dr wbrbm y'bd l'ztwd,* "May they beget very many, may they be exceedingly mighty, may they serve Azitawaddu exceedingly well." Cf. O'Callaghan in *Orientalia* 18 (1949), 179, and Levi Della Vida in *Rendiconti Lincei* 8 (1949), 286. It now becomes much easier to understand a Punic phrase which M. Lidzbarski, *Ephemeris für semitische Epigraphik,* (Giessen, 1915), III, p. 281, found extremely baffling: *kšm' ql' 'd p'mt brbm,* "For he heard his voice very many times." Lidzbarski (p. 282) proposed either *"unter vielen (Menschen)"* or *"unter den Rabs."*

For the expression *yhbyh* in Jewish incantations of the seventh century A.D., see Albright, *From the Stone Age to Christianity,* p. 260, n. 84.

5. *shivers the cedars.* Moshe Held, "The YQTL-QTL (QTL-YQTL) Sequence of Identical Verbs in Biblical Hebrew and Ugaritic," in *Studies and Essays in Honor of Abraham A. Neuman,* eds. M. Ben-Horim et al. (Leiden, 1962), pp. 281–90, proposes to read piel perfect *šibbēr* for MT *šōbēr,* as suggested by the construction found in Pss xxxviii 12, xciii 3, etc., as well as in Ugaritic, but one must also consider the stylistic device of using the same root in different conjugations in the same verse. Thus in Ps xxiv 7, qal imperative *śᵉ'ū* is balanced by niphal imperative *hinnāśᵉ'ū,* while Ps xxxviii 3 collocates piel *niḥᵃtū* and qal *tinḥat.* The MT sequence *šōbēr-yᵉšabbēr* is probably to be classed in the latter category.

the cedars of Lebanon. These trees were praised for their strength and durability in Canaanite poetry of the second millennium. When the palace of Baal was to be built, workers repaired "to Lebanon and its timbers, to Shirion and its choicest cedars"; UT, 51:VI:20–21, *llbnn w'ṣh lšryn mḥmd arzh.*

7. *cleaves with shafts of fire.* The sense and position of vs. 7 have been much debated, but if one grants a measure of probability to the present version, its position immediately after vs. 5 seems natural. With the bolts of lightning that accompany the thunder Yahweh splinters the mighty cedars. *lahᵃbōt 'ēš* is parsed as an accusative of means; this construction may have been prompted by the fact that *ḥōṣēb* ends in *b*. The usage is well attested in Ugaritic; e.g., UT, 'nt:II:15–16, *mṭm tgrš šbm,* "With two maces she drives out the *šbm,*" and 'nt:IV:86–87, *wtrḥṣ ṭl šmm,* "And she washes with the dew of heaven."

6. *Lebanon . . . Sirion.* For the Ugaritic parallelism of these geographic terms, see second NOTE on vs. 5.

skip like a calf. Reading *wayyarqēd-mi* for MT *wayyarqīdēm,* as first proposed by Ginsberg (he read *-ma* for *-mi*) in 1935 (see general NOTE, p. 175); this was the first of several hundred instances of enclitic *mem* found in the Bible. After twenty-four years, several articles on the subject, and scores of examples, *La Bible de la Pléiade,* II, p. 948, buoyantly unaware of the existence of the enclitic *mem,* recommends the deletion of the *mem* of *yrqdm.*

Charles Clermont-Ganneau, *Recueil d'Archéologie Orientale* (Paris, 1888), I, p. 94, proposed to find in the verb *rāqad* an allusion to the Hellenistic cult of Baal Marcod, "Baal of the Dance." In an unpublished tablet from Ras Shamra which lists several musical instruments familiar from the Bible, there is mention of *mrqdm,* "dancers"; see CRAIBL, 1962 (appeared 1963), 109. The occurrence of this root in ancient Canaanite texts further confirms the thesis that Psalm xxix is an adaptation of an older composition.

8. *the steppe of Kadesh.* Being mentioned in UT, 52:65, *mdbr qdš* should be sought in the environs of Lebanon and Anti-Libanus, perhaps near Kadesh on the Orontes. It should be recalled that *midbār* does not connote "desert" in our sense, but rather "land without permanent settlements." While conceding some formal parallels with Ugaritic, Weiser, *Die Psalmen,* p. 175, n. 3, voices a protest against simply labeling the psalm as Canaanite, since vs. 8 contains, according to Weiser, a reference to the Sinai tradition. But he fails to mention that nowhere is the wilderness of Sinai called *midbar qādēš,* and he equally fails to record that *mdbr qdš* is mentioned in Ugaritic.

9. *makes the hinds writhe.* Though R. Lowth's (*De Sacra Poesia Hebraeorum Praelectiones Academicae Oxonii Habitae. Cum Notis et*

Epimetris Ioa. Dav. Michaelis. Edidit Ern. Frid. Car. Rosenmüller. [Lipsiae, 1815], p. 316) reading *yeḥōlēl 'ēlōt,* "makes the oaks bend," has found wide acceptance, MT *yeḥōlēl 'ayyālōt* too closely resembles Job xxxix 1, *ḥōlel 'ayyālōt,* "the writhing of the hinds," to be abandoned in favor of Lowth's reading. The pronounced Canaanite associations of ch. xxxix of Job suggest that we are dealing with the same phrase. To be sure, there is no evidence that wild or domestic animals are so affected by a storm that they calve prematurely, but this does not foreclose the possibility that the ancients may have had some such belief.

strips the forests bare. The verb *ḥāsap,* "to strip," has correctly been identified with Phoen. *ḥsp* in the Ahiram Inscription, *tḥtsp ḥṭr mšpṭh,* "May the scepter of his judicial authority be stripped off"; see Harris, *A Grammar of the Phoenician Language,* p. 103, and Gevirtz in VT 11 (1961), 147. Though this is the only instance of feminine plural *ye'ārōt,* the Ugaritic place name *y'rt* and the gentilic *y'rty* bespeak a double gender of this substantive, just as the unique occurrence of feminine plural *'ōlāmōt* in Ps xlviii 15 is sustained by Ugaritic plural *'lmt.*

in his temple. As in Pss xi 4, xviii 7, xxvii 4; Isa vi 1; Mic i 2; Jon ii 8; Hab ii 20, *hēkāl* refers to the heavenly temple. On Ugar. *hkl,* "heavenly temple," in UT, 51:v:124, etc., see Norman C. Habel, *Yahweh versus Baal: A Conflict of Religious Cultures* (New York, 1964), p. 76.

Thus the glory of Yahweh filled both the heavens and the earth; this, too, is the burden of Isa vi 1–4, "I saw Yahweh sitting upon a throne, high and uplifted, with his robes [?] filling the (heavenly) temple . . . Holy, holy, holy, is Yahweh of Hosts; the whole earth is full of his glory."

all of it. Frequently deleted as dittographic of the final two consonants of *hēkālō, kullō* should be retained as a constitutive element of a divine theophany in the heavenly temple, to judge from the description of the Inaugural Vision in Isa vi 1–6. In vs. 1 it is stated that *šūlāyw melā'īm 'et hāhēkāl,* "His robes [?] filled the (heavenly) temple," while vs. 3 reads *mālō'* (MT *melō'*) *kol hā'āreṣ kebōdō,* "filling all the earth with his glory." Cf. Exod xl 34, "And the glory of Yahweh filled the tabernacle."

a vision. Reading *'ōmer* for MT *'ōmēr,* and understanding *'mr* in the Akkadian-Ugaritic sense "to see," the meaning discussed at Ps xi 1, and in *Biblica* 42 (1961), 383 f., and 44 (1963), 295 f. Though the context is not decisive, a strong case can be made for defining *'ōmer* as "vision" in Ps lxxvii 9, *he'āpes lāneṣaḥ ḥasdō gāmar 'ōmer ledōr wādōr,* "Has his kindness ceased forever, has vision come to an end for generations and generations?" Cf. I Sam iii 1, "And the word of Yahweh was rare in those days; there was no frequent vision."

of the Glorious One. On the divine appellative *kābōd,* see NOTE on Ps iii 4.

Understood in this manner, *'ōmer kābōd,* "a vision of the Glorious

One," semantically and structurally balances vs. 2, *hadrat qōdeš,* literally "the appearance of the Holy One," which comes fourteen beats after the open of the hymn, while *'ōmer kābōd* is fourteen beats removed from the ending of the psalm.

10. *from the flood.* Grammatically, *lammabbūl* should be compared with UT, 1 Aqht:176, *lyrḫm lšnt,* "from months to years." Cf. Ps cvi 7, *wayyāmrū 'ēlīm* (MT *'al yam*) *b^eyam sūp,* "And they rebelled against the Most High from the Sea of Reeds." There are numerous cases where *l^e* denotes "from" in a temporal sense; see NOTE on Ps ix 8 and cf. Pss xlv 3, lxxviii 69, cxi 8, cxix 152, cxxx 6, cxlviii 6. The psalmist alludes not to the Flood in the days of Noah, but to the motif of the struggle between Baal, lord of the air and genius of the rain, and Yamm, master of sea and subterranean waters. UT, 68, explicitly treats this combat. In lines 9–10 Baal is informed that when he destroys his enemy, Prince Sea, he will receive his eternal dominion: *tqḥ mlk 'lmk.* After having discomfited his rival Yamm, Baal becomes king: *ym lmt b'lm ymlk* (32), "Yamm is truly dead, Baal will reign." By his victory over the primeval forces of chaos, Yahweh is mythopoeically conceived as acquiring full dominion over earth and sea. This theme also underlies Pss xcii 9–10 and xciii 2–3.

has sat enthroned . . . from eternity. The Masoretic sequence *yāšab . . . wayyēšeb* is grammatically faultless when it is seen that *l^e'ōlām* means "from eternity," as in Pss ix 8, xxxiii 11, xlv 3, lxxviii 69, etc. Cf. Kirst in FuF 32 (1958), 216, n. 46. Here the term "eternity" really means "primeval time, *Urzeit,*" as in a number of other biblical passages; several scholars have lately studied this problem, most recently Lipiński in *Biblica* 44 (1963), 435 f., with bibliography. Cf. also Kraus, *Psalmen,* II, p. 649 (on Ps xciii 2).

11. *will give his people victory.* Just as Yahweh achieved a signal triumph over the forces of chaos, so will he grant his people mastery over their foes. This nuance of *'ōz* is present in I Sam ii 10; Pss lxviii 29 (Albright in HUCA 23 [1950], 31), lxxxix 18, cx 2, and possibly in UT, 49:VI:17, *mt 'z b'l 'z,* "Mot is victorious, Baal is victorious."

with peace. Victory without subsequent peace cheats the hope of the people.

PSALM 30

(xxx 1–13)

1 *A psalm, a song for the dedication of the temple; of David.*

2 I shall exalt you, O Yahweh,
for you drew me up,
Nor let my Foe rejoice over me.
3 O Yahweh my God, I cried to you, [2]*
and you healed me.
4 O Yahweh, you lifted me from Sheol, [3]
you restored me to life
as I was descending the Pit.
5 Sing to Yahweh, O his devoted ones, [4]
and praise his holy name.
6 For death is in his anger, [5]
life eternal in his favor;
In the evening one falls asleep crying,
but at dawn there are shouts of joy.
7 I said in my insouciance, [6]
"I will never stumble."
8 O Yahweh, by your favor you made me [7]
more stable than the mighty mountains;
You turned away your face,
I was greatly shaken.
9 To you, O Yahweh, I call, [8]
and to my Lord I plead for mercy.
10 What gain is there in my tears, [9]
in my descent to the Pit?
Will the Slime praise you,
or publish abroad your fidelity?
11 Hear, O Yahweh, and have mercy on me, [10]
Yahweh, be my helper!

* Verse numbers in RSV.

12 Turn my weeping into dancing, [11]
unlace my sackcloth and gird me with happiness,
13 So that my heart might sing to you, [12]
and weep no more.
O Yahweh, my God, forever will I thank you.

Notes

xxx. A tightly structured psalm of thanksgiving for recovery from an illness that brought the psalmist to death's door. In the translation proposed here, the following structure emerges: vss. 2–5 are the thanksgiving proper; 6–8 are moralizing, warning against the sin of overconfidence; vss. 9–13a form the text of the lament sung by the psalmist when he prayed for healing. Verse 13b is a doxology, resuming the thought of vs. 2.

2. *drew me up*. The verb primarily means to "draw up a bucket of water from the well," but since in vs. 4 the nether world is called *bōr,* which properly denotes a "well, pit," *dillītanī* is an apposite verb.

my Foe. Parsing, *'ōyᵉbay* as *plurale excellentiae* referring to Death, the archfoe of the stricken poet; other instances of this usage are discussed under Ps xviii 4.

4. *you restored me to life*. Reading *ḥiyyītanī-m* (enclitic *mem*) *yārᵉdī bōr*. More difficult than kethib *yōrᵉdī, yārᵉdī* is probably original and dialectal; cf. the participle in Ugaritic, pronounced *yāridu*. The final -*ī* is paragogic, as frequently with participles; see Joüon, GHB, § 93n.

the Pit. A poetic name for the infernal regions.

6. *death is in his anger*. The prevailing antithetic parallelism of this poem indicates that *rega'* must connote the opposite of *ḥayyīm,* "life eternal." This inference finds confirmation in Job xxvi 12, *bᵉkōḥō rāga' hayyām ūbītᵉbūnātō māḥaṣ rāhab,* "With his strength he annihilated the sea, and with his skill he smote Rahab." Comparison with UT, 67:i:1–2, *ktmḫṣ ltn bṯn brḥ tkly bṯn 'qltn,* "When you smote Lotan the primordial serpent, made an end of the twisting serpent," shows that *rg'* and *kly,* both of which are synonymous with *mḫṣ,* are in turn synonyms. In numerous passages, LXX understood *rg'* as "destroy"; cf. I. L. Seeligmann in VTS, I (1953), p. 169, n. 2; G. R. Driver, VTS, III (1955), p. 75.

It is also possible that *rega'* here might denote "Perdition," i.e., "the place of Death," just as *māwet,* "death," not infrequently refers to the realm of Death. In Ps vi 11 and Num xvi 21 *rega'* denotes "Perdition," another name for Sheol. In the context of the present psalm this would make effective contrast to *ḥayyīm,* "life eternal," which implies "Paradise." Thus the anger of God results in death while his favor produces life. Cf. El Amarna, 169:7–9, "You give me life and you give me death."

life eternal. For this definition of *ḥayyīm,* see NOTE on Ps xxi 5.

in the evening. In contrast to "dawn," night is a symbol of death.

falls asleep. Symbolic language for "to die"; cf. Pss xlix 13 and xiii 4, "Avert the sleep of death."

crying. Cf. Gen xlii 38, "You would bring down my hoary head to Sheol in sorrow," and for the connection between tears and sleep, UT, Krt:31–32, *bm bkyh wyšn bdm'h nhmmt,* "While he weeps he falls asleep, while he cries, deep slumber."

at dawn. Dawn is a symbol of resurrection and immortality; cf. Ps xxvii 4, "awaking each dawn in his [heavenly] temple." D. N. Freedman has called my attention to the death-life, evening-morning sequence that is echoed in Michelangelo's sculptures for the Medici Chapel in Florence. This sequence is not a simple contrast between life and death but rather the contrast between death, which is inevitable, and eternal life, which will follow. The psalmist is convinced that eternal life will follow; this conviction finds expression in numerous texts of the Psalter. Consult NOTES on Pss i 3, 5, xvi 10–11, xvii 15, xxi 5, xxvii 4, xxxvi 10, etc.

8. *you made me more stable.* The suffix for *he'ᵉmadtāh* is really supplied by the second-colon phrase *hāyītī,* which contains the first person. On *'āmad,* "to stand firm," see Pss xviii 34, xxvi 12.

than the mighty mountains. Parsing *lᵉ* of *lᵉharᵉrī 'ōz* as *lamedh comparativum.* For this usage in Mic v 1, see J. M. Fitzmyer CBQ 18 (1956), 10–13; in Song of Sol i 3, W. F. Albright in *Hebrew and Semitic Studies Presented to Godfrey Rolles Driver,* eds. D. Winton Thomas and W. D. McHardy (Oxford, 1963), p. 2; in Nah i 7, Dahood in *Biblica* 45 (1964), 288. Another instance may be remarked in Ezek xvi 13, *wattiṣlᵉḥī līmᵉlūkāh,* "And you prospered more than royalty." The curious form *harᵉrī* might well be an archaic plural in the oblique case; this tallies with the dialectal form in vs. 4, *yārᵉdī.*

You turned away. The root of *histartā* is probably *sūr,* "to turn aside," and the conjugation infixed *-t-;* cf. treatment in NOTE on Ps x 11.

10. *in my tears.* Gunkel, *Die Psalmen,* p. 129, has acutely noted that this psalm does not deal with violence and that *dmy* does not refer to "blood" but only to "suffering." Hence it is better to vocalize as infinitive construct *dommī,* to balance infinitive construct *ridtī,* and to derive *dommī* from *dmm,* "to weep," well known from Akkadian and now attested in Northwest Semitic, as proposed at Ps iv 5. A most relevant parallel is Isa xxxviii 10, "I said as I wept (*bᵉdommī*), 'I have completed my days, I have been consigned to Sheol for the rest of my

years'." See Dahood in CBQ 22 (1960), 401–2; *Biblica* 45 (1964), 402 f.; Georg Fohrer, *Das Buch Jesaja* (Zürcher Bibelkommentar, 1962), II, p. 183.

the Slime praise you. Gunkel, *Die Psalmen,* p. 128, is probably correct in his rendition of *'āpār,* usually translated "dust," as *Kot.* This falls in better with Northwest Semitic motifs which describe the nether world as a place of mud and filth; cf. NOTE on Ps xxii 16, and for the theme of Sheol as a place where there is no praise of Yahweh, Pss vi 6, lxxxviii 11–12.

12. *Turn my weeping . . . unlace my sackcloth.* Parsing *hāpaktā* and *pittaḥtā* as precative perfects to balance the vs. 11 imperatives *šᵉma'* and *hᵉyēh;* cf. NOTE on Ps iii 8. LXX is at least consistent in taking all the verbal elements in vss. 11–12 as perfects, but a better coherence is obtained by understanding them all as expressing wishes; these verses (9–13) contain the lament which the poet sang in the hope that he might be healed from his sickness. On the use of the optative perfect to continue an imperative, cf. NOTE on Ps iii 8.

13. *So that. lᵉma'an* introduces a final clause; see Michel, TSP, § 26, 1, p. 174.

my heart. Vocalizing *kābēd,* literally "my liver," for MT *kābōd.* The same Masoretic confusion between these words is evident in Gen xlix 6 (cf. LXX; Dahood, *Biblica* 36 [1955], 229) and Ps vii 6. As frequently in Ugaritic (see NOTE on Ps xvi 4), pronominal suffixes with names of parts of the body are sometimes omitted in biblical Hebrew; hence *kābēd* can mean "my liver." Cf. UT, 1 Aqht:I:34–35, *tbky pǵt bm lb tdm' bm kbd,* "Pughat weeps in her heart, she cries in her liver." Note the lack of pronominal suffix with *lb* and *kbd.*

and weep no more. See NOTE on vs. 10, and G. Schick in JBL 32 (1913), 239. LXX reads *mē katanugô,* "lest I be absorbed in grief."

O Yahweh, my God. yhwh 'ᵉlōhay forms an *inclusio* with vs. 3, *yhwh 'ᵉlōhāy.*

PSALM 31

(xxxi 1–25)

1 *For the director. A psalm of David.*

2 In you, O Yahweh, have I trusted,
let me not be humiliated, O Eternal One!
In your fidelity rescue me!
3 Incline your ear to me,
speedily deliver me!
Be mine, O mountain of refuge!
O fortified citadel, save me!
4 For you are my crag and my fortress,
and for the honor of your name
You will lead me and guide me.
5 You will free me from the net
which they hid for me,
For you are my refuge.
6 Into your hand I entrust my life;
ransom me, O Yahweh God!
7 Truly I hate those who keep worthless idols,
and I put my trust in Yahweh;
I shall rejoice and be happy because of your kindness.
8 When you saw my affliction,
you took care of me against the Adversary;
9 You did not put me into the hand of the Foe,
nor set my feet in the broad domain.
10 Have pity on me, O Yahweh, [9]*
for distress is mine!
My eye is wasted with sorrow,
my throat and my belly.
11 Indeed my life is spent with grief, [10]
and my years in groaning.

* Verse numbers in RSV.

My strength fails through affliction,
my bones are wasted away,
my vitals are consumed.
12 I have become an object of scorn [11]
even to my neighbors;
a calamity and a fright to my friends;
Those who see me in the street flee from me.
13 I have shriveled up [12]
like a dead man, senseless,
become like a jar that is broken.
14 For I hear the whispering of many, [13]
terror all around;
When they counsel together against me,
when they plot to take my life.
15 But in you have I trusted, O Yahweh, [14]
I said, "You are my God;
my life-stages are in your hand."
16 Rescue me from the hand of my foes, [15]
and from my pursuers.
17 Let your face shine upon your servant; [16]
save me in your kindness.
18 O Yahweh, let me not be humiliated, [17]
when I call you.
Let the wicked be humiliated,
hurled into Sheol!
19 Let lying lips be muzzled,
that speak against the Ancient Just One, [18]
with presumption and scorn.
20 How many are the good things, [19]
that you have stored for those who fear you!
That you have gathered for those who rely upon you,
in the sight of the sons of men.
21 You shield them in the shelter of your presence, [20]
from the slanderings of men;
You shelter them in your abode,
from the wranglings of tongues.
22 Praise to Yahweh, [21]
for he has shown me wondrous kindness
from the fortified city.
23 Once I thought in my dismay, [22]
"I am cut off from your sight."

But you heard my plea for mercy,
 when I cried out to you.
24 Love Yahweh, all you devoted to him! [23]
 Yahweh preserves his faithful ones,
 but abundantly requites whoever acts presumptuously.
25 Be strong and let your heart be stout, [24]
 all you who hope in Yahweh.

Notes

xxxi. A personal lament. This psalm divides into three sections. Verses 1–12 include the cries for help and the description of the illness which put the psalmist at death's door; vss. 12–20 describe the mental anguish brought on by being abandoned by his friends and slandered by his foes; and vss. 20–25 are a hymn of thanksgiving for rescue from both death and slander.

2. *O Eternal One*. Parsing *l*ᵉ*'ōlām* as vocative *lamedh,* discussed in Note on Ps iii 9, followed by the divine name *'ōlām,* recorded in Note on Ps xxiv 7. Vocative *l*ᵉ*'ōlām* forms a perfect counterpart to vocative *yhwh* of the first colon and recalls the stylistic equipoise of Ps xxxiii 1, where vocative *lay*ᵉ*šārīm,* with vocative *lamedh,* is the opposite number of *ṣaddīqīm,* without vocative particle, in the first colon. Cf. Ps lxxxvi 12, where vocative *l*ᵉ*'ōlām* of the second half verse balances vocative *'*ᵃ*dōnāy '*ᵉ*lōhay* of the first colon. The same analysis is valid in Ps lxxi 1.

In your fidelity. The *b* of *b*ᵉ*ṣidqat*ᵉ*kā* seems to be causal, as in Phoenician Karatepe I:12 f., *bṣdqy wbḥkmty,* "because of my justice and my wisdom." Since the psalmist has put his full trust in him, Yahweh is in fidelity obliged to rescue the psalmist. See Jean and Hoftijzer, *Dictionnaire . . .*, I–II, p. 31, line 27. For this nuance of *ṣ*ᵉ*dāqāh,* see Zorell, ZLH, p. 684a.

3. *Be mine. h*ᵉ*yēh lī* recalls Hos i 9, *lō' 'ehyeh lākem,* "I will not be yours," and Exod xx 3, "Other gods shall not be yours [*lō' yihyeh l*ᵉ*kā*]."

O mountain of refuge. The *lamedh* of *l*ᵉ*ṣūr mā'ōz* is vocative; cf. following Note. I am indebted to D. N. Freedman for this observation. Imperative *h*ᵉ*yēh lī* at the beginning of vs. 3 balances imperative *l*ᵉ*hōšī'ēnī* at end of verse.

O fortified citadel. The *lamedh* of *l*ᵉ*bēt* is again the vocative particle as frequently in Ugaritic and often enough in Hebrew; e.g., Pss iii 9, xvi 2, xxxii 5, xlii 10, cxl 7. Cf. Note on Ps iii 9 for full listing.

save me. Gunkel has rightly seen that *lᵉhôšîʿēnî,* parsed as preposition followed by hiphil infinitive construct, is a prosaic addition, but when analyzed as emphatic *lamedh* followed by an imperative, his observation becomes irrelevant. From this parsing emerge five successive imperatives; the last being climactic, it is preceded by an emphatic particle. The same invocation occurs in Isa xxxviii 20, *yhwh lᵉhôšîʿēnî,* "O Yahweh, save me!" as noticed by Paul Haupt in *The Book of Proverbs,* eds. A. Müller and E. Kautzsch (Leipzig, 1901), p. 52.

4. *You will lead me and guide me.* The sequence *tanḥēnî ûtᵉnahᵃlēnî* confirms my analysis of Ps xxiii 4, *tnḥmny* which forms an inclusion with vs. 2, *yᵉnahᵃlēnî.*

6. *my life.* Literally "my spirit."

ransom me. pādîtāh is precative perfect; see Notes on Pss iii 8 and iv 2, while a discussion of precative perfects with the *scriptio plena* may be found in Note on Ps iv 8.

The verb *pādāh,* so pregnant with theological meaning in the Old Testament, appears in a Ugaritic contract of emancipation studied by Virolleaud, *Palais royal d'Ugarit,* II, pp. 18 f.

O Yahweh God. yhwh 'ēl, the original, full form of Yahweh, is found in Pss x 12 and xviii 3, where it is separated in the parallel cola.

7. *Truly I hate.* Explaining *'ᵉmet* as the emphatic substantive found in Ugaritic, Phoenician, and biblical Hebrew; full discussion in CBQ 22 (1960), 406. Good examples include Isa xlii 3, xliii 9, liii 10; Ezek xviii 9; Ps cxxxii 11. On Isa liii 10 see R. de Vaux, *Les sacrifices de l'Ancien Testament* (Paris, 1964), p. 100, n. 7.

The verb *śānē'tî* is a *terminus technicus* used in the formal repudiation of idolatry or charges of idolatry; cf. Note on Ps v 6. The psalmist takes pains to protest his innocence of the sin of worshiping or keeping idols in his possession. Among the Israelites this was believed to be one of the chief causes of sickness or other misfortunes.

worthless idols. For discussion of the phrase *hablē šāw',* consult Note on Ps xxiv 4.

8. *When you saw.* For this meaning of *'ᵃšer,* see BDB, p. 82b.

you took care of me. This nuance of *yāda'* has been discussed in Note on Ps i 6.

against the Adversary. Death is the adversary par excellence; hence the poet employs the *plurale excellentiae, ṣārôt,* in precisely the same way as his Canaanite poet predecessors. When Baal girds for his mortal combat with Yamm, the god of ocean and nether waters, the artisan-god Kothar, who had forged two clubs for him, instructs him in the following terms: UT, 68:8–9, *ht ibk b'lm ht ibk tmḫṣ ht tṣmt ṣrtk,* "Now your Foe, O Baal, now your Foe will you smite, now will you destroy your Adversary." Specialists in Ugaritic have often taken both *ibk* and *ṣrtk* as semantically plural forms, but this appears to be incorrect; in text 68 Baal is locked in combat with a single foe, Yamm. Both vocables must accordingly be understood as singular forms, one being a concrete noun, the other, *ṣrt,* probably a plural abstract, but with a concrete singular denotation.

9. *the Foe.* Another reference to Death. He receives this epithet *'ōyēb,* "Foe," in Pss vii 6, xiii 3, xviii 4, xli 3, lxi 4. The poetic balance between a concrete and an abstract noun has been examined on the NOTE to Ps v 8; the most germane parallels are Ps cxxxviii 7 and the Ugaritic text cited in the previous NOTE. Compare the expression *yad* *š^{e}'ōl,* "the hand of Sheol," in Ps xlix 16 and Job xvii 16, *baddē š^{e}'ōl, t^{e}rēdannāh,* "Into the hands (Ugar. *bd*) of Sheol will it descend."

nor set my feet. The consideration that synonymous, not antithetic, parallelism characterizes this psalm requires that the force of the negative *lō'* in the first colon be understood as carrying over into the second colon and negativing the verb *he'^{e}madtā.* Joüon, GHB, § 160q, finds other instances of this usage in Pss ix 19, xxxv 19, xxxviii 2, xliv 19, lxxv 6. Similar usage obtains in Ugaritic 76:II:4–5, *in b'l bbht*[*t*] *il hd bqrb hklh,* "Baal is not in his house, the god Hadd is not inside his palace."

the broad domain. merḥāb is a poetic name for the nether world, discussed in connection with Ps xviii 20.

10. *with sorrow.* Some MSS read *mikka'as* for *b^{e}ka'as,* an indication that their scribes no longer were familiar with the meaning "from" for *b.* The bearing of the Ras Shamra tablets on biblical philology is most widely felt in the study and interpretation of prepositions. In Ps vi 8 the same phrase does occur with *min: 'āš^{e}šāh mikka'as 'ēnī.*

my throat. Ugar. *npš,* "throat," merely confirms the long-standing observation that in about a dozen passages *nepeš* denotes precisely this; e.g., Jon ii 6. Cf. *Biblica* 42 (1961), 384, and UT, 67:II:18–19, *npš blt ḥmr,* "My throat is wasted from fever." To delete, with Kraus and others, the phrase "my throat and my belly" is gratuitous.

11. *through affliction.* Reading (for MT *'^{a}wōnī*) *'ōnī,* a *scriptio plena* found again in Ps cvii 41. Cf. Ps lxxxviii 10, *'ēnī dā'^{a}bāh minnī 'ōnī,* "My eye wastes away through affliction."

my vitals are consumed. Attaching *m* of *mikkol* to preceding *'āšešū* as enclitic, and vocalizing *kālū ṣōr^{e}ray;* this expression has been studied in NOTE on Ps vi 8.

12. *even to my neighbors.* The *waw* preceding "to my neighbors" is emphatic, as in Ugaritic. See NOTE on Ps iv 5.

a calamity. Attaching the *mem* of MT *m^{e}'ōd* to the previous word as enclitic and vocalizing *'ēd,* "disaster, calamity." Hummel in JBL 76 (1957), 99, has adopted this reading; as here, the balance between *'ēd* and *paḥad* in Job xxxi 23 and Prov i 26 sustains the proposal.

13. *have shriveled up. niškaḥtī* can scarcely derive from *šākaḥ,* "to forget," since the psalmist was anything but forgotten by his avid enemies. Ugar. *ṯkḥ,* "to wither," parallel to *rpy,* "to wilt," provides the sense called for by the immediate context as well as by the tenor of the entire lament. The root can be documented in Pss cii 5, cxxxvii 5, and elsewhere in the Bible. See W. F. Albright in BASOR 84 (1941), 15; Dahood in CBQ 19 (1957), 148; PNWSP, p. 12; Thomas, *The Text of the Revised Psalter,* p. 52.

dead man, senseless. If *millēb* denoted "out of mind" (RSV), it should immediately follow *niškaḥtī.* That not being the case, it must be understood as modifying *mēt;* in other words, *kᵉmēt millēb* syntactically and semantically balances *kīkᵉlī 'ōbēd.* Cf. Ps xlv 6, *yippᵉlū bᵉlēb 'ōyᵉbē hammelek,* "Senseless will fall the foes of the king," and I Sam xxv 37, "And his heart died within him and he became like a stone."

14. *terror all around.* Consult the interesting remarks on *māgōr missābīb* by Bright, *Jeremiah* (The Anchor Bible, vol. 21), pp. 132 ff.

15. *my life-stages.* Literally "my times." An early reference to the sevenfold division of life may possibly be found in UT, 67:I:20–21, *hm šb' ydty bṣ',* "Behold, the seven parts (of my life) are cut off." So Albright in BASOR 83 (1941), 42. Other allusions to this theme may be present in Pss ciii 5, cxxxix 16; Dan iv 22; and I Chron xxix 30. The theme has been briefly examined by Dahood in *Biblica* 40 (1959), 168 f. The early Christians used to distinguish the seven epochs of history which marked the great stages of salvation.

17. *your face shine.* This is epistolary language; Virolleaud, *Palais royal d'Ugarit,* II, 15:9–10, *wpn špš nr by mid,* "And the face of the Sun [i.e., the Pharaoh] shone brightly upon me."

your servant. A polite substitute for the personal pronoun, discussed in NOTE on Ps. xix 12.

18. *hurled into Sheol.* The versions differ considerably in their comprehension of consonantal *ydm lš'l,* but on the strength of Exod xv 16, *yuddūm* (encl. *mem*) *kā'eben,* "They were hurled like a stone," (Dahood, *Biblica* 43 [1962], 248 f.; supported by Neh ix 11, as noted by S. E. Loewenstamm; see *Elenchus Bibliographicus* in *Biblica* 43 [1962], 170*, No. 2301), one is justified in vocalizing *yuddūm lišᵉ'ōl,* from the verb *nādāh,* "to hurl, cast," well known from Akkadian and fully attested in Ugaritic. See Virolleaud in GLECS 8 (1960), 90. LXX *katachteíesen,* "they are driven down," evinces a similar understanding of the phrase, while Ps lv 16 and Ezek xxxi 16 express equally unholy sentiments.

19. *lying lips be muzzled.* As H. Lesêtre in *Dictionnaire de la Bible,* ed. F. Vigouroux (Paris, 1908), IV, col. 1347, has pointed out, the Greek text of Sirach xx 31 (28) reads *phīmos,* "muzzle," where Vulg. has *mutus,* "dumb." He correctly infers that the Hebrew original must have

contained a substantive from the verb *'ālam,* "to bind," which Jerome read as *'illēm,* "mutus," a reading that yields no sense in the context. It also follows that Isa lvi 10, *kelābīm 'illēmīm* denotes "muzzled dogs" rather than "dumb dogs." Cf. also Ps xxxix 2, 10, and Isa liii 7.

the Ancient Just One. Vocalizing *'attīq* for MT *'ātāq;* cf. Dan vii 9, 13, 22, *'attīq yōmīn,* "the Ancient of Days," and Ps lxxv 6, *ṣ'ūr 'attīq* (MT *ṣawwā'r 'ātāq*), "the Ancient Mountain." Cf. the Ugaritic divine title *ab šnm,* "the Father of Years," used of El, the head of the pantheon.

20. *the good things.* The suffix of *ṭūbekā* functions as the definite article; cf. NOTE on Ps xvii 12 and compare the opposite practice of using the article in the function of pronominal suffix in such passages as Pss xxxiii 17 and lxxxv 13.

That you have gathered. In association with *ṣāpan,* "to store, treasure up," *pā'altā* takes on a kindred nuance, as in Prov xi 18, xxi 6, and Phoenician Karatepe I:6–7, *wp'l 'nk ss 'l ss,* "And I gathered horse upon horse" (cf. *Biblica* 44 [1963], 70), and in the Phoenician phrase *mp'l 'gdr,* "the arsenal of Agadir," as interpreted by Torrey in JAOS 57 (1937), 401.

in the sight of. In other words, the blessings bestowed on his favorites will arouse the envy of Yahweh's enemies; cf. NOTE on Ps xxiii 5.

21. *slanderings of men.* The hapax legomenon phrase *ruksē 'īš* becomes explicable, it would seem, when the semantic relationship between "to bind, join together," which is what *rakāsu* (Ugar. *rks*) denotes in Akkadian, and "to spin tales" is appreciated. Cf. discussion concerning *gedīlōt,* "distortions," from *gādal,* "to weave," in NOTE on Ps xii 4. On this hypothesis, Isa xl 4, *rekāsīm* would denote "twisting, tortuous terrain."

in your abode. Suffixless *sukkāh* shares the suffix of parallel *pānekā;* cf. NOTE on Ps iii 4.

22. *from the fortified city.* As so frequently in Hebrew poetry, *b* denotes "from." "The fortified city" is a poetic name for the heavenly abode of Yahweh. Compare Ps xviii 7, "My voice was heard in his [heavenly] palace." Kraus, *Psalmen,* I, p. 247, can find no sense in the phrase *be'īr māṣōr.* A probable parallel to this theme of heaven the fortress is in Ps lxxiv 20, *habbēṭ labbīrāt* (MT *labberīt*), "Look down from the fortress."

23. *Once I thought.* On this meaning of *'āmartī,* see C. J. Labuschagne, "Some Remarks on the Translation and Meaning of *'āmartī,*" in *New Light on Some Old Testament Problems* (Papers read at fifth meeting of Die Ou Testamentiese Werkgemeenskap in Suid-Afrika held at the University of South Africa, Pretoria, 1962), pp. 27–33, especially p. 29.

I am cut off. Though the closely related passage in Jon ii 5 reads *nigraštī,* and Ps lxxxviii 6 *nigraztī,* there is no need to alter *nigraztī,* whose root and meaning are made clear by the context and by *garzēn*, "ax," from *gāraz*, "to cut."

24. *his faithful ones.* The pronominal suffix of *'emūnīm* is provided by that of *ḥasīdāyw* on the principle of the double-duty suffix, while the concrete meaning of *'amūnīm* emerges from its balance with concrete *ḥasīdāyw*. This poetic device is analyzed under NOTE on Ps v 8. Cf. NOTE on Ps xii 2.

PSALM 32
(xxxii 1–11)

1 *Of David. A maskil.*

How blest is he whose transgression is forgiven,
whose sin has been remitted.
2 How blest the man
to whom Yahweh imputes no guilt,
And in whose spirit there is no guile.
3 But I had become like a potsherd,
my bones had wasted away
through my groaning all day long.
4 For day and night, O Most High,
your hand was oppressive;
I was ravaged, O Shaddai,
as by the drought of summer. *Selah*
5 My sin I made known to you,
and did not hide my guilt from you.
I said, "I shall confess, O Most High,
my transgressions, O Yahweh!"
Then you forgave my sinful guilt. *Selah*
6 And so let every devoted one pray to you.
When an army approaches,
or violent waters rush on,
These will not reach him.
7 You are my shelter,
from the besieger protect me!
My refuge, save me, enfold me! *Selah*
8 I will instruct you and show you
the way you must go;
My eye is never closed on you;
9 Don't be like a horse, a mule—without sense.
With muzzle and straps
must his petulance be curbed;

Then you can approach him.
10 How many are the torments of the wicked!
But who trusts in Yahweh,
with love will he enfold him.
11 Rejoice in Yahweh and be glad, you just,
and shout for joy, all you upright of heart!

Notes

xxxii. A psalm of thanksgiving for recovery from illness. Since disease was believed to be punishment for sin, healing is proof that the transgression is forgiven. Because of the several didactic elements, some would label this a Wisdom psalm.

1. *A maskil.* A sense-giving harmony; it bears a double, intellectual-exegetical and artistic-musical meaning. See M. Gertner, BSOAS 25 (1962), 22–24.

is forgiven. As frequently remarked, the unusual spelling *n^{e}śūy* (cf. vs. 5b) was prompted by the desire for rhyme with *k^{e}sūy*.

2. *the man.* Brigg's observation that *'ādām* is used of an individual only here and in lxxxiv 6, 13 in the Psalter is illuminated by Phoenician practice where *'dm* normally appears in this function; cf. Z. S. Harris, *The Development of the Canaanite Dialects* (New Haven, 1939), p. 52.

3. *become like a potsherd.* The acknowledged similarity of vss. 3–4 to Ps xxii 15–16 suggests the reading *heḥ^{e}raśtī* for MT *heḥ^{e}raštī* and its parsing as a denominative verb from *ḥereś*, "potsherd." In other words, it is the semantic equivalent of xxii 16, *yābēš kaḥereś kōḥī*, "My strength is dried up like a potsherd." See also Ps xxxi 13 and Prov xvii 22.

had wasted away. On *bālū*, see UT, 2064:22–23, *blym alpm*, "The oxen are worn out."

4. *O Most High.* Vocalizing *'ēlī* for MT *'ālay;* consult Note on vs. 5.

your hand was oppressive. Cf. I Sam v 11, *kāb^{e}dāh m^e'ōd yad '^{e}lōhīm šām*, "The hand of God was very oppressive there," and UT, 54:11–13, *w yd ilm p kmtm 'z mid*, "And the hand of the gods is like death here, very powerful."

I was ravaged. Parsing *nehpak* as the niphal participle whose subject is contained in the verb of vs. 3, *heḥ^{e}raštī*, "I had become like a potsherd." This nuance of the verb *hāpak*, "to overturn," is present in Job xii 15, as noted by BDB, p. 245b.

O Shaddai. Pointing *l^{e}šadday* for MT *l^{e}šaddī*, and analyzing the *lamedh* as the vocative particle, studied in the Note on Ps iii 9, and identifying consonantal *šdy* with the divine name Shaddai. The pairing of the divine names *'ēlī,* "Most High," and *šadday,* "Shaddai," is the equivalent of that found in Ps xci 1, where *'elyōn,* "Most High," balances *šadday,* "Shaddai."

5. *I made known to you.* LXX "I acknowledged my sin and did not conceal my iniquity" achieves perfect symmetry by omitting the dative suffix of *'ōdī'ᵃkā.* A symmetry that is more faithful to the exigencies of the Hebrew text can be gained by invoking the principle of the double-duty suffix (cf. NOTE on Ps iii 4) and rendering *lō' kissītī,* parallel to suffixed *'ōdī'ᵃkā,* as "I did not hide (my guilt) from you." Employing this principle, the poet was able to count seven syllables in the first colon and eight in the second.

and did not hide . . . from you. See previous NOTE.

O Most High. The construction *'ōdeh 'ālē* being elsewhere unexampled (BDB, p. 392a), consonantal *'ly* is more suitably pointed as *'ēlī,* the divine appellative studied in NOTE on Ps vii 9. A similar situation obtains in Ps cxxxix 14, *'ōdᵉkā 'al kī nōrē'tā* (MT *nōrā'ōt*), "I shall praise you, O Most High [cf. NOTE on Ps vii 11], since you are so awesome." See NOTES on vs. 4.

O Yahweh. The *lamedh* of *lyhwh* is vocative, a particle treated in NOTE on Ps iii 9. The two cola of vs. 5b are tightly interwoven by the poetic device of enjambment; cf. NOTES on Pss vii 3 and xi 4, and Mowinckel, *The Psalms in Israel's Worship,* II, p. 265.

my sinful guilt. *'ᵃwōn ḥaṭṭā'tī* may be taken either as a case of hendiadys or as another instance of the double-duty suffix to be rendered, "my guilt, my sin."

6. *every devoted one.* The psalmist includes himself in *kōl ḥāsīd,* just as in Ps iv 7 the poet refers to himself as *ḥāsīd* and in Ps v 13 as *ṣaddīq.*

an army approaches. For *rīq,* "army" (MT reads *raq*), see NOTE on Ps ii 1; *māṣā',* "to reach, approach," was studied by Dahood in BCCT, p. 57. In Isa viii 7–8 the three ideas of "army," "overflowing waters," and "reaching" are associated. There is similar imagery in Jer xlvii 2 and Nah i 7, *ṭōb yhwh lᵉmā'ōz bᵉyōm ṣārāh wᵉyōdēᵃ' ḥōsē bō ūbᵉšeṭep 'ōbēr,* "In time of siege Yahweh is better than a fortress, and he cares for those who trust in him when the flood rushes on."

reach him. I.e., the *ḥāsīd,* in this instance the psalmist himself.

7. *my shelter.* Numerous commentators have remarked, and BH³ registers the proposal, that the pronominal suffixes of vs. 7 should all agree with vs. 6, *'ēlāyw.* This agreement is attained when *'ēlāyw* is seen to refer to the poet and when account is taken of the sudden shifts of person commented upon at Ps v 10.

the besieger. Relating consonantal *ṣr* to *ṣwr* or *ṣrr,* "to besiege." This etymology fits better in the immediate context, even though generic "adversary" is quite passable.

My refuge. Consonantal *rny,* pointed *ronnī,* receives a satisfactory etymology and meaning from **rnn,* "to find refuge, to rest," a root that needs to be postulated in Ps lxiii 8 if MT is to be retained: "O that you would be my help, that I might find refuge (*'ărannēn*) in the shadow of your wings." In other words, Ps lxiii 8 expresses the same sentiment as Ps xxxvi 8, *beṣēl kenāpekā yeḥesāyūn,* "(Gods and men) find refuge in the shadow of your wings." In Ps lxxviii 65 the nuance of "rest" is more prominent: *kegibbōr mitrōnēn miyyāyin,* "like a warrior resting after wine." Cf. further Isa xliii 14, "the Chaldaeans whose refuge (*rinnātām*) was in ships."

save me. The object of *pallēṭ* is forthcoming from the suffix of *tesōbebēnī;* cf. NOTE on vs. 5.

enfold me. tesōbebēnī is a jussive continuing imperative *pallēṭ,* a stylistic sequence examined at Ps x 15.

8\. *I will instruct you.* The speaker is Yahweh and the person addressed is the psalmist.

the way you must go. The archaic relative pronoun *zū* equals Ugar. *dū.*

is never closed. Reading *'ī 'āṣāh,* with *'ī* the negative particle that is found in Job xxii 30; Prov v 17, Ugaritic-Phoenician, Mishnaic-Hebrew, Ethiopic, and Akkadian. Cf. Goetze, "Ugaritic Negations," in *Studia Ioanni Pedersen . . . dicata,* pp. 122 f. For *'āṣāh,* "to close the eyes," see Prov xvi 30; Isa xxix 10, xxxiii 15; both Isaian forms are followed by enclitic *mem.* See GB, p. 610a.

9\. *Don't be.* The speaker is still Yahweh; the person addressed, the poet, *tihyū,* which looks like a plural form, is explained as the second-person singular with the archaic ending *-ū,* as in Ugaritic and in Ps x 2. According to the apparatus in BH^3, two MSS do read the singular —apparently an attempt to modernize the text.

a mule. Hitherto unattested in the other Semitic languages, *pered* now makes two appearances in the Ras Shamra tablets, in UT, 2044:10 and 2101:12, *rṭ l ql d ybl prd,* "A garment for the courier who travels by mule," badly misconstrued by C. Virolleaud in GLECS 7 (1955), 21, who took *ybl prd* as "*qui apporte* (*ou 'amène, conduit'*)." Syntactically more probable is the parsing of *ybl* as qal passive with *prd* an accusative of means; hence literally, "who is borne by mule." Ugaritic-Hebrew *pered* further points up the strict lexical relationship subsisting between these two dialects.

muzzle. The correct meaning of *meteg,* usually rendered "bridle," is preserved in Vulg. and *Juxta Hebraeos, camus,* "muzzle." The same meaning of *meteg* is found in Isa xxxvii 29 ‖ II Kings xix 28, "Because you raged against me and your gnashing of teeth reached my ears, I shall put a hook in your nose, *ūmitgī bīśepātekā.*" Here *mitgī* can scarcely denote "bridle," since this will not silence an animal, nor is it placed upon the lips; it is put between the lips or in the mouth. The hapax legomenon MT *ša'ᵃnanᵉkā,* which is written in 1QIsª *šnnkh* with superscript *aleph,* derives from *šnn,* "to gnash the teeth," in Ugaritic. Job xvi 9 pairs the two ideas of "rage" and "gnashing of teeth," just as here. Once *šnnk* is correctly derived, the true sense of *meteg* follows; the "muzzle" serves to prevent a beast from biting or from raising his voice; see Lesêtre in *Dictionnaire de la Bible,* IV, col. 1347. Cf. also Prov xxvi 3, where Vulg. renders *meteg* by *camus.* On *resen,* "muzzle, straps," see Zorell, ZLH, p. 777b.

his petulance. The root of consonantal *'dy* (pointed *'uddī*) is doubtless *'dd,* Arabic-Ugaritic *ġadda,* "to swell up, be irritated." For example, UT, 'nt:II:25, *tġdd kbdh bṣḥq,* "Her liver swells with laughter," while Arabic IV, *'aġadda 'ala,* "he was irritated with," brings out the other aspect of the verb. The parallelism in Job x 17, however, clinches the meaning: *tᵉḥaddēš 'dyk negdī wᵉtereb ka'aśᵉkā 'immādī,* "You intensify your petulance toward me, and increase your irritation with me." The balance with *ka'aś,* "irritation," reinforces the value of *'dyk.* In the psalm, J. Calès, *Le livre des Psaumes* (Paris, 1936), I, p. 350, correctly rendered the substantive *pétulance.* Cf. Ps ciii 5, and Sigmund Mowinckel, *Psalmenstudien* (see Selected Bibliography) I, pp. 52 f.

Then you. As in Ugaritic-Arabic, *bal* sometimes has positive force in Hebrew; cf. NOTE on Ps x 15 and Dahood, PNWSP, p. 31.

can approach him. Parsing *qᵉrōb* as imperative, attaching *kaph* of *'lyk* to following *rabbīm,* and parsing *'ly* as containing third-person singular suffix *-y* (cf. NOTE on vs. 4). The same false division of consonants can be seen in Isa lii 14a, *ka'ᵃšer šāmᵉmū 'ālēy kī* (MT *'āleykā*) *rabbīm,* "As many indeed were appalled at him." Here the *kī* is emphatic; cf. R. Gordis, "The Asseverative *kaph* in Ugaritic and Hebrew," JAOS 63 (1943), 176–78, for general orientation.

10. *How many.* Identifying *kī* of *kī rabbīm* with superlative *kī* in such expressions as Gen i 12, *kī ṭōb,* "How good!," and Isa xxii 9, "And he saw the breaches of the City of David, *kī rabbū,*" which is probably to be rendered "how they have multiplied" or "how great they have become," as proposed by W. F. Albright in *Mélanges André Robert* (Paris, 1957), pp. 22–26. Albright's new and convincing parallel to the biblical expressions comes from the cuneiform letters from Ras Shamra published by J. Nougayrol which contain many typically Canaanite usages. This equation further points up the ill-advised separation of Ugaritic from Hebrew and Phoenician by Moscati and others; cf. Moscati, *An Introduction to the Comparative Grammar of the Semitic Languages, Phonology and Morphology,* pp. 9 f., and Alfred Haldar, "The Position of Ugaritic among the Semitic Languages," in BO 21 (1964), 267–77, especially p. 276.

with love. The fondness of the psalmists for the accusative of means preceding its verb (cf. NOTE on Ps v 10) favors the adoption of the version put forth by Baethgen, Gunkel, and others, *"den umgibt er mit Gnade,"* as against CCD and RSV, "But steadfast love surrounds him who trusts in the Lord."

11. *you just . . . you upright of heart.* These parallel vocatives bear on the grammatical analysis of the opening verse of the next psalm.

PSALM 33

(xxxiii 1–22)

1 Exult, you just, in Yahweh,
 in lauding, O upright, the Glorious One!
2 Praise Yahweh with the harp,
 on the ten-stringed lyre play to him.
3 Sing to him a song that is new,
 play sweetly with sounds of gladness.
4 For the word of Yahweh is direct,
 and every work of his is truth itself.
5 He loves what is just and right,
 of Yahweh's kindness the earth is full.
6 By the word of Yahweh
 were the heavens made,
And by the breath of his mouth
 all their host.
7 He gathers into a jar
 the waters of the sea,
He puts the deeps into storehouses.
8 Let all the earth fear Yahweh,
 all the world's inhabitants revere him.
9 For he spoke and it was,
 he commanded and it stood forth.
10 Yahweh frustrates the plan of nations,
 brings to naught the designs of peoples.
11 But the plan of Yahweh
 has stood fixed from eternity,
The designs of his mind
 are for generation upon generation.
12 How blest the nation
 Yahweh its God has blest;
The people he has chosen
 for his own patrimony.

13 From heaven Yahweh looks down,
he sees all the sons of men.
14 From the throne where he sits
he intently gazes
Upon all the inhabitants of the world.
15 The Creator inspects their intention,
the Observer all their works.
16 No king gives himself victory
through the size of his army,
No warrior delivers himself
through his massive strength.
17 Useless for victory is his horse,
and he cannot rescue himself
By his military might.
18 Mark well: The eye of Yahweh
is on those who fear him,
on those who rely on his kindness,
19 To rescue them from Death,
to preserve their lives from the Hungry One.
20 Our soul is waiting for Yahweh,
our warrior, our shield is he.
21 For in him our heart rejoices,
in his holy name we trust.
22 May your kindness, O Yahweh, be upon us,
since we have put our trust in you.

Notes

xxxiii. A hymn to Yahweh, the Creator and Master of history.

1. *in lauding.* The preposition *b* with *nā'wāh* is forthcoming from *b-yhwh* in the first colon on the strength of the principle of the double-duty preposition studied below in Note on vs. 7.

The form *nā'wāh* is piel infinitive construct (GK, §§ 52p, 45d) of the root *n'w*, a by-form of *nāwāh* (GB, p. 491a) which in Exod xv 2 is reproduced by LXX as *doksásō* and by Vulg. as *glorificabo*. The two other occurrences of *nā'wāh* in the Psalter fit this definition: xciii 5, *l^{e}bēt^{e}kā na'^{a}wāh qōdeš yhwh l^{e}'ōrek yāmīm,* "In your house will be lauding by the saints for days without end, O Yahweh"; cxlvii 1, *kī ṭōb zamm^{e}rāh '^{e}lōhēnū kī nā'īm nā'wāh t^{e}hillāh,* "How good it is to hymn our God, how delightful to laud our Glorious One!" The pairing with the infinitive construct *zamm*^{e}*rāh* reveals the infinitival nature of *nā'wāh,* while the balance with *'*^{e}*lōhēnū* shows *t*^{e}*hillāh* to be a divine appellative sharing the double-duty suffix (see NOTE on Ps iii 4).

O upright. The *lamedh* of *lay*^{e}*šārīm* is parsed as vocative, a particle discussed at Ps iii 9. I am indebted to D. N. Freedman for this observation. Notice the two parallel vocatives *ṣaddīqīm* and *yišrē lēb* in the preceding verse (Ps xxxii 11).

the Glorious One. See end of NOTE on vs. 19 below and the annotation to Ps xxii 4, *t*^{e}*hillōt yiśrā'ēl,* "the Glory of Israel."

2. *ten-stringed lyre.* On *kinnōr,* Ugar. *knr,* see NOTE on Ps xlix 5.

3. *play sweetly. hēṭībū naggēn* may profitably be compared with Ezek xxxiii 32, *kaššīr* (MT *k*^{e}*šīr*) *'ūgābīm* (MT *'*^{a}*gābīm*) *y*^{e}*pēh qōl ūmēṭīb naggēn,* "a skillful flutist, fine-voiced, and a maker of sweet music," and with UT, 'nt:I:20, *yšr ǵzr ṭb ql,* "The sweet-voiced lad sings." Cf. *Biblica* 44 (1963), 531 f.

4. *is truth itself.* The *b* of *be'*^{e}*mūnāh* serves an intensifying function; cf. NOTE on Ps xxix 4.

5. *Yahweh's kindness.* Parsing *ḥesed* as an accusative of material-with-which, as in Ps xlviii 12; for the position of *ḥesed* before its verb, see NOTE on Ps v 10. Especially relevant parallels include Ps xxxii 10 and Amos vi 6.

6. *all their host.* I.e., the stars. That *ṣābā',* "army, host," could also refer to the "stars" resides in the poetic tradition that the stars were warriors who executed the Lord's commands; cf. Judg v 20 and Ps ciii 20–21.

7. *into a jar.* Vocalizing *kened* instead of MT *kannēd* and identifying it with Ugar. *knd,* Akk. *kandu,* "jar, pitcher," which C. Bezold, *Babylonisch-Assyrisches Glossar* (Heidelberg, 1926), p. 143, tentatively describes as a West-Semitic loanword in Akkadian (the Ras Shamra tablets sustain his opinion). Cf. Aistleitner, WuS, No. 1337. As Briggs has pointed out, the parallelism is better served when consonantal *knd* is understood with LXX and most ancient versions as "flask." While these doubtless read *nō'd,* "water-skin." Ugaritic-Akkadian proffer a solution requiring no consonantal alterations.

As a corollary, the imagery is to be dissociated from Exod xv 8, "The streams stood up in a heap," and related to that found in Job xxxviii 8–10, 22, 37; Ps cxxxv 7; Isa xlv 3; Jer x 13, which mention storehouses of snow, hail, and water in the heavens. The figure of storing water in a jar is an apt one, since ancient Palestinians stored their water in earthen jars.

The lack of a preposition with *kened* is to be explained on the principle of the double-duty preposition (mentioned above in connection with vs. 1), a poetic practice to be subsumed under the general heading of ellipsis; cf. GK, § 119hh. Other instances are examined in the NOTES on Pss xii 3, xxxviii 23, xl 5, xlii 5, 1 8, lii 3, lxv 5, lxvii 5, cxxxv 6; cf. Isa xlviii 14; Jon ii 4, *wattašlīkēnī m^eṣūlāh bīl^ebab yammīm,* "For you cast me into the deep, into the heart of the seas." The standard insertion of *b* before *m^eṣūlāh* is made unnecessary by the recognition that one preposition can suffice for two nouns in tandem. An equally good example is found in Hab iii 8b.

For Ugaritic usage, see UT, p. 97, n. 2, and on 126:III:9–10, *n'm lḥṭt b'n bm nr ksmm,* "Sweet to the wheat in the furrow, to the emmer in the tilth," see Ginsberg, LKK, p. 47, and M. H. Pope in JCS 5 (1951), 126. Gordon, UT, p. 143, seems to have disregarded this poetic practice when rendering 125:14–15, *bḥyk abn nšmḫ blmtk ngln,* "We rejoice, O our father, in thy life; thine immortality, we are glad therein." It seems quite clear that the power of *b* in *bḥyk* extends to the corresponding substantive *blmtk,* which should accordingly be rendered, "In your immortality we are glad." To be sure, one may argue that the *b* of *blmtk* is elided, as in *bt* = *bbt,* but the translation would remain the same. In neither case can Gordon's version be sustained.

11. *from eternity.* This interpretation of *l^e'ōlām* is examined in the NOTES on Pss ix 8 and xxix 10.

12. *God has blest.* The relative *'ašer* is often deleted since the opposite number *hā'ām bāḥar* does without it, but the problem might be resolved by the verbal pointing *'iššēr,* which uncovers a theological wordplay on *'ašrē* and *'iššēr,* as in Deut xxxiii 29; cf. NOTE on Ps xlvii 10. See further *Biblica* 44 (1963), 298. D. N. Freedman proposes (unpublished) to associate *'ašer* with both *gōy* and *'ām* and to make *bāḥar* the predicate of both cola of the interlocking verse, so as to read, "How blest the nation whom its God Yahweh, the people (whom its God Yahweh) has chosen for his own patrimony."

14. *the throne where he sits.* Since in Pss lxxxix 15 and xcvii 2 it signifies the "dais of a throne," *mākōn* by metonymy may have come to mean here the throne itself. If such be the case, then *m^ekōn šibt^ekā* (also in Sirach xxxvi 13) might be compared with UT, 'nt:VI:15, *ksu ṯbth,* "the throne where he sits." Cf. Exod xv 17 and Isa xviii 4.

15. *inspects their intention.* Reading (for MT *yaḥad,* hitherto unexplained in this context) *yeḥde,* the Canaanite form of *yeḥze* studied at Ps xxi 7 and in *Biblica* 45 (1964), 407 f. This error may be ascribable not only to the dialectal nature of the form but also to the defective spelling *yḥd* for *yḥdh.* The punctuators similarly confused *yeḥde* with *yaḥad* in Ps xlix 11, where the balancing verb is *yir'eh,* and in Job xxxiv 29, where *yḥd* is found in connection with *yašqīṭ* and *y^ešūrennū,* both verbs of seeing. Consult, on the last passage, Samuel Terrien, *Job* (Neuchâtel, 1963), p. 230, n. 3; the proposed analysis of the psalm

text has been accepted by Brekelmans, *Ras Sjamra en het Oude Testament,* p. 8.

The connotation "intention" found in *lēb* recurs in Ps lv 22, *ūqᵃrab libbō,* "But his intention was war."

16. *gives himself victory.* Understanding niphal *nōšā'* in a reflexive sense.

17. *his horse.* The article of *hassūs* serves as a pronominal suffix parallel to *ḥēlō.* Cf. NOTE on Ps xxxi 20 and the usage in Ps lxxxv 13, *haṭṭōb,* "his rain." The steed of the king is intended by *hassūs.*

rescue himself. Reading, with LXX, Targ. niphal *yimmālēṭ,* with reflexive force, for MT piel *yᵉmallēṭ.*

19. *from the Hungry One.* "The Hungry One" is a poetic name for Death. Either vocalizing *rā'ēb* (see comment below on Job xviii 12) or retaining MT *rā'āb* and explaining it as abstract "Hunger" for concrete "Hungry One" according to the poetic usage treated in NOTE on Ps v 8.

The insatiable appetite of Death was proverbial in both Ugaritic and Hebrew literatures. Gaster, *Thespis,* 1961, p. 206, gathers the relevant texts, e.g., Isa v 14; Hab ii 5; and Prov i 12. To these may be added: (a) Deut xxxii 24, as interpreted in JAOS 63 (1943), 178, where Robert Gordis renders *rā'āb* as personified "Hunger"; (b) Jer xviii 21, *tēn 'et bᵉnēhem lᵉrā'āb,* "Give their children to the Hungry One"—the verse later on mentions *hᵃrūgē māwet,* "those slain by Death," thus witnessing the same pairing that is found in the present verse; (c) perhaps the most telling new example, Job xviii 12, a notoriously obscure text: *yᵉhī rā'ēb 'ōnō wᵉ'ēd nākōn lᵉṣal'ō,* "Let the Hungry One face him ['ōnō is qal participle of *'ānāh,* "to meet," followed by accusative suffix], with Death stationed at his side" (cf. NOTE on Ps xxxviii 18). On *'ēd,* "Death," cf. NOTE on Ps xviii 19.

Notice in the present passage that the preposition *min* of *mimmāwet* is balanced by *b,* "from," in *bᵉrā'āb;* cf. NOTE on Ps xx 7.

20. *our warrior.* Cf. NOTE on Ps xxxv 2.

21. *our heart rejoices.* With *yiśmaḥ libbēnū,* compare UT, 'nt:II:25–26, *ymlu lbh bšmḫt,* "Her heart is filled with joy."

PSALM 34
(xxxiv 1–23)

1 *Of David, who feigned madness before Abimelech who compelled him to leave.*

2 I will bless Yahweh at all times,
his praise will ever be in my mouth.
3 In Yahweh my soul will glory, [2]*
let the humble hear and rejoice.
4 Glorify Yahweh with me, [3]
let us extol his name together.
5 I sought Yahweh and he answered me, [4]
and from all my terrors he rescued me.
6 They looked at him [5]
and their faces shone;
They will never be humiliated.
7 This poor man called and Yahweh heard him, [6]
and from all his anguish he saved him.
8 The angel of Yahweh is encamped [7]
around those who fear him,
that he might liberate them.
9 Taste and drink deeply, [8]
for Yahweh is sweet;
How blest the man who trusts in him!
10 Oh, fear Yahweh, you his saints, [9]
for those who fear him will lack nothing.
11 The rich will grow poor and hungry, [10]
but they who seek Yahweh will lack no blessing.
12 Come, children, listen to me, [11]
the fear of Yahweh will I teach you.
13 What man is there who desires life, [12]
longs for days to enjoy prosperity?

* Verse numbers in RSV.

14 Then keep your tongue from evil, [13]
and your lips from speaking guile.
15 Shun evil and do good, [14]
seek peace and pursue it.
16 The eyes of Yahweh are on the just, [15]
and his ears are toward their cry.
17 The fury of Yahweh is with the evildoers, [16]
to root out their memory from the earth.
18 When they cry, Yahweh hears them, [17]
and from all their anguish rescues them.
19 Close is Yahweh to the brokenhearted, [18]
and those crushed in spirit he saves.
20 Many are the trials of the just, [19]
but from them all Yahweh rescues him.
21 He watches over all his bones, [20]
not one of them shall be broken.
22 Evil will slay the wicked, [21]
and those who hate the just will perish.
23 Yahweh ransoms the life of his servants, [22]
and they who trust in him will not perish.

Notes

xxxiv. A psalm of thanksgiving composed by an individual whose prayer for deliverance from tribulations was heard by Yahweh. The grateful poet invites the afflicted to join him in his hymn of praise.

Being acrostic in form, the psalm offers a sequence of sentiments whose logical connections are not always immediately evident. The reader and the exegete must accordingly take into account the formal element and its logical consequences.

The psalm heading alludes to an episode of David with Achish, the king of Gath (I Sam xxi 11–16). Instead of Achish the psalm heading reads Abimelech, which many commentators consider an historical inaccuracy on the part of the psalmist or psalm editor, but it is quite possible that Abimelech was the Semitic name of the king of Gath. The author of Gen xxvi 1 mentions an Abimelech "king of the Philistines" in Gerar.

7. *Yahweh heard him.* Though not furnished with an accusative suffix, *šāmē*^{a}*ʿ* is entitled to one by virtue of its balance with *hōšīʿō*.

See NOTE below on vs. 18 and NOTES on Pss iii 4 and especially iv 4, where other instances of the double-duty suffix with *šāma'* are given.

9. *Taste.* Failure to grasp the nature of the metaphor has led *La Bible de la Pléiade,* II, p. 960, to render *ṭa'ᵃmū,* which really means "taste, savor!" by *constatez,* a dubious translation. The correct version is found in the citation in I Pet ii 3, "you have tasted."

and drink deeply. Assigning imperative *rᵉ'ū,* often deleted, to *yr'* II, "to be fat, sated, drink deeply," semantically cognate with *rāwāh,* "to be saturated, drink one's fill," studied by Dahood in PNWSP, p. 23, in connection with Prov xi 25, where *yūrā'* (MT *yōrē'*) is paired with *tᵉduššān.* Texts studied there includes Ps xci 16; Isa liii 11; Job x 15, where in each instance the synonymous verb is *śāba',* "to be sated, satisfied."

For the exegesis of the present verse, Prov xxiii 31 is perhaps most suitable: *'al tīre' yayin kī yit'addām,* "Drink not deeply of wine when it is red." G. R. Driver in *Biblica* 32 (1951), 187, recognized that the verse was a warning not to drink red wine unless it had been cut with water, but he needlessly emended *tīre'* to *tirweh.* Another occurrence of the root is studied at Ps l 23.

Yahweh is sweet. Vulg. correctly renders *quoniam suavis est Dominus.* For this nuance of *ṭōb,* cf. UT, 1084:1, *yn ṭb,* "sweet wine," and Song of Sol i 2, *kī ṭōbīm daddekā* (MT *dōdekā*) *miyyayin,* "For your breasts are sweeter than wine." See further, Albright, "Archaic Survivals in the Text of Canticles," *Hebrew and Semitic Studies presented to Godfrey Rolles Driver,* p. 2, and Aistleitner, WuS, p. 119.

10. *will lack nothing.* Found but once in the Psalter, *maḥsōr* occurs in El Amarna, 287:16, and as an economic term in UT, 1137:1, *mḫsrn,* with the meaning "deficit."

11. *The rich.* This is how LXX, Vulg., and Syr. understood *kᵉpīrīm,* which is capable of two explanations. Either it is the word for "young lions," used metaphorically (some twenty-four animal names are employed metaphorically in the Bible; cf. NOTE on Ps ii 5 and *Biblica* 40 [1959], 161 f.), or *kᵉpīrīm* is a by-form of *kabbīrīm,* "the great, magnates," and hence to be pointed likewise. See Ezek xxxviii 13, *šᵉbā' ūdᵉdān wᵉsōḥᵃrē taršīš wᵉkol kᵉpīrehā yō'mᵉrū lᵉkā,* "Sheba and Dedan and the merchants of Tarshish and all its magnates will say to you." The submission that *kᵉpīrehā* be emended to *rōkᵉlehā,* "its traders," is drained of all plausibility by the occurrence of the same substantive here.

15. *Shun evil.* The phrase *sūr mēra'* is important for the correct interpretation of Prov xxii 3, which will now be seen to contain an infixed *-t-* form of the verb *sūr: 'ārūm rā'āh rā'āh wᵉyistār ūpᵉtāyīm 'ābᵉrū wᵉne'ᵉnāšū,* "A shrewd man sees trouble coming and avoids it,

/ While simpletons keep on and pay the penalty" (Scott, The Anchor Bible, vol. 18).

17. *The fury of Yahweh.* For this sense of *pānīm* and parallels, see *Biblica* 44 (1963), 548 and NOTE on Ps xxi 10; the most relevant parallels are Lam iv 16, *p^enē yhwh ḥill^eqām lō' yōsīp l^ehabbīṭām,* "The fury of Yahweh destroyed them [identifying *ḥill^eqām* with Ugar. *ḫlq,* "to perish, die"], he shall look upon them no more," and Ps lxxx 17, "At your angry rebuke they perish."

with the evildoers. A possible counterpart to *p^enē yhwh b^e'ōśē rā'* in UT, 75:I:33, *wbhm pn b'l,* "And with them was the fury of Baal."

For the hostile sense of *b,* see Pss cxxiv 3, cxli 5, and Brockelmann, *Hebräische Syntax,* § 106h.

18. *When they cry.* The subject is "the just" of vs. 16; the acrostic arrangement of the psalm may account for the disruption of thought caused by vs. 17.

Yahweh hears them. As in vs. 7, the poet employs one pronominal suffix with two parallel verbs.

22. *Evil will slay the wicked.* Cf. Prov xxi 25, *ta'^awat 'āṣēl t^emītennū,* "The indolence of the slothful will slay him." See PNWSP, p. 41. This further rapport with Wisdom Literature tallies with the sapiential elements which scholars have identified in this psalm.

will perish. This denotation of *'āšam* has been examined at Ps v 11.

23. *ransoms the life.* The verb *pdy* occurs in UT, 1006:2.12, a juridical text which states that a certain EWRKL emancipated a family of seven by paying a hundred shekels of silver to the citizens of Beirut. Poetic metaphor depicts Yahweh paying ransom money (to Death) to assure his saints of life. Cf. Job v 20, *b^erā'āb pād^ekā mimmāwet,* "In famine he ransomed you from Death."

PSALM 35

(xxxv 1–28)

1 Attack, O Yahweh, those who attack me,
combat those who combat me.
2 Grip the shield and buckler,
and rise to my battle.
3 Ready the spear and the javelin
to confront my pursuers.
Say to my soul, "I am your victory."
4 Let those be humiliated and disgraced
who seek my life;
Let those be turned back in shame
who plan my discomfiture.
5 Let them be like chaff before the wind,
with the angel of Yahweh driving them;
6 Let their destiny be Darkness and Destruction,
with the angel of Yahweh pursuing them.
7 For they secretly hid a pit for me,
with their net
They stealthily spied on my life.
8 May the pit come upon him unawares,
and the net which he hid ensnare him;
Into the pit let him fall.
9 But my soul shall rejoice in Yahweh,
exult in his victory.
10 All my bones shall say,
"O Yahweh, who is like you,
Who rescues the afflicted
from one too strong for him,
Both the afflicted and the needy
from his despoiler."
11 Malicious witnesses testify against me,
they whom I know not interrogate me.

12 They repay me evil for good,
ravaging my soul.
13 But I—when they played the pipe,
my garment was sackcloth;
I afflicted myself through fasting,
and my prayer rested upon my bosom;
It was like a friend,
like a brother to me.
14 I went about like one grieving his mother,
I was bent over in mourning.
15 When I stumbled they gathered with glee,
smiters gathered about me,
And they whom I did not know
tore me to pieces,
And did not desist from slandering me.
16 My encircling mockers gnashed their teeth at me.
17 How long, O Lord, will you idly watch?
Rescue my life from their pits,
my face from the young lions.
18 I will thank you in the great congregation,
in the mighty throng will I praise you.
19 Let not my treacherous foes rejoice over me,
my stealthy enemies who wink their eye.
20 For they do not speak of peace,
but attack the oppressed in the land.
21 They conceive treacherous plans,
and they open wide their mouth against me
saying, "Aha, Aha! our own eye has seen him."
22 Look, O Yahweh, be not silent;
Lord, be not far from me.
23 Bestir yourself and awake to my defense,
My God and my Lord, to my combat.
24 Defend me as befits your justice, O Yahweh;
my God, let them not rejoice over me.
25 Lest they boast in their heart,
"Aha, our throat!"
Lest they boast, "We have engorged him."
26 Let all be put to shame and confusion,
who rejoice at my misfortune;

Let them be clothed with shame and infamy,
who calumniate me.
27 May they shout for joy and be glad,
who desire my vindication;
And may they ever say, "Yahweh is great,
who desires the well-being of his servant."
28 Then my tongue will proclaim your justice,
all the day long your praise.

NOTES

xxxv. An individual lament in which the psalmist prays for deliverance from personal enemies.

1. *Attack . . . who attack me.* W. F. Albright in JPOS 14 (1934), 118, No. 73, has compared the cognate accusative construction *rībāh . . . yᵉrībay* with UT, 1 Aqht:196, *imḫṣ mḫṣ aḫy,* "I will smite the smiter of my brother." In the psalm, the martial language is purely figurative; the poet's enemies are those who slander him and accuse him of serious crimes. The morphologically unusual substantive *yᵉrībay,* with preformative *yodh,* comports with Canaanite morphology as reflected in the Ugaritic nouns *ypḥ,* "witness," and *yṣḥ,* "herald" (probable meaning).

2. *to my battle.* Deriving *'ezrātī* from *'zr* II, Ugar. *ǵzr,* "lad, warrior," rather than from *'zr* I, Ugar. *'ḏr,* "to help." The root has been widely recognized in Hebrew; e.g., Ginsberg in JBL 57 (1938), 210 f., who cited Job vi 13, ix 13; Ezek xii 14; I Chron xii 1; Driver, in CML, p. 142, n. 17; M. Dahood in *Biblica* 43 (1962), 225 f. To be added to the list is Judg v 23, *kī lō' bā'ū lᵉ'ezrat yhwh baggibbōrīm,* "Since they did not come to Yahweh's war as warriors." This is the motif of the holy war. Equally convincing is the usage in Nah iii 9, *pūṭ wᵉlūbīm hāyū bᵉ'ezrātēk,* "Put and the Libyans were in your army," which is to be interpreted in the light of Ezek xxvii 10, "Persia and Lud and Put were the men of war in your army (*bᵉḥēlēk*)." A comparison of these two statements reveals the synonymy of *'ezrātēk* and *ḥēlēk.*

3. *Ready the spear.* A spear attached to a chariot was kept in a sheath, so that one could correctly use the phrase "draw the spear," but it seems preferable to associate *hārēq* with *rīq* II, "to prepare, mobilize," studied in the NOTE on Ps ii 1.

and the javelin. Much-contested *sᵉgōr* (probably to be vocalized *seger*) occurs in 1 Qumran Milḥamah, 5:7, with the meaning "socket of a javelin." By metonymy, it denotes "pike" or "javelin" in the present text. See J. Carmignac in VT 5 (1955), 359; Yadin, *The Scroll of the War of the Sons of Light against the Sons of Darkness*, pp. 137, 281. On p. 137, n. 3, Yadin correctly observes that there is no longer need for dragging in Scythian *sagaris* or emending to *seghodh* (Akk. *šukudu*) to explain the etymology of *seger*.

confront my pursuers. A related motif in UT, ʻnt:II:3–5, *klat ṯǵrt bht ʻnt wtqry ǵlmm bšt ǵr*, "Anath closed the gates of the mansion and encountered the warriors at the foot of the mountain."

your victory. The military context favors this nuance of *yešūʻātēk* over "your salvation" (CCD).

4. *be humiliated*. Contrast Ps cxxvii 5, "They shall not be humiliated but shall drive the foes from the gate," as proposed in TS 14 (1953), 85–88.

my discomfiture. Generic *rāʻātī*, "my misfortune," is specified by the military context.

5. *driving them*. Though formally without a suffix, *dōḥeh* acquires one in translation by reason of its parallelism with suffixed *rōdepām* in vs. 6 on the principle of the double-duty suffix studied at Ps iii 4.

6. *their destiny*. This sense of *darkām* is discussed briefly in the Note on Ps xlix 14.

Darkness and Destruction. These are poetic names for the underworld. Thus *ḥōšek* in I Sam ii 9; Ps lxxxviii 13; Job xxii 11, etc., denotes Sheol, analogous to *'apēlāh*, "Darkness," in Jer xxiii 12, while *ḥalaqlaqqōt* probably stems from *ḥlq*, Ugar. *ḫlq*, "to perish," which recurs in Ps lxxiii 18, *'ak baḥalāqōt tištelēmō* (MT *tāšīt lāmō*), "Surely in Destruction will you plant them"; cf. *Biblica* 44 (1963), 548; 45 (1964), 408 and Note on Ps v 10. A cognate is Jer xxiii 12, *lākēn yihyeh darkām lāhem kaḥalaqlaqqōt ba'apēlāh yiddāḥū wenāpelū bāh*, "And so their way shall be like Perdition to them; they shall be thrust into Darkness and fall into it."

7. *with their net*. *rištām* is an accusative of means preceding its verb, an element of style remarked at Ps v 10.

They stealthily. Consonantal *ḥnm* should perhaps be dissociated from *ḥinnām*, "without cause." The basis for this assertion lies chiefly in Prov i 17, *kī ḥnm* (MT *ḥinnām*) *mezōrāh hārāšet beʻēnē kol baʻal kānāp*, "For stealthily is the net spread out, out of sight (*beʻēnē* equals *mēʻēnē*) of every winged creature." In Prov i 11, *ḥnm*, in conjunction with *ne'erebāh* and *niṣpenāh*, evidently contains a kindred notion, such as "sneakily" or "stealthily." In other words, Prov i 11, *niṣpenāh lenāqī ḥnm*, "Let us stealthily hide for the innocent," is the equivalent of Ps xxxvii 7, *ḥnm ḥāperū lenapšī*, "They stealthily spied on my life." In a very cryptic Ugaritic letter, UT, 1020:8–10, one reads, *im mlkytn yrgm aḫnnn wiḫd*, "If Milkyaton gives the word, I will ambush him (?) and seize him." The root, then, would be *ḫnn*, and thus to be distinguished from *ḥnn*, "to be gracious." The parallelism in vs. 17 points to the same meaning for *ḥnm: 'ōyᵉbay šāqer śōnᵉ'ay ḥnm*, "my treacherous foes, my stealthy enemies."

spied on my life. For this nuance of *ḥāpar*, Deut i 22 and Josh ii 2, where it means "to spy out" or "reconnoiter" the land, and Job xxxix 29, *miššām ḥāpar 'ōkel lᵉmērāḥōq 'ēnāyw yabbīṭū*, "Thence he spies out the prey, / His eyes see it from afar" (Pope, The Anchor Bible, vol. 15). In other words, *ḥāpᵉrū lᵉnapši* is synonymous with Ps iii 3, *'ōmᵉrīm lᵉnapši*, "who eye my life."

8. *pit come upon him*. For the sense of *šō'āh, fosse, piège* (*Fallgrube*), see Milik, *Biblica* 38 (1957), 249 f. LXX reads *pagís*, and there is good reason to question the standard assumption that *pagís*, "trap," reflects Heb. *šūḥā*, "pit, trap," since *šō'āh*, "trap, pit," occurs in a Qumranic text. The suffix of *tᵉbō'ēhū* is datival, a usage greatly clarified by Ugaritic-Phoenician syntax; see Bogaert, *Biblica* 45 (1964), 220–47.

10. *the afflicted and the needy*. Though usually deleted, most recently by Kraus, *Psalmen*, I, pp. 274 f., *wᵉ'ānī* is needed to form, with *wᵉ'ebyōn*, a "ballast variant" to *'ānī* of the first colon. If a major word in the first colon is not balanced in the second, then one or more words in the second tend to be longer than their parallels in the first colon. In the present instance, the participle *maṣṣīl* in the first colon finds no counterpart in the second; this lack is compensated for by *wᵉ'ānī wᵉ'ebyōn*, which is, of course, longer than parallel *'ānī* of the first colon. Ugaritic poetry offers numerous examples; e.g., UT, 1 Aqht: 42–44, *šb' šnt yṣrk b'l ṯmn rkb 'rpt*, "Seven years may Baal fail, eight the Mounter of the Clouds." For full discussion, see UT, § 13.116, pp. 135 ff.

11. *Malicious witnesses*. The specific force of *ḥāmās* is difficult to establish; LXX renders it "false," while some modern versions prefer "unjust."

testify against me. Being parallel to *yiš'ālūnī*, with a pronominal suffix, *yᵉqūmūn* may be assumed to have one on the principle of the double-duty suffix. For this meaning of *qūm*, see Ps xxvii 12; Deut xix 15–16.

they . . . interrogate me. In Virolleaud, *Palais royal d'Ugarit*, II, 161:5, *šal* is a *terminus technicus* for "investigation." Cf. Eissfeldt in JSS 5 (1960), 49. T. H. Gaster in VT 4 (1954), 73, understands *yiš'ālūnī* as "to question a witness in a law court," while W. F. Albright in JBL 75 (1956), 257, is of the opinion that the name Sheol originally meant "ordeal, examination." In the Akkadian texts from Ras Shamra published by Nougayrol in *Palais royal d'Ugarit*, III, 16.157, lines 25–28, p. 84, one reads the following curse: "And he who shall annul this gift, may the storm-god, the lord of Mount Casius, interrogate him (*li-iš-al-šu*)"; see Gevirtz, "West-Semitic Curses and the Problem of the Origins of Hebrew Law," VT 11 (1961), 137–58.

12. *ravaging my soul.* Reading *šaklēl napšī* for MT *šᵉkōl lᵉnapšī*, a shaphel infinite absolute from *kālāh*, "to be spent, destroyed." The form can scarcely be dissociated from Ugar. *škllt*, an obscure personage in a class with *š'tqt*, "she who makes (disease) pass away." The continuation of a finite verb by an infinitive absolute can be seen in UT, 126:v:10–11, *my bilm ydy mrṣ gršm zblm*, "Which of the gods can expel the sickness, exorcizing the disease?"

13. *played the pipe.* I.e., while they celebrated, the psalmist fasted. Reading (for MT *ḥᵃlōtām*) *ḥallōtām*, from *ḥll*, "to play the pipe," Akk. *ḫalālu*, "to pipe, wheeze," a root that recurs in Pss xli 4, lxxxvii 7; I Kings i 40; and probably in I Sam xviii 6. On the unusual infinitival form which seems based upon a *lamedh he* verb, cf. GK, § 67r, where such forms as Ps lxxvii 10, *ḥannōt* from *ḥnn*, lxxvii 11, *ḥallōtī* from *ḥll*, and Ezek xxxvi 3 *šammōt* from *šmm* are discussed. Though virtually all modern versions relate consonantal *ḥlwtm* to the verb "to be sick," LXX rendered it *parenochlein*, "when they molested me," which lends indirect support to my interpretation.

afflicted myself. I.e., stifled the desire for revenge.

through fasting. Or "while fasting"; cf. Ps lxix 11, *wā'ebbᵉkāh* (MT *wā'ebkeh*) *baṣṣōm napšī*, "And I poured out [root is *nbk/npk*] my soul while fasting."

rested upon my bosom. In other words, my prayer was like a close friend. Cf. John xiii 23, "There was at the table reclining in Jesus' bosom one of his disciples whom Jesus loved."

Deriving *tāšūb* from *šwb*, a by-form of *yšb*, "to sit, rest," discussed in the NOTES on Pss vii 8 and xxiii 6. Cf. Eccles vii 9, "For vexation resides (*yānūᵃḥ*) in the bosom of fools."

friend . . . brother. Comparing *kᵉrēᵃ' kᵉ'āḥ* with UT, 1019:8, *laḫy lr'y*, "to my brother, to my friend."

14. *grieving his mother.* With LXX and Syr., vocalizing *'ābēl 'ēm* for MT *'ᵃbel 'ēm*.

15. *gathered with glee.* Evoking imagery of wolves closing in on their victim. The two verbs *śāmᵉḥū wᵉne'ᵉsāpū* form a hendiadys.

smiters gathered about me. Reading *ne'esᵉpū 'ālay nōkīm* (MT *nēkīm*), thus forming a three-beat colon to balance 3-beat *ūbᵉṣal'ī śāmᵉḥū wᵉne'esāpū*. That the qal of *nky*, "to smite," was also used in addition to the hiphil is clear from UT, 125:89, *km nkyt tǵr*, and from South Arabic *nky*, which means "to smite, cause pain." See A. Jamme in *Cahiers de Byrsa* 8 (1958 f.), 165 f.

they whom I did not know. lō' yāda'tī is a relative clause without the relative pronoun; in meaning it is the same as vs. 11, *'ᵃšer lō' yāda'tī*, "they whom I knew not." On the omission of the relative, see C. Brockelmann, *Grundriss* (Berlin, 1913), II, pp. 552–56; for Phoenician example, Donner and Röllig, KAI, II, p. 45. Biblical examples include

Job xviii 21, xxix 12, and especially xxix 16, *'āb 'anōkī lā'ebyōnīm wᵉrīb lō' yāda'tī 'eḥqᵉrēhū,* "I was a father to the needy, and the cause of someone whom I knew not I investigated." Cf. further, GK, § 155n.

tore me to pieces. Metaphorical for slander, as in English. Apply here the principle of the double-duty suffix; cf. NOTE on Ps iii 4.

did not desist from slandering me. Dividing to read *wᵉlō' dammū bᵉḥonpī* (MT *ḥanpē*); explaining *ḥonpī* as infinitive construct with accusative suffix, and with a connotation probably found in El Amarna, 288:7, *ḫanpa ša iḫnupu,* "The slander they uttered against me." Though CAD, VI, p. 76b, defines *ḫanpu* as "villainy," and W. von Soden, *Akkadisches Handwörterbuch* (Wiesbaden, 1965), I, p. 320a, as *Gemeinheit,* GB, p. 246a, is probably correct with *verleumden.* The context itself is not decisive. There is, however, a Ugaritic text which seems to support GB's definition of *ḫanpu* as "slander, defamation." UT, 3 Aqht:rev(?):17 calls the goddess Anath *bt ḫnp,* which may fairly be translated "daughter of defamation" in view of 2 Aqht:VI:51 which states of her: *tlšn aqht ǵzr,* "She slandered Aqhat the hero."

16. *My encircling mockers.* Reading *lō'ᵃgay mā'ōg,* literally "my mockers of a circle," for MT *la'ᵃgē mā'ōg.* The pronominal suffix intervenes in a construct chain precisely as in vs. 19, *'ōyᵉbay šeqer,* "my treacherous foes." See NOTE there and bibliographical reference. For the sense of *mā'ōg,* from *'wg,* "to draw a circle," in Mishnaic-Hebrew, see Milik, *Biblica* 38 (1957), 254 f.

gnashed their teeth. Kraus, *Psalmen,* I, p. 275, among others, proposes emending the infinitive absolute *ḥārōq* to finite *ḥārᵉqū,* but this proposal betrays an unfamiliarity with the revolution that the syntax of the infinitive absolute has undergone as the result of Ugaritic-Phoenician discoveries. See John Huesman, "Finite Uses of the Infinitive Absolute," *Biblica* 37 (1956), 271–95; "The Infinitive Absolute and the Weak Waw Perfect Problem," *ibid.,* 410–34; Solá-Solé, *L'infinitif sémitique, passim.*

17. *idly watch.* This nuance of *tir'eh* is preserved in Gen xlii 1, *wayyō'mer ya'ᵃqōb lᵉbānāyw lammāh titrā'ū,* "And Jacob said to his sons, 'Why do you idly watch?'." LXX has "Why do you sit still?"

from their pits. For etymology, see NOTE on vs. 8, and for imagery, Job xxxiii 30, *lᵉhāšīb napšō minnī šāḥat,* "To turn back his soul from the Pit" (Pope, The Anchor Bible, vol. 15).

my face. On *yᵉḥīdātī,* cf. NOTE on Ps xxii 21.

the young lions. Namely, the enemies of the psalmist. On the extensive metaphorical use of animal names in Ugaritic and Hebrew, cf. my observations in *Biblica* 40 (1959), 161 f., and NOTE on Ps ii 5.

19. *my treacherous foes. 'ōyᵉbay šeqer* forms a construct chain with the pronominal suffix interposed between the *regens* and *rectum.* Cf. NOTES on vs. 16 and Ps xviii 18.

my stealthy enemies. For the construction *śōnᵉʾay ḥinnām*, see preceding NOTE; the sense of *ḥinnām* has been examined in the NOTE on vs. 7.

wink their eye. Though formally lacking a suffix, *ʿayin* receives one in translation, since Canaanite and biblical poets often omitted the suffix with names of parts of the body; cf. NOTE on Ps xvi 4.

20. *but attack the oppressed*. From the point of view of style, consonantal *wʿl* should express a verb antithetic to "speak of peace." This desideratum can be obtained by pointing *wᵉʿālū*, and by comparing the verb with Phoenician Ahiram: 2, *wʾl mlk bmlkm wskn bs[k]nm wtʾ mḥnt ʿly gbl*, "If any king whatever, or any governor whatever, or camp commandant should attack Byblos." To explain the syntax of *ʿly gbl*, W. F. Albright in JAOS 67 (1947), 155, felt obliged to insert the preposition *ʿl*, "against," after *ʿly*, but this now appears unnecessary. The verb *ʿly* can govern a direct object. A recently discovered Ras Shamra text reflects similar usage: RŠ 24.277, *hm qrt tuḫd* (?) *hm mt yʿl bnš*, "Either the city will be seized or Death will attack man." See UT, Glossary, No. 773, p. 391. Cf. Gen xlix 4 and Prov xxi 22.

the oppressed in the land. *rigʿē ʾāreṣ* is a hapax legomenon. The root is *rgʿ*, "to oppress, destroy," discussed in the NOTE on Ps xxx 6.

21. *open wide their mouth*. Expressing the image of a ravenous monster, well illustrated by Canaanite texts; see Gaster, *Thespis*, 1961, pp. 206 f., and the NOTE on Ps xxxiii 19.

Aha, Aha. The etymology of *heʾāḥ* becomes apparent upon comparison with *ʾābī*, "Good grief," in Job xxxiv 36, and with Ps xlix 8, *ʾāḥ*, "Alas!" Hence *heʾāḥ* has been analyzed into the interjection *hēʾ*, "Lo, behold," and *ʾāḥ*, "Brother!" Cf. English "O brother!"

has seen him. In other words, has witnessed the committing of the crime of which the poet has been falsely accused.

22. *Look, O Yahweh*. *rāʾītāh* may be parsed as an optative perfect, followed by the jussive *ʾal teḥᵉreš*; cf. NOTE on Ps iv 2.

23. *Bestir yourself and awake*. The unusual parallelism claims a word of comment. The two imperatives *hāʿīrāh* and *hāqīṣāh* are placed in the first colon while the two vocatives *ʾᵉlōhay* and *ʾᵃdōnāy* are found in the second half verse. A similar arrangement was remarked at Ps xxvii 2b.

25. *Lest they boast*. On *ʾal*, "lest," see NOTE on Ps ix 20.

our throat. In association with *pī* of vs. 22 and *billaʿᵃnūhū*, "we have engorged him," of the present verse, such is the meaning of *napšēnū*, as in Ugaritic-Hebrew; see *Biblica* 44 (1963), 105.

We have engorged him. This is a literal translation of *billaʿnūhū* which I analyze as a denominative verb from *blʿ*, "gorge, throat," that is probably found in Prov xxiii 2. The use of this verb evokes the image of Belial, a poetic name for Sheol discussed in the second NOTE on Ps xviii 5.

26. *who calumniate me*. This meaning of *gādal* has been studied under Ps xii 4. The *Messale quotidiano dei fedeli* a cura del P. A. Bugnini, 2d ed. (Roma, 1963), p. 369, renders *magdīlīm ʿālāy "che mi calunniano,"* which is remarkably exact.

27. *my vindication*. This nuance of *ṣidqī* has been noticed at Ps iv 2.

who desires. The article of *heḥāpēṣ* functions as a relative pronoun; see GK, § 138i–k, and Joüon, GHB, § 145d–e; compare Ps xviii 33.

PSALM 36

(xxxvi 1–13)

1 *For the director; of the servant of Yahweh, of David.*

2 Perversity inspires the wicked man
within his heart;
There is no dread of God
before his eyes.
3 But his God will destroy him with his glance [2]*
having discovered his impious slander.
4 The words of his mouth are sinful deceit, [3]
too crass is he to act prudently,
to do good.
5 He plans iniquity on his bed, [4]
takes his stand on the path of crime,
evil he never shuns.
6 From the heavens, O Yahweh, is your kindness, [5]
your fidelity is to the clouds.
7 Your generosity is like the towering mountains, [6]
your providence like the vast abyss;
You make man and beast thrive.
8 O Yahweh, how precious is your kindness! [7]
Gods and men find refuge
in the shadow of your wings.
9 They are sated with the fatness of your estate, [8]
from the stream of your delicacies
you give them to drink.
10 Truly with you is the fountain of life, [9]
in your field we shall see the light.
11 Prolong your kindness to those who know you, [10]
and your generosity to the upright of heart.
12 Let not the foot of the presumptuous overtake me, [11]
nor the arm of the wicked fling me down.

* Verse numbers in RSV.

13 See how the evildoers will fall! [12]
hurled down,
They will be unable to rise.

NOTES

xxxvi. A psalm of mixed type, with Wisdom elements in vss. 2–5, a hymn in vss. 6–11, and the language of a lament in vss. 12–13. To classify it with Giorgio Castellino, *Libro dei Salmi* (see Selected Bibliography), p. 798, as a Wisdom psalm is to make the opening verses decisive; on the other hand, *The Oxford Annotated Bible*, p. 681, is of the opinion that "since the last section seems to determine the character of the whole, the psalm should probably be classified as a liturgy of lament." The coexistence of three literary types within a poem of thirteen verses points up the limitations of the form-critical approach to the Psalter.

1. *servant of Yahweh.* With *'ebed yhwh*, compare the Canaanite personal names *'bdil* (UT, 80:I:3) and *'bdb'l* (146:21).

2. *Perversity inspires.* An adequate exegesis of the phrase *n*ᵉ*'ūm peša'* must take into account the consideration that *n*ᵉ*'ūm*, "utterance, whisper," is elsewhere used only in connection with prophets in an ecstatic condition, or before divine names. Whether there is a trace of dualism here can hardly be determined on the basis of the present context. On the dualistic elements in Qumran see F. M. Cross, Jr., *The Ancient Library of Qumran*, rev. ed. (New York, 1961), pp. 210 f., for general orientation.

The frequent alteration of *n'm* to *n'm*, lately sustained by Kraus, is too clever by half.

within his heart. The suffix of *libbī* is third-person singular masculine, as in Phoenician; consult excursus in NOTE on Ps ii 6.

3. *his God.* Explaining *'ēlāyw* as plural of majesty *'ēlīm*, "God," followed by pronominal suffix; cf. NOTE on Ps vii 7.

will destroy him. No suffix is needed with *heḥ*ᵉ*līq* since the immediately following word is equipped with one. The verb is here derived from *ḥlq*, Ugar. *ḫlq*, "to die, perish," studied in the NOTE on Ps v 10. In the present passage God causes death by his glance, whereas in Lam iv 16 it is the wrath of Yahweh that destroys: *p*ᵉ*nē yhwh ḥill*ᵉ*qām lō' yōsīp l*ᵉ*habbīṭām*, "The fury of Yahweh destroyed them; he shall look upon them no more."

with his glance. Literally "with his eyes."

having discovered. Parsing *limṣō'* as circumstantial infinitive construct, a usage discussed in the NOTES on Pss viii 3 and xxvii 4. For the thought, compare Ezek xxviii 15, *'ad nimṣā' 'awlātāh bāk,* "Until guilt was discovered in you."

his impious slander. Literally "his iniquity, his slander," a case of hendiadys, as in the next verse. Reading for MT *liśnō'* piel infinitive construct *laššᵉnō'* from *liššēn,* "to slander," and explaining final *aleph* as variant spelling for suffix *-ō* or *ōh.* The proposed reading *lᵉšōnō,* "of his tongue," is also possible, but then it becomes difficult to account for the Masoretic misunderstanding, whereas an examination of the passages where *liššēn* purportedly occurs reveals a Masoretic unsureness about it.

Since the wicked man did not fear God, he would have few qualms about slandering him; note the following phrase, "The words of his mouth are sinful deceit."

4. *sinful deceit.* Literally "iniquity and deceit," another instance of hendiadys.

too crass is he. On *ḥdl* II, "to be fat, dull," see Philip J. Calderone in CBQ 23 (1961), 451–60; 24 (1962), 412–19, especially p. 417, for discussion of Isa liii 3, *nibzeh waḥᵃdal 'īšīm,* "the most despicable and stupid of men." For the semantic relationship between the idea of "be fat" and moral obtusity, see Deut xxxii 15; Isa vi 10, and Ps cxix 70. Another consideration militating against the traditional rendition of *ḥādal* as "he ceased," is the observation that the Hebrew sages appear to divide all mankind into two great classes, the wise and the fools; they do not imagine a passage from one class into the other, once a man has definitely chosen one or the other. Our wicked man seems to be long established in his business of evil-doing, to judge from the preceding and subsequent descriptions, so there is scant likelihood of *ḥādal* signifying "to cease" in the present context. In other words, *ḥādal* expresses a habitual condition, not a transition from the state of virtue to that of crime. On the division of men into two classes, see J. L. McKenzie, *The Two-Edged Sword* (Milwaukee, 1956), pp. 217 f.

5. *on his bed.* Bed is the place for the expression of one's inmost thoughts; cf. UT, Krt:25–29; Pss iv 5, cxlix 5. The most essential thoughts of the wicked are those of mischief.

the path of crime. A stronger synonym of the substantive *rā', lō' ṭōb,* literally "no-good," is preferably understood as a composite noun, not an adjective, like Deut xxxii 21, *lō''ēl,* "a no-god." Hence *derek lō' ṭōb* is a construct chain. An equally clear example of the composite noun *lō' ṭōb* appears in Prov xx 23: *tō'ᵃbat yhwh 'eben wā'āben ūmō'znē mirmāh lō' ṭōb,* "Diverse weights are an abomination to Yahweh, and false scales are a crime." From its balance with the substantive *tō'ēbāh,* and from the argument that were it an adjective, *lō' ṭōb* should be dual or plural in form since it follows the dual noun *mō'znayim,* which it modifies, one may conclude that *lō' ṭōb* is a composite substantive, synonymous with *ra'* in Ps xxx and with *tō'ēbāh* in Prov xx 23. For bibliography consult NOTE on Ps v 5.

6. *From the heavens.* Briggs, CECBP, I, p. 318, remarking the similarity with Ps lxxxv 12, "Truth shall spring out of the earth, and justice shall look down from heaven," would find a probable antithesis in the poet's mind, the kindness coming down out of heaven, faithfulness ascending the heights of heaven. This insight is now rendered philologically possible by recognizing that *b* often denotes "from" in Ugaritic-Hebrew, and by noticing that vs. 7 likewise expresses a double movement, with justice said to be as high as the majestic mountains and judgments as profound as the extensive deep. A similar grammatical construction can be seen in Ps lxviii 6, "The father of orphans and the defender of widows is God from (*bīmeʻōn*) his holy dwelling." A few MSS and LXX read *mimmeʻōn,* evidence that their understanding of the description was correct. In other words, *b* can signify "from" even when no verb is expressed, a conclusion which seems to undercut the position of Hartman in CBQ 26 (1964), 105 f., that the idea "from" resides in the verb, not in the preposition.

7. *Your generosity.* The contents of the hymn in vss. 6–11 suggest that this is the nuance borne by *ṣidqātekā;* see NOTE below on vs. 11, *ṣidqātekā,* with which it forms an inclusion.

the towering mountains. In the construct chain *harerē 'ēl, 'ēl* functions as a superlative; this has been widely received. Cf. Pss l 10, lxviii 16, lxxx 11; El Amarna, *kasap ilāni,* "the very finest silver"; and Ugar. *ṯlḥn il,* "a splendid table." The frequency of the construction in Ugaritic (UT, § 13.22) shows the interpretation of the biblical expression to have been correct and speaks volumes for the Canaanite classification of Ugaritic. Cf. UT, 51:II:35–36, where *hr il* is apparently parallel to *bym il.*

your providence. Once the true value of *ṣidqātekā* is brought out, it becomes rather evident that the idea of governance contained in *mišpāṭekā* more specifically refers to the foreseeing care and guardianship of God over his creatures.

like the vast abyss. No conjunction *ke* is needed before *tehōm* on the principle of the double-duty conjunction; in this case it is supplied by *keharerē 'ēl.* See NOTE on Ps xxxiii 7 on the double-duty preposition, and compare the relevant passage in UT, 128:I:5–7, *arḫ tẓǵ l'glh bn ḫpṯ lumthm ktnḥn udmm,* "As the wild cow moans for her calf, as the young of the flock for their mothers, so do the Udumians groan." Note that no conjunction precedes *arḫ* and *bn ḫpṯ;* it is forthcoming from *ktnḥn.* Contrast non-elliptical 49:II:28–30, *klb arḫ l'glh klb ṯat limrh km lb 'nt aṯr b'l,* "Like the heart of a wild cow for her calf, like the heart of a ewe for her lamb, so was the heart of Anath toward Baal."

In the biblical expression *tehōm rabbāh,* "the vast abyss," *rabbāh* is the superlative element corresponding to *'ēl* in *harᵉrē 'ēl,* "the towering mountains."

You make . . . thrive. For this connotation of the root *yš',* Ar. *wasi'a,* "to be capacious," and in the fifth and eighth forms, "to be or live in abundance," see II Sam xxiii 5; Ps xii 6; Job v 4, 11, xxx 15; and J. Pedersen, *Israel I–II* (Copenhagen, 1926), pp. 330 ff. S. Mowinckel, *He That Cometh,* tr. G. W. Anderson (Oxford, 1956), p. 47, writes that *yeša'* "means not only deliverance from earthly, cosmic and demonic enemies, and from distress and misfortune, but good conditions, well-being, outward and inward prosperity, fertility in field, flock, and nation, quietness and order in the state, 'peace,' and the like."

man and beast. Merismus for every living creature; see NOTE on Ps viii 8.

8. *O Yahweh.* The exigencies of the 3+3 meter, which is dominant in this psalm, require that *yhwh* begin vs. 8 rather than terminate vs. 7; this has often been proposed.

how precious. Common Semitic *yqr* refers to El in an unpublished Ras Shamra tablet, according to Virolleaud as cited in UT, Glossary, No. 1144a.

Gods and men. The current practice has been to attach *'ᵉlōhīm* to the preceding colon as vocative (RSV, "How precious is thy steadfast love, O God!"), but the *Wortfeld* of vss. 7–9 militates against a breakup of the phrase *'ᵉlōhīm ūbᵉnē 'ādām,* "gods and men," which formally balances vs. 7, *'ādām ūbᵉhēmāh,* "man and beast." There is extra-biblical evidence to support this reading. In UT, 51:VII:49–52, the god Mot issues his claim to supreme divinity in these terms: *aḥdy dymlk 'l ilm dymru ilm wnšm dyšb' hmlt arṣ,* "I alone will rule over the gods, will fatten gods and men, sate the multitudes of the nether world." This theme is re-echoed in Jotham's fable in Judg ix 9, *heḥᵃdaltī 'et dišnī 'ᵃšer bī yikbᵉdū* (MT *yᵉkabbᵉdū*) *'ᵉlōhīm wa'ᵃnāšīm,* "Shall I give up my fatness through which [*bī* contains third-person suffix *-y,* as at Ps ii 6] gods and men grow fat?" Thus *'ᵉlōhīm ūbᵉnē 'ādām* answers to Ugar. *ilm wnšm* and to Judges *'ᵉlōhīm wa'ᵃnāšim; dešen* equals Judges *dišnī,* while *yirwᵉyūn* is synonymous with Ugar. *ymru* and *yšb'.* Yahweh manifests his supreme dominion by providing (cf. above on vs. 7, *mišpāṭekā*) for all creatures, heavenly and terrestrial.

shadow of your wings. The imagery has Canaanite antecedents; see the representation of the goddess Anath on an ivory footboard from Ras Shamra, published in *Syria* 31 (1954), Pl. VIII, and the discussion by C. F. A. Schaeffer on pp. 54–56. The motif of the outstretched wings has been treated at Ps xviii 11.

8–10. The language of these verses is of a piece with the Canaanite terms that describe the nature of immortality that Baal bestows upon certain individuals. UT, 2 Aqht:VI:30–31, *kb'l kyḥwy y'šr ḥwy y'šr wyš[q]ynh*, "For when Baal bestows eternal life, he invites the life-given to a banquet; he invites him to a banquet and gives him to drink."

In these verses of the psalm we have the background of the messianic banquet which figures so prominently in the Qumran literature, the other intertestamental literature, and, of course, in the New Testament; cf. NOTE on Ps 1 23.

9. *They are sated.* Referring to gods and men. Cf. Ugar. *dymru ilm wnšm*, "who will fatten gods and men." The use of the pagan term "gods" recurs in poetic metaphor in Pss xxix 1, xlvii 2, lxviii 5, xcvii 7, cxxxvi 2, etc.

fatness of your estate. The arrangement of vss. 9–10, with *naḥal* *'ᵃdānekā* chiastically paired with *mᵉqōr ḥayyīm*, indicates that as the counterpart to *'ūr*, "field," *bētekā* is more properly understood as "your estate," a meaning touched upon in the NOTE on Ps 1 9. D. N. Freedman has called my attention to this signification in Exod xx 16.

stream of your delicacies. Compare the theme of the stream of eternal life issuing from the temple in Ezek xlvii 1 ff.; Joel iv 18; Zech xiv 8.

The root of *'ᵃdānekā* is witnessed in Ugar. *'dn*; cf. Driver, CML, p. 141a.

give them to drink. The clause *wᵉnaḥal 'ᵃdānekā tašqēm* lends itself to two syntactic analyses. Either *naḥal* shares the preposition of corresponding *middešen*—this comports with *šāqāh*, which often is construed with *min*—or *šāqāh* here, as frequently elsewhere, governs a double accusative. The question cannot be decisively resolved, but I would direct attention to the latter construction in UT, 1 Aqht:222, *tšqy msk hwt*, "She proffers him the bowl to drink." On *msk*, "bowl," usually rendered "mixed drink," see Dahood, *Mélanges Eugène Tisserant*, p. 95, and PNWSP, p. 49.

10. *with you.* Perhaps *'immᵉkā* denotes "in your estate/house," as in Pss xxvi 4, xxxix 13, cxx 5; Job xxix 18. Compare UT, 2 Aqht: vi:28–29, *aššprk 'm b'l šnt*, "I shall make you count years with (in the house of) Baal."

fountain of life. Though *mᵉqōr ḥayyīm* occurs elsewhere (Prov x 13, xiii 14) with no such overtones, here *ḥayyīm* seems to allude to "eternal life." In UT, 2 Aqht:vi:27–28, *ḥym* by itself denotes "eternal life": *irš ḥym watnk blmt wašlḥk*, "Ask for life eternal and I will give it to you, immortality and I will bestow it upon you." See NOTE on Ps xxi 5 and compare Ar. *kawṯar*, the copious fountain in Paradise.

in your field. Since the received translation, "In your light we shall see the light," has not yielded to satisfactory interpretation, one may be allowed to propose a distinction between the homographs *'wr* (*'ōr*), "light," and *'wr* (*'ūr*), "field." The following texts enter into discussion: (a) Isa xxvi 19, "Your dead shall live, their bodies will rise; those who dwell in the dust will awake and will sing for joy: *kī ṭal 'ūrōt* (MT *'ōrōt) ṭallekā wā'āreṣ r^{e}pā'īm tappīl,* For your dew is the dew of the fields, but the land of the Shades will be parched" (on *tappīl,* "be parched," see Dahood, PNWSP, p. 24)—in this text, *'ūrōt,* which is contrasted with "the land of the Shades," must signify the Elysian Fields, especially since the context deals with resurrection and immortality. (b) Ps lvi 14, *l^{e}hithallēk lipnē '^{e}lōhīm b^{e}'ūr* (MT *'ōr*) *haḥayyīm,* "to walk before God in the field of life"—the sense of the verse is neatly illustrated by Ps cxvi 9, *'ethallēk lipnē yhwh b^{e}'ārṣōt haḥayyīm,* "I shall walk before Yahweh in the fields of life"; it is clear from these two texts that *'ūr* and *'^{a}rāṣōt* are synonyms. (c) Ps xcvii 11, *'ūr* (MT *'ōr*) *zārū^{a}' laṣṣaddīq ūl^{e}yišrē lēb śimḥāh,* "A sown field awaits the just, and happiness the upright of heart." (d) Job xxxiii 30, which much resembles Ps lvi 14, reads, *l^{e}hāšīb napšō minnī šāḥat l^{e}'ōr b^{e}'ūr* (MT *'ōr*) *haḥayyim,* "To turn back his soul from the pit, that he might be resplendent in the field of life." The occasional emendation of *'wr* to *'ereṣ,* while showing a fine feeling for the needs of context, becomes unnecessary on the present hypothesis. The vocalization *'ūr* assumes that the correct tradition was preserved in the expression *'ūr kaśdīm,* which occurs in Gen xi 28, 31, xv 7; and Neh ix 7. In all four instances, LXX translated *'ūr* by *chôra,* "land, region." What is more, Gen xxiv 4, 7, puts Abraham's birthplace in Upper Mesopotamia, so storied Ur in Lower Mesopotamia can scarcely be intended by *'ūr kaśdīm.* In the poetic passages, then, we have the motif of the Elysian Fields, the abode of the blessed after death. In UT, 1 Aqht:66.73, *ur* may well denote "field," but the obscure context precludes certainty.

we shall see the light. I.e., the light of your face in the beatific vision; see NOTE on Ps xvii 15. Contrast Ps xlix 20, "Never more shall they see the light." In Isa liii 11, the LXX reading has found confirmation in 1QIs^{a}, *yir'eh 'ōr,* "He shall see the light," i.e., the suffering servant will be rewarded with immortality for his vicarious sufferings. There is a radiant description of the future life in 1QS:IV:7–8, "And the reward of all that walk in its ways is health and abundant well-being, with long life and fruition of seed along with eternal blessings and everlasting joy in the life everlasting, and a crown of glory and a robe of honor amid light perpetual (*'wr 'wlmym*)" (Gaster, *The Dead Sea Scriptures in English Translation,* p. 44).

11. *Prolong your kindness.* The construction *m^{e}šōk ḥasd^{e}kā l^{e}yōd^{e}'ekā* bears on the disputed syntax of the kindred sentiment in Jer xxxi 3, *'al kēn m^{e}šaktīkā ḥāsed,* "And so for you have I prolonged kindness." The suffix of *m^{e}šaktīkā* expresses the indirect object, in this case a *dativus commodi,* while *ḥased* is the direct or accusative object. See Bogaert, *"Les suffixes verbaux non accusatifs dans le sémitique nord-occidental et particulièrement en hébreu," Biblica* 45 (1964), 220–47, especially p. 238, n. 2.

to those who know you. I.e, who have received your revelation; cf. Amos iii 2, "You only have I known of all the families of the earth." But *yāda'* expresses more than knowledge; nuances of "care for, love" are also present, as is clear from Pss i 7, ix 10, etc.

your generosity. This sense of *ṣ*^{e}*dāqāh* is treated in the NOTE on Ps xxiv 5. Cf. NOTE above on vs. 7.

12. *foot of the presumptuous.* Being parallel to concrete *yad r*^{e}*šā'īm,* "the arm of the wicked," *regel ga'*^{a}*wāh* must likewise be understood concretely. This is the poetic device of pairing a concrete noun with an abstract substantive which was treated under Ps v 8. To strike a more perfect balance, Gunkel followed Gressmann's suggestion in emending concrete *r*^{e}*šā'īm* to abstract *reša',* but Ugaritic poetic practice now shows Gunkel to have been ill-advised.

overtake me. The suffix of *t*^{e}*bō'ēnī* is datival, as in Ps xxxv 8. The imagery is that of the chase, as also in Ps xxxv 8.

arm of the wicked. This meaning of *yad* has been examined by W. F. Albright in VTS, IV (Congrès de Strasbourg, 1957), p. 251. The determination of the root of the predicate and a comparison with Exod xv 16, "By your powerful arm they are hurled like a stone," further serve to bring out the force of *yad* in the present context.

fling me down. The root of consonantal *tndny* is much contested, but *ndy,* "to cast, hurl," is a strong candidate. Akk. *nadū,* Ugar. *ndy* are well attested, and its presence in biblical Hebrew is gradually emerging. See Dahood, "Nādâ 'to hurl' in Ex 15, 16," in *Biblica* 43 (1962), 248 f. Hence vocalizing piel, *t*^{e}*naddēnī.*

13. *See how.* Equating *šām* with El Amarna *šumma,* "behold." Cf. NOTE on Ps xiv 5. The CCD version also renders *šām,* "See how," though without the benefit of El Amarna.

hurled down. The correct exegesis of this verse depends, it would seem, on the overtones carried by *dāḥāh,* "to hurl." Usage in several texts indicates thrusting, with special reference to Sheol. Thus Jer xxiii 12, *bā'*^{a}*pēlāh yiddāḥū w*^{e}*nap*^{e}*lū bāh,* "They will be hurled into the Darkness and will fall into it." Cf. also Pss v 11, xxxv 5, and Prov xiv 32. In Ps lvi 14 *d*^{e}*ḥī* is a name of the nether world.

unable to rise. Cf. Ps cxl 11, *b*^{e}*mah*^{a}*mārōt bal yāqūmū,* "From the miry depths they shall not rise."

PSALM 37

(xxxvii 1–40)

1 *Of David.*

Be not wrought up over evildoers,
nor indignant with those who do wrong.
2 For like grass they soon will wither,
and like green herbs fade away.
3 Trust in Yahweh and do good,
reside in the land
And feed on its riches.
4 Take your delight in Yahweh,
and he will grant your heart's request.
5 Commit to Yahweh your destiny,
trust in him and he will act.
6 And he will make your justice
shine like the sun,
And your cause like the noonday.
7 Wait for Yahweh and hope in him.
Be not wrought up over one
who makes his fortune flourish,
Who succeeds in his evil plans.
8 Desist from anger and forsake wrath,
be not wrought up, it only brings harm.
9 For evildoers shall be cut down,
while those who invoke Yahweh—
Lo, they shall inherit the land.
10 Yet a little while and the wicked man
shall cease to be;
If you peer into his house,
he will not be there.
11 But the meek shall inherit the land,
and shall delight in abundant prosperity.

12 The wicked has evil designs on the just man,
and gnashes his teeth at him.
13 The Lord laughs at him,
for he sees that his day is coming.
14 The wicked draw their sword and bend their bows
to fell the afflicted and the poor,
To slaughter those who walk the straight path.
15 Their sword shall enter their own heart,
and their bows shall be shivered.
16 Better is the poverty of the just
than the wealth of the wicked rich.
17 For the resources of the wicked shall be shattered,
but Yahweh will support the just.
18 Yahweh looks after the possessions
of the honest,
And their patrimony will last forever.
19 They shall not wither up in time of drought,
but in time of famine will have plenty.
20 But the wicked shall shrivel,
and Yahweh's foes be consumed
Like the burning of the hollows.
More quickly than smoke shall they vanish.
21 The wicked man borrows but never repays,
but the just man is open-hearted in giving.
22 For those blessed by him shall inherit the land,
but those cursed by him shall be cut down.
23 A man's steps are made steady by Yahweh,
who makes sure his stride.
24 If he should charge,
he will not be pitched headlong,
For Yahweh holds fast his hand.
25 I have been young and now am grown old,
but I have never seen a just man forsaken,
Or his children begging bread.
26 He is always open-hearted in lending,
and his children are destined for blessing.
27 Turn from evil and do good,
that you may abide forever.
28 For Yahweh loves the just man,
and never deserts his devoted ones.

Forever shall they be safeguarded,
 but the children of the wicked shall be cut down.
29 The just man shall inherit the land
 and dwell upon it forever.
30 The mouth of the just talks wisdom,
 and his tongue speaks what is right.
31 The law of his God is in his heart,
 and his feet never slip.
32 When the wicked man spies on the just,
 seeking to slay him,
33 Yahweh will not put him into his hand,
 nor have him found guilty when he is tried.
34 Wait for Yahweh and keep to his way,
 for he will raise you up to inherit the land;
When the wicked are cut down you can exult.
35 I have seen a wicked man thriving,
 and flourishing like a luxuriant native tree.
36 But he passed away and, lo, he was no more;
 I sought him but he could not be found.
37 Heed Sir Honest and mark Sir Upright
 for there is a future for the man of integrity.
38 But perverse men shall wholly be destroyed,
 and the future of the wicked shall be cut off.
39 While the safety of the just
 will be from Yahweh,
Their stronghold in time of siege;
40 Yahweh will save and rescue them,
 he will rescue them from the wicked;
And he will give them safety
 because they seek refuge in him.

Notes

xxxvii. An acrostic Wisdom psalm which seeks to counsel and encourage those depressed by the apparent success of the ungodly. Retribution will be meted out to them in due season. As in Ps xxxiv, the acrostic structure of the composition occasionally interferes with the logical flow of ideas.

1. *Be not wrought up.* Referring to the ardor of jealousy; similar counsel is given in Prov xxiv 19.

2. *will wither.* The theme struck here will serve as the basis for the new version proffered at vs. 19.

3. *in the land.* I.e., Palestine; cf. Deut xi 1–32.

its riches. LXX reads *ploútō,* "riches." This is semantically and grammatically more fitting than traditional "feed in security." Hence I must postulate a substantive *'āmōn,* followed by the feminine singular suffix *-āh,* "riches," related to vs. 16, *hāmōn,* with the same signification. Notice that *hāmōn* in II Kings xxv 11 appears as *'āmōn* in the doublet of Jer lii 15. For cognate phraseology, cf. Prov x 21, *śiptē ṣaddīq yirᵉʿū rabbīm,* "The lips of the just will feed on wealth." Both *hāmōn* and *'āmōn* are kin to Ps ii 8, *māmōn,* "riches"; note the wordplay in Luke xvi 11, "So if you were not reliable (*'mn*) in using your ill-gotten wealth (*mmn*), who will trust (*'mn*) you with true riches?"

5. *your destiny.* This sense of *derek* is touched upon in the NOTES on Pss xxxv 6 and xlix 14. A cognate usage is found in vs. 7.

he will act. Compare the absolute use of *'āśāh* in Pss xxxix 10 and cxviii 24, "This is the day Yahweh acted."

6. *shine like the sun.* S. Esh in VT 4 (1954), 307, has identified the true force of *hōṣī'* in the present context. On this meaning, see NOTE on Ps xvii 2, and for a closely allied sentiment, Isa lxii 1, "until her justice shine [*yēṣē'*] like the sun and her vindication burn like a torch."

Though the standard Hebrew lexicons usually cite only Job xxxi 26 for *'ōr* "sun," progress in Northwest Semitic philology uncovers this meaning in Hab iii 4; Job xxxvii 11, 21, xli 10, and possibly in UT, ʿnt:III:3, *pdry bt ar,* "Pidrayu, daughter of the sun." A hitherto unknown goddess of Canaanite mythology is named *pḥlt bt špš,* "Pḥlt, the daughter of the sun"; C. F. A. Schaeffer in *Annales archéologiques de Syrie* 13 (1963), 131.

9. *who invoke Yahweh.* On *qāwāh* II, "to gather, call," see NOTE on Ps xix 5. To be sure, the customary version "who wait upon the Lord," is also defensible, but since the poet employs the construction *qawwēh 'el yhwh* in vs. 34 but *qōwē yhwh* in vs. 9, one may assume that he was probably using two different verbs.

Lo, they shall inherit. On *hēmmāh,* "look, lo," cf. NOTE on Ps ix 7–8.

10. *his house.* Literally "his place," *mᵉqōmō* carries this connotation in Ps xxvi 8; cf. NOTE there.

12. *gnashes his teeth.* In rage, because the meek prosper.

13. *his day.* I.e., that of death and judgment.

14. *their sword.* On the use of the double-duty suffix with *ḥereb,* see Brekelmans in *Jaarbericht . . . Ex Oriente Lux* 17 (1963), 203.

bend their bows. In vs. 15 singular *ḥereb* is paired with plural *qaštōtām,* and some commentators have proposed reading *qaštōtām* in the present verse. To achieve this harmony between vss. 13 and 14, it suffices to retain the consonantal text but to vocalize it *qᵉšōtām*. In Ugaritic the plural of *qaštu*, "bow," is *qašātu* (UT, § 8.12) and this form recurs in Ps cxli 9, where its recognition resolves the two difficulties besetting the verse: *šomrēnī mīdē paḥ yāqᵉšū lī ūmiqqᵉšōt* (MT *ūmōqᵉšōt*) *pōʿᵃlē ʾāwen*, "Protect me from the trap they laid for me, and from the bows of evildoers." Here, then, is another point on which Hebrew and Ugaritic morphology agree.

to fell the afflicted. The balance between the verbs *nāpal* and *ṭābaḥ* is equivalently found in UT, 124:12–13, *ṭbḫ alpm ap ṣin šql ṯrm wmri ilm*, "He slaughtered oxen and small cattle, he felled bulls and fatted rams."

16. *the wealth.* Here, in Isa lx 5; Ezek xxix 19, xxx 4; and Eccles v 9, *hāmōn* may have to be distinguished from *hāmōn*, "sound, confusion," and identified as a dissimilated form of *māmōn*, studied at Ps ii 8.

the wicked rich. Though usually emended to singular *rab* to agree with *hāmōn*, which it putatively modifies, *rabbīm* should be retained and parsed as an adjective modifying *rᵉšāʿīm*.

The plural reading is further sustained by 4Qp (Q pesher) Ps 37 II, *rby*[*m*]. In a number of passages *rab* carries the connotation "rich, wealthy"; e.g., Hab ii 8 (fully cited in the NOTE on Ps xvii 14); Prov x 21 (quoted above in connection with vs. 3), xxviii 20, 27, *nōtēn lārāš ʾēn maḥsōr ūmaʿlīm ʿēnāyw rab mᵉʾērōt*, "He who gives to the poor shall not lack, but he who shields his eyes will be rich in curses."

17. *the resources.* Literally *zᵉrōʿōt* means "arms," but here and in Job xxii 8, 9, the stress is on "resources." A good analogy is proffered by plural *yādāyw*, "hands, arms," but which in Ps lxviii 32 and Deut xxxiii 7 connotes "possessions, resources."

18. *possessions of the honest.* Inasmuch as *yᵉmē*, "days," makes a poor parallel to "their patrimony," and since LXX reads *hodoùs*, "ways," one may be permitted to depart from the current translation and propose that consonantal *ym* contains the root *ymm*, "to create," discussed at Ps xiii 3. The semantic nexus between "create" and "possessions" is apparent in *miqneh*, "property," from *qānāh*, "to create." If, on the other hand, there is a basis for the LXX reading, we may assume an original *darkē* but in the Canaanite sense of "dominion, power," discussed at Ps i 1. In Prov xxxi 3 *dᵉrākekā* specifically denotes "your wealth."

19. *shall not wither.* Vocalizing *yībāšū* for MT *yēbōšū*. The confusion between *yābēš*, "to be dry," and *bōš*, "to be ashamed," has been established by N. H. Tur-Sinai in *Studies in the Bible* (Scripta Hierosolymitana, VIII), p. 157. Herein would seem to lie the solution for Jer xii 13, *ūbāšū-m* (*ūbōšū*) *tᵉbūʾōtēkem* (MT *mittᵉbūʾotēkem*) *mēḥᵃrōn ʾap yhwh*, "And your crops will shrivel up because of Yahweh's blazing

wrath." See also Jer xvii 13; Hos xiii 15; and Joel i 11, where the roots *ybš* and *bwš* are confused in the Masoretic tradition.

time of drought. Just as *ṭōb*, "good," concretely denotes "rain" in several passages (see NOTE on Ps iv 7 and *Biblica* 45 [1964], 401) so in certain contexts *rā'āh*, "evil," concretely means "drought," the evil par excellence in Palestine. In association with *yābēš* and *rē'ābōn*, "hunger," *rā'āh* almost inescapably signifies "drought." The sustained agricultural metaphor in Jer xvii 6–18 likewise makes it highly probable that vs. 17, *b*ᵉ*yōm rā'āh*, is to be translated "in time of drought."

20. *shall shrivel*. Generic *yō'bēdū*, "shall perish," more specifically denotes "to shrivel, sear," when predicated of the land, as in Jer ix 11, where *'ābad* balances *nāšat*, "to burn," or when asserted of the harvest as in Joel i 11. In UT, 2031:3, 4, 5, 8, 10, *šd ubdy* probably refers to a "parched field," though another interpretation may be possible.

Like the burning. The frequent emendation of *kīqar* to *kīqōd* may prove unnecessary in view of the evidence, albeit exiguous, for a root *yqr/qrh* "to burn." Consider the following texts: Job xxx 17, *laylāh 'ᵃṣāmay niqqar mē'ālāy*, "At night my bones are more inflamed than a caldron," equals Job xxx 30, *'ōrī šāḥar mē'ālāy w*ᵉ*'aṣmī ḥārāh minnī ḥōreb*, "My skin is blacker than a caldron, and my bones burn with heat"; Prov xxix 8, *'anšē lāṣōn yāpīḥū qiryāh waḥᵃkāmīm yāšībū 'āp*, "Scoffers enkindle wrath, but wise men turn away anger." Though the context is much too damaged to inspire confidence, UT, 'nt:pl. x:v:14, *l tqr mtnh* may express the same idea as 75:II:39, *bmtnm yšḫn*, "In his loins he is fever-racked."

of the hollows. Disputed *kārīm* finds a satisfactory etymology in *kārāh*, "to dig, hollow out," and proves neatly analogous to Num xxxiii 32, *ḥōr*, "a hollow," from *ḥrr*, "to bore, pierce." The vocable recurs in Ps lxv 14, *lāb*ᵉ*šū kārīm haṣṣō'n wa'ᵃmāqīm ya'aṭ*ᵉ*pū bār*, "The hollows are clothed with green [*ṣō'n* with afformative is related to Isa xxxiv 1, *ṣe'*ᵉ*ṣā'*, "produce," and Job xxxviii 27, *mōṣā' deše'*, "green grass"] and the valleys are covered with wheat." The balance with "valleys" notably clarifies the meaning of *kārīm*.

The figure drawn by the psalmist is that of a grass fire whose smoke quickly vanishes.

More quickly than smoke. Understanding the *b* of *be'āšān* as *beth comparativum*, as in Pss li 8, 9, lxviii 35, lxxxix 3, 8, 38, xcix 2, cxix 89; Ezek xxvi 17; Hab iii 4; Job vii 14; Prov iv 7, xxiv 5; Eccles ii 24, iii 12, ix 3; I Chron v 2; cf. *Biblica* 44 (1963), 299 f. Especially relevant is Ps cii 4, *kī kālū b*ᵉ*'āšān yāmāy*, "For my days are more transitory than smoke." On *kālāh*, "be swift, transitory," see Job vii 6, 9.

22. *blessed by him*. No need to read piel *m*ᵉ*bārākāyw* with LXX for pual *m*ᵉ*bōrākāyw*.

23. *who makes sure*. With Perles, *Analekten zur Textkritik des Alten*

Testaments, p. 76, deriving *yeḥpāṣ* from *ḥāpaṣ* II, which in Job xl 17 describes the action of the hippopotamus or crocodile which stiffens its tail like a cedar. Being paired with *kōnānū*, "are made steady," and occurring in a sapiential psalm, *ḥāpaṣ* is surely related to the root in Job xl 17. Hence *yeḥpōṣ* is vocalized as in Job xl 17.

24. *If he should charge*. If God is holding the hand of the man, it is difficult to see how *yippōl* can mean "fall"; more likely it means "to fall on someone else, to make a charge." Cf. Job i 15, *wattippōl šᵉbā' wattiqāḥēm*, correctly rendered by RSV, "And the Sabeans fell upon them and took them," and by Pope, "When the Sabeans attacked and took them" (The Anchor Bible, vol. 15). The description of the warrior in vs. 23 lends support to this interpretation of *yippōl*. An instructive analogy is provided by *kāšal*, "to stumble," but which in Nah ii 6 denotes "to hurtle, rush headlong": *yizkōrū* (MT *yizkōr*) *'addīrāyw yikkāšᵉlū bahᵃlīkōtām yᵉmahᵃrū ḥōmātāh*, "His captains are strong [cf. NOTE on Ps xx 8 for this meaning of *zākar*], they hurtle in their march, they speed toward the wall."

26. *his children*. Also possible is the vocalization *zᵉrō'ō*, "his arm," for MT *zar'ō*, in which case the translation would be "and his arm is for blessing."

28. *the just man*. Abstract *mišpāṭ*, "justice, rectitude," assumes a concrete meaning by virtue of being matched with concrete *ḥᵃsīdāyw*, "his devoted ones"; cf. NOTE on Ps v 8, and note the perfect parallel in Prov ii 8, an instance recognized by V. van der Weiden who will publish an article on this subject in a near number of *Verbum Domini*.

31. *his feet*. The balance between *libbō*, "his heart," and a study of the nouns occurring in parallelism with it, show that *'ᵃšūrāyw* more properly denotes "legs, feet" than "steps"; cf. NOTE on Ps xvii 4.

never slip. He never veers from the path of truth. On feminine singular *tim'ad* with dual subject, see GK, § 145k. In Ugaritic, dual nouns prefer a verb with *t-* preformative, though the lack of vocalization makes it difficult to ascertain if the verb is singular or plural; e.g., UT, 1003:5–7, *lšnm tlḥk šmm tšrp ym d̲nbtm*, "The two (forked) tongues lick the heavens, the two tails swish (?) the sea."

33. *will not put him*. *ya'azᵉbennū* derives from *'āzab* II, "to put," Ugar. *'db*, discussed in connection with Ps xvi 10. Instances of this root in Job were examined by Dahood in JBL 78 (1959), 303–9, and in *Biblica* 43 (1962), 542. Compare Gen xxxix 6, *wayya'ᵃzōb kol 'ᵃšer lō bᵉyad yōsēp*, "he also put him [Joseph] in charge of his household and entrusted to him all his possessions" (Speiser, The Anchor Bible, vol. 1) with xxxix 4, *kol 'ᵃšer yēš lō nātan bᵉyādō*, "Everything he had he put in his charge." The synonymy of *'āzab* and *nātan* likewise appears in Neh ix 27–28 and in Ps xvi 10.

35. *wicked man thriving*. This translation is problematical.

37. *Sir Honest . . . Sir Upright.* MT *tām,* usually revocalized abstract *tōm,* and MT *yāšār,* often repointed abstract *yōšer,* are evidently appellative adjectives that refer to the two divine messengers who lead the way to virtue. They are either the titles of two gods or the compound name *tām wāyāšār,* like *kṯr wḫss,* "Sir Skillful and Cunning," which is broken up into its components for the sake of poetic parallelism, as in UT, 62:48–49, *kṯrm ḥbrk wḫss d'tk,* "Sir Skillful is your colleague, Sir Cunning is your friend."

The motif of the two messengers has been treated in the NOTES on Pss xxiii 6 and xxv 21. In Ps xxv 21 the process of demythologizing the mythical messengers is complete, since there they have become abstract *tōm wāyōšer,* "integrity and uprightness," but an earlier stage of the process may be seen in the present passage.

a future. I.e., a future life, a denotation of *'aḥarīt* propounded by Dahood in PNWSP, pp. 48 f. Cf. NOTE on Ps i 3.

38. *future of the wicked.* The destiny of the wicked will be Sheol, where the minimal existence of its denizens does not merit the term "future life." In this sense the future of the wicked is said to be cut off.

39. *the safety.* The metaphor in vss. 39–40 dictates this interpretation of generic *tešū'at.*

Their stronghold. Cf. NOTE on Ps xxviii 8.

in time of siege. This nuance of *beyōm ṣārāh* is illustrated in the NOTE on Ps xx 2 in the light of Nah i 7.

40. *will save and rescue them.* H. L. Ginsberg in *Orientalia* 7 (1938), 3, has remarked a similar parallelism between *'āzar* and *pālaṭ* in UT, 3 Aqht:rev:13–14, *aqht ypltk bn dnil wy'ḏrk,* "And (call) Aqhat and let him save you, Daniel's son, and let him rescue you."

give them safety. *yōšī'ēm* forms an inclusion with vs. 39, *tešū'at.*

PSALM 38

(xxxviii 1–23)

1 *A psalm of David. For remembrance.*

2 O Yahweh, do not reprove me in your anger,
nor chastise me in your wrath.
3 For your arrows have sunk into me, [2]*
and your arm descended upon me.
4 There is no soundness in my flesh, [3]
because of your indignation;
There is no wholeness in my bones,
because of my sin.
5 For my crimes have lit upon my head, [4]
like a heavy burden, they are too heavy for me.
6 My wounds stink and fester, [5]
because of my foolishness.
7 I am utterly bowed down and prostrate, [6]
all the day long I go about in gloom.
8 For my loins are filled with inflammation, [7]
and there is no soundness in my flesh.
9 I am spent and utterly crushed, [8]
I groan and moan in my heart.
10 O Lord, all my sighing is before you, [9]
and my groaning never leaves your presence.
11 My heart is fever-racked, my strength fails me, [10]
and the light of my eyes—
Alas, even this has left me.
12 My friends and fellows stand far off from my plague, [11]
and my neighbors stand far off.
13 Those who seek my life lay snares, [12]
they who desire my misfortune pursue me;
Ruin and treachery
they ponder all day long.

* Verse numbers in RSV.

14 But I am like a deaf man, [13]
who does not hear;
And like a dumb man,
who opens not his mouth.
15 And I have become like a man [14]
who does not hear,
And from whose mouth
no recriminations come.
16 But for you, O Yahweh, do I wait, [15]
you will answer, My Lord, my God,
17 When I say, "Let them not rejoice over me; [16]
when my foot slips,
Let them not calumniate me."
18 For my iniquity is stationed at my side, [17]
my grief is ever before me.
19 Indeed, I hold my guilt before me, [18]
I am apprehensive because of my sin.
20 My mortal foes are powerful, [19]
my treacherous enemies are numerous.
21 Those who repay me evil for good, [20]
slander me when I seek their good.
22 Do not forsake me, O Yahweh, [21]
my God, be not distant from me!
23 Make haste to help me, [22]
O Lord, to save me!

NOTES

xxxviii. An individual lament; the psalmist is afflicted by a grave disease. The common belief that illness was a punishment for sin was an unexcelled opportunity to the psalmist's enemies, ever eager to slander, to speculate on the nature of his guilt.

The psalm has an alphabetic structure (twenty-two verses) without the alphabetic acrostic. This may have been the reason for placing this lament after Ps xxxvii. The twenty-two-verse structure is a literary convention which characterizes laments (e.g., Lamentations). A well-ordered plan can be traced in the poem. Verses 2–11 describe the illness; 12–17 detail the reaction of others; 18–19 summarize vss. 2–11;

20–21 summarize vss. 12–17, while the final two verses form a conclusion.

2. *nor chastise me.* On double-duty negative *'al,* see NOTE on Ps ix 19, and contrast the doublet in Ps vi 2, where *'al* appears in both members of the verse.

3. *your arrows.* The Canaanite god of pestilence is named in UT, 1001:3, *b'l ḥẓ ršp,* "Resheph the archer," while a fourth-century Phoenician inscription calls him simply *ršp ḥṣ,* "Resheph of the arrow." This theme has been adopted by Hebrew poets to express the belief that illness comes from Yahweh. The theme recurs in Deut xxxii 23–24; Job vi 4, xvi 12–13.

your arm. On *yad,* "arm," see NOTE on Ps xxxvi 12. Here the most pertinent parallels are Deut xxxiii 27, *muttaḥēt* [!] *zᵉrō'ōt 'ōlām,* "One who lowers his arms is the Eternal," and Isa xxx 30, *naḥat zᵉrō'ō,* "the descent of his arm."

4. *no soundness.* As the substantive *mᵉtōm* is morphologically unusual, I am reading *'ēn-m* (enclitic *mem*) *tōm,* as proposed by Hummel in JBL 76 (1957), 99. The sense remains the same. Joüon, GHB § 88j, describes the two *'ayin-'ayin* nouns *mᵉtōm* and *mōrek* as *anormales,* but J. Croatto (unpublished, I believe) would eliminate the second of these, the hapax legomenon *mōrek* in Lev xxvi 36, by attaching the purported performative *mem* as enclitic to the preceding verb, *wᵉhēbē'tī-m rōk.* The substantive *rōk* is attested in Deut xxviii 56 and conforms to a standard morphological pattern; see Bauer and Leander, *Historische Grammatik der hebräischen Sprache,* § 61h', p. 455.

8. *loins are filled with inflammation.* Cognate expressions are found in Ps cvii 20; Mic vi 14; Lam iv 20; UT, 75:II:39, *bmtnm yšḫn,* "In his loins he is fever-racked."

9. *I groan and moan.* Reading *šā'agtī-m* (encl. *mem*) *nāhamti* (MT *minnahᵃmat*) *libbī,* to achieve a better balance with the two verbs of the first colon. The presumed substantive *nᵉhāmāh* is a dis legomenon, whereas verbal forms of *nāham,* "to groan," are attested in Ezek xxiv 24 and Prov v 11. For the spelling *nāhamti,* without final *-y,* cf. Ps xvi 2, *'āmarti* for *'āmartī,* and GK, § 44i.

in my heart. libbī may be parsed either as an accusative of specification or an accusative of place.

10. *my sighing.* Not "my longing" (RSV); see NOTE on Ps ix 13 for this definition of *ta'ᵃwātī.*

leaves your presence. The root of *nistārāh* is probably *sūr,* "to turn aside," and the conjugation is infixed *-t-*. See NOTE on Ps x 11, and Dahood, PNWSP, pp. 45, 54. For the parallelism of the roots *ngd* and *sūr,* cf. Ps xviii 23, *kī kol mišpāṭāyw lᵉnegdī wᵉḥuqqōtāyw lō' 'āsīr mennī,* "For all his judgments are before me, his laws I have never put aside."

11. *My heart is fever-racked.* The hapax legomenon *seḥarḥar* can satisfactorily be explained as a de-emphaticized form of *ṣḥr,* "to burn," which appears in UT, 52:44–45, *'ṣr tḥrr lišt wṣḥrrt lpḥmm,* "The bird is roasting on the fire, is being broiled upon the coals." The root *ṣḥr/sḥr* is evidently related to Song of Sol i 6, *šeḥarḥōret,* "black." For other instances of de-emphaticized roots, see GB, p. 533a, and compare Ugar. *qlṣ,* "derision," with Heb. *qeles.* The theme of the fever-racked heart is found in Pss xxxix 4, cii 4–5; Ezek xv 4.

Alas, even this. With Patton, CPBP, p. 37, understanding *hēm* as the particle of exclamation treated at Ps ix 7–8. Contrast the psalmist's abatement of strength and dimming of his eyes with the condition of Moses at his death as described in Deut xxxiv 7, "His eye was not dimmed nor his forces abated."

12. *stand far off.* For this sense of *minneged,* see Ps x 5. The sequence of the verbs *ya'amōdū* and *'āmedū* has been examined in light of Ugaritic practice by Moshe Held, in *Studies and Essays in Honor of Abraham A. Neuman,* pp. 281–90.

13. *pursue me.* On *dibbēr,* "to pursue," see NOTE on Ps ii 5. The accusative pronominal suffix must be supplied from *rā'ātī.* Understood thus, the verse scans into four cola totaling ten stresses: 3+3 followed by 2+2.

14. *who does not hear.* The balance with *yiptaḥ* requires that *'ešma'* also express third-person singular. The popular pronunciation of initial *ya* as *e* in Amorite opens up the possibility for a similar explanation of the several cases that have been noted in Hebrew. For the Amorite phenomenon, consult W. F. Albright in BASOR 99 (1945), 12, and bibliography cited there, and I. Gelb, *Rendiconti Lincei* 13 (1958), 157; for biblical examples, consult GK, p. 126, n. 1, and H. L. Ginsberg in *Mordecai M. Kaplan Jubilee Volume,* English Section (New York, 1953), p. 257, who discusses such instances as Isa x 12, xiv 30. I am indebted to Charles Krahmalkov for the last reference.

15. *from whose mouth.* The preposition *be* of *bepīū* denotes "from," as often in Ugaritic-Hebrew. Cf. UT, 1 Aqht:75, *bph rgm lyṣa,* "The word had not gone out of his mouth."

17. *when my foot slips.* In other words, when I fall into misfortune, as in the present illness.

calumniate me. For *gādal,* "to weave, calumniate," see NOTE on Ps xii 4 and *Biblica* 45 (1964), 367. Within a religious structure where men believed that sickness and sin are causally related, the illness of the psalmist would grant his enemies an excellent occasion to spin tales about the heinous crime he must have committed.

18. *my iniquity.* Namely, the sin causing the poet's illness. Reading (for MT *'anī*) *'ōnī,* from *'āwen,* "trouble, iniquity," followed by pronom-

inal suffix. The balance with *mak'ōbī,* "my grief," is perfect. Note the sequence A+B+C // Á+B́+Ć.

at my side. In Ugaritic, some prepositional phrases are formed of *l* followed by the name of a part of the body: *lriš* and *lẓr,* both denoting "above, upon." To this pattern belongs *l*ᵉ*ṣela',* literally, "at my rib." Its parallelism with *negdī,* "before me," supplies the lacking pronominal suffix on the basis of the double-duty suffix. Cf. NOTE on Ps iii 4. Cf. Job xv 23, *yāda' kī nākōn b*ᵉ*yādō yōm ḥōšek,* "He knows that stationed at his side is the day of darkness," and xviii 12, *y*ᵉ*hī rā'ēb 'ōnō w*ᵉ*'ēd nākōn l*ᵉ*ṣal'ō,* "Let the Hungry One [cf. NOTE on Ps xxxiii 19] face him [*'ōnō* is derived from *'ānāh,* "to meet," followed by accusative suffix], with Death stationed at his side."

19. *I hold my guilt before me.* Explaining *'aggīd* as a denominative verb from *neged,* "front, face." This etymon is supported by the general tendency of Ugaritic-Hebrew to form denominative verbs from nouns signifying parts of the body. See NOTE on Ps xv 3.

I am apprehensive. The pairing with *yārē',* "to fear," in Isa lvii 11 and Jer xvii 8 suggests that the burden of *dā'ag* is foreboding for the future, not grief over a past offense.

20. *My mortal foes.* It is possible to either vocalize with Hummel in JBL 76 (1957), 99, *'ōy*ᵉ*bē ḥayyay-m* (with enclitic *mem*), or preferably, retain MT and analyze the phrase as another instance (at least a dozen have been identified) of a pronominal suffix intervening in a construct chain. See NOTE on Ps xviii 19. The balance with *śōn*ᵉ*'ay šāqer,* "my treacherous enemies," proves the second alternative to be preferable.

21. *slander me.* A reprise of vs. 17, *'ālāy higdīlū.* LXX correctly translated *yiśṭ*ᵉ*nūnī* as *endiéballón me,* "they slandered me." The parallelism in Pss lxxi 13 and cix 4, 20, further shows this to be the sense of *śāṭan,* and of the cognate *śāṭam* in Gen xlix 23 (cf. LXX).

when I seek their good. Literally "for my pursuing good," whose ambiguity is relieved by a comparison with Ps cix 4–5, "For my love they slander me . . . And my assailants give evil for good and hatred for my love." Here "my love for them" is intended by "my love."

23. *to save me.* Literally "to my salvation." The preposition *l*ᵉ before *y*ᵉ*šū'ātī* is forthcoming from parallel *l*ᵉ*'ezrātī,* "to help me," on the principle of the double-duty preposition studied in NOTE on Ps xxxiii 7. Contrast Ps xxxv 23, where *l* precedes both *mišp*ᵉ*ṭī* and *rībī.*

PSALM 39

(xxxix 1–14)

1 *For the director; for Jeduthun. A psalm of David.*

2 I said, "I will heed my steps,
lest I stumble over my tongue.
I will keep a muzzle on my mouth,
while the wicked man is full of glee before me."
3 I was muzzled to total silence, [2]*
I refrained from speaking,
I was deeply stirred by anguish.
4 My heart burned within me; [3]
when I thought about it, a fire blazed.
5 I spoke with my tongue, [4]
"O Yahweh, teach me my destiny,
and my span of days, what is it?
That I may know how transitory I am."
6 Look, you have made my days but a few handbreadths, [5]
and my lifetime is nothing before you;
Alas, every man is but vapor,
every man a false image. *Selah*
7 Alas, as a mere phantom does man go about; [6]
alas, for nought is he in turmoil.
He heaps up but does not know
who will gather.
8 And now, what shall I exclaim, O Lord? [7]
My hope is in you!
9 From all my transgressions deliver me; [8]
make me not the taunt of a knave.
10 I was muzzled, opened not my mouth, [9]
Oh that you would act!
11 Remove your scourge from me, [10]
by the club in your hand am I forspent.

* Verse numbers in RSV.

12 With reproofs for his guilt you chastise a man, [11]
and you consume his body like a moth;
Alas, every man is but vapor. *Selah*
13 Hear my prayer, O Yahweh, [12]
and give ear to my cry, O El;
Be not deaf to my tears,
for I am a guest in your house,
a client like all my ancestors.
14 Turn your gaze from me, [13]
that I may be glad,
Before I depart and am no more.

NOTES

xxxix. A lament in which the psalmist prays for healing from a serious sickness. When the poet was stricken, the skeptical, who doubted God's concern for justice and goodness, indulged in *Schadenfreude*. At first the psalmist refrains from complaining about the apparent injustice of God (vss. 2–3), but when no longer able to contain himself, he bursts into a frank expression of his feelings and asks for deliverance from his affliction (8–9).

2. *I will heed my steps.* That *derākāy*, "my steps," often emended to *debārāy*, "my words" (latterly by Kraus, *Psalmen*, I, p. 299), is the *mot juste* emerges when *ḥaṭō'* is seen to carry a physical rather than a moral connotation.

I stumble over my tongue. I.e., utter rash statements. This problematic translation depends, in large measure, upon the accuracy of the interpretation of Ps xv 3, *lō' rāgal 'al lešōnō*, "Who does not trip over his tongue." The imagery, somewhat bizarre from the modern point of view, has mythological antecedents in UT, 1003:5–9, *lšnm tlḥk šmm tšrp ym d̲nbtm tnn lšbm*, "The two (forked) tongues licked the heavens, the two tails swished (?) the sea, (but) Tannin has indeed been muzzled." Humorous formulations are used in pedagogic psalms; see NOTE on Ps xv 3 and Hempel, IDB, III, p. 954a.

For *ḥāṭā'*, "to stumble," note Prov xix 2, *'āṣ raglayim hōṭē'*, "He who makes haste stumbles"; cf. Zorell, ZLH, p. 236a. It is possibly also in Exod v 16, *'abādekā mukkīm weḥāṭā't 'ammekā*, "Your servants are beaten and your people stumble."

I will keep. With the recognition that Ps cxli 3, *šomrāh*, and Job vii 12, *mišmār*, very probably signify "muzzle" (see JBL 80 [1961], 270), proposals to emend *'ešmᵉrāh* to *'āśīmāh, 'āšītāh,* or *'ettᵉnāh* appear singularly ill-advised. In fact, the locution *'ešmᵉrāh lᵉpī maḥsōm* is virtually a cognate accusative construction which could defensibly be rendered, "I muzzled a muzzle on my mouth." *maḥsōm,* "muzzle," is found in a fourth-century B.C. Phoenician inscription studied by Benjamin Maisler in OLZ 11 (1936–37), 239 f.

is full of glee. Relating the infinitive construct *'ōd* to *ǵdd,* "be gleeful," in UT, 'nt:II:25–26, *tǵdd kbdh bṣḥq ymlu lbh bšmḫt,* "Her liver is gleeful with laughter, her heart is filled with joy." Cf. Pss cxlvi 9, cxlvii 6; Job viii 21, xxxi 29; *Biblica* 38 (1957), 319 f.; and P. Joüon in *Mélanges de l'Université de St. Joseph* 6 (1913), 175. This version sharpens the contrast between the afflicted believer and the smirking skeptic.

3. *I was muzzled.* The mention of "muzzle" in vs. 2 suggests that *ne'ᵉlamtī* is a denominative verb from *'elem,* "muzzle, bridle," discussed in the NOTE on Ps xxxi 19.

total silence. The ending of *dummīyāh,* an accusative of specification, may be the intensifying element *yāh.* Other instances of this emphatic afformative have been examined by Morris Jastrow in ZAW 16 (1896), 1–7; his conclusions are supported indirectly by the frequent use of *il* in Ugaritic as a superlative element; see UT, § 13.22.

I refrained from speaking. Deriving *miṭṭōb* from *nāṭab,* a by-form of *nāṭap,* "to drop, drip," figuratively, "to discourse." Compare the brace *nāšab* and *nāšap,* "to blow." Numerous Ugaritic-Hebrew examples of non-phonemic interchange between *b* and *p* have been collected in Dahood, PNWSP, pp. 32 f. Especially relevant to the present discussion is Prov xv 2, *lᵉšōn ḥᵃkāmīm tēṭīb dā'at ūpī kᵉsīlīm yabbīᵃ' 'iwwelet,* "The tongue of the wise drops knowledge, but the mouth of fools pours out folly." In Amos vii 16; Mic ii 6, etc., the hiphil of *nāṭap* takes no object, just as the qal infinitive construct here governs no accusative. See BDB, p. 643a.

The frequently proposed emendation of *miṭṭōb* to *mibbaṭṭē',* "from rash speech," while neatly meeting the exigencies of context, becomes unnecessary.

4. *My heart burned.* See NOTE on Ps xxxviii 11.

when I thought about it. Namely, my miserable condition and the prosperous condition of the ungodly man.

5. *teach me . . . That I may know.* Many MSS and commentators insert a *waw* before *'ēdᵉ'āh,* but this is not necessary as the construction *hōdī'ēnī . . . 'ēdᵉ'āh* is identical with that of UT, 127:37–38, *rd lmlk amlk ldrktk aṯbnn,* "Come down from your royal seat that I may reign, from your throne that I may sit thereon." In Ugaritic, one would vocalize *rid . . . amluka;* the latter is the subjunctive or volitive mode, which suggests that *'ēdᵉ'āh* is also subjunctive or volitive rather than

cohortative. Cf. Brockelmann, *Hebräische Syntax*, § 176c; W. L. Moran, "Early Canaanite *yaqtula*," *Orientalia* 29 (1960), 1–19. Cf. also Pss xxii 23, lxi 5.

6. *every man*. Reading *kōl* for MT *kol;* cf. Ugar. *kl*, "every man," in UT, 2 Aqht:VI:38, *mt kl amt*, "The death of every man will I die." Cf. Dahood, PNWSP, pp. 39 f., for other biblical examples of *kōl*, "every man."

a false image. Vocalizing *nāṣāb* for MT *niṣṣāb*. For Palmyrene *mṣb'*, Nabatean *nṣb*, Punic *nṣb*, "statue, image," see Jean and Hoftijzer, *Dictionnaire . . .*, p. 184. In *Muséon* 71 (1957), 130–32, G. Ryckmans examines the meaning of Sabean *nṣb*, which he concludes signifies "stela" rather than "image." The semantic nexus between "image" and "semblance" comes out in vs. 7, *ṣelem*, "statue, empty image, semblance" (the definitions are those of BDB, pp. 853 f.).

7. *as a mere phantom*. The *bᵉ* of *bᵉṣelem* is the emphatic preposition commented upon at Ps xxix 4.

is he in turmoil. Reading the energic form *yehᵉmāyannā* for grammatically difficult MT *yehᵉmāyūn*. The Masoretic unfamiliarity with this mode may easily account for the mispointing. On the frequency of energic forms in Ugaritic and Hebrew, see NOTE on Ps viii 2.

who will gather. The final *mem* of consonantal *'spm* is enclitic, or *'spm* is a defectively written plural participle, *'ōsᵉpīm*.

8. *what shall I exclaim*. Deriving *qiwwītī* from *qāwāh*, "to cry," discussed in NOTE on Ps xix 5 and recurring in Ps xl 2. To be sure, "What shall I hope for?" is defensible in view of parallel *tōḥaltī*, "my hope," but the sustained and anguished cry of vss. 9–14 is more fittingly introduced by the proposed version.

10. *Oh that you would act*. Since *'āśītā* is used absolutely with no suffix in sight to warrant an appeal to the principle of the double-duty suffix, the traditional version, "For it is thou who hast done it" (RSV), is grammatically vulnerable. More suitably, *kī 'attāh 'āśītā* analyzes into emphatic *kī*, the emphatic independent pronoun *'attāh*, and the precative perfect *'āśītā*. Cf. NOTE on Ps iii 8. Other texts employing a similar construction include Pss iii 8, lvi 9, and lxi 6. Among the texts which use *'āśāh* absolutely, the most relevant to our purpose are Ps xxxvii 5, "Trust in him and he will act" (*wᵉhū' ya'ᵃśeh*), which equivalently collocates the same two ideas that are found in the present verse; Ps cix 21, "But you, O Yahweh, my Lord, act on my behalf" (*'ᵃśēh 'ittī*); and Isa xxxviii 15, *mah 'ᵃdabbēr wᵉ'ōmar* (MT *wᵉ'amar*) *lī wᵉhū' 'āśāh*, "What shall I speak and say to him that he might act?"

11. *the club in your hand*. To judge from the substantives which elsewhere balance *nega'*, "scourge," we should expect the hapax legomenon *tigrāh* to signify something like *šēbeṭ*, "club," paired with *nega'* in Ps lxxxix 33. In Jer xviii 21 (cf. Ezek xxxv 5; Ps lxiii 11) *haggīrēm*

'al yᵉdē ḥāreb, the most natural version seems to be, "Smite them with the edge of the sword." The attempts to relate the verbal form to *nāgar,* "to flow," are somewhat forced. Cf. Ps lxxvii 3, *yādī laylāh niggᵉrāh wᵉlō' tāpūg,* "At night his hand [third-person singular suffix *-y*] strikes me without surcease." The possible Ugaritic cognates are much too ambiguous, because of the lack of vocalization, to inspire confidence. For example, UT, Krt:11, *wgr nn 'rm,* "And smite the cities," and 125:47–48, *[m]rḥh yiḫd byd wtg(!) rh bm ymn,* "He took his spear in his left hand and his club in his right hand."

12. *his guilt. 'āwōn* shares the suffix of parallel *ḥᵃmūdō;* cf. NOTE on Ps iii 4.

his body. Where MT reads *ḥᵃmūdō,* LXX has "his life." This approximates the sense desiderated by the context, while a comparison with Job xx 20 makes greater precision possible: *lō' yāda' šālēw bᵉbiṭnō baḥᵃmūdō lō' yᵉmallēṭ,* "He knows no rest in his bosom, in his body he finds no relief." The balance with *beṭen* points to the meaning of *ḥᵃmūdō,* while Job xix 20 and Ps cvii 20 illustrate the meaning of *millēṭ,* "to find relief." The semantic relationship between "desire" and the "seat of desire" is reasonably clear. This colon, then, resumes the thought of vs. 11.

13. *O El.* Reading the divine name *'ēl* for MT preposition *'el,* and attaching it to the second colon. This pointing reveals both vocative *'ēl* in balance with vocative *yahweh,* "O Yahweh," and the original form of the Tetragrammaton, *yahweh 'ēl,* here separated into its components that are placed in parallel cola. See NOTE on Ps x 12. Another example of Masoretic confusion between the divine name *'ēl* and the preposition *'el* may be seen in Deut xxxiii 28 where Freedman, IEJ 13 (1963), 125–26, has shown that the correct reading is *ya'ᵃqōb 'ēl,* "Jacob-El," the original, unapocopated name of Jacob. For the Masoretic confusion (or alteration) of *'ēl* and *'el* in Job xli 1, consult Pope, *Job* (The Anchor Bible, vol. 15), p. 282.

deaf to my tears. For adverbial accusative with *ḥāraš,* see Job xli 4.

in your house. This nuance of *'im* appears in Pss xxxvi 10, cxx 5; Job xxxi 5; and Prov xxiv 21.

14. *Turn your gaze.* This verse is kindred to Job vii 19, x 20 f., xiv 6.

PSALM 40

(xl 1–18)

1 *For the director. A psalm of David.*

2 Constantly I called Yahweh,
and he stooped to me and heard my cry.
3 He drew me up from the pit of Destruction, [2]*
from the miry bog.
He set my feet upon a rock,
making my legs secure.
4 And put a new song into my mouth, [3]
a hymn of praise to our God.
Many will see and be awed,
and so will trust in Yahweh.
5 Happy the man who makes Yahweh his trust, [4]
who turns not to pagan idols,
or to fraudulent images.
6 Great deeds have you achieved, O Yahweh, [5]
my God, you have worked wondrous miracles.
Your thoughts are of us—you have no peer;
Were I to declare and tell them,
they would be too numerous to number.
7 In sacrifice and offering you were not interested, [6]
so you made my ear receptive;
Burnt offering and sin offering,
you did not request.
8 Then I promised, "Look, I come; [7]
in the inscribed scroll
it is written to my debit.
9 To perform your will, O my God, is my concern, [8]
and your law that is inside my heart."
10 I announced the glad news of your deliverance, [9]
in the great congregation;

* Verse numbers in RSV.

Lo, I did not restrain my lips,
  Yahweh, you yourself know.
11 Your generosity I did not conceal [10]
  inside my heart;
Your fidelity and your saving action
  I announced.
I did not hide your kindness,
  nor your fidelity from the great congregation.
12 You, O Yahweh, did not withhold your love from me; [11]
  your kindness and fidelity
  have always safeguarded me.
13 Alas, evils have encompassed me, [12]
  till they are without number;
My iniquities have overtaken me,
  and I am unable to escape.
They are more numerous than the hairs of my head,
  and my heart fails me.
14 Run, O Yahweh, to rescue me, [13]
  O Yahweh, make haste to help me.
15 Let all be humiliated and put to confusion, [14]
  who seek to snatch away my life;
Let them recoil in disgrace
  who desire my ruin.
16 Let them be appalled over their shame, [15]
  who say to me, "Aha, aha!"
17 May they rejoice and be glad in you, [16]
  all who seek you.
May they who love your salvation ever say,
  "Great is Yahweh."
18 Though I am afflicted and poor, [17]
  the Lord will think of me;
You are my helper and my deliverer,
  O my God, do not tarry.

Notes

xl. A composite psalm of two distinct parts. Verses 2–11 are a hymn of thanksgiving for healing from a mortal illness, while vss. 12–17, almost identical with Ps lxx, are a lament. Originally, the component parts were probably independent poems.

2. *Constantly I called.* The synonymity with *šāwʻātī,* "my cry," in the second colon, shows that Jacob Barth was correct in relating *qawwōh qiwwītī* to *qāwāh* II, "to call," discussed in NOTE on Ps xix 5. Yahweh does not hear a "waiting" (CCD, RSV), but he does hear a cry for help.

3. *the pit of Destruction.* This is one of the thirty-odd appellatives of the nether world found in biblical poetry. As in the lament Ps xxx 4, the psalmist was on the verge of death, but Yahweh's miraculous intervention restored him to life.

miry bog. That Sheol was believed to be a place of mud and filth appears from several ancient sources; see NOTE on Ps xlvi 3. According to the testimony of Philo Byblius, some ancient writers held that Mot "death," signified "mud," while others maintained that it meant "filth"; cf. Pope, in *Wörterbuch der Mythologie,* p. 301.

my legs. On this sense of *'ašūrāy,* cf. NOTES on Pss xvii 5, xxxvii 31.

4. *a new song.* By restoring the stricken psalmist to health, God has given him a new motive and a new theme for singing.

5. *pagan idols.* The usual derivation of *reḥābīm* from *rāhab,* "to be arrogant," is supported by analogous *zēdīm,* a term for pagan deities in Ps xix 14 deriving from *zyd,* "to act stormily, arrogantly." Hence the mythical sea monster Rahab is "the Arrogant One." Note too that LXX translates *reḥābīm* by *mataiótētas* which elsewhere reproduces Hebrew words for "idols, gods."

or to fraudulent images. The force of the preposition *'el* carries over from the first colon to the second; see GK, § 119hh. Cf. UT, 126: III:9–10, *nʻm lḥṭt bʻn bm nr ksmn,* "It was sweet to the wheat in the furrow, in the tilth to the emmer"; note that the *l* of *lḥṭt* also serves with parallel *ksmn.* Cf. NOTE on Ps xxxiii 7.

The exact sense of *śāṭē kāzāb* is difficult to determine, but the clearer parallelism in Ps ci 3 may point the way out of the impasse: *lō' 'āšīt leneged ʻēnay debar beliyyāʻal ʻaśōh sēṭīm śānē'tī lō' yidbaq bī,* "I will not set before my eyes any base thing; I hate the making of images, it shall never cling to me." With the recognition of the technical usage of *śānē'tī,* as in Pss xxvi 5 and xxxi 6–7, where this verb is used in the repudiation of idols, and with the appreciation that the "base thing" must be an idol since it is something held up to view, a strong case can be made for defining *śāṭē kāzāb* as "fraudulent images," or "fraudulent idols or gods." The proposal is likewise valid in Hos v 2, *wᵉšaḥᵃṭāh śēṭīm heʿmīqū,* "They are in the depths of slaughtering to images." The phrase *šaḥᵃṭāh śēṭīm* (or possibly *šᵃḥōt haśśēṭīm*) yields to understanding with the knowledge that in Ezek xvi 21, xxiii 39, and Isa lvii 5, *šāḥaṭ* describes the slaughter to false gods.

6. *have you achieved.* Transposing *'attāh* and *yhwh* and then vocalizing *'ātᵉtāh,* from *'ōt,* "to work wonders," a denominative verb from *'ōt,* "sign, wonder." This pointing thus provides the verb needed for the second colon to balance *ʿāśītā* in the first. The same denominative verb occurs in Ps xliv 3, parallel to *pāʿaltā.*

you have no peer. Literally "none compares to you"; cf. NOTE on Ps xvi 2.

7. *you were not interested.* This nuance of *ḥāpēṣ* comes to the fore in Ps li 18, 21; I Kings xiii 23; Hos vi 6; Job xxxiii 32; I Chron xxviii 9.

made my ear receptive. I.e., open to divine inspiration. Reading (for MT *kārītā*) *kārattā,* from *kārat,* "to cut, circumcise." Contrast Exod vi 12, *ʿᵃral śᵉpātāyim,* "of uncircumcised lips," and Jer vi 10, *ʿᵃrēlāh 'oznām,* "Their ears are uncircumcised," i.e., are unattentive.

8. *the inscribed scroll.* The phrase *mᵉgillat sēper* is of a piece with UT, 138:6–7, *lḥt spr,* "the tablet of the letter, *Brieftafel.*"

to my debit. The economic sense of *ʿālāy,* well illustrated by Ras Shamra commercial texts (UT, § 10.14), has been studied by the writer in connection with Job xiii 26, *tiktōb ʿālāy mᵉrōrōt,* "You write to my debit acts of violence," in BCCT, pp. 59 f. Cf. II Kings xxii 13.

10. *announced the glad news.* Referring to his recovery from the mortal illness. D. J. McCarthy in *Verbum Domini* 42 (1964), 26–33, has traced the pre-Israelite history of the root *bśr.*

11. *your saving action.* In the present *Sitz im Leben, tᵉšūʿātᵉkā* doubtless refers to the poet's delivery from death.

nor your fidelity. The stereotyped phrase *ḥasdᵉkā wa'ᵃmittᵉkā* should perhaps be broken up so that the pause comes after *ḥasdᵉkā;* two parallel cola of two beats each thus emerge. Cf. NOTE on Ps xi 4. Job xxxi 13 also illustrates the same poetic device: *'im 'em'as mišpaṭ ʿabdī // wa'ᵃmātī bᵉrībām ʿimmādī,* "If I despised the claim of my slave, / Or my slave girl, when they complained" (Pope, The Anchor Bible, vol. 15). Contrast RSV, "If I have rejected the cause of my manservant or my maidservant, when they brought a complaint against me." In both texts, MT fails to recognize the breakup of a stereotyped phrase.

from the great congregation. With verbs of refusing, withholding, etc., *l* denotes "from," as in Ugaritic; for other instances, see Dahood, CBQ

16 (1954), 302. Unfamiliarity with this image led to the imprecise CCD version, "in the vast assembly." If this were meant, one would expect *b^{e}qāhāl rāb*. Just as God did not withhold his love from the psalmist (vs. 12, *mimmennī*), so the psalmist did not conceal God's kindness toward him *from* the vast assembly.

12. *kindness and fidelity*. Personified as two attendants who protect the psalmist against sundry dangers—in the present context, against the danger of wild animals; cf. the metaphor in following verse. The theme of the two guides or attendants has been remarked at Ps xxiii 6, but the most pertinent parallel here is Ps xxv 21, since it employs the same verb *yiṣṣ^{e}rūnī*, "Let integrity and uprightness safeguard me."

13. *have encompassed me*. Balanced by "overtaken me," *'āp^{e}pū* describes the action of dogs or wolves closing in on their quarry. Compare a similar metaphor in Ps xxii 13–17.

unable to escape. Reading (for MT *lir'ōt*, "to see") *lid'ōt*, "to fly, escape." The same confusion between *daleth* and *resh* has been documented in II Sam xxii 11, which reads *wayyērā'*, while the doublet in Ps xviii 11 correctly reads *wayyēde'*, "and he flew"; similarly in Deut xiv 13, incorrect *hr'h* is correctly read *hd'h* in the doublet of Lev xi 14. See Dahood, *Biblica* 45 (1964), 401.

my heart fails me. In the metaphor of the chase in Ps xxii 15 the heart is said to have become like wax.

14. *Run, O Yahweh*. Pointing *rūṣāh* for MT *r^{e}ṣēh*, "be pleased." The energic imperative *rūṣāh* creates a perfect parallel to energic imperative *ḥūšāh* of the second colon. In other words, we have an *inclusio* with the verse beginning and closing with energic imperatives. The desire to avoid a strong anthropomorphism may readily explain the MT pointing. The verb *rūṣ* is predicated of God the warrior in Job xvi 14.

15. *recoil in disgrace*. Hendiadys; literally "Let them turn back and be disgraced."

16. *Aha, aha*. For the etymology of the interjection *he'āḥ*, see NOTE on Ps xxxv 21.

17. *Great is Yahweh*. This clause is interposed between the verb and the subject. A translation following the Hebrew word order would read, "Let them always say, 'Great is Yahweh,' who love your salvation."

18. *my helper*. Paired with concrete *m^{e}pal^{e}ṭī*, abstract *'ezrātī* acquires a concrete meaning on the strength of the poetic practice clarified by Ugaritic usage. Consult remarks in NOTE on Ps v 8. The doublet in Ps lxx 6 reads *'ezrī*, "my help," often emended to *'ōz^{e}rī*, "my helper."

PSALM 41

(xli 1–14)

1 *For the director. A psalm of David.*

2 How blest the man prudent in speech,
in time of danger may Yahweh deliver him.
3 May Yahweh protect him, [2]*
give him long life,
bless him upon the earth,
Do not put him into the maw of his Foe!
4 May Yahweh support him [3]
on his bed of illness;
Sustain his confinement,
overthrow the sickness itself!
5 And I said, "O Yahweh have pity on me, [4]
heal me though I have sinned against you."
6 My foes speak maliciously against me, [5]
"When will he die and his name perish?"
7 If one comes to visit, [6]
he utters lies from his heart;
He stores up malice for himself,
goes outside and gossips.
8 They whisper about me together; [7]
all my enemies, O Most High,
Plot evil against me.
9 "Pour a lethal substance into him, [8]
that he who lies ill may rise no more."
10 Even my colleague in whom I trusted, [9]
he who ate my bread
Spun slanderous tales about me.
11 But you, O Yahweh, have pity on me, [10]
and raise me up
That I may repay them.

* Verse numbers in RSV.

12 Then shall I know that you love me, [11]
if my Foe does not triumph over me.
13 But I in my integrity— [12]
grasp me
And set me before you forever!
14 Praised be Yahweh, the God of Israel, [13]
from eternity and to eternity.
Amen and Amen.

Notes

xli. A prayer for healing from sickness which closes (vs. 13) with a prayer for eternal life with Yahweh.

In *Interpretation* 18 (1964), 20–38, especially p. 29, Loren Fisher has made the plausible suggestion that this ancient psalm may relate to a time when the king was ill and his enemies tried to overthrow him. The basis for his proposal comes from the similar situation described in UT, 127:43–57, which relates the attempt of Prince Yaṣṣib to dethrone his bedridden father King Keret (or Kirta). The language of the lament is very archaic (probably Davidic era) and difficult, so that the translation of several clauses is doubtful.

2. *prudent in speech.* Since the customary version of *maśkīl dāl,* "who considers the poor," does not harmonize with the contents of the poem, one is permitted to submit that *dāl* is elliptical for Ps cxli 3, *dal śᵉpātāy,* "the door of my lips." Cf. Prov xvi 23, *lēb ḥākām yaśkīl pīhū,* "The mind of a wise man renders his speech prudent."

Having been the victim of a whispering campaign and slanderous attacks, the psalmist is disposed to commend the man who is circumspect in speech.

3. *give him long life.* This too may be the connotation of the Canaanite salutation in UT, 76:II:20, *ḥwt aḫt,* "May you have a long life, O my sister!"

bless him. Reading piel *yeʾaššēr* for MT pual *yeʾuššar* and supplying the accusative suffix from the preceding verb on the principle of the double-duty suffix treated at Ps iii 4. The three verbs of the blessing in vs. 3a semantically coincide with the three verbs that comprise the Canaanite blessing often found at the beginning of Ugaritic letters. For example, UT, 1019:2–4, *ilm tǵrk tšlmk tʿzzk,* "May the gods protect you, keep you hale, strengthen you."

into the maw. On *nepeš,* "throat," see Note on Ps xxvii 12. Since biblical poetry teems with mythical imagery, the present task of scholars is to recover these mythological allusions. The prominence in Canaanite poetry of the theme, "the maw of Mot," is the basis for assuming that the motif was not unknown to biblical bards.

The prayer, "Do not put him into the maw of his Foe," is synonymous with Ps xvi 10, "Since you will not put me in Sheol, nor allow your devoted one to see the Pit," and is a request for the same gift that was accorded Enoch and Elijah, namely, the privilege of being assumed by God (see NOTE on Ps xlix 16) directly without experiencing death. The sentiment is taken up again in vs. 13, "Grasp me and set me before you forever!"

of his Foe. I.e., Death. Plural *'ōyᵉbāyw* is here taken as the plural of excellence, since the psalmist's chief foe was Death. The same usage is found in Pss xviii 4 and xlii 10.

4. *his bed of illness.* As Ginsberg, LKK, p. 49, has remarked, *'ereś dᵉwāy* equals UT, 127:35, *'rš mdw.*

Sustain his confinement. In other words, make his sickness bearable. Reading (for MT *kol*) *kūl* from the root *kwl,* "to sustain, support," which, while usually employed in the pilpel conjugation, does appear as qal in Isa xl 12. Imperative *kūl* is thus in balance with jussive *yis'ādennū,* "may he support him."

overthrow. Parsing *hāpaktā* as precative perfect, in balance with the preceding jussive and imperative, a topic treated at Ps iii 8. Cf. UT, 127:v:20–21, [*my*] *bilm ydy mrṣ gršm zbln,* "Which of the gods will cast out the sickness, exorcising the disease?"

the sickness itself. Explaining the *bᵉ* of *bᵉḥōlī* as the emphasizing particle investigated at Ps xxix 4. Cf. Isa i 5b, where *laḥᵒlī,* "very sickness," preceded by the emphatic *lamedh,* parallels *dawwāy.* The final *waw* of consonantal *ḥlyw* in the present passage is transferred to the following word as the conjunction.

5. *And I said.* The conjunction *waw* has been detached from the preceding word and joined to *'ᵃnī.* The poet begins both his prayer for healing and his prayer for eternal life in vs. 13 with the same formula, *wa'ᵃnī.*

6. *against me.* Commentators have experienced difficulty in accounting for *lī* where *'ālāy* would have been expected. The same problem recurs in vs. 8, *yaḥšᵉbū rā'āh lī,* "They plot evil against me." The hostile force of *lᵉ* is mentioned in NOTE on Ps xvii 4.

his name perish. In other words, when will his family vanish from the earth? In fact, *šēm,* "name," does denote "offspring" in a number of texts; see O'Callaghan, VT 4 (1954), 164 f. Cf. Job iv 20, *mibbᵉlī-m šēm* (MT *mibbᵉlī mēśīm*) *lāneṣah yō'bēdū,* "They perish forever nameless" (Pope, The Anchor Bible, vol. 15).

7. *he utters lies from his heart.* Literally "His heart utters lies." Cf. Ps xix 15, *hegyōn libbī,* "the utterance of my heart."

goes outside and gossips. Having left the patient, he goes to spread the slander abroad. Since the psalmist was sick, his supposed friends concluded that he must have committed some heinous crime and now begin to speculate on it. For *dibbēr,* "to gossip," see Pss lvi 6, 11, lix 13.

8. *They whisper.* The root of *yitlaḥ*^{a}*šū* is attested in Ugaritic-Phoenician *lḥšt,* "whisper, incantation," and in an unpublished incantation text from Ras Shamra in *mlḥš,* "enchanter." See C. Virolleaud in GLECS 10 (1964), 5–6.

O Most High. Vocalizing MT *'ālay* as *'ēlī,* the divine appellative studied at Ps vii 9. It may here be noted that in his lament, King Hezekiah invokes the Exalted One (*mārōm*): Isa xxxviii 14, *dallū 'ēnay l*^{e}*mārōm* (MT *lammārōm*), "My eyes have grown weak, O Exalted One." Cf. also Ps lvi 3. I am indebted to D. N. Freedman for the reading *'ēlī.*

against me. See NOTE on vs. 6.

9. *Pour.* Reading either imperative *y*^{e}*ṣōq* or infinitive absolute *yāṣōq* serving the function of an imperative for MT *yāṣūq.* Compare imperative *y*^{e}*ṣōq,* preserving the initial consonant, in Ezek xxiv 3, *š*^{e}*pōt hassīr š*^{e}*pōt w*^{e}*gam y*^{e}*ṣōq bō māyim,* "Set the pot, set it on, and also pour water into it." Cf. UT, 55:9, *dk aḥdh wyṣq baph,* "Grind them together and pour them into his nostrils."

a lethal substance. Literally "a substance of destruction." A synonym of *d*^{e}*bar b*^{e}*liyya'al* can be seen in Ps lxiv 4, *dār*^{e}*kū ḥiṣṣām dābār mār,* "They tipped their arrows with a poisonous substance."

that he who. Parsing *'*^{a}*šer* as a compound relative. The unique occurrence of Ugar. *aṯr* finds it in the role of a compound relative; UT, 2060:34–35, *aṯr iṯ bqṯ w štn ly,* "Find out what is available and write to me."

may rise no more. I.e., from his sickbed; see NOTE below on vs. 11.

10. *Even my colleague.* In other words, even he who was in compact with me. For expression *'īš š*^{e}*lōmī,* see NOTE on Ps vii 5 and W. F. Albright, BASOR 163 (1961), 52, n. 75.

who ate my bread. Referring to part of the covenant rite. Cf. Gen xxvi 30, xxxi 54; Num xviii 17–19; and especially Ps lxix 23, "May their table before them be a trap and even their colleagues a snare" (Exod xxiv 12).

Spun slanderous tales. Literally "spun slander." On *gādal,* "to weave, spin," cf. NOTE on Ps xii 4 and *Biblica* 45 (1964), 397. Compare the cognate imagery in Ps l 19, *ūl*^{e}*šōn*^{e}*kā taṣmīd mirmāh,* "And with your tongue you weave deceit."

That the stem *'qb* denotes "to malign, traduce, slander" ensues from these texts: Jer ix 3, *kī kol 'āḥ 'āqōb ya'qōb w*^{e}*kol rē*$^{a'}$ *rākīl yah*^{a}*lōk,*

"For every brother constantly maligns, and every fellow man is a traducer" (the balance with *rākīl* leaves little doubt as to the force of *'āqab*)—what should be borne in mind is the consideration that Jer ix 1–4 is a catalogue of the sins of speech; and Ps lxxxix 52, *'ᵃšer ḥērᵉpū 'ᵃqābōt* (MT *'iqqᵉbōt*) *mᵉšīḥekā,* "Who insultingly malign your anointed one"—the phrase *ḥērᵉpū 'ᵃqābōt,* literally "they insult by slanderous remarks,"—is an example of hendiadys.

In a highly ironic passage in UT, 3 Aqht:rev:19, the god El assures the goddess Anath that *dṯ ydṯ m'qbk,* "He who maligns you will surely be crushed underfoot." The irony of El's words becomes apparent in light of UT, 2 Aqht:VI:51, where Anath is said to have slandered Aqhat the hero, *tlšn aqht ǵzr.* The pun in the words *dṯ ydṯ m'qbk* has been brought out by Gaster, *Thespis,* 1950, p. 452. One may proceed further and propose that the root of *'āqab,* "to malign," is *'āqēb,* "heel," just as *rāgal* and *riggēl,* "to slander," stem from *regel,* "foot." Such an etymology agrees with the distinct tendency of Ugaritic and Hebrew to coin denominative verbs from names of parts of the body; cf. NOTE on Ps xv 3. Here then is a further criterion for assessing the linguistic position of Ugaritic.

For a similar semantic relationship between "heel" and "slander," cf. Ar. *'aqqaba,* "to criticize sharply, tear to pieces," from *'aqib,* "heel," and consult A. Guillaume, JSS 9 (1964), 285.

11. *raise me up.* Indicating from my sickbed (cf. NOTE on vs. 9) as well as from the brink of Sheol (cf. NOTE on Ps XXX 2).

That I may repay them. For subjunctive *'ᵃšallᵉmāh,* cf. NOTE on Ps xxxix 5.

12. *Then.* This sense of *bᵉzō't,* a dis legomenon, was noticed at Ps xxvii 3, where the usual version "by this" does not fit.

my Foe. On singular *'ōyᵉbī* as a name for personified Death, cf. NOTE on Ps xxxi 9.

13. *in my integrity.* Or, "because of my integrity." Compare Karatepe, I:12–13, *bṣdqy wbḥkmty,* "because of my justice and because of my wisdom."

grasp me. Parsing *tāmaktā* as precative perfect in balance with vs. 11 imperative *ḥonnēnī;* cf. NOTE on Ps iii 8. By the use of the precative perfect the poet seems to hark back to the precative perfect *hāpaktā* in vs. 4.

The psalmist not only prays for recuperation from illness but boldly requests the privilege of being assumed by God and placed in his presence for eternity. Thus *tāmak* is a synonym of *lāqaḥ,* the technical term for "assume" discussed in the second NOTE on Ps xlix 16.

set me before you. Implying so that I might enjoy the beatific vision; consult NOTES on Pss xvi 11, xvii 15, xxi 5, 7, xxvii 4, xxxvi 10, xlix 16. This petition resumes the thought of vs. 3, "Do not put him into the throat of his Foe": instead of putting me into Sheol after death, directly take me to yourself that I might encounter you face to face for all eternity.

14. *Praised be Yahweh.* A doxology closing the first of the five books into which the Psalter was divided (see Introduction, The Structure of the Psalter). Cf. Pss lxxii 19–20, lxxxix 53, cvi 48. It did not form part of the original poem.

PSALM 42

(xlii 1–12)

1 *For the director. A maskil of the sons of Korah.*

2 As a hind cries aloud for running streams,
so my soul cries aloud for you, O God.
3 My soul thirsts for God, [2]*
for the living God.
When shall I begin
to drink in deeply the presence of God?
4 My tears have been my food [3]
day and night,
When it was being said to me
all day long,
"Where is your God?"
5 These things I shall remember, [4]
and shall pour out my soul before him
When I cross the barrier,
and prostrate myself near the temple of God,
Amid loud shouts of thanksgiving,
amid a festal throng.
6 Why are you so sad, O my soul? [5]
And why do you sigh before me?
Wait for God, for I shall still praise him,
my Savior, my Presence, and my God.
7 My soul before me is very sad [6]
because I remember you,
From the land of descent and of nets,
from the mountains at the rim;
8 Where deep calls to deep, [7]
at the peal of your thunderbolts;
And all your breakers and your billows
pass over me.

* Verse numbers in RSV.

9 By day Yahweh had sent his grace [8]
and his vision to me at night.
10 My prayer to my living God: [9]
I shall say: "O El, my Rock,
why have you forgotten me?
why must I go in gloom
because of harassment by the Foe,
because of the Assassin within my bones?"
11 My adversaries taunt me [10]
saying to me all day long,
"Where is your God?"
12 Why are you so sad, O my soul? [11]
And why do you sigh before me?
Wait for God, for I shall still praise him,
my Savior, my Presence, and my God.

Notes

xlii. Psalms xlii–xliii form a single lyric consisting of three stanzas, each of which is followed by a refrain (xlii 5, 11, xliii 5). Ps xlii may fairly be described as the biblical version of "The Dark Night of the Soul." The psalmist, who had enjoyed God's consoling grace, finds himself in a state of extreme desolation because God has withdrawn his spiritual favors. He compares his wretchedness to the cheerless existence of Sheol.

2. *As a hind.* Reading (for MT *k*^{e}*'ayyal ta'*^{a}*rōg,* which is grammatically discordant) *k*^{e}*'ayyelet 'ārōg,* and with Huesman in *Biblica* 37 (1956), 290, parsing *'ārōg* as infinitive absolute functioning as a finite verb, as in Pss xvii 5, xxxv 16, xlix 4. This analysis is preferable to the supposition that a *t* was lost through haplography, as proposed by H. L. Ginsberg in BA 8 (1945), 56. Consult further Solá-Solé, *L'infinitif sémitique,* § 58*bis,* pp. 95 f.

For the sequence *k . . . kn,* cf. UT, 49:II:28–30, *klb arḫ l'glh klb ṯat limrh km lb 'nt aṯr b'l,* "Like the heart of a wild cow for her calf, like the heart of ewe for her lamb, so was the heart of Anath toward Baal."

Biblical *'ayyelet,* "hind," appears as Ugar. *aylt.*

cries aloud. A. B. Ehrlich, *Die Psalmen* (Berlin, 1905), p. 95, has shown, in view of Joel i 20, that *'ārag* is related to Ar. *'ajja,* "to cry aloud." This proposal was adopted by J. A. Bewer, in *A Critical and Exegetical Commentary on Obadiah* (ICC; Edinburgh, 1912), p. 92, and *The Prophets in the King James Version with Introduction and Critical Notes* (New York, 1949), p. 603, who corroborated the proposal by remarking the synonymy of Joel i 20, *ta'ᵃrōg 'ēlekā,* and i 19, *'ēlekā yhwh 'eqrā'.*

The motif of an animal crying appears in a fragment mentioned by Virolleaud in GLECS 8 (1960), 90: *arḫ td rgm bǵr,* "The wild cow throws her voice from the mountain." Numerous scholars have noted the similarity of the biblical simile with UT, 67:I:16–17, *hm brky tkšd rumm 'n kḏd aylt,* "Lo, the wild oxen make for the pools, the hinds make for the spring."

for you, O God. In Pss xlii–lxxxiii, the divine name *'ᵉlōhīm* occurs some 210 times, *yhwh* only 45 times. In the rest of the Psalter, however, the Tetragrammaton appears some 584 times, *'ᵉlōhīm* but 94 times. The striking contrast between the frequencies of *yhwh* and *'ᵉlōhīm* in Pss xlii–lxxxiii in comparison with the rest of the Psalter has been considered the result of a "late" revision of the text. For instance, CCD, III, p. 155, states, "In the Second Book of the Psalms the proper name of God, Yahweh, 'The Lord', was changed in almost all places by some early scribe to read Elohim, 'God'." Why some early scribe undertook to do this has never been satisfactorily explained. R. Boling, "'Synonymous' Parallelism in the Psalms," JSS 5 (1960), 221–55, especially pp. 253–55, has challenged the prevailing opinion by arguing that the frequencies of *yahweh* and *'ᵉlōhīm* in the Yahwistic and the Elohistic psalms represent opposing stylistic preferences.

3. *the living God.* Some would read *'ēl ḥayyay,* on the strength of vs. 9, *'ēl ḥayyay,* but this emendation overlooks the allusive power of *ḥay* which, associated with *ṣāmᵉ'āh,* "thirsts," is doubtless meant to evoke the image of *mayim ḥayyīm,* "living waters," predicated of God in Jer ii 13 and elsewhere.

When shall I begin. In the phrase *'ābō' wᵉ'ērā'āh, 'ābō'* serves as an inchoative verb, a topic briefly treated in first NOTE on Ps xxii 32.

to drink in deeply. In a context that describes the thirst of a hind for running waters, and the thirst of a soul for living waters, the verb *'ērā'āh* (MT *'ērā'eh*) is more meaningfully derived from *yārā'* or *yārē',* "to be fat, to drink deeply," examined in connection with Ps xxxiv 9, "Taste and drink deeply, for Yahweh is sweet," than from *rā'āh,* "to see."

4. *tears have been my food.* Cf. Ps lxxx 6; Lam iii 15; and particularly Jer viii 14c, "For Yahweh our God has made us weep and has given us tears to drink, because we have sinned against Yahweh." For details of this version, cf. Dahood in *Biblica* 45 (1964), 402, and for

Canaanite analogy, UT, 62:10, *tšt kyn udmʿt,* "She drinks tears like wine."

day and night. The unit-phrase *yōmām wālāylāh* recurs in vs. 9 where, however, it is broken up and the components placed in the parallel cola.

5. *shall pour out my soul before him.* Explaining the suffix of *'ešpekāh ʿālay* as third-person masculine singular as in Phoen. *ʿly,* "upon it"; cf. NOTE on Ps ii 6. For the thought, cf. Ps lxii 9, *šipekū lepānāyw lebabekem,* "Pour out your heart before him"; Job x 1, *'eʿezebāh ʿālay śīḥī,* "I shall set my complaint before him" (cf. LXX); and Ps cii 1. For *ʿal,* "before, in presence of," see Suárez in *Verbum Domini* 42 (1964), 71–80.

the barrier. Perhaps the barrier separating the temple enclosure from the court of the Gentiles. Deriving *sāk* from *sākak,* "to screen, cover"; it is related to *śūk,* "to hedge, fence in," and to Lam ii 6, *śukkō,* probably denoting "fence." See Tsevat, *A Study of the Language of the Biblical Psalms,* p. 83.

prostrate myself. The root underlying difficult *'eddaddēm* is taken to be *ndd,* "to bow down," followed by enclitic *mem.* The root probably occurs in UT, 76:II:17–18, *lpnnh ydd wyqm lpʿnh yqrʿ wyql;* the apparent parallelism with *ykrʿ,* "he bows down," points to the meaning of *ydd.* In UT, 51:III:11–12, *ydd* seems to balance *yqdd,* "he prostrates himself." Other biblical instances of *ndd* may be present in Ps lxviii 13; Isa xxxviii 15. Cf. Ps cxxxviii 2, "I prostrate myself near your holy temple."

near the temple. For this sense of *ʿad,* consult H. L. Ginsberg, BASOR 124 (1951), 29 f., and S. Speir, BASOR 126 (1952), 27, who pointed out that in the last century S. D. Luzzatto recognized this value of *ʿad* in Gen xiii 12b, xxxviii 1b, and Judg iv 11b.

loud shouts of thanksgiving. Literally "loud shouts and thanksgiving," a case of hendiadys.

amid a festal throng. The principle of the double-duty preposition, considered at Ps xxxiii 7, permits *hāmōn ḥōgēg* to share the preposition of *beqōl rinnāh wetōdāh.*

6. *before me.* For *ʿal,* "before," see first NOTE above on vs. 5. From this translation the literary genus known as "the dialogue of a man with his soul" more clearly comes to light. See Pss lxii 2, ciii 1, cxvi 7, cxlii 4, cxliii 4.

my Savior. A *plurale majestatis, yešūʿōt* is most simply understood as a divine name, as in Ps xxviii 8. There may be an analogy in Prov ix 10, *teḥillat ḥokmāh yir'at yhwh wedaʿat qedōšīm bīnāh,* "The beginning of wisdom is to hold the Lord in awe, / And knowledge of the Holy One is understanding." A number of modern versions, following LXX *hagíōn,* take *qedōšīm* as a plural of majesty with a singular meaning. The most recent discussion may be found in A. Barucq, *Le Livre des Proverbes* (Paris, 1964), p. 98.

The suffixes of the ensuing divine appellatives supply that of *yᵉšûʻōt*, "my Savior," according to the practice cited in NOTE on Ps iii 4. Cf. also Ps xli 3, where the first two verbs have suffixes whereas the third of the series is without one.

my Presence. Reading *pānay* for MT *pānāyw* and attaching the final *waw* to next word as the conjunction; this reading is imposed by vs. 12 and Ps xliii 5, *yᵉšûʻōt pānay wē'lōhāy*. This looks like proof positive that some biblical texts were written without word dividers and that word division posed a not insignificant problem. For *pānīm,* "Presence," see NOTE on Ps xxiv 6.

7. *before me.* See NOTES on vss. 5 and 6 on *ʻālay,* "before me."

because I remember. *ʻal kēn,* "because," as in Ps xlv 3, introduces the reason for the poet's despondency.

the land of descent. A poetic name for the nether world. In his desolate state, the psalmist imagines himself in the depths of Sheol at the farthest possible remove from God. Similar imagery is found in Ps lxi 3. Compare the phrase *'ereṣ yardēn* with UT, 51:VIII:8–9, *tspr byrdm arṣ,* "Be numbered among those who go down into the nether world." The mention of *tᵉhōm,* "deep, abyss," in the next verse confirms the substantial correctness of this interpretation, namely, that the poet pictures himself in Sheol. A similar motif occurs in Jon ii 3, *mibbeṭen šᵉ'ōl šiwwaʻtī,* "From the bosom of Sheol I cried out." Cf. further Pss xviii 5–7, lxix 2–3, lxxxviii 5–7.

D. N. Freedman finds a connection between the geographical name Jordan and the noun here postulated as the name of the nether world. After all, the Jordan makes a precipitous descent to the lowest point in the world, a region that must have provided some of the imagery associated with the nether regions.

and of nets. Explaining *ḥermōnīm* as a by-form of *ḥērem,* "net." The morphological relationship between *ḥrm* and *ḥrmn* is that which subsists between, say, Heb. *mḥsr,* "lack," and Ugar. *mḫsrn;* Heb. *bṣqln* (II Kings iv 42), and Ugar. *bṣql;* Ugar. *drb,* "goad," and Heb. *drbn* (Eccles xii 11).

The motif of Sheol as a place of snares and nets appears in Ps xviii 6 and Job v 5.

mountains at the rim. Reading plural (or dual) *hārē-m ṣʻr* for MT *har miṣʻar,* and explaining *ṣʻr* as metathetic for *ʻṣr,* which occurs in UT, 51:VIII:4–8, *ʻm tlm ǵṣr arṣ ša ǵr ʻl ydm ḫlb lẓr rḥtm wrd btḫptṯ arṣ,* "Toward the two mounds at the edge of the nether world. Lift the mountain upon your hands, the wooded hill upon your palms and go down to the infirmary of the nether world." Cf. Jon ii 7, *lᵉqiṣbē hārīm yāradtī hā'āreṣ,* "At the edges of the mountains I descended into the nether world." It should be remarked, however, that not all Ugaritic specialists agree in their definition of *ġṣr;* some relate it to Ar. *ġaḍira,* "thriving" (Ginsberg, Gordon), while others connect it with Ar. *ġaḍura,* Heb. *'āṣar,* "to retain, enclose" (Albright, Aistleitner, Gaster, Driver).

8. *deep calls to deep.* In other words, even the subterranean waters reverberate to the lightning bolts of Yahweh. Cf. Ps lxxvii 19. Patton, CPBP, p. 46, has remarked that the phrase *t^ehōm 'el t^ehōm* recalls the duality expressed by the Ugaritic form *thmtm,* "the two deeps."

your thunderbolts. This sense of *ṣinnōr* has been clarified by E. L. Sukenik in JPOS 8 (1928), 126. It is the trident with which God strikes the sea and creates its breakers. Ugar. *ṣnr* evidently denotes "pipe, shaft." Verses 7b, 8a, and 8b form a strophe in 3+2 meter.

9. *By day . . . at night.* The pairing of adverbial *yōmām* with the prepositional phrase *ballaylāh* is analogous to the Ugaritic practice of balancing a preposition in one parallel member by *-m* in the other: Krt:159–61, *lqh imr dbḥ bydh lla klatnm,* "He took a lamb of sacrifice in his left hand, a kid in both hands"; cf. *lẓr // ṯkmm* (Krt:166–67), *krpnm // bks* (51:III:43–44), UT, § 11.6. Cf. also Ps cxxi 6.

The breakup of the stereotyped phrase *yōmām wālāylāh* (vs. 4) does not mean that the psalmist enjoyed God's grace only by day and his visions only at night; it is merely the poetic way of saying that he constantly received the gracious visitations of Yahweh. Now that these visitations have ceased, the psalmist is extremely desolate and compares his spiritual depression to that experienced by the denizens of Sheol.

had sent. In several texts *ṣiwwāh,* "to command," denotes "to send," just as *šālaḥ,* "to send," frequently denotes "to command, commission"; cf. Bogaert, *Biblica* 45 (1964), 227, concerning Phoen. *šlḥ,* "to commission," and Zorell, ZLH, pp. 847 f., for biblical examples. There is a good instance in Ps xci 11 of *ṣiwwāh,* "to send." *La Bible de la Pléiade,* II, p. 985, accurately renders the present passage, *"Iahvé mandait sa grâce durant le jour."*

his vision. T. H. Gaster in JBL 73 (1954), 237 f., has correctly identified consonantal *šyrh* with Ugar. *ḏrt,* "vision," parallel to *ḥlm,* "dream." Hence the collocation of "vision" and "night" in the biblical passage tallies with the Ugaritic balance of "vision" and "dream," which presumably took place at night.

The suffix of *ḥasdō* serves to limit consonantal *šyrh,* "his vision," precisely as in Ps lxxvii 9, *he'āpēs lāneṣaḥ ḥasdō gāmar 'ōmer l^edōr wādōr,* "Has his grace ceased for eternity, his vision [cf. NOTE on Ps xxix 9] come to an end for all generations?"

to me. In Ugaritic the more common meaning of *'m* is "to, toward"; see UT, § 10.14, and Aistleitner, WuS, No. 2041, p. 233. Cf. UT, 138:8, *spr d likt 'm ṯryl,* "The letter that you sent to ṮRYL."

10. *O El.* Parsing *l*[e]*'ēl* as *lamedh vocativum* (cf. NOTE on Ps iii 9) and the personal name of the divinity rather than generic "God."

my Rock. There is added relevance in this epithet in that Sheol was considered a vast quagmire with no firm footing (Ps lxix 3). Similar imagery is used in Ps lxi 3, "From the edge of the nether world I called to you when my courage failed. Onto a lofty rock you led me from it."

forgotten me. As appears from Pss vi 6, lxxxviii 6, one of the most poignant sorrows of consignment to Sheol was to be forgotten by God. Though the psalmist is not physically in Sheol, his desolation is no less acute.

the Foe. Death is signified; cf. NOTE on Ps xxxi 9 for *'ōyēb,* an epithet of Death.

the Assassin within my bones. b[e]*reṣaḥ b*[e]*'aṣmōtay* is puzzling, but when the Foe is identified, it becomes likely that *reṣaḥ,* "murder," may be another designation of the archenemy of the psalmist. That Death was thought to reside in the body of a sick person may be gathered from UT, 127:13–14, *mt dm ḫt š'tqt dm lan,* "Death on the one hand is shattered, Shataqat [literally "she who makes depart"] on the other is victorious."

12. *my Savior.* Cf. NOTE on vs. 6.

PSALM 43

(xliii 1–5)

1 Defend me, O God, and plead my case!
From an ungodly nation,
from deceitful and impious men deliver me!
2 For you are my Fortress-God,
why have you rejected me?
Why must I go in gloom
because of harassment by the Foe?
3 Send forth your light and your truth;
behold, let them lead me;
Let them bring me to your holy mountain
and to your dwelling.
4 I would come to the altar of God,
to El, the joy of my life;
And I would praise you with the lyre,
O God, my God!
5 Why are you so sad, O my soul?
And why do you sigh before me?
Wait for God, for I shall still praise him,
my Savior, my Presence, and my God.

NOTES

xliii. This untitled psalm is the continuation of Ps xlii. It closes with the refrain that appears in xlii 6 and 12.

1. *deliver me.* Imperatives *šopṭēnī* and *rībāh* followed by jussive *t^{e}pall^{e}ṭēnī* are a type of sequence well documented in Ugaritic poetry, as noted at Ps x 15. Friedrich, PPG, § 42*, p. 162, commenting upon Yaudian (a Phoenician dialect) *plṭ*, "to rescue, deliver," observes that the verb in Hebrew is limited to poetry and further queries whether the usage is not to be termed an *Aramaismus*. The negative reply was given three decades ago with the publication of UT, 3 Aqht:rev:13,

wypltk bn[*dnil*]. Since the Aqhat Legend dates to the early second millennium in its composition, one would hardly be disposed to speak of *plṭ* as an Aramaism. The root also occurs in the Ugaritic personal name *ypltn* of the fourteenth century B.C.

2. *my Fortress-God.* Literally "the God of my fortress."

the Foe. Cf. NOTE on Ps xlii 10.

3. *Send forth your light.* Indicating what is so desperately needed in the poet's spiritual darkness.

your light and your truth. An adaptation of the ancient Near Eastern belief that the gods were accompanied by two attendant deities; see NOTE on Ps xxiii 6. Of especial relevance for the present passage is UT, 51:IV:16–17, *qdš yuḫd šb'r amrr kkbkb lpnm,* "Qudshu begins to shine, Amrur is like a star in front." To be sure, *qdš wamrr* refers to a single deity (see Ginsberg, BASOR 95 [1944], 25), but his double-barreled name would readily lend itself for adaptation into *'ōr,* "light," and *'ᵉmet,* "truth." The essential point of the comparison I wish to make here, however, is that *qdš wamrr* guides the goddess Asherah to the abode of El where the two deeps erupt, while divine light and truth are sought to lead the psalmist to the holy mountain where God resides.

behold. See Note on Ps xxiii 4 for discussion of *hēmmāh,* "behold."

let them lead me. The verb *yanḥūnī* from *nāḥāh* shows that Ps xxiii 4, *ynḥmny,* likewise predicated of two guides, is to be analyzed into the verb *nāḥāh,* followed by an "internal" enclitic *mem* and then by the pronominal suffix.

bring me. The kethib of the Oriental Mss. reads qal *yᵉbō'ūnī* where MT has hiphil *yᵉbī'ēnī.* The qal form, here being more difficult, may be correct since this form of *bw'* does mean "to bring" in Pss lxv 3, cxxxii 7, cxliii 2; Deut xxxii 17; Isa xxxv 4, lx 5; Amos v 10; Prov xviii 6.

your dwelling. Though plural in form, *miškᵉnōtekā* is singular in meaning, like Ugar. *mšknt;* see UT, § 13.17. Cf. Pss lxxxiv 2, cxxxii 5, 7; Job xviii 21, xxxix 6. This similarity of usage might be considered when the question of the linguistic classification of Ugaritic is explored further.

4. *I would come.* Explaining *'ābō'āh* as subjunctive; cf. NOTE on Ps xxxix 5.

El, the joy of my life. Deriving *gīl,* "life," from *gīl,* "to live," studied at Ps ii 11. LXX reads "the joy of my youth," which is equally possible since *gīl,* used in Dan i 10 in a context dealing with young men, more specifically refers to a period of life.

The phrase *'ēl śimḥat* compares with UT, 49:III:14, *šmḫ lṭpn il dpid,* "The benign and kindly El rejoiced."

5. *before me.* Consult NOTE on Ps xlii 6.

my Savior. See annotation to Ps xlii 6.

PSALM 44

(xliv 1–27)

1 *For the director. A maskil of the sons of Korah.*

2 O God, with our own ears we have heard,
our fathers have told us;
The deeds you performed in their days,
in days of old your hand worked wonders.
3 Nations you dispossessed, [2]*
but you planted them;
Peoples you dispersed,
but you made them send forth shoots.
4 For not by their sword did they seize the land, [3]
nor did their arm bring them victory.
But it was your right hand and your arm,
and the light of your face,
since you loved them.
5 You are my King, my God, [4]
my Commander, the Savior of Jacob.
6 Through you we butted our adversaries, [5]
through your name we trampled our assailants.
7 For not in my bow did I trust, [6]
nor did my sword bring me victory.
8 But you gave us victory over our adversaries, [7]
and put to shame our enemies.
9 In God we have continually boasted, [8]
and your name we will praise forever. *Selah*
10 But you rejected and humiliated us, [9]
and no longer went forth with our armies.
11 You made us retreat before our adversary, [10]
and our enemies pillaged us.
12 You made us a flock to be devoured, [11]
and scattered us among the nations.

* Verse numbers in RSV.

13 You sold your people for a trifle, [12]
and did not consider them of much value.
14 You made us the taunt of our neighbors, [13]
the derision and scorn of those about us.
15 You made us a byword among the nations, [14]
a laughingstock among the peoples.
16 My disgrace is continually in front of me, [15]
and my shamefacedness is exposed before me.
17 Because of the voice of the taunter and the reviler, [16]
because of the foe and the avenger.
18 Every indignity has come upon us, [17]
but we have not forgotten you,
or been disloyal to your covenant.
19 Our heart has not turned back, [18]
nor our feet strayed from your path.
20 Though you crushed us with festering of the loins, [19]
and covered us with total darkness.
21 If we had forgotten the name of our God, [20]
or stretched out our palms to an alien god;
22 Would not God discover this, [21]
since he knows the dark corners of the heart?
23 No, because of you we are slain [22]
the whole day long,
accounted as sheep for the slaughter.
24 Arise! Why do you sleep, O Lord? [23]
Awake! Be not angry forever!
25 Why did you turn away your face, [24]
and forget our affliction and oppression?
26 For our neck is bowed down to the dust, [25]
our belly cleaves to the ground.
27 Rise up, help us! [26]
Ransom us as befits your kindness.

Notes

xliv. A national lament. The community prays for deliverance from her enemies who have inflicted a shattering defeat upon her. The lack of clear historical allusions precludes an approximate dating of the composition.

2. *The deeds you performed.* Paul Humbert in ZAW 65 (1953), 35–44, has shown that the verb *pā'al* (here *pō'al pā'altā*)—the normal verb "to do, make" in Phoenician and Ugaritic, which, however, uses the dialectal form *b'l* though a recently published personal name *yp'l* conforms to the Phoenician pattern—is essentially a poetic verb in Hebrew. The heaviest concentration of derivatives from this root is in Psalms, followed by the Wisdom Literature. As Tsevat, *A Study of the Language of the Biblical Psalms,* p. 144, n. 456, has remarked, the verb *pā'al* and its substantives have probably been assimilated by the Hebrew language from Canaanite dialects.

your hand worked wonders. Reading *'ātāh yādekā* for MT *'attāh yādᵉkā;* for the verb *'ātāh,* see Note on Ps xl 6.

3. *Nations you dispossessed. hōraštā* is an example of hiphil privative; see Bergsträsser, *Hebräische Grammatik,* II Teil, *Verbum,* § 19g, p. 104, and Note on Ps xxv 17. Cf. UT, Krt:24–25, *wbtmhn špḥ yitbd wbpḫyrh yrt,* "And in its entirety a posterity perished, and in its totality dispossessed."

you planted them. Cf. Ps lxxx 9–12; Jer i 10, xlv 4. The antecedent of "them" is vs. 2, *'ᵃbōtēnū,* "our fathers."

Peoples you dispersed. Vocalizing *tārōᵃ'* for MT *tāra',* and deriving the verb from *r'',* "to smash." The semantic kinship between "smash" and "scatter" comes out in *nāpaṣ,* "to shatter, disperse." Zorell, ZLH, p. 525a, appears to be correct in assuming but one root, as against BDB, pp. 658 f., who distinguish between *nāpaṣ,* "to shatter," and *nāpaṣ,* "to disperse." There may have been, however, some interchange between the roots *r''* and *r'w/y,* both denoting "to scatter," if one may judge from Isa xxiv 19 and Eccles i 14, *rᵉ'ūt rūᵃḥ,* "dissipation of the spirit."

made them send forth shoots. The consistency of the metaphor is maintained when *tᵉšallᵉḥēm* is parsed as a piel denominative verb from *šelaḥ,* "sprout, shoot," as in Ps lxxx 12; Jer xvii 8; and Ezek xvii 6c. A fine analogy is proffered by *šātal,* "to transplant," from *šātīl,* "transplanted shoot, slip."

5. *my God, my Commander.* Reading *'ᵉlōhay mᵉṣawweh* for MT *'ᵉlōhīm ṣawwēh,* and invoking the principle of the double-duty suffix treated in Note on Ps iii 4; there is a good parallel in Ps xlii 6.

the Savior of Jacob. The divine name *yᵉšûʿôt* is studied in Note on Ps xlii 6.

6. *we butted our adversaries*. Cf. UT, 49:vi:17–18, *mt ʿz bʿl ʿz ynghn krumm*, "Mot now prevails, now Baal prevails; they butt like wild buffaloes." Many modern versions unnecessarily obscure the underlying metaphor by rendering *nᵉnaggēᵃḥ* "we push down" (RSV) or something similar.

10. *But you rejected*. Like the conjunction *pa* to which it is related, *'ap* has here adversative force. R. Yaron in VT 13 (1963), 237–39, would equate *zānaḥtā* here and in several other texts with Akk. *zenû*, "to be angry." Thanks to the parallelism, Ps lxxiv 1 is a convincing example of the Akkadian sense, but the present usage is less clear.

11. *before our adversary*. The suffix of parallel *mᵉśanᵉ'ênû* serves also for *ṣar* on the principle of the double-duty suffix; cf. Note on Ps iii 4. LXX reads "our adversaries," but this does not mean that a suffix stood in the original. On this point see G. R. Driver in JRAS, 1948, 165, who points out "That the ancient Vrss. of the O.T. do not recognize this rule but provide both of two such parallel nouns with the pronominal suffix is no proof that the suffixes may have stood in the original text; for the idiom of the languages in which they are written will not have tolerated what is to Western eyes so intolerable an ellipse." It is clear from Jerome's *Juxta Hebraeos, vertisti terga nostra hosti et qui oderant nos dirupuerunt nos* that the original Hebrew text put no suffix after *ṣar*.

pillaged us. No need to emend *lāmô* to *lānû*, given that *lāmô* does express the first plural relationship in at least six texts that are listed in Note on Ps xxviii 8.

12. *flock to be devoured*. Cf. UT, 51:viii:17–18, *al yʿdbkm kimr bph*, "Lest he put you like a lamb into his mouth."

13. *consider them of much value*. Contrast the sentiments in Ps xx 4, *ʿōlātekā yᵉdaššannāh*, "May he consider your burnt offering generous," and Ps lxxi 21, *tereb gᵉdālātī* (MT *gᵉdullātī*), "May he consider my large head of cattle of great value."

14. *and scorn*. *qeles* is probably a dissimilated form of Ugar. *qlṣ*, "scorn." Compare Ps xxxviii 11, *sḥrḥr* with Ugar. *ṣḥrr*.

15. *a laughingstock*. Literally "a shaking of the head."

16. *is exposed before me*. Consonantal *kstny* is elusive, but the parallelism and syntax are well served by the pual pointing *kussᵉtanī*. The pual of *kāsāh*, "to cover," bears a privative sense in Ps cxliii 9; Hos ii 11 (courtesy Maurice Bogaert); Job xxxvi 30; Prov x 18, xxvi 26. The pronominal suffix would be *dativus incommodi;* in vs. 18 a dative suffix occurs in *bā'atnû*.

18. *Every indignity*. This definition of *zō't* is examined at Ps vii 4.

has come upon us. The suffix of *bā'atnû* is datival, as in Ps cix 17, *t^e^bō'ēhū;* cf. Bogaert in *Biblica* 45 (1964), 239. Under vs. 16 above, another instance of datival suffix was noted.

disloyal to your covenant. D. Winton Thomas in JSS 5 (1960), 283, has compared *šiqqarnū bīb^e^rīteka* with Aramaic Sefire Stela I, B, line 38, *šqrt b'dy',* "You will have been disloyal to (this) treaty."

19. *Our heart has not turned back.* I.e., our intention has never wavered.

our feet strayed. For *'ašūr,* "foot," cf. NOTE on Ps xvii 5, and for the syntax of *wattēṭ,* Ps xxxvii 31. There is a literary parallel in UT, 'nt:III:30, *bh p'nm tṭṭ,* "Her feet stagger," and related sentiment in Ps xvii 5, "From your tracks my feet never swerved."

20. *you crushed us.* That *dikkītānū,* sometimes emended, is the *mot juste,* may be gathered from the frequent occurrence of the motif of crushing the legs to express extreme anguish; Ginsberg, LKK, p. 46. What is more, the association of the ideas of "crushing" and "inflammation of the loins" recurs in Ps xxxviii 8–9.

festering of the loins. With no consonantal changes, reading *b^e^mōq motnayim* for MT *bim^e^qōm tannīm,* and parsing *mōq* as infinitive construct of *māqaq,* "to decay, fester," predicated of flesh in Zech xiv 12, and of wounds in Ps xxxviii 6, also a lament. Texts mentioning fever and inflammation of the thighs have been collected by me in PNWSP, p. 28, n. 2. These include Ps cvii 20; Mic vi 14; Lam iv 20; UT, 75:II:39, *bmtnm yšḫn,* "In the loins he is fever-ridden." The collocation of the two ideas of festering and darkness suggests that the poet is alluding to the curses described in Deut xxviii 27–29, "Yahweh will smite you with the boils of Egypt, and with the ulcers . . . and you shall grope at noonday as the blind grope in darkness." On the other hand, these expressions may be standard components of the language of laments, with no historical allusions intended; e.g., Job xvi 16, "My face is flushed with weeping, upon my pupils there is total darkness" (*ṣalmāwet,* as in the psalm).

22. *dark corners of the heart.* The precise value of *ta'alūmōt* has not been determined, though a derivation from *'ālam,* "to be dark," is generally agreed upon. The above version has been suggested by a comparison with Job xxviii 11, *mabb^e^kī n^e^hārōt ḥibbēš w^e^ta'alūmāh yōṣī' 'ōr,* "He explores the sources of the rivers, and makes dark places shine with light." This sense of *yōṣī'* has been studied at Ps xvii 2.

23. *because of you.* Compare *'āleka* with UT, 49:v:12–13, *'lk pht dry bḥrb,* "Because of you I have seen hacking by the sword."

sheep for the slaughter. *ṣō'n ṭibḥāh* compares with UT, 124:12, *ṭbḫ alpm ap ṣin,* "Large cattle and small cattle were slaughtered."

24. *Why do you sleep.* Cf. Elijah's taunt addressed to the prophets of Baal in I Kings xviii 27, *'ūlay yāšēn hū' w^e^yīqāṣ,* "Perhaps he is asleep and needs to be awakened." Widengren in *Myth, Ritual, and*

Kingship, p. 191, argues from this formula of Ps xliv to a dying and rising Yahweh, but a merely formal parallel does not permit one to infer a parallel meaning; cf. W. L. Moran in *Biblica* 40 (1959), 1027. Mythical formulas must be interpreted in light of the dominating Hebrew concept of history, and vivid poetic images can scarcely be made the basis for serious theological discussion. The sleep of God, who really does not and cannot sleep (Ps cxxi 4), simply means that by remaining inattentive to the prayers of his people he gives the impression of being asleep.

Be not angry. On this meaning of *tiznaḥ,* see NOTE on vs. 10.

25. *turn away your face.* Deriving *tastīr* from *sūr,* as proposed in the NOTE on Ps x 11.

26. *our neck.* For *nepeš,* "neck, throat," see Koehler and Baumgartner, *Lexicon,* p. 626b, and NOTE on Ps vii 3.

cleaves to the ground. Referring to a posture of supplication. A relief from the Egyptian tomb of Horemhab (fourteenth century B.C.) shows Canaanite, Libyan, and Ethiopian slaves with their necks and chins touching the ground. For the representation, see Avi-Yonah and Kraeling, *Our Living Bible,* p. 172.

27. *help us.* Altering MT pointing *'ezrātāh* to *'āzartā,* a precative perfect balancing the two imperatives *qūmāh* and *p^{e}dēnū;* cf. NOTES on Pss iii 8 and iv 2. The full writing of the final syllable *-āh* agrees with the nine other examples of precative perfects, listed in NOTE on Ps iv 8, which employ the full spelling. The construction *'āzar l* is well attested: II Sam viii 5; Isa l 7, 9 (with Yahweh as subject, as here). Cf. BDB, p. 740a–b. This analysis finds confirmation in Jerome's *Juxta Hebraeos, surge auxiliare nobis.*

PSALM 45

(xlv 1–18)

1 *For the director. According to "Lilies"; a maskil of the sons of Korah. A love song.*

2 My heart has composed a sweet melody;
I shall recite my work, O king!
my tongue the pen of a skillful scribe.
3 You are the fairest of the children of men; [2]*
charm flows from your lips,
because God has blessed you from eternity.
4 Gird your sword upon your thigh, [3]
prevail by your splendor
and conquer completely by your majesty.
5 Ride triumphantly in the cause of truth, [4]
and defend the poor.
And let your right hand's awesome wonders,
your sharpened arrows,
point you out.
6 The peoples shall fall at your feet, [5]
senseless the foes of the king.
7 The eternal and everlasting God has enthroned you! [6]
The scepter of your kingdom
must be a scepter of equity.
8 You must love justice and hate iniquity, [7]
because God, your God, has anointed you.
9 Your garments are the oil of rejoicing, [8]
all your robes are myrrh, aloes, and cassia.
10 How many are the ivory palaces!
How many shall rejoice you!
Daughters of kings shall be stationed in your mansions, [9]
the queen at your right hand in gold of Ophir.

* Verse numbers in RSV.

11 Listen, O daughter, and see, and turn your ear: [10]
"Forget your people and your father's house;
12 For the king desires your beauty; [11]
indeed, he is your lord, pay homage to him.
13 A Tyrian robe is among your gifts, [12]
the guests seek your favor."
14 All her robes are royal garb, [13]
inside brocaded with gold;
Her wardrobe comes from the women
who weave threads of gold.
15 Let the maiden be led to the king, [14]
let her companions be brought after her.
16 Come, let her be led with joy and gladness, [15]
let her be brought into the palace of the king.
17 In place of your fathers shall be your sons, [16]
you shall make them princes over all the earth.
18 I shall sing your name through all generations, [17]
and peoples will praise you from age to age.

Notes

xlv. This psalm is an epithalamion, a wedding song, which extols a king and his bride on the occasion of their marriage. Being addressed to the king (vs. 2, "O king"), the poem may be classed as a royal psalm. It readily divides into two parts. Verses 3–10 praise the virtues of the king, while vss. 11–16 exhort the queen to heed her husband and describe her wardrobe and the procession of the queen and her attendants to the king's palace. The final two verses are a blessing upon the king and form an inclusion with vss. 2–3.

2. *My heart has composed.* Explaining the hapax legomenon *rāḥaš* as a metathetic form of *ḥāraš* II, "to engrave, work metal," but here denoting "to compose, improvise." This latter sense of *ḥāraš* can be seen in Zeph iii 17b; Job xi 3. The conceptual relationship between "work metal" and "compose songs" is reflected in Hebrew-Syriac *qīn,* "to lament, sing," and Ar. *qayn,* "smith." See H. L. Ginsberg in BASOR 72 (1938), 13; Gaster, *Thespis,* 1961, p. 339; Zorell, ZLH, p. 722a.

a sweet melody. For this nuance of *ṭōb,* see Note on Ps xxxiii 3. "Melody" should be understood as a "poem suitable for singing."

O king. Parsing *l* of *l^emelek* as *vocativum* (cf. NOTE on Ps iii 9), since vs. 3 begins with the direct address, "You are the fairest."

a skillful scribe. With *sōpēr māhīr,* compare the Punic personal name *bn mhrb'l spr,* "the son of Mahirbaal, the scribe."

3. *You are the fairest.* The curious form *yopyāpītā,* often emendated, may be a genuine dialectal form. A recent addition to Northwest Semitic morphology is Ugar. *d' d',* "know well," from *yd';* GLECS 8 (1957–1960), 65. Cf. also UT, 51:IV:15, *ysmsmt,* "beauty."

from your lips. Another instance of *b,* "from"; cf. NOTE on Ps ii 4, and NOTE below on vs. 6.

because God has blessed you. The king is handsome *because* God has favored him. Similar signs were present in Saul and pointed to the fact that he was to be the king of Israel; cf. I Sam ix 2, x 23 f., and Gaster, *Thespis,* 1961, p. 218. Hence *'al kēn* expresses the cause of the things that have been previously stated, as in Ps xlii 7; Gen xviii 5; on this point, see Philip J. King, *A Study of Psalm 45* (*44*) (Rome, 1959), p. 68.

from eternity. In *l^e'ōlām, l* has the Ugaritic sense "from," like *b* in "from your lips." Cf. NOTES on Pss ix 8 and xxix 10 for listing of texts where *l^e'ōlām* denotes "from eternity."

Other texts setting forth the belief in predestination of certain individuals include Ps cxxxix 16; Isa xlix 1, 5; Jer i 5; Gal i 15.

4. *upon your thigh.* No suffix is needed after *yārēk*—either on the principle of the double-duty suffix (see NOTE on Ps iii 4), or because it is the name of a part of the body—where it is often omitted, both in Ugaritic and in Hebrew, a fact which further points up the close rapports between these Canaanite dialects. Other instances of lack of suffix with names of parts of the body are discussed in NOTES on Pss xvi 4 and xvii 4.

prevail by your splendor. Reading imperative *g^ebar* for MT *gibbōr* to balance imperative *ḥ^agōr.* The splendor of a king was often sufficient to strike terror into his enemies. Compare Akk. *pulḫu melammu šarrutiya isḫup,* "The terrifying glory of my kingship threw down (my enemies)." See Oppenheim in JAOS 63 (1943), 31–34.

hōd^ekā is explained as an accusative of means.

conquer completely by your majesty. Reading *w^ehadrēk h^adārekā* for MT *wah^adārekā wah^adār^ekā.* On *hadrēk* see Judg xx 43 and Albright, JBL 63 (1944), 219, n. 82. The hiphil form *hadrēk* could support the version "make your majesty conquer," but the parallelism suggests that *hadrēk* be rendered as proposed and parsed as a hiphil elative; on the elative function of hiphil, see Speiser, *Genesis* (The Anchor Bible, vol. 1), p. 273.

5. *Ride triumphantly.* Literally "succeed, ride," an example of hendiadys. Speiser, *Genesis,* p. 145 and *passim,* comments on the extensive

use of hendiadys in biblical Hebrew. Canaanite antecedents for the practice can be seen in UT, ʿnt:IV:47, *lnḫt lkḥṯ drkth,* "upon the peaceful bench of his authority"; cf. Albright, JAOS 67 (1947), 156, n. 26.

defend the poor. Reading, with no consonantal changes, *weʿānāw haṣdēq* for MT *weʿanwāh ṣedeq;* compare Ps lxxxii 3, *ʿānī wārāš haṣdīqū,* "Defend the afflicted and the poor." The Old Testament king was supposed to be solicitous for the poor; Pss xxii 27, lxxii 4; Prov xxix 14, etc. In Canaanite literature Prince Yaṣṣib is said to have taxed his father with failure to defend the rights of the poor and the widows and should accordingly abdicate his throne. The text is UT, 127:45–50, "You judge not the cause of the widow, nor adjudicate the case of the wretched. You do not drive out those that prey on the poor (*dl*), nor feed the fatherless in front of you, the widow behind your back." Consult F. Charles Fensham, "Widow, Orphan, and the Poor in Ancient Near Eastern Legal and Wisdom Literature," JNES 21 (1962), 129–39. For the terms *ʿānī,* and *ʿānāw,* see Kraus, *Psalmen,* I, pp. 82 f.; P. Van den Berghe, "ʿANI et ʿANAW dans les Psaumes," in *Le Psautier,* ed. R. De Langhe (Orientalia et Biblica Lovaniensia, IV; Louvain, 1962), pp. 273–95. For a different approach to this phrase, see C. Schedl, "Neue Vorschläge zu Text und Deutung des Psalmes XLV," VT 14 (1964), 310–18, especially p. 312.

your sharpened arrows. Stands in apposition with "your right hand's awesome wonders." The king's arrows were so terrifying because they possessed preternatural powers; this reflects the theme of divinely made weapons treated in NOTE on Ps xviii 35.

point you out. The construction of the third-person feminine singular *tōrekā* with plural subject should be compared with Job xii 7, *šeʾal nāʾ behēmōt wetōrekkā,* "Now ask the beasts, they will teach you" (Pope, The Anchor Bible, vol. 15). Other examples are presented in GK, § 145k; C. H. Gordon in JBL 70 (1951), 160.

Heroic achievements will signalize the king.

6. *at your feet.* This version of *taḥtekā* seems preferable to "under you"; cf. Exod xxiv 4, *taḥat hāhār,* "at the foot of the mountain," and UT, Aqht:115–16, *tqln tḥt pʿnh,* "They fell at his feet." Consult NOTE on Ps viii 7.

senseless. The prepositional phrase *belēb* equals Ps xxxi 13, *millēb,* inasmuch as both *b* and *min* denote "from"; see NOTE above on vs. 3 and Sarna, JBL 78 (1959), 310–15. D. N. Freedman calls attention to I Sam xxv 37, "His heart died within him and he become a stone."

the foes of the king. In CRAIBL, 1962 (appeared 1963), 94, n. 1, Virolleaud reports that an unpublished tablet from Ras Shamra mentions *ib mlk,* "the foe(s) of the king," which equals *ʾōyebē hammelek* in the present verse.

7. *The eternal and everlasting God.* Reading *ʾelōhē-m* (with enclitic

mem as in *'elōhē-m ṣebā'ōt*) *'ōlām wā'ed,* a construct chain in which the genitive is the composite noun *'ōlām wā'ed* examined in NOTE on Ps x 16, for MT *'elōhīm 'ōlām wā'ed.* Cf. Isa xl 28, *'elōhē 'ōlām yhwh,* "Yahweh is the Eternal God." That *'ōlām wā'ed* is a genitive and not an accusative of time ensues from comparison with vs. 18, *le'ōlām wā'ed;* in fact, some MSS do insert the preposition in our verse.

The topic of composite nouns has been treated in NOTES on Pss x 16 and xxxvi 5.

has enthroned you. Vocalizing *kissē'akā,* a denominative piel from *kissē',* "throne." The only evidence for this proposal is its manifest good sense, its concordance with the Ugaritic-Hebrew proclivity for coining such verbs (*Biblica* 44 [1963], 204 f.) and, negatively, the unsatisfactory nature of the numberless solutions which have been proffered on behalf of this *crux interpretum.*

In other words, *kissē'akā 'elōhīm* is stylistically parallel to vs. 3, *bērākekā 'elōhīm,* "God has blessed you," and stylistically and semantically parallel to vs. 8, *mešāḥakā 'elōhīm,* "God has anointed you." Some commentators (as early as 1790) have felt that a verb is needed here and have accordingly supplied *hēkīn* or something similar; cf. King, *A Study of Psalm 45 (44)*, p. 79.

8. *You must love justice.* Or simply, "love justice," with *'āhabtā* parsed as precative perfect (see NOTE on Ps iii 8), followed by jussive *tišnā';* an equivalent verbal sequence is commented upon at Ps x 15.

and hate iniquity. In the Phoenician Inscription of Karatepe I:9, King Azitawaddu assures us that he fulfilled this obligation of a king: *wtrq 'nk kl hr' 'š kn b'rṣ,* "And I cleared out all the evil that was in the land."

because. See NOTE above on vs. 3.

God, your God. Contrary to the prevailing view, there is no need to assume dittography here; the meter requires the repetition. Verses 7–9 are comprised of four cola of four (2+2) beats each.

9. *oil of rejoicing.* Referring to the oil used on festive occasions. Cf. Eccles ix 8, "At all times let your clothing be white, and the oil on your head not be lacking" (Scott, The Anchor Bible, vol. 18).

The identification of the garments with the oil with which they are scented is hyperbolic language which characterizes much of Canaanite and biblical poetry. Freedman in IEJ 13 (1963), 125 f., correctly analyzed and interpreted Deut xxxiii 28, but left something to be desired in his translation of the clause *'ereṣ dāgān wetīrōš,* "His land is (one of) grain and must," or "Whose is a land of grain and must." These versions partially obscure the lush quality of Canaanite poetry. The text literally reads, "His land is grain and must," and since this does not offend English idiom, it should be retained.

your robes. The ostensible balance with *bigdōtekā,* "your garments," suggests that consonantal *mḥbryk* contains a cognate vocable. An etymological basis is provided by *ḥābar,* "to join, unite," *ḥōberet,* "drapery," in Exod xxvi 4, 10, and *maḥberet,* "place of joining" (of curtains, parts of dress), in Exod xxviii 27.

10. *How many.* Reading *man* for MT *min* and equating it with Ugar. *mn,* "who, how many?" Cf. Aistleitner. WuS, No. 1593, p. 188, and UT, 125:81, *mn yrḫ kmrṣ,* "How many months has he been sick?" Cf. Deut xxxiii 11, *man,* "Which, how many?"

ivory palaces. Amos iii 15 speaks of "houses of ivory," and remains of a palace with ivory inlay have been discovered at Samaria. For the list of Samaria ivories, see C. Decamps de Mertzenfeld, *Inventaire commenté des ivoires phéniciens et apparentés, découverts dans le Proche Orient,* Texte (Paris, 1954), pp. 62–75.

How many shall rejoice you. Reading *man yeśammeḥūkā,* the piel causative, for MT *minnī śimmeḥūkā.*

Daughters of kings. Cf. Phoen. *mlkyt,* "royal women"; see Donner and Röllig, KAI, II, pp. 15 f.

stationed in your mansions. niṣṣebāh is possibly niphal, third-person feminine plural ending in *-āh;* for Hebrew examples, see GK, § 145k, n. 2, and for Ugaritic possibilities, UT, p. 70, n. 3. That *niṣṣebāh* is the predicate of preceding *benōt melākīm,* and not of following *šegel,* may be inferred from metrical considerations; the proposed analysis and word division result in two parallel cola of four beats each. The vocable *yiqqerōt,* doubtless related to *qīr,* "wall of a house," may be found in the Palmyrene phrase *yqr bt 'lm'* (Corpus Inscriptionum Semiticarum II, 4192), studied at length by P. Joüon, "Glanes Palmyréniennes," *Syria* 19 (1938), 99–102. It is perhaps also found in Ps xlix 13 and Isa xxviii 16, *pinnat yiqrat,* "the cornerstone of the mansion."

gold of Ophir. I.e., the finest gold. The location of Ophir is still a matter of dispute, with the southwest coast of Arabia or the Somali coast the most likely identifications. A Hebrew ostracon from Tell Qasile, just north of Tel Aviv, dating from the eighth century B.C., mentions *zhb 'pr,* "gold of Ophir." See Benjamin Maisler, "Two Hebrew Ostraca from Tell Qasile," JNES 10 (1951), 266.

13. *A Tyrian robe.* Identifying *bot,* MT *bat,* with the vocable in II Kings xxiii 7, *'ašer hannāšīm 'ōregōt šām bottīm la'ašērāh.* There is wide agreement that *bottīm* means "robes" or something kindred. Zorell, ZLH, p. 135a, defines it as *textura quaedam vestis vel velum pro ašeris,* while W. F. Albright, *Archaeology and the Religion of Israel* (Johns Hopkins Press, 1942), p. 165, writes: "Most intriguing is the reference in II Kings 23:7 to the destruction of the house (?) of the *qedeshim* in which women wove robes (?) for Asherah." The Lucianic recension of LXX translated *stolás,* "garments." The much-contested phrase in Isa iii 20, *bottē hannepeš,* may well signify "perfumed robes." Tyrian robes

had already acquired international fame in Homeric times. An economic text from Ras Shamra lists a *ktn d ṣr pḥm bh,* "a Tyrian tunic inlaid with rubies"; Virolleaud, *Palais royal d'Ugarit,* II, 110:4, p. 144.

the guests. Inasmuch as traditional "wealthiest of the people" is not particularly meaningful in the context, and since the poem was composed for a wedding feast, one is permitted to propose, with due reservation, that *ʿašîrē ʿām* derives from *ʿšr* II, a rather frequent root in Ugaritic denoting "to invite to a banquet," identical with Ethiopic *ʿaššara.* Cf. Ginsberg, LKK, p. 45; Albright in BASOR 94 (1944), 33, n. 10; and T. H. Gaster in JNES 7 (1948), 191.

seek your favor. Referring to the presentation of the Tyrian robe.

14. *are royal garb.* See NOTE above for the phrase *bot melek.*

inside brocaded. The adverb *penîmāh,* "inside," compares with Ugar. *pnm* according to Aistleitner, WuS, No. 2230, p. 257; UT, Glossary, No. 2065.

from the women who weave. Vocalizing *lerōqāmōt* (cf. Ps lxviii 7, *kōšārōt*) for MT *lirqāmōt,* and interpreting the preposition as "from." The *rōqāmōt* would be professional brocaders, like the professional weavers mentioned in II Kings xxiii 7. There may be a reference to the art of brocading cloth in Virolleaud, *Palais royal d'Ugarit,* II, 109:6, p. 143, *lpš d sgr bh,* "a garment with gold in it." The meaning of *sgr* is not beyond doubt, though an identification with Job xxviii 15, *segōr,* "gold," parallel to *kesep,* appears very probable.

15. *the maiden.* That *betûlōt* is singular is evident from the suffixes of *'aḥarehā* and *rēʿōtehā,* which suppose an antecedent in the singular. Hence the morphology of *btlwt* is Phoenician, like that of Prov ix 1, etc., *ḥokmōt,* "Wisdom," which has been rightly explained by W. F. Albright in VTS, III (1955), p. 8, where he compares *ḥokmōt* with Phoen. *milkōt* (for **milkāt*), "Queen" (name of a deity). Further discussion is found in Friedrich, PPG, § 288, and F. L. Moriarty, *Gregorianum* 46 (1965), 86 (on Ezek xxvii 3). See NOTE below on Ps xlix 12.

after her. Or, "with her," since *'aḥarē* can also denote "with," especially with verbs of coming; cf. *Biblica* 44 (1963), 292 f., with bibliography, and UT, Glossary, No. 158, p. 356.

16. *Come, let her be led.* Reading imperative singular *lēk* (cf. NOTE on Ps xxvii 8) for MT *lāk* and *modus energicus* third-person feminine singular *tûbālannāh* for *tûbalnāh.* Discussion of the energic mood in Hebrew appears at Ps viii 2.

joy. Plural *śemāḥōt* is a dis legomenon, the other occurrence being in the very Phoenicianizing Ps xvi 11.

let her be brought. Reading hophal third-person feminine energic *tûbāʾannāh* instead of the grammatically inexplicable *tebōʾnāh;* see first NOTE on this verse, above.

17. *your fathers . . . your sons.* The suffixes in Hebrew being mascu-

line, the poet refers to the fathers and sons of the king. Mentioning both ancestors and descendants, the poet intends to stress the continuity of the line. With this blessing contrast the Phoenician curse in Eshmunazar, 8–9, *'l ykn lm bn wzr' tḥtnm,* "May they have no son nor seed in their stead."

PSALM 46

(xlvi 1–12)

1 *For the director; of the sons of Korah, according to "Maidens," a song.*

2 God is our shelter and stronghold,
found from of old to be help in trouble.
3 Therefore we will not fear the jaws of the nether world, [2]*
nor the toppling of the mountains
into the heart of the sea,
4 Though its waters rage and foam, [3]
the mountains heave in its midst,
the river and its channels stand in a heap.
5 God brings happiness to his city, [4]
the Most High sanctifies his habitation.
6 With God in her midst, [5]
she shall not be toppled;
He will help her
at break of dawn.
7 Nations tremble, kingdoms totter; [6]
he gives forth his voice,
the earth melts away.
8 Yahweh of hosts is with us, [7]
our stronghold is the God of Jacob. *Selah*
9 Come, observe the works of Yahweh, [8]
who has put fertility in the earth;
10 He makes wars to cease, [9]
to the edge of the earth.
The bow he breaks, and snaps the spear,
the shields he burns with fire.
11 Be still and know that I am God: [10]
exalted above the nations,
exalted above the earth.

* Verse numbers in RSV.

12 Yahweh of hosts is with us, [11]
our stronghold is the God of Jacob. *Selah*

Notes

xlvi. A song of Zion whose refrain of reassurance, "Yahweh of hosts is with us," could also justify its classification as a psalm of confidence.

2. *our shelter and stronghold.* See Note on Ps xxviii 8.

found from of old. Reading *mē'ād,* the Canaanite form of *mē'āz,* for MT *me'ōd.* Ugar. *id,* "time, then," equals Ar. *'iḏ* and Heb. *'āz,* while Ugar. *idk* answers to Ar. *'iḏāk,* "then"; cf. Driver, CML, p. 135a. Other dialectal words involving the interchange of *d* and *z* have been noted at Ps xxi 7 and in PNWSP, p. 32. Another dialectal form can be seen in vs. 9, where consonantal *šmwt* equals Ugar. *šmt,* "oil, fatness," and where classical Hebrew has *šemen* and *šemēnāh* (Gen xlix 20).

This assumption brings within reach a solution of the long-standing crux in Ps cxxxix 14, *wenapšī yāda'tā* (MT *yōda'at*) *mē'ād* (MT *me'ōd*) "And my soul you knew from of old." The standard emendation *mē'āz* becomes unnecessary. Very frequent in Isaiah, the adverb *mē'āz* is found in Pss lxxvi 8 and xciii 2, *nākōn kis'akā mē'āz,* "Your throne has been established from of old." Ps xciii 5, *m'd* is Canaanite for xciii 2, *mē'āz,* "from of old."

3. *we will not fear.* Notice the rare construction *nīra' be,* found elsewhere only in Jer li 46 and possibly in Ps xlix 6. Were Ugaritic to employ *yr'* with a preposition, it would be with *b* (or, less likely, with *l*), since *min* is extremely rare in that dialect. The motif of the fear of death is mentioned in UT, 67:II:6–7, *yraun aliyn b'l ṯt'nn rkb 'rpt,* "Victor Baal feared him (i.e., Mot), filled with dread of him was the Mounter of the Clouds."

jaws of the nether world. Explaining *hamīr* (pointing uncertain) *'āreṣ* through UT, 67:I:6–8, *lyrt bnpš bn ilm mt bmhmrt ydd il ǵzr,* "Indeed you must descend into the throat of divine Mot, into the jaws of El's beloved, Ghazir," and UT, 51:VIII:8–12, *tspr byrdm arṣ idk al ttn pnm tk qrth hmry,* "Be numbered among those who descend into the nether world, be now on your way toward his city Hmry." Both *mhmrt* and *hmry* can derive from *hmr,* which in Arabic denotes "to pour down." Scholars (e.g., Cassuto in IEJ 12 [1962], 81) have correctly identified *mhmrt* with Ps cxl 11, *mahamārōt,* usually rendered "miry depths," and it is here proposed that *hamīr* be associated with the name of Mot's city *hmry.* Fuller discussion may be found in *Biblica* 40 (1959),

167 f., and, more recently, in M. H. Pope, JBL 83 (1964), 277, who arrives at the same conclusion as Cassuto regarding the meaning and etymology of Ugar. *mhmrt,* biblical *mhmrwt.* This root has recently been recognized by Nicholas Tromp (unpublished) in a "Northern" dual form in Job xvii 2, *'im lō' hattillēm* (MT *hatūlīm*) *'immādī ūbehamīrōtēm* (MT *ūbehammerōtām*) *tālīn* (MT *tālan*) *'ēnī,* "Indeed the two mounds are before me, and in the twin miry deeps my eye will sleep." For the vocalization *tillēm,* see UT, 51:VIII:4, *'m tlm ǵṣr arṣ,* "toward the two mounds at the edge of the nether world." That this is the general sense of the verse in Job is tolerably clear from the preceding verse, "My spirit is broken, my days are snuffed out, the grave is mine."

toppling of the mountains. Referring to the cosmic upheaval of the latter days. The imagery would readily spring to mind along the Phoenician littoral where the Lebanon Mountains in many places begin their rise at the edge of the Mediterranean waters. Briggs, CECBP, I, p. 394, suggests that the poet may have seen portions of Mount Carmel falling into the Mediterranean Sea. An originally geographical description had become a part of mythological language so that any poet could have used it. The images of the "jaws of the nether world" and the "toppling of the mountains" belong to the picture of the great final catastrophe.

heart of the sea. Hebrew lexicons point out that *belēb* is seldom used of things. Its use with *yam* may reflect a mythopoeic origin; in Canaanite mythology, personified Yamm or Sea was one of Baal's chief rivals. Consonantal *ymym* may be parsed as either a plural of majesty or as singular *yam* followed by enclitic *mem.* The suffixes in vs. 4 point back to a singular antecedent, as the customary version, "sea," recognizes.

4. *in its midst.* Namely, of the sea. Identifying *ga'awātō* with *ga'awāh,* "back," in Ps lxxxix 10; Deut xxxiii 26 (according to my analysis in *Biblica* 45 [1964], 399); Job xli 7; and Prov xiv 13 (LXX, some commentators). The double meaning is also found in *gēw,* "back, midst." On *gē',* "midst," see NOTE on Ps xxiii 4. Ps lxxxix 10 claims a word of comment: *'attāh mōšēl bega'awat* (MT *gē'ūt*) *hayyām beśō' gallāyw 'attāh tešabbeḥēm,* "You rule upon the back of the sea; when he lifts up his waves, you check them." The verb *šābaḥ* is closely related to Ugaritic-Hebrew *šbm,* "to muzzle" (Ps lxviii 23), and actually occurs in parallelism with it in UT, 'nt:III:37, *lištbm tnn išbḥnh,* "Indeed, I muzzled Tannin, I checked him." That *išbḥnh* is to be read for *editio princeps išbm*[*n*]*h* follows from the operation of the Barth-Ginsberg law: when the vowel of the first syllable in the qal conjugation of the verb is *i,* the thematic vowel must be *a.* In the present instance a laryngal must be read for Virolleaud's *m;* since the text is badly damaged and since the signs for *m* and *ḥ* are very similar in the Ugaritic script, one must opt for *ḥ.* Moreover it seems very unlikely that the infixed

-t- conjugation of *šbm* would be followed by a qal form. With the proposed rendition of Ps lxxxix 10 cf. Job ix 8, "Alone he stretched out the heavens, / Trod on the back of the Sea" (Pope, The Anchor Bible, vol. 15).

the river and its channels. Attaching vs. 5, *nāhār pᵉlāgāyw* to vs. 4. One would expect the copula *wᵉ*, but ellipsis characterizes the style of this hymn, e.g., vss. 4a, 7, 8, 9. Here *nāhār* signifies the ocean current, as in Ugaritic; cf. NOTE on Ps xxiv 4. Notice the rhyme of *mēmāyw* and *pᵉlāgāyw,* which suggests that consonantal *g'wtw* might more correctly be vocalized as plural *ga'ᵃwātāw;* the meaning would remain the same.

stand in a heap. As the result of an earthquake. For MT *selāh,* reading the verb *sālāh,* "to heap up." Similar imagery is found in Exod xv 8, "The waters piled up, the rivers stood in a heap."

5. *brings happiness.* The plural vocalization *yᵉśammᵉḥū* may be retained, since the plural of majesty *'ᵉlōhīm* can govern a plural predicate, as in Gen xx 13 or Exod xxii 8. Cf. GK, § 145h; Brockelmann, *Hebräische Syntax,* § 50; Speiser, *Genesis,* p. 150.

his city. Being parallel to *miškᵉnī,* "his habitation," *'īr* needs no suffix by right of the double-duty suffix; cf. NOTE on Ps iii 4.

sanctifies his habitation. That is, by his presence. With LXX, Vulg., vocalizing *qiddēš* to balance *yᵉśammēᵃḥ;* and for doubtful *miškᵉnē,* which is a masculine plural construct not used elsewhere (Baethgen, *Psalmen,* p. 135), reading *miškᵉnī* with third-person singular suffix *-y.* This version is supported by LXX *hēgíase to skênoma autoú ho hýpsistos,* "The Most High has sanctified his dwelling." A perfect parallelism of the two cola emerges: A+B+C // Á+B́+Ć, with 3+3 meter, with seven syllables in the first half verse and seven in the second. This verse also illustrates the breakup of the divine composite title *'ᵉlōhīm 'elyōn* (Ps lvii 3) into its components, *'ᵉlōhīm* being placed at the end of the first colon and *'elyōn* at the end of the second, with the result that the two cola are ever more tightly interlocked. On third-person suffix *-y,* see NOTE on Ps ii 6.

Contrast this treatment with that of H. Junker in *Biblica* 43 (1962), 197–201, who on p. 199 proposes, *"Ein Strom, dessen Arme die Stadt Gottes erfreuen, ist das heiligste im Gezelt des Allerhöchsten"* ["The holy of holies in the tent of the Most High is a river whose streams gladden the city of God"].

Note the sequence *yqtl* (*yᵉśammᵉḥū*) and *qtl* (*qiddēš*); cf. Ps viii 7.

6. *shall not be toppled.* I.e., unlike the mountains in vs. 3.

at break of dawn. I.e., the time when attacks were made. Cf. UT, Krt: 118–21, "And lo! with the sun (*špšm*) on the seventh day King Pabil will not sleep for the rumble of the roaring of his buffaloes." This was the result of the approach of King Kirta's troops who moved to attack the city, since in lines 133 ff. we are informed that Kirta was requested, "Do not attack Great Udm, etc." The assault had been planned for dawn, and this may be relevant for the exegesis of our phrase, especially since military metaphors appear in vss. 2, 11, and 12. Consult J. Ziegler, "Die Hilfe Gottes am Morgen," in *Alttestamentliche Studien F. Nötscher gewidmet* (Bonn, 1950), pp. 281–88.

7. *Nations tremble, kingdoms totter.* Nations and kingdoms are personified in order to develop the motif of a person going to pieces upon sensing that bad news is in the offing. The classic Canaanite description is UT, ʿnt:III:29–32, *bh pʿnm tṭṭ bʿdn ksl tṯbr ʿln pnh tdʿ tǵṣ pnt kslh anš dt ẓrh,* "Her feet totter; behind, her loins do break; above, her face does sweat. The joints of her loins shake, weakened are those of her back." Cf. Ginsberg, LKK, p. 46; Dahood, PNWSP, pp. 29 f. Other biblical texts with this theme include Pss lx 10, xcvii 4–5; Exod xv 15; Isa xv 4; Ezek xxi 11; Mic iv 9; Prov xiii 20.

he gives forth his voice. Namely, as thunder. Cf. UT, 51:v:70, *wtn qlh bʿrpt,* "And he gave forth his voice from the clouds." Other texts where *qōl* equals "thunder" are Ps xviii 14; Exod xix 16; Isa xxx 30, etc.; see Moshe Held in *Studies and Essays in Honor of Abraham A. Neuman,* p. 287, n. 4.

the earth melts. Within the context of "the shattering of the loins" motif, *tāmūg* connotes "to melt with sweat," the counterpart of *tdʿ* in the above-cited Ugaritic text.

9. *the works of Yahweh.* Hummel in JBL 76 (1957), 103, may be correct in moving back the purported preformative *mēm* to the previous word as enclitic *mem;* ditto in Ps lxvi 5.

who has put fertility. The context hints that consonantal *šmwt* is the antonym of *milḥāmōt,* "wars"; Budde long ago proposed the emendation *šālōm.* This inference evokes the theme of UT, ʿnt:III:11–15, *qryy barṣ mlḥmt št bʿpr[ ] ddym sk šlm lkbd arṣ arb dd lkbd šdm,* "Banish war from the earth, put love in the land; pour peace into the bowels of the earth, rain down love into the bowels of the fields." Consonantal *šmwt* is identified with Ugar. *šmt,* "oil, fat," from **šmnt;* cf. Heb. *šᵉmēnāh,* "fatness" (Gen xlix 20); UT, § 8.3.

10. *to the edge of the earth.* With *qᵉṣeh hāʾāreṣ,* compare UT, 126: III:3, *sb lqṣm arṣ,* "Pour to the edges of the earth," a reading communicated to me by W. F. Albright in a letter of 1953. Gordon's UT reads *sblt ʿṣm arṣ,* which is meaningless, but Herdner, *Corpus des tablettes en cunéiformes alphabétiques découvertes à Ras Shamra-Ugarit de 1929 à 1939,* p. 74, correctly reads *sb lqṣm arṣ.* The phrase *qṣm arṣ* illustrates the enclitic *mem* interposed in a construct chain.

the shields. 1QM, VI:15, states that the horsemen were armed with *mgny ʿglh,* "round shields"; cf. Yadin, *The Scroll of the War of the Sons of Light against the Sons of Darkness,* p. 121.

he burns with fire. Shields were often made of leather stretched over a wooden frame (like the Roman *scutum*), or of wickerwork. The leather surface had to be regularly oiled to guard against cracking (II Sam i 21; Isa xxi 5). Ezek xxxix 9 also mentions the burning of shields. The verb *śrp* occurs several times in Ugaritic.

The chiasmus of *qešet yešabbēr weqiṣṣēṣ ḥanīt* should be noted, as well as the sequence of *yqtl-qtl,* commented upon at vs. 5. Hence the proposed emendation of *weqiṣṣēṣ* to *yeqaṣṣēṣ* is drained of whatever plausibility it may have possessed.

11. *Be still.* Namely, do nothing; do not enter into military alliances with other nations, since Yahweh controls history. This is the military policy advocated by Isa xxx 15, "By sitting still and keeping quiet will you be saved." On this passage, see Dahood in CBQ 20 (1958), 41–43, and G. von Rad, *Der heilige Krieg im alten Israel,* 2d ed., (Göttingen, 1952), pp. 57 f. This exegesis, if sound, might bear on the dating of the psalm.

exalted above the nations. From the stylistic point of view, *'ārūm* is preferably parsed as a passive participle from *'rm,* a by-form of *yrm* and *rwm* discussed at Ps xviii 47.

PSALM 47

(xlvii 1–10)

1 *For the director; of the sons of Korah, a psalm.*

2 All you strong ones, clap your hands,
acclaim, you gods, with shouts of joy.
3 For Yahweh Most High is awesome, [2]*
the Great King over all the earth.
4 He made nations prostrate beneath us, [3]
and peoples under our feet.
5 He chose for himself our kingdom, [4]
the pride of Jacob whom he loves. *Selah*
6 God has gone up amid shouts of joy, [5]
Yahweh to the sound of a trumpet.
7 Sing praises, you gods, sing praises, [6]
sing praises to our king, sing praises.
8 For he is king of all the earth, [7]
O gods, sing a skillful song.
9 For God is king over the nations, [8]
has taken his seat upon his holy throne;
O nobles of the peoples, gather round!
10 The God of Abraham is the Strong One; [9]
truly God is Suzerain of the earth,
greatly to be extolled.

* Verse numbers in RSV.

NOTES

xlvii. A hymn celebrating God's enthronement as king of all the gods and of all nations.

2. *All you strong ones.* Namely, heathen gods. The term *'ammīm* has been examined at Ps xviii 28. The *'ammīm* of the pagans are contrasted with vs. 10, *'am 'elōhē 'abrāhām,* "The God of Abraham

is the Strong One"; note the singular *'am* against plural *'ammīm* and the *inclusio* which comes to light with this analysis. The invitation to the pagan deities should be compared with Ps xxix 1, *hābū l^eyahweh b^enē 'ēlīm hābū l^eyahweh kābōd wā'ōz,* "Give Yahweh, O gods, give Yahweh glory and praise," and with Ps lxviii 33, cited in NOTE below on next colon.

clap your hands. kāp, without suffix, may be considered a good example of mention of parts of the body without a suffix, a practice remarked in NOTE on Ps xvi 4.

acclaim, you gods. Despite the recurrence of the formula *hārī'ū lē'lōhīm* in Pss lxvi 1 and lxxxi 2, and *hārī'ū l^eyahweh* in xcviii 4 and c 1, several considerations favor the analysis of *l* in *lē'lōhīm* as *lamedh vocativum.* First, the parallelism with vocative *hā'ammīm,* "you strong ones"; the gods addressed are those worshiped by the gentile nations. The occurrence of vocative *lamedh* in only the second of two parallel cola accords with the usage in Ps xxxiii 1 where vocative *ṣaddīqīm* without the morphologic indicator is balanced by *lay^ešārīm,* "O upright." Similarly in Ps lxviii 33, *maml^ekōt hā'āreṣ šīrū lē'lōhīm zamm^erū 'adōnāy,* "O kings of the earth, sing! O gods, sing praises to the Lord!" This grammatical analysis (i.e., of Ps lxviii 3) results in 3+3 meter, with eight syllables in the first colon and nine in the second, instead of the purported 4+2 meter.

Second, in a solemn address of this kind, strict parallelism seems to be favored; e.g., Deut xxxii 1 (cf. Isa i 2), "Give ear, O heavens, and I shall speak; and hear, O earth, the words of my mouth." Third, this interpretation places in vs. 3 the entry of Israel's God with the solemn title Yahweh Elyon; mention of him in vs. 2 would seem unduly anticipatory. Finally, this appeal to the gods to acknowledge the supremacy of Yahweh is repeated in vss. 7a and 8b.

3. *the Great King. melek gādōl* is another term for "suzerain" or "overlord." In fact, one encounters in Ugaritic correspondence the formula, *špš mlk rb,* "the suzerain, the great king"; e.g., UT, 118:25–26; 108:1–2. The Akkadian equivalent is *šarru rabū.* Cf. Hos v 13 and x 6, *l^emalkī rāb* (MT *melek yārēb*), "to its (Assyria's) great king." On the third-person singular suffix *-y* see NOTE on Ps ii 6.

all the earth. With *melek gādōl 'al kol hā'āreṣ,* compare UT, 49:I:37, *wymlk barṣ il klh,* "And he reigns in the vast (nether) earth, all of it."

4. *made nations prostrate.* See NOTE on Ps xviii 48.

under our feet. Longer *taḥat raglēnū,* with five syllables, is the ballast variant of shorter *taḥtēnū,* with three syllables, in the first colon. This difference compensates for the lack of a verb in the second colon. The ample documentation of this stylistic device in Ugaritic poetry sheds welcome light on the history of Israelite usage. See UT, § 13.116, especially 2 Aqht:I:26–27, where *bqrb* is the ballast variant of *b: wykn bnh bbt šrš bqrb hklh,* "And may his son be in the house, a root in the midst of his palace."

5. *He chose for himself.* The unique phrase *yibḥar lānū* runs counter to the standard Hebrew idiom of using *bāḥar,* "to choose," with a reflexive pronoun; in the Hebrew mode of speech, one chooses for himself, not for others. Hence *lannū* from *lanhū* should be read for MT *lānū* and *ln* equated with Ugaritic *ln,* the longer form of *l.* In Northwest Semitic (Ugaritic-Hebrew-Phoenician), two sets of prepositions were in use: *b+bn; b'd+b'dn; l+ln; 'l+'ln; 'm+'mn; tḥt+tḥtn.* The double series of prepositions with and without *-m* is analogous; e.g., *l* and *lm; b* and *bm,* and conjunctions such as *k* and *km.* See UT § 6.8; Albright in BASOR 150 (1958), 38, for Ugaritic usage; for Phoenician practice, Cross and Freedman in JNES 10 (1951), 229, and Donner and Röllig, KAI, II, pp. 18 f. In other words, *yibḥar lannū* is the syntactic equivalent of Ps cxxxv 4, *kī ya'aqōb bāḥar lō yāh,* "For Yahweh chose Jacob for himself." Cf. also Ps xxxiii 12.

our kingdom. In a hymn celebrating the kingship of Yahweh, this seems to be the nuance borne by *naḥalāh.* But cf. NOTE on Ps ii 8. In UT, 51:VIII:12–14, *ksu ṯbth,* "the throne on which he sits," is paired with *arṣ nḥlth,* "the land which he rules." This connotation points up the gratuitousness of emendating *tinḥal* in Ps lxxxii 8 to *timšōl: qūmāh 'elōhīm šōpṭāh hā'āreṣ kī 'attāh tinḥal bekol haggōyīm,* "Arise, O God, govern the earth, for you are the ruler over all the nations."

pride of Jacob. A poetic name for the kingdom of Israel.

6. *has gone up.* I.e., has ascended his throne on Mount Zion. See Lipiński, "Yahweh *mālāk,*" *Biblica* 44 (1963), 405–60, especially p. 443. The word order is identical with that of vs. 4: A+B+C // B́+Ć. Johnson, *Sacral Kingship in Ancient Israel,* p. 66, n. 2, has noticed that *'ālāh* is a theological wordplay on the divine appellative *'elyōn* of vs. 3. A similar wordplay involving this root recurs in Ps xcvii 9. Though the play on many of Marduk's fifty names has long been appreciated (e.g., E. A. Speiser in *Ancient Near Eastern Texts . . . ,* p. 62, nn. 34 ff.; p. 93, n. 190; p. 94, n. 202; Tsevat, *A Study of the Language of the Biblical Psalms,* p. 81), the extent of this practice in biblical literature remains to be determined. Here we may direct attention to Gen xiv 20 and xv 1, where *miggēn,* "to hand over, bestow," and *māgān* (MT *māgēn*), "Benefactor, Suzerain," are the elements of the wordplay, and Ps lxxv 6, *'al tārīmū lammārōm qarnekem,* "Raise not your horn against the Exalted One."

7. *Sing praises, you gods.* These are the deities mentioned in vs. 2, who also figure in other enthronement psalms, such as xcvi 6, *nōrā' hū' 'al kol 'elōhīm,* "He is more awesome than all the gods." The fact that no preposition precedes *'elōhīm* in the first colon, as it does in

the second, suggests in itself that *'ᵉlōhīm* serves a different function. Some scribes have attempted to set the text to rights by inserting the preposition, but such a reading, being *facilior,* is obviously secondary. Furthermore, the chiastic arrangement of vss. 7–8 reveals that *'ᵉlōhīm* in vs. 7a is the opposite number of vocative *'ᵉlōhīm* in vs. 8b.

After completing the first draft, I came across Gaster's version of Ps xlvii 7 in *Thespis,* 1950, p. 421, "Make music ye gods, make music," a welcome confirmation of my independent conclusion.

8. *is king of all the earth.* Referring to Yahweh, not Baal or other Canaanite gods. The polemical tone can be sensed upon comparison with such Canaanite professions of faith as UT, 51:IV:43–44 = 'nt: v:40–41, *mlkn aliyn b'l ṯpṭn in d'lnh,* "Our king is Victor Baal, our ruler who is without peer."

O gods. Contrary to the usual practice, attaching *'ᵉlōhīm* to the second colon and parsing it as vocative. This division produces 3+3 meter, the prevailing beat of the hymn, with seven syllables in the first half verse and eight in the second.

sing a skillful song. This is the only example of *maśkīl* within the context of a psalm (as opposed to its appearance in psalm titles). That gods are invited to sing a *maśkīl* may have some significance for the meaning and history of this much-canvassed term, whose precise sense has not been agreed upon; see Gertner, in BSOAS 25 (1962), 23, who renders "sing instructively."

9. *God is king.* Though *yhwh mālak* in Pss xciii 1, xcvii 1 probably denotes "Yahweh has become king," it is much less clear that *mālak 'ᵉlōhīm* is to be interpreted inchoatively. The phrase seems to be a repetition in verbal form of the sentiment expressed in a nominal sentence in vs. 8, *kī melek kol hā'āreṣ.* What the phrase probably means is that Yahweh has proved himself to be a king by his victories over his rivals; hence he is king now.

his holy throne. kissē' qodšō is a hapax legomenon, though its components do occur separately in the parallel members of Ps xi 4a.

O nobles of the peoples. The position of *nᵉdībē 'ammīm* at the head of the sentence suggests that it is a vocative. There may be a wordplay on *'ammīm,* "strong ones (gods)," in vs. 2, and *'ammīm,* the pagan nations who worship many *'ammīm* as against the "Strong One of Abraham" (singular *'am*).

gather round. I.e., in order to worship the true *'am,* "the Strong One." Parsing *ne'ᵉsāpū* as precative perfect, discussed in NOTES on Pss iii 8 and iv 8.

10. *the Strong One.* The divine epithet *'am* is fully treated in NOTE on Ps xviii 28.

truly God is Suzerain. The proclamation *kī lē'lōhīm magnē* (MT *maginnē*) *'ereṣ* is very similar to Ps xxii 29, *kī lyhwh hammᵉlūkāh,*

"For truly is Yahweh the king," and lxxxix 19, *kī lyhwh m^e^gānēnū* (MT *maginnēnū*), "For truly is Yahweh our Suzerain."

Suzerain of the earth. Vocalizing *magnē* (MT *maginnē*) *'ereṣ,* and explaining the plural form as *plurale majestatis.* This sense of *māgān* was studied at Ps iii 4.

greatly to be extolled. Compare *m^e^'ōd na'^a^lāh* with UT, 128:III:13, *mid rm* [*krt*], "Be greatly exalted, O Kirta!" The root of *na'^a^lah* is that of vs. 3, *'elyōn,* and is meant to form an *inclusio* as well as a theological wordplay, a topic discussed above at vs. 3.

PSALM 48

(xlviii 1–15)

1 *A song. A psalm of the sons of Korah.*

2 Great is Yahweh,
and much to be praised.
In the city of our God
is his holy mountain;
3 The most beautiful peak, [2]*
the joy of all the earth.
Mount Zion is the heart of Zaphon,
the city of the Great King.
4 God is her citadel, [3]
has shown himself her bulwark.
5 For, behold, the kings assembled, [4]
together they stormed;
6 Lo! they looked, were sore astounded, [5]
terror-struck they were ready to flee.
7 Panic seized them, [6]
alas, anguish like a woman in labor.
8 As when by the east wind [7]
the ships of Tarshish are shattered.
9 As we have heard, so have we seen [8]
in the city of Yahweh of Hosts,
in the city of our God.
God will make her secure forever. *Selah*
10 We have reflected on your kindness, O Yahweh, [9]
in the midst of your temple.
11 As your heavens, O God, [10]
so your praise reaches the ends of the earth.
12 Your right hand is full of generosity, [11]
let Mount Zion rejoice;
let the daughters of Judah be glad
Because of your acts of providence.

* Verse numbers in RSV.

13 Encircle Zion and walk around her, [12]
count her towers;
14 Consider her wall, [13]
and examine her citadels,
That you may tell the generation to come:
"This is God's."
15 Our eternal and everlasting God— [14]
he will guide us eternally.

NOTES

xlviii. A hymn celebrating the beauty and impregnability of Zion, as well as the kingship of God who resides on Zion.

2. *much to be praised.* See NOTE on Ps xlvii 10.

In the city of our God. My stichometric division diverges sharply from the standard versions by considering the opening four words of vs. 2 as an invocation conceptually distinct from the description that follows.

his holy mountain. The phrase, recurring in royal Ps ii 6, *har qodšī,* "his holy mountain," with third-person suffix *-y,* shows that the present poem contains elements of the royal psalms. Again, there is a mixing of types; cf. introductory NOTE on Ps xxxvi.

3. *The most beautiful peak.* *yᵉpēh nōp* is much-contested, but some light, however dim, is cast by UT, 'nt:VI:7–9, [*'b*]*r gbl 'br q'l 'br iht np šmm,* "Cross over the mountain, cross over the ridge, cross over the *iht* of the peak touching the heavens." F. Løkkegaard in *Studia Orientalia Ioanni Pedersen . . . dicata,* p. 230, n. 15, understands *np šmm* as "zenith." Gunkel, *Die Psalmen,* p. 207, is probably correct in seeing in *yᵉpēh nōp* a superlative expression though his emendation to plural *nāpōt* seems uncalled for; *nōp* may be parsed either as an accusative of specification or understood as collective. A similar construction seems to underlie Ps xcix 4, *'ōz melek mišpāṭ 'āhēb 'attāh kōnantā mēšārīm,* "The strongest king, the lover of justice, you established equity." Cf. also Ps xxii 7, *bᵉzūy 'ām,* "the most despicable of the people," and Isa liii 3, *nibzeh waḥᵃdal 'īšīm,* "the most despicable and stupid of men"; Prov xv 20, *ūkᵉsīl 'ādām bōzeh 'immō,* "But he who despises his mother is the most brutish of men."

heart of Zaphon. Mount Zion is to Yahwism what Mount Zaphon (present day Mount Casius) is to Canaanite religion; namely, the dwelling of God and the most hallowed spot of the land. Scholars generally agree that *yarkᵉtē ṣāpōn* is the semantic equivalent of Ugar. *ṣrrt ṣpn,* but differ in their etymological derivations of the vocables. A common element comes to the fore if we accept Driver's equation (CML, p. 150, n. 18) of Ugar. *ṣrrt* with Akk. *ṣurru,* "insides (of the human body), heart, center (of an object)." Since Heb. *yārēk* denotes "loins, insides" (Gen xlvi 26), it may be maintained that *yarkᵉtē ṣāpōn* is a paraphrase of *ṣrrt ṣpn.* The substantive *ṣrrt,* "insides," is found in Hebrew, as maintained in NOTE on Ps vi 8.

The present passage should be compared with UT, ʿnt:III:26–28, *btk ǵry il ṣpn bqdš bǵr bnʿm bgbʿ tliyt,* "In the midst of my mighty mountain, Zaphon; on the holy mountain of my governance, on the beautiful hill of my dominion." Though *ṣāpōn* came to mean "North" in Hebrew, there are three other poetic passages where the ancient Canaanite sense as the name of a specific mountain is still preserved: Ps lxxxix 13; Isa xiv 13, where *yarkᵉtē ṣāpōn* stands in apposition to *har mōʿēd,* "the mountain of assembly"; and Job xxvi 7. See Otto Eissfeldt, *Baal Zaphon, Zeus Kasios und der Durchzug der Israeliten durchs Meer* (Halle, 1932), pp. 13 ff.; Oswald Mowan, "Quattuor Montes Sacri in Ps. 89:13," in *Verbum Domini* 41 (1963), 11–20.

In terming Zion the "heart of Zaphon," the poet may be alluding to the theme of the navel of the earth, a motif commented upon in connection with Ps xxii 28. A full bibliography is available in Gaster, *Thespis,* 1961, p. 183. In the Jewish Diaspora, in stages marked by LXX, Aristeas, the Sibylline writings, and Philo, there was a tendency to place Jerusalem on the highest mountain in the world, in its center or navel. Cf. J. A. Seeligmann, "Jerusalem in Jewish-Hellenistic Thought," in *Judah and Jerusalem* (The Twelfth Archaeological Convention, Israel Exploration Society; Jerusalem, 1957), especially pp. vi and 202. For Jewish ideas about the cosmic north, see Julian Morgenstern, "Psalm 48," HUCA 16 (1941), 47–87.

the Great King. I.e., the Suzerain; cf. NOTE on Ps xlvii 3. Verses 2–3 form a strophe, beginning with *gādōl yhwh* and closing with *melek rāb,* a neat example of *inclusio.*

4. *God is her citadel.* Understanding *b* of *bᵉʾarmᵉnōtehā* either as *beth essentiae* or as *beth emphaticum,* a particle examined in NOTE on Ps xxix 4. The credit for this parsing is due to D. N. Freedman. The plural form, here rendered singular (also in vs. 14), coincides with the Canaanite poetic practice of using plural forms of the names of habitations and fortifications; see NOTE on Ps xliii 3.

her bulwark. Though formally without a suffix, *miśgāb* is entitled to one by reason of its balance with suffixed *ʾarmᵉnōtehā.* Cf. NOTE on Ps iii 4 and the recent article by Brekelmans, in *Jaarbericht . . . Ex Oriente*

Lux 17 (1963, appeared, however, in January 1965), 202–6, especially p. 204.

5. *the kings assembled.* A similar description is found in royal Ps ii 2. Attempts to identify these kings historically appear to be misplaced. For example, Leo Krinetzki, "Zur Poetik und Exegese von Ps. 48," in BZ 4 (1960), 70–97, especially p. 82, proposes that these verses refer to Sennacherib's invasion of 701 B.C. More probably, the kings are mere literary foils in hymns celebrating the power of the Yahwistic king or the invulnerability of the sacred city whose citadel is Yahweh himself. Consult W. F. Albright in JBL 64 (1945), 285 f.

they stormed. Deriving *'ābᵉrū* from *'br* II, "to rage, infuriate oneself," appearing in the noun *'ebrāh,* "rage, arrogance."

6. *Lo! they looked.* Identifying *hemmāh* with Ugar. *hm,* "lo, behold!" Serving no evident useful purpose as an independent pronoun, *hemmāh* does make a fine parallel to vs. 5, *hinnēh,* just as UT, 52:42–43, *whm aṯtm tṣḥn,* "Lo, the two wives shout," is a variation on line 46, *whn aṯtm tṣḥn,* "And lo, the two wives shout." Cf. NOTE on Ps ix 7–8 for other examples of this interjection, and Dahood, "The Language and Date of Psalm 48," CBQ 16 (1954), 15–19, especially p. 16. Equate *hēmmāh rā'ū* with II Kings xiii 21, *hinnēh rā'ū,* and Isa xxxv 2, *hēmmāh yīrᵉ'ū kᵉbōd yhwh,* "Behold, they shall see the glory of Yahweh."

7. *alas.* If *šām* is an adverb, it has no correlative to which it responds. It is lacking in Syriac and Symmachus; hence *šām* has been distinguished from the adverb "there" and identified with El Amarna *šumma,* "behold!" noted at Ps xiv 5.

anguish . . . labor. Compare *ḥīl kayyōlēdāh* with UT, 75:I:25, *ḫl ld,* and Phoenician Arslan Tash, 22, *ḥl wld.* It is difficult to understand why UT, Glossary, No. 955, omits to cite the Phoenician parallel.

8. *As when by the east wind.* Preceded by *kayyōlēdāh* and followed by *ka'ᵃšer, bᵉrūᵃḥ* need not be furnished with *kᵉ* to express a simile; the principle of the double-duty conjunction remarked at Ps xxxvi 7 operates here. A very instructive analogue is present in UT, 128:I:5–7, *arḫ tẓǵ l'glh bn ḫpṯ lumthm ktnḥn udmm.* In prose one would expect a *k* before *arḫ* and before *bn.* The presence of merely one element of the simile *ktnḥn,* "so do they moan," sufficed to show that the other elements were to be supplied by the listener or reader.

ships of Tarshish. Probably large refinery ships that plied the metal trade between the western Mediterranean and Phoenicia. Tarshish, famous for its mines and refineries, has long been identified with Tartessos in southern Spain, but in recent decades a strong case for situating it in Sardinia has been presented by Albright in *Archaeology and the Religion of Israel,* pp. 133 f. He further suggests that *taršīš* may originally have been a common noun signifying "metal refinery." The poet himself seems to have placed it in the west, since he collocates it with *rūaḥ qādīm,* "the east wind," just as the collocation in vs. 3 of *ṣīyyōn* and *ṣāpōn* is intended to evoke the southern and northern points of the compass; see the note by M. Palmer in *Biblica* 46 (1965), 357–58.

The term "ships of Tarshish" apparently belongs to the same category as "Byblos-ships," frequently mentioned in Egyptian literature. The name may simply imply use for travel to Byblos, or may also refer to the fact that the ship was built in Byblos; consult R. Giveon, "A Ramesside 'Semitic' Letter," in *Rivista degli Studi Orientali* 37 (1963), 167–73, especially p. 172.

are shattered. Reading niphal *tiššābēr* with collective plural *'onīyyōt,* the subject, for MT piel *tešabbēr*. For this syntax, see NOTE on Ps xliv 19 and Ps lxviii 3, *tinnādēp* (MT *tindōp*), "May they be put to flight," as read by Albright in HUCA 23 (1950), 17.

To judge from a recently published Ugaritic letter, the destruction of ships through sudden storms may have occurred frequently. The text is UT, 2059:10–15, *any kn likt mṣrm hndt bṣr mtt by gšm adr nškḥ,* "The sturdy ship you sent to Egypt foundered near Tyre, having been caught in a violent downpour."

9. *secure forever.* Stylistically, *'ad 'ōlām* closes the first stanza and corresponds to vs. 15, *'ōlāmōt,* "forever." These separated elements are found joined in UT, 1008:14–15, *'d 'lm šḥr 'lmt,* "forever, an eternal dawn."

10. *midst of your temple.* Compare *beqereb hēkālekā* with UT, 76: II:5, *hd bqrb hklh,* "Hadd is in the midst of his palace." As noticed at Ps xxvi 8, Hebrew cultic terms for sacred dwellings were borrowed from the Canaanites.

11. *your heavens.* The long-standing proposal to read *šāmekā* (in *scriptio defectiva, šmk*) for MT *šimekā* (in *scriptio defectiva, šmk*) finds some confirmation in the motif expressed in UT, 'nt:III:21–22, *tant šmm 'm arṣ thmt 'mn kkbm,* "The meeting (Ar. *'anā,* Heb. *'ānāh,* 'to meet') of heaven with the nether world, of the deeps with the stars." Heaven meets earth at the horizon where the stars sink daily into the subterranean ocean. Cf. Albright in BASOR 150 (1958), 38, n. 13, for a brief study of the Anath text.

Cf. Amos ix 6, "The one who builds his chambers in the heavens, and establishes his vault upon the earth." The rim of this vault was thought to rest upon the edges of the earth. As the heavens extend over the whole earth, from one end to the other, so does your praise, a sentiment akin to the refrain, "the earth is full of your glory."

12. *full of generosity.* Gunkel, *Die Psalmen,* p. 208, argued well that generic *ṣedeq* did not mean "justice"; he proposed *Gnade, Treue.* A clearer understanding of such passages as Pss xxiii 3, xxiv 5, xxxvi

7, 11, lxxxv 15 and Joel ii 23 indicates that "generosity" may be the nuance the poet meant to bring out.

rejoice . . . be glad. The parallelism of the verbs *śāmēᵃḥ* and *gīl* in both Ugaritic and Hebrew was noted at Ps xvi 9.

the daughters of Judah. Hebraic for the villages of Judah.

acts of providence. Singular *mišpāṭ,* "providence," has been discussed at Ps xxxvi 7; the plural form *mišpaṭekā* may refer to many acts of providence just as plural *ḥᵃsādīm,* "deeds of kindness," refers to the historic displays of kindness shown Israel by Yahweh. In the present context, the acts of providence are the deliverances from Israel's military foes.

Note the chiastic arrangement of vs. 12 as well as the *inclusio* started by *ṣedeq* and ending in *mišpāṭekā.*

13. *Encircle Zion.* I.e., form a procession around Zion after worship in the temple.

14. *her wall.* On the lack of *mappiq* in *ḥēlāh,* see GK, § 91e. The substantive *ḥl* in UT, 113:40 and 2027:rev:11 probably means "wall."

and examine. The MT hapax legomenon *passᵉgū,* which has received no viable explanation, is probably to be divided to read *pa,* "and," and imperative *sīgū,* a by-form of *śīg,* "to examine, meditate"; cf. Calderone in CBQ 23 (1961), 456–58, for full discussion of *sīg* and *śīg.* Though well known from Arabic, the existence of *pa,* "and," in the Canaanite dialects was not firmly established until the Ras Shamra discoveries. Its presence in Hebrew is now widely received. Further discussion may be found in Dahood, in *Biblica* 38 (1957), 310–12, and PNWSP, p. 53; Jirku in FuF 32 (1958), 212; Garbini, *Il Semitico di Nord-Ovest,* p. 167, n. 3. Other instances appear in Ps l 10–11; Hos iv 2, vii 1; Amos i 11 (courtesy W. L. Moran); Job ix 12, 20, xvi 14.

This is God's. Literally "the one of God," referring to vs. 3, *har ṣīyyōn,* which belongs to God. It is comparable to *zeh sīnay, zeh dōr,* etc., treated in NOTE on Ps xxiv 6, only in this instance it does not refer to God as the One, but rather to something that belongs to him.

15. *Our eternal and everlasting God.* Analyzing *'ᵉlōhēnū 'ōlām wā'ed* as a construct chain with interposing pronominal suffix, a construction examined in NOTES on Pss xviii 18 and xxxv 19. Cf. NOTE on Ps x 16 regarding the composite noun *'ōlām wā'ed.*

eternally. With LXX^{A}, reading *'ōlāmōt* for MT *'al mūt,* as proposed by Krinetzki in BZ 4 (1960), 73, on the basis of Ugar. *'lmt.* Good analogies to the double plurals *'ōlāmīm* and *'ōlāmōt* are offered by Heb. *šānīm* and *šānōt, dōrīm* and *dōrōt.* There should now be less hesitation (manifested by some, including myself) in translating the Ugaritic divine title *ab šnm* as "Father of Years," though all the other instances of plural "years" in Ugaritic are feminine plural *šnt.*

Just as the first stanza ended with *'ad 'ōlām* (vs. 9), so the poet closes the second stanza and the poem with the synonym *'ōlāmōt*. This stylistic observation makes serious inroads into my earlier proposal, "He will lead us from death" (CBQ 16 [1954], 18), and into that of Johnson, "He is our leader against Death" (*Sacral Kingship in Ancient Israel,* p. 81).

PSALM 49

(xlix 1–21)

1 *For the director; of the sons of Korah, a psalm.*

2 Hear this, all your peoples,
give ear, all your dwellers in the world,
3 Of lowly birth or high degree, [2]*
rich and poor alike.
4 My mouth shall speak wisdom, [3]
and my heart shall proclaim insight.
5 I will incline my ear to a proverb, [4]
will breathe out my riddle on the lyre.
6 Why should I fear the evil days, [5]
or the malice of the slanderers who surround me,
7 Who trust in their wealth, [6]
and of their ample riches boast?
8 Alas, a man can in no wise redeem himself, [7]
or pay to God his ransom price.
9 But the Mansion shall be the redemption of his soul, [8]
and he shall cease forever,
10 When he could have lived jubilant forever, [9]
and never have seen the Pit.
11 If he looks at the wise, they die; [10]
if he gazes upon fools,
They straightway perish,
and leave to others their wealth.
12 Inside their eternal home, [11]
their dwelling place for all generations,
While upon the earth
they invoke their names.
13 For man in the Mansion will sleep indeed, [12]
become like beasts that cease to be.

* Verse numbers in RSV.

14 This is the destiny of those who had wealth, [13]
and the final end
Of those who indulged their taste. *Selah*
15 Like sheep they will be put into Sheol, [14]
Death will be their shepherd;
When they descend into his gullet like a calf,
their limbs will be devoured by Sheol,
consumed by the Devourer.
16 But God will ransom me, [15]
from the hand of Sheol
Will he surely snatch me. *Selah*
17 Be not envious when a man grows rich, [16]
when the wealth of his house increases;
18 For when he dies, nothing will he take, [17]
his wealth will not descend with him,
19 Though he worshiped his appetite while he lived. [18]
20 And though they praise you when you prosper,
you will enter the circle of your fathers, [19]
Who will never more see the light.
21 Man in the Mansion will nothing sense,
become like beasts that cease to be.

Notes

xlix. A Wisdom psalm reflecting on the transitory nature of wealth and pleasure. One should not envy the rich, for the grave awaits them, where their lot will be that of the beasts who perish. Paradise with Yahweh, however, awaits the just man who places his confidence in him rather than in earthly riches and pleasure. The poem is marked by a subtle irony throughout, while the language is probably the most dialectal in the Psalter.

3. *rich and poor*. The Targum identified these with the "unjust" and the "just," respectively, an interpretation warranted by several biblical passages. Thus Isa liii 9 makes *rāšā‘*, "the wicked man," synonymously parallel to *‘āšīr*, "the rich man," while Job xxiv 6 (like Isa liii 9, often the victim of the emendators) *kerem rāšā‘*, "the vineyard of the wicked man," really means the rich man's vineyard. Cf. further Prov xi 7, where *rāšā‘* balances *’ōnīm*, "riches."

4. *speak wisdom*. Ugaritic-Phoenician *ḥkmt*. MT *ḥokmōt,* like *’ᵃdāmōt*

in vs. 12, is the Phoenician form of classical Heb. *ḥokmāh,* as analyzed by Ginsberg and accepted by Albright in VTS, III (1955), p. 8, and by Barucq, *Le livre des Proverbes,* p. 96, as a possibility. Barucq prefers to explain *ḥokmōt* as a *plurale majestatis,* but then it should be pointed *ḥakāmōt.*

my heart shall proclaim. Reading infinitive absolute *wehāgōt* for MT *wehāgūt;* a verbal form is needed to keep the sentence moving. To be sure, the normal infinitive absolute is *hāgō* (Isa lix 13), but the poet may have chosen this unusual form to create a rhyming sequence with *ḥokmōt* and *tebūnōt.* Rhyme, wordplay, assonance, alliteration figure prominently in this riddle. In Ps xc 15 (and Deut xxxii 7), the poet, for the sake of rhyme with *šenōt,* "years," employs the rare plural *yemōt* (two occurrences; Phoen. *ymt*). Other infinitives absolute like *hāgōt* include Isa xxii 12, *šātōt,* Isa xlii 20, *ra'yōt,* and Hab iii 13, *'aryōt;* see Solá-Solé, *L'infinitif sémitique,* p. 78, and Huesman in *Biblica* 37 (1956), 290.

5. *incline my ear.* In other words, to catch the inspiration, he will in turn murmur to the accompaniment of the lyre. Cf. Job iv 12, "Now a word came to me quietly, / Just a whisper caught my ear" (Pope, The Anchor Bible, vol. 15).

breathe out my riddle. Parsing *'eptaḥ* as infixed *-t-* conjugation from *pūḥ,* "to blow, breathe," occurring again in this conjugation in Jer i 14, *miṣṣāpon tiptāḥ* (MT *tippātaḥ*) *hārā'āh,* "Evil will blow down from the north." Particularly corroborative is Ps cxix 130, *pētaḥ debārekā yā'īr mēbīn petāyīm,* "The mere uttering of your words gives light, giving intelligence to the uninstructed." Other cases of infixed *-t-* forms have been examined by Dahood, in ZAW 74 (1962), 207 f., *Orientalia* 32 (1963), 498 f., and PNWSP, pp. 45 f. Cf. further Prov viii 6, *miptaḥ śepātay,* "the utterance from my lips," and xvii 19, *magbīah pitḥō,* "he who speaks proudly" (courtesy J. Swetnam).

on the lyre. kinnōr appears in a recently discovered Ugaritic text which also lists *tp,* "tambourine, drum," and *mṣltm,* "cymbals"; C. Virolleaud in CRAIBL, 1962 (appeared 1963), 94. Hence it is amusing to read in IDB, p. 474b, that biblical *kinnōr* perhaps derives from Persian-Arabic *kunnār,* "lute," or from the root meaning "lotus plant." Cf. now UT, Glossary, No. 1274.

6. *the evil days.* I.e., when death approaches. The construction *yārē' be* instead of *yārē' min* was commented upon at Ps xlvi 3.

the slanderers. To judge from the present context and from Ps xli 5–9, a man's maligners were wont to gather round when he lay on his deathbed.

For MT *'aqēbay,* possibly read *'ōqebay;* for the meaning, cf. discussion at Ps xli 10. The pronominal suffix has the force of the article or demonstrative; cf. NOTE on Ps xvii 15.

who surround me. With Origen, vocalizing plural *y^e^subbūnī* instead of MT *y^e^subbēnī.* For the picture of slanderers surrounding their victim, see Pss iii 7, xxxi 14, xxxv 16, xli 5–9.

7. *trust . . . boast.* Note the superb example of chiasm: A+B // B́+Á.

8. *Alas, a man.* The modern penchant for forming interjections from words expressing blood relationship (e.g., Italian *mamma mia,* literally "My mother!", an exclamation of wonder or of fear) enjoys biblical analogues in *'āḥ,* "alas," recurring in Ezek vi 11, xxi 20, and in *'ābī* in Job xxxiv 36, *'ābī yibbāḥēn 'iyyōb 'ad neṣaḥ,* "Good grief, must Job be tested perpetually?" Proposals to delete *'ābī* (e.g., BH^3) should quietly be consigned to the museum of text-critical aberrations.

9. *But . . . soul.* With Hummel in JBL 76 (1957), 102, reading (for MT *napšām*) *napšō-m* with enclitic *mem,* a formation that recurs in Ps cix 13, *š^e^mō-m,* "his name," and vs. 15, *zikrō-m,* "his memory."

the Mansion. A poetic name of Sheol; see NOTE below on vs. 13.

the redemption. I.e., the minimal existence of Sheol will be the only redemption the rich man can hope for.

10. *jubilant forever.* Relating *'ōd* to Ugar. *ǵdd,* "to expand, rejoice," in UT, 'nt:II:25–26; cf. NOTE on Ps xxxii 9 and Ps xxxix 2, *b^e'^ōd rāšā' l^e^negdī,* "while the wicked man is full of glee before me." In the present passage, parse *'ōd* as stative participle of *'dd.*

and never have seen the Pit. Cf. Ps xvi 10, "Since you will not put me in Sheol, nor allow your devoted one to see the Pit." Immortality is offered to all men who are willing to put their confidence in Yahweh and not in riches.

the Pit. One of the five poetic names for Sheol in this psalm.

11. *If he looks.* God is the subject.

if he gazes. The force of conditional *kī* in the first colon extends to the parallel member; cf. NOTE on Ps iii 2. Reading (for MT *yaḥad*) *yāḥad,* an apocopated form of *yaḥ^a^deh,* as in Job xxxiv 29, *'al gōy w^e'^al 'ādām yāḥad,* "Upon nation and men he gazes." The root is Ugar. *ḥdy* discussed at Ps xxi 7. Terrien, *Job,* p. 230, n. 3, correctly grasped the sense of Job xxxiv 29, but needlessly emended *yāḥad* to *yāḥaz.*

They straightway perish. Reading (for MT *ba'ar*) *bā'īr,* an adverb discovered by W. F. Albright (private communication) in Ps lxxiii 20; Hos xi 9; Eccles viii 10. For the thought, note Ps xxxvi 3, "But his God will destroy him with his glance."

12. *Inside their eternal home.* Compare *qirbām battēmō* with UT, 1 Aqht:74, *bm qrbm asm,* "in the midst of the granary," and 51:v:76, *bqrb hklk,* "inside your palace." Akk. *qirbum* may suggest another pointing of *qirbām.*

eternal home. A poetic name for Sheol. This phrase is the semantic equivalent of Eccles xii 5, *bēt 'ōlāmō,* "his eternal home"; Phoen. *bt 'lm;* Palmyrene *bt 'lm'.*

Plural *battēmō* with singular meaning follows the principle mentioned at Ps xliii 3.

eternal . . . for all generations. The synonymous parallelism *'ōlām // dōr wādōr* equals Ugar. *'lm // dr dr.*

their dwelling place. For the plural form, cf. previous NOTE. The association of *miškān* with the nether world can be seen in Isa xxii 16, *miškān,* "tomb," and in Qumran Copper Scroll, VI:11; cf. J. T. Milik in M. Baillet, J. T. Milik and R. de Vaux, *Discoveries in the Judaean Desert,* III (Oxford, 1962), p. 249.

the earth. The hapax legomenon *'ᵃdāmōt* is doubtless the Phoen. feminine singular ending in *-ōt;* cf. vs. 4, *ḥokmōt,* and NOTE on Ps xlv 15.

they invoke. Namely, the heirs who inherited their wealth. Subtle irony pervades this psalm.

13. *the Mansion.* Another of the thirty-odd names of the nether world heretofore recognized in biblical poetry. In Palmyrene funerary inscriptions one encounters the phrase *yqr' bt 'lm',* which is surely related to *yᵉqar* in the present verse, especially since vs. 12 speaks of *battēmō lᵉ'ōlām.* For full study of *yqr,* see *Syria* 19 (1938), 99–102, where Joüon defines Palmyrene *yqr'* as *"monument d'honneur";* cf. NOTE on Ps xlv 10.

will sleep. The verb *yālīn* connotes "to sleep the sleep of death" in Ps xxx 6 and Job xvii 2.

indeed. Understanding *bal* in the affirmative sense as in Arabic-Ugaritic and occasionally in the Bible; cf. UT, § § 9.18; 11.10; and Pss x 15, xxxii 9; Prov xiv 7.

that cease to be. This phrase harks back to vs. 9, "and he shall cease forever." Deriving *nidᵉmū* from *dāmāh* II, "to cease, cause to cease"; see BDB, p. 198b. The subject of *nidᵉmū* is plural *bᵉhēmōt;* on Ugar. *bhmt,* see NOTE on Ps viii 8.

14. *the destiny.* The parallelism here and the context of Ps xxxv 6 serve to pinpoint the value of *darkām.* There is an instructive analogy in UT, 2 Aqht:IV:35–36, *mt uḫryt my yqḥ mh yqḥ mt aṯryt,* "What will man receive as his final end, what will man receive as his destiny?" The balance between *uḫryt* and *aṯryt* is semantically the same as that between *darkām* and *'aḥᵃrēhem,* since both *aṯr* and *drk* signify "to tread, walk."

who had wealth. The paronomasia involves *kēsel,* "wealth," and vs. 11, *kᵉsīl,* "fools." The semantic range of the root *ksl* partially coincides with that of *kbd.* From the latter derive vocables signifying "liver," "dull," and "wealth," while derivatives of *ksl* include words for "loins," "stupid," and, presumably, "wealth." The clinching argument is supplied by Prov xix 1, *ṭōb rāš hōlēk bᵉtummō mē'iqqēš śᵉpātāyw wᵉhū' kᵉsīl,*

"Better a poor man who lives virtuously / Than a dissembler who is rich" (Scott, The Anchor Bible, vol. 18) The antithesis to *rāš* leaves little doubt as to the connotation of *k*ᵉ*sīl*. Of course, there are numerous critics who will emendate *k*ᵉ*sīl* to *'āšīr* on the strength of the doublet in Prov xxviii 6, which reads *'āšīr,* "rich man." But *lectio difficilior potior.*

*the final end. 'aḥ*ᵃ*rēhem* equals Ugar. *uḫryt* with the same meaning; cf. Dahood, PNWSP, pp. 48 f.

who indulged their taste. Literally "who found pleasure in their mouth." Of course, the sin of gluttony is meant.

15. *Like sheep they will be put.* Reading *šītū,* qal passive of *šīt,* as in Ps iii 7, for MT *šattū.* The syntax of *liš*ᵉ*'ōl šītū* recalls that of Ps xvi 10, *lō' ta'*ᵃ*zōb napšī liš*ᵉ*'ōl,* "You will not place me in Sheol," while the imagery is much elucidated by UT, 51:VIII:15–18, *al tqrb lbn ilm mt al y'dbkm kimr bph,* "Do not approach divine Mot lest he put you like a lamb into his mouth."

Death will be their shepherd. The psalmist waxes ironic. See previous NOTE and compare the euphemism in UT, 67:VI:6, *ln'my arṣ dbr,* "to the pleasant places of the land of grazing." This phrase is a euphemistic description of the nether regions, as rightly noticed by Aistleitner, WuS, No. 1806, p. 208. In the Egyptian Magical Papyrus Harris, the chthonic deity Horon is called the "valiant shepherd"; see Albright, *Archaeology and the Religion of Israel,* p. 80.

When they descend. Pointing *w*ᵉ*yār*ᵉ*dū,* from *yrd,* instead of MT *wayyirdū.* This root is very frequent in contexts concerned with the underworld; e.g., Ps lxxxviii 5, *yōr*ᵉ*dē bōr,* and UT, 51:VIII:8–9, *yrdm arṣ.*

into his gullet. A doubtful translation. Reading *b*ᵉ*mēšārīm* for MT *bām y*ᵉ*šārīm.* This sense of *mēšārīm* is inferred from the context and from the examination of two other passages: Prov xxiii 31–32, *yithallēk b*ᵉ*mēšārīm,* "It (the wine) flows down the throat"; and Song of Sol vii 10, *w*ᵉ*ḥikkekā k*ᵉ*yēn haṭṭōb hōlēk l*ᵉ*dōdī l*ᵉ*mēšārīm,* "And your palate is like sweet wine flowing down the throat of my beloved." Cf. Song of Sol i 4. The root *yšr,* "to be straight," provides a passable etymology, while the imagery relates to UT, 67:I:6–7, *lyrt bnpš bn ilm mt,* "Indeed I shall go down into the throat of divine Mot."

like a calf. Reading *l*ᵉ*bāqār* for MT *labbōqer,* a prepositional phrase occurring in plural form in Ps ci 8, *lib*ᵉ*qārīm* (MT *labb*ᵉ*qārīm*) *'aṣmīt kol riš'ē 'āreṣ,* "Like cattle I will destroy all the wicked in the land." Cf. UT, Krt:93, *wlrbt,* "and by the ten thousands," for a similar prepositional formation. Stylistically, *l*ᵉ*bāqār* balances *k*ᵉ*ṣō'n* at the beginning of the sentence; the balance between *bāqār* and *ṣō'n* is very frequent.

their limbs. Relating *ṣīrām* to the verb *yāṣar,* "to form, fashion," used in connection with the formation of the human body in Isa xliv 2, xlix 5, etc., and underlying Job xvii 7, *yᵉṣūray,* "my limbs."

will be devoured. Literally "are for devouring." Deriving *ballōt* from *bālāh,* "to wear out, consume," attested in UT, 67:I:18, *npš blt,* "my life is wasted away," and 2064:22–23, *blym alpm,* "The oxen are worn out" (i.e., are unfit for plowing). It should not be overlooked that the biblical text uses *ballōt* in connection with *ṣō'n* and *bāqār.*

by Sheol. Sheol is like the shepherds of Ezek xxxiv 3 who, instead of feeding the flock, feed on it.

consumed by the Devourer. An uncertain version. Reading (for MT *mizzᵉbūl lō*), with no consonantal changes, *mᵉzē bōleh lō,* literally "consumed by the one who devours for himself," with *lō* understood as *dativus commodi.* Cf. Deut xxxii 24, *mᵉzē rā'āb,* "consumed by the Hungry One" (cf. NOTE on Ps xxxiii 19).

16. *the hand of Sheol.* Since Death was personified, it is more correct to understand *yad* literally than to obscure the image by rendering it "power" (CCD). Cf. Hos xiii 14 and Job xvii 16, "Into the hands of Sheol will it (my hope) descend, when together we go down upon the slime."

Will he surely snatch me. The correct stichometric division is owed to the Ugaritic specialists, who identified in *kī yiqqāḥēnī* the emphasizing particle *kī* which often causes the postposition of the verb. Thus in his *Ugaritic Grammar* (Rome, 1940), p. 54, C. H. Gordon listed the present passage among those exhibiting the syntactic phenomenon placed in such clear light by, e.g., UT, 62:I:14–15, *lktp 'nt ktšth,* "Upon the shoulders of Anath she surely puts him." This usage is attested five times in the Bible and not once was it correctly understood by any of the ancient versions. Though widely accepted today for the present passage (see Muilenburg, HUCA 32 [1961], 135–60, especially p. 143; Brekelmans, *Ras Sjamra en het Oude Testament,* p. 10), this analysis seems to have escaped J. van der Ploeg in his long study, "Notes sur le Psaume XLIX," in *Studies on Psalms* (Oudtestamentische Studien, XIII; Leiden, 1963), pp. 137–72, especially p. 158. Among recent commentators, Kraus, *Psalmen,* I, pp. 362 f., gives the correct explanation, but recent translations have not been alive to this syntactic refinement.

What the psalmist is professing is his firm conviction that God will take him to himself, just as he took Enoch and Elijah; in other words, he is stating his belief in "assumption." Most commentators find this meaning in the psalmist's words; for a full listing, see Van der Ploeg, *Studies on Psalms,* p. 163. The verb *lqḥ* is precisely that used in Gen v 24; II Kings ii 3, 5, 9; Sirach xlii 15, xlviii 9; as well as in Ps lxxiii 24. Consult Robert Martin-Achard, *De la mort à la résurrection* (Neuchâtel, 1956), pp. 56 ff.

A recently published Ugaritic letter sheds some light on the history of *lqḥ* in the context of death. The text is UT, 2059:21–22, *wklhm bd rb tmtt lqḥt,* "And I snatched all of them from the hand(s) of the Master of Death (=Mot)."

17. *Be not envious.* Vocalizing *tēre'* for MT *tīrā',* from *rā'āh,* "to see." The shade of meaning "to envy," which translators normally fail to detect here, can be established from the following texts: (a) Ps lxxiii 3, *kī qinnē'tī bahōlelīm šelōm rešā'īm 'er'eh,* "For I was jealous of the arrogant, the prosperity of the wicked I envied"; (b) Deut xxxiii 21, *wayyar' rē'šīt lō kī yiššōm ḥelqat meḥōqēq,* "And he covets the best for himself, indeed he pants after a commander's share"—cf. Cross and Freedman in JBL 67 (1948), 195; (c) Isa liii 2, *lō' tō'ar lō welō' hādār wenir'ēhū welō' mar'eh weneḥmedēhū,* "He had no form nor charm that we should envy him, no beauty that we should desire him"; (d) Deut xxxii 19, *wayyar' yhwh wayyin'āṣ mikka'as bānāyw ūbenōtāyw,* "And Yahweh grew envious and spurned them, because he was vexed with his sons and daughters"—the sense of the verse becomes clear when compared with vs. 21, "They provoked me to jealousy with a no-god, they vexed me with their idols"; (e) Song of Sol i 6, *'al tire'ūnī še'anī šeḥarḥōret,* "Do not envy me in that I am black." Analogous is *'yn,* "to see," but in I Sam xviii 9, "to envy"; see Zorell, ZLH, p. 590b.

wealth of his house. kābōd denotes "wealth" in Gen xxxi 1; Isa x 3, xxii 24, lxvi 11, 12; Nah ii 10, while the qal of *kābēd* signifies "to be rich" in Gen xiii 2. On the last text, see Gevirtz in VT 11 (1961), 141, n. 5. Song of Sol viii 7, *hōn bētō,* "the substance of his house," is synonymous with the present phrase.

18. *nothing will he take.* A similar sentiment in Eccles v 14, "Nothing whatever he shall take of his gains, that he could take with him."

descend with him. So LXX; for *'aḥarē,* "with," see R. B. Y. Scott in JTS 50 (1949), 178 f.; Dahood in *Biblica* 44 (1963), 293. Scott's observation is borne out by UT, 77:32–33, *'mn nkl ḫtny aḫr nkl yrḫ ytrḫ,* "With Nikkal will be my marriage; with Nikkal will Yariḫ enter into wedlock." The parallelism with *'mn* appears decisive for the meaning of *aḫr.* For the thought of the verse, note Job xv 29, *lō' yiṭṭēh lā'āreṣ minlō-m* (MT *minlām*), "He will not be rich, nor his wealth endure / Nor his possessions reach the nether world" (Pope, The Anchor Bible, vol. 15), as I proposed in BCCT, pp. 60 f.

19. *he worshiped his appetite.* The phrase *napšō . . . yebārēk* recurs in Ps x 3, *napšō ūbōṣēa' bērēk,* "The despoiler worships his appetite." The root is denominative from *berek,* "knee," as in Ps xcv 6; see A. Jirku, FuF 32 (1958), 212. The thought is also Pauline: Philip iii 19, "whose god is their belly."

20. *they praise you.* The subject of *yōdūkā* is indefinite plural, while the suffix indicates that the psalmist shifts from the third person (the wealthy man in vss. 17–18) to a direct address of the rich man himself.

the circle. This meaning of *dōr* is noted at Ps xiv 5. Here, however, the realm of the dead is meant.

your fathers. Reading (for MT *'ᵃbōtāyw*), with no change of consonants, *'ᵃbōtī*, the oblique plural as in Ugaritic, and attaching the final *waw* to the next word. The suffix is forthcoming from *yōdūkā* on the principle noted at Ps iii 4.

Who will. Explaining the *waw* of *wᵉʿad* as explicative; cf. GK, § 154N(b) and Albright in BASOR 164 (1961), 36, in his comments on *kṯr wḫss*, which he understands as "Kothar who is Ḫasis."

never more see the light. I.e., enjoy immortality, an idiom notably clarified by a new appreciation of Ps xxxvi 10. The light of God's face in the fields of life will be denied those who put their trust in riches and boast of financial success. Their lot will be the direct opposite of the prospects set forth in vs. 10.

21. *the Mansion*. See NOTE on vs. 13.

will nothing sense. Parsing *waw* of *wᵉlō'* as *emphaticum*, considered in NOTE on Ps iv 5.

like beasts that cease to be. See vs. 13 and NOTE.

PSALM 50

(1 1–23)

1 A *psalm of Asaph.*

The God of gods is Yahweh,
he spoke and summoned the earth,
From the rising of the sun to its setting.
2 Out of Zion, the perfection of beauty,
God shone forth.
3 Our God is coming and will not be silent.
Before him a devouring fire,
around him a raging tempest.
4 He summoned the heaven above,
and the earth, to the trial of his people. *Selah*
5 "Gather before him his devoted ones,
who made a covenant with him
in the presence of a sacrifice.
6 Let the heavens announce his just claim,
for he is the God of justice."
7 "Listen, my people, and I will speak,
Israel, and I will testify against you,
Yahweh, your God, am I.
8 Not for your sacrifices do I reprove you,
nor for your burnt offerings
that are ever before me.
9 I ask no bullocks from your estate,
nor goats from your folds;
10 Since mine are all the animals of the forest,
the beasts in the towering mountains;
11 For I know all the mountain birds,
and what moves in the field
is present before me.

12 Were I hungry, I would not tell you,
mine being the world and all it holds.
13 Do I eat the flesh of bulls,
or drink the blood of goats?
14 Offer to God praise as your sacrifice,
and fulfill your vows to the Most High.
15 Then call me in time of distress;
I will rescue you and you will be feasted by me."
16 But to the wicked man God says:
"But how can you recite my commandments,
and raise my covenant upon your lips?
17 For you hate my instruction,
and cast my words behind your back.
18 When you see a thief, you vie with him,
and with adulterers you make common cause.
19 With your mouth you forge evil itself,
and with your tongue you weave deceit.
20 You sit speaking against your brother,
against your own mother's son you spread gossip.
21 These things have you done:
Am I to remain silent?
You harbor evil desires:
Am I like you?
I will accuse you and draw up a case
before your eyes.
22 Consider this well, you who forget God,
lest I snatch and there be none to rescue.
23 He who offers the sacrifice of praise
will be feasted by me;
The one who is set in my way
will I make drink deeply
of the salvation of God."

Notes

l. A prophetic liturgy of divine judgment. In the tradition of the prophets, the psalmist stresses the futility of sacrifice divorced from true morality.

1. *The God of gods*. The grammatical relationship between the words

'ēl '^{e}lōhīm yhwh is uncertain, and its interpretation is tied up with that given to this cluster in Josh xxii 22.

Several possibilities present themselves, but the most attractive is to understand *'^{e}lōhīm* as numerical plural, as in Ugaritic (UT, p. 357, *ilhm*) and in Hebrew (Zorell, ZLH, pp. 53 f.) and to construe the phrase as superlative in meaning: "the God of gods," like "the king of kings." I am indebted to D. N. Freedman for this observation. In the use of the term *'ēl* there may be a reference to Canaanite *'ēl,* who was the chief deity and head of the Canaanite pantheon. In the Psalter, the phrase *'ēl '^{e}lōhîm,* "the God of gods," recurs in lxii 2 and lxxvii 2 (*bis*).

to its setting. *'ad m^{e}bō'ō* equals Phoenician Karatepe I:5, *'d mb'y,* "to its setting."

2. *God shone forth.* Relating the root of *hōpī^{a}'* to Ugar. *yp',* "to rise up," as proposed by F. L. Moriarty in CBQ 14 (1952), 62; cf. UT, Glossary, No. 1133, p. 413.

3. *Before him . . . around him.* This imagery is important for the correct understanding of Ps xcvii 3, *'ēš l^{e}pānāy tēlēk ūt^{e}lāhēṭ sābīb ṣārāyw.* "A fire goes before him and flashes round his back." Usually taken as "adversaries," plural *ṣārāyw,* balancing plural *pānāyw,* is identical with Ugar. *ẓr,* "back." A cognate description is found in Hab iii 5, *l^{e}pānāyw yēlek dāber w^{e}yēṣē' rešep l^{e}raglāyw,* "Before him went pestilence, and fire shone at his back." On *yṣ',* "to shine," see Dahood, PNWSP, p. 52, and NOTE on Ps xvii 2.

4. *the heaven . . . the earth.* Heaven and earth are summoned by God to function as witnesses (Gunkel would make them judges) in his controversy with Israel. G. Ernest Wright, *The Old Testament against Its Environment* (London, 1950), p. 36, has suggested that heaven and earth, invoked in the literary genus known as the "lawsuit," can best be interpreted in light of the divine assembly, the members of which constitute the host of heaven and earth. H. Huffmon in JBL 78 (1959), 291, takes exception to this interpretation since, in his opinion, there is no direct evidence that heaven and earth were members of the divine assembly. Though there is still no direct evidence, a recently discovered Ugaritic tablet does counter Huffmon's position. A list of offerings to different gods includes the phrase *arṣ wšmm š,* "Earth and Heaven, one sheep" (cited from UT, Glossary, No. 959, p. 401). If one compares the offering list published as UT, 1:6–7, which, among the gods listed, specifically mentions *dr il wpḫr b'l,* "the family of El and the assembly of Baal," as recipients of a large head of cattle, one is on safe ground when inferring that for the Canaanites Earth and Heaven were deities who formed part of the divine assembly.

5. *Gather before him.* These are not the words of Yahweh, but rather of the speaker for the plaintiff, Yahweh. The speech of Yahweh begins in vs. 7 with the solemn formula, "Listen, my people, and I will speak."

Both LXX and Syriac assume third-person suffixes; with the knowledge that Hebrew possessed a third-person suffix *-y,* we can retain MT *lī,* "before him."

his devoted ones. I.e., those bound by covenant obligations. This suffix of *ḥsdy* is third-person singular following a plural noun; cf. Ps ii 6.

a covenant with him. Literally "his covenant," but the genitive suffix often expresses a datival relationship; see NOTE on Ps ii 8.

in the presence of. This frequent Ugaritic-Hebrew sense of *'alē* may be intended here; see NOTE on Ps xxiii 2. The oath made in the presence of the slaughtered animal was the formality which made the covenant valid. The Alalakh tablets relate that in the treaty made between Abban and Yaram Lim, Abban slaughtered a sheep to make a covenant with Yaram Lim and accompanied this act by placing himself under oath. The oath to the gods was taken almost simultaneously with the act of slaughtering. See D. J. Wiseman in JCS 12 (1958), 126, 129. This translation of *'alē* brings out an unnoticed affinity of the present verse with the description of the covenant made with Abraham in the presence of the sacrificed animals (Gen xv 17–18).

6. *his just claim.* Within the literary framework of a lawsuit, this seems to be the connotation borne by *ṣidqō;* see Job xxxiii 32.

the God of justice. With Ehrlich, Gunkel, and others, reading *'elōhē mišpāṭ* for MT *'elōhīm šōpēṭ.* God being just, his claim must be legitimate.

7. *Yahweh.* Substituting *yahweh* for *'elōhīm* in the Elohistic Psalter; cf. Exod xx 2; Deut v 6.

8. *Nor for your burnt offerings.* The second colon of vs. 8 may be cited as an instructive example of the extent to which ellipsis could be carried in biblical poetry. Ginsberg, LKK, p. 44, cites Ps cxiv as a beautiful illustration of ellipsis, but the present brief colon, being elliptical in three respects, is no less instructive. It lacks the negative *lō',* which must be supplied from the first half verse, as well as the preposition *'al,* which must likewise be understood as carrying over from the first colon. The lack of a relative pronoun is treated in following NOTE, while other examples of double-duty negatives in the Psalter have been cited at Ps ix 19 and those of double-duty prepositions at Ps xxxiii 7.

that are ever before me. An elliptical relative clause, a rather frequent phenomenon in the Psalter; cf. NOTE on Ps xviii 28.

9. *from your estate.* Closely cognate senses of *bayit* occur in Jewish Aramaic (Jean and Hoftijzer, *Dictionnaire . . . ,* p. 36, line 14), while in biblical place names it often signifies "village"; cf. Milik, in *Discoveries in the Judaean Desert,* III, p. 248, and NOTE on Ps xxxvi 9.

10. *the towering mountains.* Reading *harerē 'ēl* (Ps xxxvi 7) for MT *harerē 'ālep,* and attaching final *pe* to the following verb as the conjunction *pa* discussed in second NOTE on Ps xlviii 14. This analysis,

proposed in *Biblica* 38 (1957), 312, has been adopted by Jirku in FuF 32 (1958), 212, and Brekelmans, *Ras Sjamra en het Oude Testament*, p. 12. A new instance of *pa* has turned up in Job xvi 14, *yiprᵉṣēnī pereṣ ʿal pānāy* (MT *pᵉnē pāreṣ*) *rōṣ yārūṣ ʿālay kᵉgibbōr*, "He rends me rift on rift, / Rushes at me like a warrior" (Pope, The Anchor Bible, vol. 15). The cognate accusative of the first colon, *yiprᵉṣēnī pereṣ*, is balanced by a similar, though not identical, construction in the second colon, *rōṣ yārūṣ*.

11. *mountain birds*. Though *ʿōp hārīm* does not ring fully authentic, the objection of Gunkel, *Die Psalmen*, p. 220, that *hārīm* alongside of *harᵉrē* is impossible, founders on such texts as UT, 2001:rev:5, where *kbkbm* is followed in line 6 by feminine plural *kbkbt*, or Prov xxxi 3–4, where plural *mᵉlākīm* follows on the heels of *mᵉlākīn*, or Prov xvi 16, which employs two different infinitives construct, *qᵉnō* and *qᵉnōt*.

present before me. The association of vs. 10 *lī* with vs. 11 *ʿimmādī* resembles that found in Job xvii 1–2, *qᵉbārīm lī ʾim lōʾ hattillēm* (MT *hᵃtūlīm*) *ʿimmādī*, "The grave is mine, indeed, the twin mounds are before me" (courtesy Nicholas Tromp).

13. *eat the flesh . . . drink the blood*. According to one opinion, there is an allusion here to the primitive belief that regarded sacrifice as satisfying the god's hunger but, more immediately, there seems to be an allusion to the carnivorous goddess Anath. In a fragmentary text recently published by C. Virolleaud in CRAIBL, 1960 (appeared 1961), 180–86, and studied by Astour in RHR 164 (1963), 1–15, Anath is described as devouring the flesh of her brother Baal and drinking his blood: *tspi širh lbl ḥrb tšt dmh lbl ks*, "She devours his flesh without a knife, she drinks his blood without a cup." The similarity with the present verse becomes even more striking with the observation that Baal is sometimes (e.g., UT, 76) said to assume the form of a bull, *ibr*, which is Heb. *ʾabbīr*, one of the words found in the present verse. One may note in passing that the palatal sibilant in *šir* rules out the possibility of understanding *ṯar* in UT, Krt:15, as "flesh," a translation adopted by a number of scholars (Driver, Virolleaud, Ginsberg), but at the same time shows that *širh* in UT, 49:III:35, is to be rendered "his flesh."

15. *you will be feasted by me*. Pointing as pual *tᵉkubbᵉdēnī* instead of MT piel. The suffix is datival and expresses agency. The resemblance of the present verse with Ps xci 15 favors this vocalization, as proposed by Bogaert in *Biblica* 45 (1964), 241. With passive verbs, the pronominal suffixes express agency in Pss lxiii 11, lxxxi 8; Isa xliv 21; Job xxxi 18. For *kbd*, "to feast," see NOTE below on vs. 23.

16. *recite . . . lips*. The association of *spr* and *py* is found in UT, 77:45–46, *bpy sprhn*, "In my mouth is their story."

17. *you hate my instruction*. *mūsār*, "my instruction," receives its suffix from *dᵉbārāy*, "my words"; cf. NOTE on Ps v 4. Other examples

of ellipsis in this psalm are remarked in vss. 8 and 23. Failure to detect the operation of the double-duty suffix has resulted in the frequent emendation of Prov viii 10, *qeḥū mūsārī we'al kesep weda'at mēḥārūṣ nibḥār;* the apparatus of BH³ advises us to read *mūsar* with LXX, Syr., Targ., and one MS on the strength of its balance with suffixless *da'at*. The opposite procedure is to be followed: extend the suffix of MT *mūsārī* to *da'at* and render, "Accept my instruction instead of silver, and knowledge of me in preference to choicest gold." In Zeph iii 7, *mūsār,* "my instruction," receives its suffix from *'ōtī,* "me."

18. *you vie with him.* With LXX, Syr., and Targ., vocalizing *wattāroṣ* for MT *wattireṣ;* compare UT, 49:I:22–24, *lyrẓ 'm b'l ly'db mrḥ 'm bn dgn,* "He cannot vie with Baal, he cannot hold a javelin with Dagan's son."

19. *With your mouth.* Explaining *pīkā* as an accusative of means; note that the accusative of means precedes its verb, a stylistic trait of the psalmists commented upon at Ps v 10.

you forge. Deriving *šālaḥtā* from *šlḥ* II, a root discussed in light of Ugar. *šlḥ,* "to forge, hammer," in the first NOTE on Ps xviii 15. This etymology accords with the metaphor in *taṣmīd,* which also expresses the activity of an artisan, according to a widely held etymology; cf. I Sam xxiii 9, *maḥarīš rā'āh,* "fabricating mischief," and Prov iii 29, vi 14.

evil itself. The *b* of *berā'āh* can suitably be accounted for as emphatic, as proposed at Ps xxix 4. Two parallels are especially apposite: Jer xxix 9, *kī bešeqer hēm nibbe'īm lākem bīšemī,* "For falsehood itself are they prophesying to you in my name"—a few MSS and many commentators, following the ancient versions, simply drop the *b,* but in the light of the well-attested usage of the emphatic *b,* such a procedure becomes indefensible; and Prov xxxi 13, *dārešāh ṣemer ūpištīm watta'aś beḥēpeṣ kappehā,* "She selects wool and flax, and her hands create beauty itself"—syntactically, *watta'aś beḥēpeṣ* is identical with *šālaḥtā berā'āh.*

with your tongue. Parallel to *pīkā, lešōnekā* is likewise an accusative of means preceding its verb. Cf. Ps v 10, *lešōnām yaḥalīqū,* "With their tongue they bring death." This analysis keeps "you" the subject of vss. 16–21, which is rhetorically effective in a *Gerichtsrede* or "lawsuit." For a similar stylistic sequence, cf. NOTE on Ps xviii 36. Note the sequence A+B+C // Á+B́+Ć, a pattern recurring in Pss vi 8, xlvi 5, cxli 3, etc.

20. *You sit speaking.* Hendiadys. Perhaps there is a reference to those described in Ps lxix 13, "They who sit at the gate gossip about me."

brother . . . mother's son. Cf. UT, 49:VI:10–11, *aḫym ytn b'l bnm umy klyy*. Some (e.g., Briggs) would see in the parallelism a distinction between a "full brother" and a "uterine brother," but whether the psalmist had this distinction in mind is difficult to determine, since the Ugaritic parallelism suggests that we might be here dealing with a poetic cliché.

21. *You harbor*. This sense of *dimmītā* can be found in II Sam xxi 5; Num xxxiii 56; cf. BDB, p. 198a.

evil desires. Instead of MT *h^eyōt*, which many commentators admit is syntactically impossible, reading *hayyōt*, the plural of *hayyāh*, "desire," in Job vi 2, a by-form of *hawwāh*, "desire" (in pejorative sense; Ps lii 9; Mic vii 3; Prov x 3, xi 6). The most relevant text is Ps lii 9, *hawwōt taḥšōb*, "You think evil thoughts."

I will accuse you. This nuance of *'ōkī^aḥ* is most clearly present in Job xl 2, where the ancient versions understand it in this manner; see Zorell, ZLH, p. 310b.

draw up a case. The absolute use of *'ārak* recurs in Ps v 4, "I will draw up my case before you," and in Job xxxiii 5, xxxvii 19.

22. *lest I snatch*. I.e., take away your life.

23. *will be feasted by me*. For pointing and parsing of verb, see NOTE on vs. 15. Exegetically, "to honor" here denotes "to honor with a banquet." This interpretation stems from the association of *kbd* with *šlḥm* and *ššqy* in UT, 2 Aqht:v:19–20, *šlḥm ššqy ilm sad kbd hmt*, "Give food, give drink to the god; serve, feast him." This definition of *kbd* comports well with the parallel verb in the present verse, "will I make drink deeply," examined below. The same nuance of *kbd* has been remarked at Ps xv 4. The subtle irony in Prov xii 9 can fully be appreciated only with the knowledge that *kbd* bears this connotation: *ṭōb niqleh w^e'ebed lō mimmitkabbēd waḥ^asar lāḥem*, "Better a man of no rank who has a helping of food than he who gives himself airs, yet has nothing to eat." The wordplay present in *mitkabbēd* emerges in the light of the definition of *kbd* in the above texts; cf. Dahood, PNWSP, p. 26.

who is set in my way. I.e., in the way of God's commandments. MT *śām derek* is difficult, but a modicum of sense can be extracted by vocalizing consonantal *śm* as the qal passive participle, a form attested in Num xxiv 21 and Obad iv; see Zorell, ZLH, p. 795b. Other qal passive (though not participles) attestations of this verb are found in Ezek iv 2; Mic iv 14; Job xx 4; II Sam xiv 7 (Joüon, GHB, § 58c), and Phoenician Eshmunazar, line 5, *k 'y śm bn mnm*, "For nothing whatsoever has been placed in it."

The value of the suffix of *y^ekubb^edān^enī* (MT *y^ekabb^edān^enī*), a pual energic form (cf. NOTES on vs. 15 and Ps viii 2), carries over into the second colon so that *derek* can signify "my way." The ellipsis involving lack of explicit suffixes and prepositions in vss. 8 and 17 has been commented upon above.

will I make drink deeply. Alter the pointing of MT *'ar'ennū* to *'ōr'ennū*, the hiphil of *yr'* II, "to be fat, drink deeply," a root discussed at Ps xxxiv 9. This exegesis is further sustained by the similarity of the present passage with Ps xci 16, *'ōrek yāmīm 'aśbī'ēhū we'ōr'ēhū* (MT *'ar'ēhū*) *bīšū'ātī*, "With length of days will I satisfy him, and I will make him drink deeply of my salvation." Gunkel's emendation of consonantal *'r'h* to *'arwēhū* in Ps xci 16, "I will make him drink his fill," while evincing a fine feeling for the needs of context, is no longer needed. Note that the construction *yr' b*, "to drink deeply from," falls in with the syntax of *šty b*, "to drink from," in UT, 52:6, and in Gen xliv 5; Amos vi 6; Prov ix 5.

It thus develops that the balance between *yekubbedānenī* and *'ōr'ennū* is semantically equivalent to that between *ššqy*, "give to drink," and *kbd*, "fete," in UT, 2 Aqht:v:19–20.

The biblical metaphor is of a piece with such phrases as Ps cxvi 13, "I will take the cup of salvation," and Isa xii 3. Here then we propose to find the theme of the messianic banquet, as presented in Pss xvi 11, xxiii 5–6; Isa xxv 8; and taken up again in Luke xiv 16–24. Cf. Martin-Achard, *De la mort à la résurrection*, pp. 103 f.

INDEX OF BIBLICAL PASSAGES

Gen i 12, 197
Gen iii 16, 88
Gen vi 4, 97
Gen xi 28, 223
Gen xi 31, 223
Gen xiv 14, 7
Gen xiv 20, 17
Gen xv 1, 17
Gen xv 7, 223
Gen xv 17–18, 307
Gen xlix 4, 215
Gen xlix 23, 19
Exod v 16, 239
Exod xv 15, 9
Lev xxvi 36, 235
Deut i 44, xxvi
Deut xxxii 1, 30, 284
Deut xxxii 8, 90
Deut xxxii 19, 302
Deut xxxii 24, 203
Deut xxxiii 3, 112
Deut xxxiii 7, 109, 229
Deut xxxiii 21, 112, 302
Deut xxxiii 27, 115, 235
Deut xxxiii 28, 242, 273
Josh x 24, 116
Josh xviii 7, 62
Judg v 23, 210
Judg v 31, 128
Judg ix 4, 8
Judg ix 9, 221
Judg xi 3, 8
I Sam ii 3, 144
I Sam xiv 47, 158
I Sam xv 29, 139
I Sam xvii 42, 112
I Sam xxiii 9, 309
I Sam xxv 37, 36
II Sam xxiii 1, 118
I Kings xiii 23, 246
II Kings xix 28, 196
II Kings xxv 11, 228
Isa iii 20, 274
Isa vii 1, 21
Isa ix 18, 98
Isa xvi 6, 30
Isa xxii 7, 19
Isa xxii 9, 197
Isa xxii 15, 11
Isa xxii 16, 299
Isa xxvi 1, 173
Isa xxvi 12, 140
Isa xxvi 19, 222 f.
Isa xxx 15, 148
Isa xxx 20, 109
Isa xxx 30, 115, 235
Isa xxxv 2, 291
Isa xxxvii 29, 196
Isa xxxviii 10, 183 f.
Isa xxxviii 14, 251
Isa xxxviii 15, 241
Isa xl 4, 191
Isa xlii 19, 42
Isa xliii 14, 196
Isa xlvii 10, 87
Isa xlix 15, 49
Isa l 6, 64
Isa lii 13, 118
Isa liii 2, 302
Isa liii 3, 139, 219, 289

Isa liii 9, 296
Isa liii 10, 188
Isa liii 11, 223
Isa lvi 10, 191
Isa lxii 1, 228
Jer ii 28, 56
Jer v 6, 97
Jer v 25, 25
Jer vi 27, 70
Jer viii 14c, 256
Jer ix 3, 251 f.
Jer ix 20–21, 9
Jer xii 13, 229 f.
Jer xiv 14, 98
Jer xvii 6, 25
Jer xvii 13, 172
Jer xviii 21, 203
Jer xxiii 12, 211, 224
Jer xxix 9, 97 f.
Jer xxxi 3, 223
Jer xxxviii 11–12, 93
Jer lii 15, 228
Ezek xxi 11, 281
Ezek xxvii 3, 275
Ezek xxvii 10, 210
Ezek xxviii 3, 113
Ezek xxviii 14, 107
Ezek xxxviii 13, 206
Hos iv 2, 32
Hos v 2, 246
Hos vi 6, 246
Hos xi 9, 298
Amos iv 6, 85
Jon ii 4, 202
Jon ii 7, 258
Mic iv 9, 281
Mic v 13, 56
Nah i 7, 195
Nah i 7–8, 127
Nah i 9, 140
Nah ii 6, 129, 231
Nah iii 9, 210
Nah iii 18b, 61
Hab i 12, 144
Hab ii 8, 99
Hab ii 17, 77
Hab iii 3, 139
Hab iii 4, 228
Hab iii 5, 306
Hab iii 8b, 202
Zeph ii 10, 42
Zeph iii 8, 58
Ps li 8, 177
Ps li 18, 246
Ps li 21, 246
Ps lii 11, 122
Ps lv 19, 177
Ps lv 21, 42
Ps lv 22, 203
Ps lv 23, 65, 139
Ps lvi 9, 20
Ps lvi 14, 223
Ps lix 4, 94
Ps lx 10, 281
Ps lxi 3, 118, 260
Ps lxi 4, 19
Ps lxii 9, 112
Ps lxiv 4, 251
Ps lxiv 5, 69
Ps lxv 12–13, 146
Ps lxv 14, 230
Ps lxvi 7, 128
Ps lxvii 7, 26 f.
Ps lxviii 6, 9
Ps lxviii 18, 77
Ps lxviii 19, 95
Ps lxviii 21, 111
Ps lxviii 30, 46
Ps lxviii 32, 229
Ps lxviii 33, XL, 284
Ps lxviii 34, 115
Ps lxviii 35, 46
Ps lxix 11, 213
Ps lxix 14, 142
Ps lxix 23, 43
Ps lxix 28–29, 33 f.
Ps lxxi 7, XL
Ps lxxi 10, 16

Ps lxxi 21, 266
Ps lxxiii 1, XXI
Ps lxxiii 3, 302
Ps lxxiii 8, 97
Ps lxxiii 18, 3, 211
Ps lxxiii 20, 298
Ps lxxiv 11, 44
Ps lxxiv 14, 127
Ps lxxiv 18, 42
Ps lxxv 6, 45, 118, 285
Ps lxxv 7, 144
Ps lxxv 10, XXIII
Ps lxxvii 9, 179
Ps lxxvii 16, 112
Ps lxxvii 19, 109
Ps lxxviii 26, XXVI, 50
Ps lxxviii 65, 196
Ps lxxxiii 3, 272
Ps lxxxiv 12, 17
Ps lxxxv 7, 144
Ps lxxxv 13, 25, 156, 203
Ps lxxxvi 11, 156
Ps lxxxix 8, 26
Ps lxxxix 10, 279
Ps lxxxix 13, 290
Ps lxxxix 17, 77
Ps lxxxix 18, 18
Ps lxxxix 19, 143, 287
Ps lxxxix 20, 112
Ps lxxxix 51, 19, 117
Ps xc 8, 124
Ps xci 9, 162
Ps xcii 2, XL
Ps xciii 5, 200, 278
Ps xcvii 3, 306
Ps xcvii 4, 281
Ps xcvii 9, 285
Ps xcvii 11, 223
Ps xcix 2, 113
Ps xcix 4, 289
Ps ci 3, 31
Ps ci 8, 300
Ps cii 3, 64, 169
Ps civ 15, 35, 115 f.
Ps cv 11, 168
Ps cvi 43, 77
Ps cvii 20, 17, 242
Ps cx 2, 13, 109
Ps cx 4, 110
Ps cxiv 2, 138
Ps cxvi 1, 110
Ps cxvi 9, 223
Ps cxviii 5, 111
Ps cxviii 24, 144
Ps cxix 38, 33
Ps cxix 152, 56
Ps cxxvii 5, 9, 211
Ps cxxix 3, XLII
ps cxxix 4, 8
Ps cxxix 8, 43
Ps cxxxv 4, 285
Ps cxxxv 7, 109
Ps cxxxvii 3b, 173
Ps cxxxviii 6, 62
Ps cxxxviii 7, 163
Ps cxxxviii 8, 18
Ps cxxxix 1, 17
Ps cxxxix 12, 113
Ps cxxxix 14, 195, 278
Ps cxxxix 16, 133
Ps cxxxix 24, 33
Ps cxl 7, XXI, XL, 87
Ps cxl 11, 224
Ps cxli 3, 59, 239
Ps cxli 9, 229
Ps cxliii 10b–11, 34
Ps cxliv 6, 109
Ps cxlvii 1, 200
Ps cxlvii 9, 81
Ps cl 1, 50
Job ii 11, 42
Job iv 20, 250
Job v 20, 207
Job vi 4, 235
Job x 1, 257
Job x 3, 2
Job x 17, 197
Job xii 2, 113

Job xiii 14, 65
Job xiii 15, 144
Job xiii 26, 246
Job xv 23, 237
Job xv 29, 302
Job xvi 9, 46, 197
Job xvi 12–13, 235
Job xvi 13, 19
Job xvi 14, 308
Job xvii 2, 279
Job xvii 13, 122
Job xvii 16, 189
Job xviii 7, 2
Job xviii 12, 203, 237
Job xviii 20, 52
Job xix 20, 242
Job xix 22, 9
Job xxi 16, 2
Job xxii 8–9, 229
Job xxii 12, 62
Job xxii 30, 196
Job xxix 16, 214
Job xxx 17, 74, 230
Job xxx 28, 93
Job xxx 30, 74, 230
Job xxi 23, 43 f.
Job xxxiii 5, 31
Job xxxiii 30, 223
Job xxxiii 32, 246
Job xxxiv 3, 67
Job xxxiv 29, 202, 298
Job xxxvi 30, 110
Job xxxvii 11, 108, 123, 228
Job xxxvii 21, 228
Job xxxviii 10, 90
Job xl 17, 231
Job xli 1, 242
Job xli 8, 107
Job xli 10, 228
Prov i 17, 211
Prov i 21, 58
Prov i 32, 44
Prov ii 22b, 97
Prov iv 9, 17
Prov v 5, 87
Prov v 17, 196
Prov viii 10, 309
Prov viii 23, 10
Prov ix 10, 257 f.
Prov x 21, 228
Prov xi 25, 206
Prov xii 9, 310
Prov xiii 20, 281
Prov xiv 1, 13
Prov xv 2, 240
Prov xv 7, 30
Prov xv 20, 289
Prov xvi 23, 249
Prov xix 1, 299 f.
Prov xix 2, 239
Prov xx 20, 78
Prov xx 23, 220
Prov xxi 22, 215
Prov xxi 25, 207
Prov xxii 3, 206
Prov xxiii 2, 105
Prov xxiii 31, 206
Prov xxiii 31–32, 300
Prov xxvi 3, 197
Prov xxvi 21, 70
Prov xxvii 22, 74
Prov xxviii 6, 300
Prov xxix 8, 230
Prov xxx 16, 18
Prov xxxi 3, 63, 229
Prov xxxi 13, 309
Song of Sol i 2, 206
Song of Sol i 6, 236, 302
Song of Sol vii 10, 300
Song of Sol viii 7, 302
Eccles i 14, 265
Eccles v 7, 62
Eccles v 14, 302
Eccles vii 27, 26
Eccles viii 10, 298
Eccles xii 5, 299
Eccles xii 8, 26
Eccles xii 12, 7

Lam ii 18, 96 f.
Lam iii 52, 69
Lam iii 61, 45
Lam iv 16, 207
Neh ix 7, 223
Neh ix 11, 190
Luke xvi 3, 47
Luke xvi 11, 228
Luke xxii 25, 17

INDEX OF HEBREW WORDS

'ābad, to shrivel, 230
'ad, hand, 95
'ād='āz, then, 278
'ᵃdāmōt, earth, 299
'āḥ, alas, 298
'aḥᵃrē, with, 302
'ayil, ram, lieutenant, 9, 10
'al, lest, 59, 215
'ālam, to muzzle, 190 f.
'āmar, to see, 16, 24, 69
'āmōn, wealth, 12, 228
'ānāh, to meet, 237
'ap, and, 89
'āram, to be high, 282
'ᵃrešet, request, 131
'āšam, to perish, 35 f., 207
'ᵃšer, he who, 251
'āšēr, happy, 63
'āt, to work wonders, 246, 265
'ēd, death, 111
'ᵉyālūt, army, 141
'ēl, El, 46, 64, 242, 305 f.
'ēl, as superlative, 220
'elem, muzzle, 240
'ēlīm, God, xxiii, 43, 218
'ᵉlōhīm ṣaddīq, God, the Just One, xxxvii
'ᵉmet, truly, 188
'ᵉmūnīm, faithful men, 73
'ereṣ, clay, 74 f.
'ereṣ, nether world, 43, 106, 144
'ēt, weapon, 73 f.
'ī, not, 196
'īš dāmīm, man of idols, 31 f.
'īšīm, men, 13
'īšōn, sleep, 78
'ītāmār, Ithamar, 16
'ōmer, vision, 179
'ōr, sun, 228
'ūr, field, 222 f.
b, from, xxvi, 3, 9, 16, 58, 61, 65, 69, 84, 96, 99, 107 f., 122, 128, 133, 168, 189, 203, 207, 220, 230, 236, 272, 278
bāhem, then, 122
bal, surely, 197, 299
bāṭaḥ, to be tranquil, 139
bayit, heavenly house, 168
bālāh, to wear out, 93, 301
bā'īr, straightway, 298
bāśar, to announce, 246
bᵉzō't, then, 252
bᵉlēb, senseless, 272
bᵉlîyya'al, Belial, 105
bēt, within, 96
bᵉtōk, out of, 140
bᵉtūlōt, maiden, 275
billa', to engorge, 215 f.
bō', to bring, 262
bōt, robe, 274
ga'ᵃwāh, back, 279
gābar, to be strong, 73
gābōᵃh, Lofty One, 62
gādal, to weave, calumniate, 73, 216, 237, 251
gāmar, to avenge, 45
ga'ᵃrāh, roar, 110
gē', midst, 146 f.
gᵉbūrōt, fortress, 128

g^{e}dūd, well-sinewed, 114
gīl, to live, 13, 139, 262
dā'āh, to fly, 107, 247
dāl, door, 249
dāmam, to weep, 24, 57, 183
dāmīm, images, idols, 163
derek, assembly, 2, 14
derek, destiny, 211, 228, 299
derek, power, dominion, 63, 70, 114, 229
dibbēr, to pursue, drive away, 9, 236
diggēl, to raise a banner, 128
dōr, assembly, 82
dōr, eternity, 144, 151 f.
hāgāh, to recite, number, 3, 7
hāgīg, utterance, 29
hāgōt, infinitive absolute, 297
hayyāh, desire, 310
h^{a}mīr, jaw, 278 f.
hāmōn, wealth, 228 f.
hāpak, to ravage, 194
hārar, to lust, 88
he'āḥ, Aha!, 215, 247
hēkāl, heavenly temple, 106, 148 f., 179
hēmmāh, behold!, 56, 166 f., 228, 236, 262, 291
zāhar, to enlighten, 124
zākar, to be strong, 129
zānaḥ, to be angry, 266
zēdīm, presumptuous ones, 124
zeh, the one of, 152
zeh, then, 153
z^{e}rō'ōt, resources, 229
zimmāh, idol, 94, 163
zō't, indignity, 42, 266
ḥādāh, to gaze, 27, 133, 202, 298
ḥādal II, to be fat, dull, 219
ḥāwāh, to bow down, 176
ḥāṭā', to stumble, 239
ḥayyīm, life eternal, 34, 91, 132, 170, 183, 222
ḥālal, to play the pipe, 213
ḥālaq, to perish, 35, 73, 99, 207
ḥ^{a}laqlaqqōt, Destruction, 211
ḥāmūd, body, 242
ḥānap, to slander, 214
ḥāsad II, to revile, 96
ḥāsam, to muzzle, 96
ḥāpaṣ II, to stiffen, 231
ḥāpēṣ, to be interested, 246
ḥāraś, become like a potsherd, 194
ḥeleq, smoothness, 89
ḥēmāh, pavilion, 123
ḥermōn, net, 258
ḥnm, stealthily, 211 f.
ḥokmōt, wisdom, 296 f.
ḥōšek, Darkness, 211
ṭōb, rain, xxxii, 25
ṭōb, sweet, 206, 270
yābēš, to dry up, 229 f.
yād, arm, 224, 235
yād, left hand, 133, 163
yāda', to cherish, 57
yāh, intensifier, 240
yahweh 'ēl, XXXVII, 64, 104 f., 188
yāḥīd, alone, 158
yāmak, to sink, 89
**yāmam,* to create, 77, 229
yāpē^{a}ḥ, witness, 169
**yāqar,* to burn, 230
yāṣā', to shine, 93 f., 228, 306
yāram, to be high, 48, 168
yardēn, land of descent, 258
yāša', to thrive, 221
yāšār, the Upright One, 71
yātam, to be blameless, 125
y^{e}ḥīdāh, face, 141, 214
y^{e}šū'ōt, Savior, 173, 257 f., 266
yeter, wealth, 99
yir'āh, he who fears, 32
yōšēb, king, 8 f., 57
yōtēn, the Bestower, 114
yqr, mansion, 274, 299
yr' II, to be seated, to drink deeply, 206, 310 f.
kābēd, liver, 184

kābōd, Glorious One, 18, 23, 179 f.
kābōd, wealth, 302
kāzāb, idol, 23 f.
kālāh, to be at an end, 62 f.
kārat, to cut, 246
kārīm, hollows, 230
kelōb, ax, 141
kened, jar, XXIII, 201
kesel, wealth, 299 f.
kepīr, young lion, 206
kī, indeed, 65, 241, 301
kibbēd, to feast, 84, 308 ff.
kinnōr, lyre, 297
kissāh, to uncover, 266
kissē', to enthrone, 273
kōl, each one, 81, 241
kūl, to sustain, 250
l, from, XXVI, 16, 56, 74, 94, 111, 117, 183, 202, 246 f., 250, 275
lāmō, for us, 173, 266
**lannū,* for himself, 285
lāqaḥ, to assume, 33
lāqaḥ, as *terminus technicus,* 301
lē', the Victor, XXV, XXVI, 46, 144, 169 f.
lēb, intention, 203
lebāqār, like a calf, 300
leḥem, grain, 81
lēlōt, watches of night, 90
leṣela', at my side, 237
lō'-ṭōb, crime, 219 f.
lšnm, double tongue, XXVIII
māgān, Suzerain, XXXVII, 17, 45, 114
māzal, to fall, 75
maḥaneh, army, 167
māmōn, wealth, XXII, 12
man, how many, 274
ma'agāl, pasture, 146
mā'ōn, habitation, 50
māqōm, home, 162, 228
mārōm, Exalted One, XXXVII, 44 f., 63, 177
maśkīl, skillful song, 286
māšaḥ, to stretch out, 107
mē'āt, a hundred times, 167
melek gādōl, suzerain, 284, 290
melūkāh, king, 143
merḥāb, name of Sheol, XLI, 111, 189
mēšārīm, gullet, 300
mētār, bowstring, 134
meteg, muzzle, 196 f.
metōm, soundness, 235
mī'āh, repeat one hundred times, 142
milḥāmāh, troops, 167
min, in, 106
mir'āh, edict, 123 f.
mirmāh, deceit, 151
miškān, tomb, 299
mišpāṭ, just man, 231
mišpāṭ, place of judgment, 2
mišpāṭ, providence, 293
mōṭ, poetic name for underworld, 78 f.
mōsēr, band, 59
mōq, festering, 267
nā'āh, to laud, 200
nāba', to pour forth, 121
**nādad,* to prostrate, 257
nādāh, to hurl, 190, 224
nāham, to groan, 235
nāwāh, to laud, 200 f.
nāḥāh, to lead into Paradise, 33, 147
naḥalāh, kingdom, 285
nāṭab, to drop, 240
nāpal, to charge, 229
nāṣāb, false image, 241
nāqī, hungry, 85
nāšīm, men, 13
nehārōt, ocean currents, 151
nepeš, neck, 41 f., 141, 169, 189, 215, 249 f., 268
nepeš, appetite, 302
sāk, barrier, 257
sārar, to be stubborn, 81

seger, javelin, 210 f.
s^eḥarḥar, to be fever-racked, 236
sīg, to examine, 293
sōd, friendship, 158
sūk, to anoint, 10
sūr, to turn aside, 64, 123, 142, 235, 268
'ābar II, to storm, 291
'ābōt, yoke, 8
'ad, near, 257
*'*ādad,* to be gleeful, 240
*'*ādad,* to be petulant, 197
'āzab II, to put, 65, 90 f., 231
'āzar II, to be youthful, 173, 210
'al, from, XVII, 26, 85
'al, before, 257, 307
'al, near, 146
'ālāh, to attack, 215
'ālam, to conceal, 162
'ālē, to the debit of, 246
'l yhwh, Most High Yahweh, 117
'al kēn, because, 258, 273
'ām, strong, 112, 283 f.
'āmad, to participate as a member, 2
'ānāh, to triumph, 116, 128, 129
'ap'appayim, pupils, eyes, 70
'āpār, mud, 43, 140, 184
*'*āṣam,* to dig, 63 f.
'āqab, to slander, 252
'ārag, to cry aloud, 255 f.
'ărāpēl, storm cloud, 107
'ārīm, gods, protectors, 55 f.
**'āšar* II, to invite, 275
'at='attāh, now, 27
'ēdāh, pack, 140
'ezrāh, helper, 247
'^elī, caldron, 74
'ēlī, Most High, XXIII, XXV, XXXVI, 45, 79, 89, 194, 251
'ēṣāh, council, 1 f., 82
'ēṣōt, doubts, 76 f.
'ēqeb, reward, 124
'ēt, life-stage, 190
'im, toward, 111 f.
'īr, to protect, 56
'ōz, fortress, XXV, 50, 173
'ōz, triumph, 131, 180
'ōlām, Eternal One, XXIII, XXV, XXXVII, 18, 75, 153, 187
'ōlām, primeval time, 56, 180
'ōlām wā'ed, composite noun, 293
'ōlāmōt, forever, 293
'ūg, to draw a circle, 214
'ūn, to dwell, 162
pa, and, 317, 307 f.
paḥad, flock, cabal, 81 f.
pālaṭ, to rescue, 261 f.
pānīm, fury, 55, 97, 133 f., 207
pānīm, intent, will, 125
pā'al, to gather, 191
p^enīmāh, inside, 275
pered, mule, 196
peša', Perversity, 218
pū^aḥ, to breathe, 297
ṣaddīq, the Just One, XXXVII, 69
ṣaddīq 'attīq, Ancient Just One, XXXVII, 191
ṣalmāwet, utter darkness, 30
ṣārāh, siege, 127
ṣ^edāqāh, meadow, 33 f.
ṣ^edāqāh, generosity, 151, 220, 224
ṣedeq, generosity, 146, 292 f.
ṣedeq, legitimate, 25
ṣedeq, vindication, 23, 93, 99, 216
ṣiwwāh, to send, 259
ṣinnōr, thunderbolt, 259
**ṣīr,* limb, 300 f.
ṣrry, heart, innards, 38, 63, 189
ṣūr, divine appellative, 118
qādōš, holy throne, 69 f., 138 f.
qāwāh, to call, 122, 156, 228, 241, 245
qārā', to collect, harvest, 81
**qārāh,* to burn, 230
qāšōt, bows, 73, 228 f.
q^edōšīm, Canaanite deities, 87 f.
qeren, wing, 107 f.

qōdeš, the Holy One, 176
qōl, thunder, 281
rā'āh, to be envious, 302
rā'āh, to watch idly, 214
rāb, arrow, shaft, 19, 117
rab, rich, 99, 229
rābab, to shoot arrows, 19
rāgal, to trip, 84
rāgaš, to forgather, 7
rāḥaš, to compose, 270
rā', treachery, 43
rā'āh, drought, 230
rā'am, to thunder, 108
rā'eb, Hungry One (=Death), 203
rāqad, to skip, 178
rāša', rich man, 296
rega', Perdition, 182
reḥābīm, idols, 245 f.
rewaḥ, square, 117
rewaḥ, broadness, 107
rig'ē 'āreṣ, the oppressed in the land, 215
rīq, troops, 7 f., 195, 210
**rnn*, to find refuge, 196
rō'š, venom, 117
rōqāmōt, women who weave, 275
ruksē 'īš, slanderings of men, 191
rūm, to rejoice, 77, 134 f.
rūṣāh, run!, XXIII, 247
śānē', to hate, as *terminus technicus*, 31, 188, 245 f.
śāpōt, lips, 73
śemāḥōt, joy, 275
śōne'ay, my Enemy (=Death), 57
šā'al, to interrogate, 212
šābaḥ, to silence, 279 f.
šāw', idol, 151, 188
šākaḥ, to shrivel, 190
šālaḥ II, to forge, 309
šālaḥ, to forge, fire, 109
šālam, to make a covenant, 42
šām, behold!, 81, 291
šāpaṭ, to exercise authority, 13
šāpar, to trace out, 89 f.
šātal, to transplant, 3
še'ōl, Sheol, 104
šilleaḥ, send forth shoots, 265
šinnēn, to gnash the teeth, 196 f.
šīrōh, his vision, 259
šmwt, fertility, 281
šō'āh, pit, 212
šōd, sob, 74
šōḥad, compensation, 84 f.
šōḥad, bribe, 163
šomrāh, muzzle, 239 f.
šūb, to sit, 44, 148, 213
šulḥān, table, 147
taḥat, at, 116, 272
taḥtāni, beneath me, 116
ta'alūmōt, dark corners, 267
tehillāh, Glorious One, 201
tehillōt, Glory, 139
tehōm, deep, flood, XXVII
tigrāh, club, 241 f.
tillēm, two mounds, 279
tōk, absolute form, XXXVIII

SUBJECTS INDEX

Abstract noun balanced by concrete noun, XXXI f., 32 f., 38, 73, 139 f., 159, 164, 173, 224, 247
Accusative of material, 91
Accusative of means, 119, 129, 178, 271
Accusative of means preceding the verb, 35 f., 97, 115 f., 211, 309
Acrostic, 54, 155, 205, 227, 234
Adverbial *he,* 161
Afterlife: see also Immortality, Resurrection, 71, 99 f., 146, 149, 170, 232
Akkadian loanwords, XXVII f.
Amorite, 236
Animal names, metaphorical use of, 9 f., 139, 142, 206, 213
Anthropomorphism, XXIII, 247
Aphaeresis, 73
Appellatives, divine, XXIII, 18, 69 ff., 75, 104 f., 108 ff., 112, 114, 117 f., 139, 144, 153, 169 f., 176, 191, 201, 258, 260, 265
Appetite of Death, 203
Arrogance, 97
Arrows, 235
Article as relative pronoun, 216
Article in function of suffix, 203
Assonance, 45
Assumption, 100, 301

Ballast variant, 212, 284 f.
Beatific vision, 71, 99 f., 133, 167
beth emphaticum, 74, 97, 177, 201
Beauty of Yahweh, 167, 170
Boundaries, determination of, 90
Breakup of stereotyped phrases, XXXIV f., 69, 71, 104 f., 108, 176 f., 232, 242, 246, 259, 280

Canaanite hymn, 175
Canaanites, 106
Case endings, 51, 303
CCD, XXVI
Celestial weapons, 115
Chase, language of, 97 f., 140, 213, 247
Chiasmus, 42, 44, 55, 121, 134, 222, 282, 286, 293, 298
Circumstantial infinitive, 167, 218 f.
Cognate accusative, 240, 308
Composite divine titles, 104 f.
Composite nouns, XLI, 30, 66, 219 f., 272 f.
Concrete noun balanced by abstract noun, see also Abstract noun . . . , XXXIII f.
Conditional sentence without indicator, 19, 168
Confidence, psalms of, 145, 166
Consonantal text, XX ff.
Construct chain, 52
Contracted dual, 70, 88, 95, 279
Council of the gods, 5
Covenant, 133, 156 f., 251, 307
Crushing of legs, motif of, 267, 281

Dative, expressed by genitive suffix, 12, 88, 156, 307

Dative suffix, 31, 113, 132, 162, 223 f., 266
Death, XXXVI, 34, 110
Death the Shepherd, 300
Death the Swallower, 105
Defective orthography: see *scriptio defectiva,* XXXVIII
Denominative verbs, 73, 129, 131 f., 173, 237, 240
Denominative verbs from names of parts of body, 84, 118, 164
Denominative verbs from numerals, XLI
Detractors as archers, 19
Dialects, Canaanite, XVI, XVIII, XLI f., 11, 194, 278, 296 f.
Double-duty conjunctions, 18, 220, 291
Double-duty interrogatives, XXXIV, 8, 18
Double-duty negatives, 18, 58, 189, 235, 307
Double-duty prepositions, 18, 73, 200 f., 205, 237, 246, 257
Double-duty suffixes, XXII, XXXIV, 17, 36, 46, 69, 77, 94, 98, 109, 113, 125, 129, 134, 157, 168, 191 f., 195 f., 211 ff., 215, 218, 228, 237, 242, 249, 266, 271, 280, 303, 307 f., 310
Double-duty vocatives, 18
Drought, caused by sin, 24
Dual forms, contracted: see also Contracted dual, XXXVIII
Dualism, 218
Dual of adjective, 113
Dual participle, 98

Eagle, metaphor of, 97, 108
Egyptian literature, XXVI f.
El Amarna Letters, XXXII, 8
Ellipsis, 8, 16, 18, 220, 280, 307
Elysian Fields, XXXVI, 3, 33 f., 146, 222 f.
Emendation, XXI f., 52
Energic mode, XXXVIII, 12, 99, 128, 241, 275
Enjambment, XXI, XXXV, 41, 43, 156, 173
Envelope figure: see *inclusio*
Epistolary language, 190
Euphemism, 300

Fatness, connotes arrogance, 97
Feminine absolute in *-t,* 62, 167
Feminine singular verb with plural subject, 292
Foe (=Death), XXXVI, 105, 119, 182, 188, 250, 252, 260

God the Shepherd, 111
God the Warrior, 131
Great sin, the, 157

Heaven and Earth, divinities, 30
Heavenly court, 51
Hebrew grammar, XXXVII ff.
Hendiadys, 27, 50, 89, 157, 173, 195, 219, 247, 309
he-temporale, 64 f.
Hiphil privative, 158, 265
Holy war, 210
Horon, 300
Hymnodic patterns, 175

Idolatry, 31, 163, 188
Immortality: see also Afterlife, Resurrection, XXXVI, 4, 78, 91, 183, 221 ff., 303
Imperative, energic, 96
Imperative, expressed by imperfect, 29 f., 31
Imperative, followed by jussive, 261
Imperfect balanced by perfect: see also Perfect balanced by imperfect, 39, 51, 56
Imperfect *yaqtulu,* 61 f., 78

Inchoative verb, 144, 256
inclusio, 5, 14, 27, 29, 41, 43 f., 59, 99, 164, 184, 188, 232, 287
Independent pronoun, 156 f.
Infinitive absolute, xxiii f., 91, 95, 138, 213 f., 251, 255, 297
Infinitive, circumstantial, 50
Infixed *-t-* conjugation, xxxviii, 61, 64, 76, 89, 123 f., 142, 169, 206, 235, 297
Innocence, psalms of, 29, 31, 93, 161
Interchange of *b* and *p,* 90, 141, 206
Interchange of *primae yod* and *primae aleph,* 95
Interchange of *t* and *d,* 69
Internal *mem encliticum,* 147
Interposition in construct chain, xxxix f.
Ivory palace, 274

Jussive, continuing imperative, 45, 66, 196

kī, emphatic, xxv, 19, 55, 96, 161, 197
kī, interposed in construct chain, 152
kī, superlative, 197
Kingship, divine, 12, 14
Kothar, 109

lamedh comparativum, 183
lamedh emphaticum, 143, 158, 188
lamedh vocativum, xxi, xxxv, xl, 21, 87, 187, 194 f., 201, 260
Lawsuit, 306, 309
Lexicography, xli ff.
Literary dependence, xxix f., 161
Literary genus, xxxii f.
Literary types, 218

Masoretes, xx ff., 49
mem encliticum, 19, 27, 108 f., 111, 116 ff., 123 f., 138, 140, 147, 162, 176, 178, 182, 189 f., 235, 237, 281
mem encliticum, balancing a suffix, 34, 66 f., 75
merismus, 51, 221
Mesopotamian literature, xxvi ff.
Messengers, motif of two, 148, 159, 232, 247, 262
Messianic banquet, 222, 337
Metaphors, xxv f., 34, 96 f., 127, 206, 222, 265
Metonymy, 139, 202, 210
Metrical pattern, 221, 237, 280, 309
min balanced by *b,* 203
Mixing of literary types, 218, 289
Modernization of text, 114 ff., 196
Morphology, 210, 275
Motifs, mythological, xxv ff.
Mud in the nether world, 34, 43, 140, 184
Mythology, xxv, 34, 50, 113, 175, 228, 279

Name of God, 127, 129
Names of habitations, xxiii, 106
Navel of the earth, 142 f., 290
Northwest Semitic philology, xxiii, xxiv, 20, 43, 149, 228

Ophir, 274
Optative perfect: see Precative perfect, 215

Paragogic *-ī,* 182
Parallelism, xxxiii, 175 f., 256
Participle used as imperative, 98 f.
Perfect balanced by imperfect, 24, 46, 129, 177 f., 236, 280 ff.
Personification, 281, 301

Phoenician, 20, 43, 51, 87, 94, 97, 176, 191, 273, 306, 310
Phoenician feminine singular ending *-ōt,* 275, 299
Pléiade, Bible de la, IX
plurale majestatis, XXIV, 43 f., 57, 78, 105, 110, 119, 182, 250, 257, 280, 296 f.
Plural forms of names for dwellings, 128, 290
Plural subject with singular verb, 272
Poetic sequence, 38, 237, 309
Poisoned arrows, 117, 251
Polite substitute for personal pronoun, 124, 190
Polytheists, 163
Postposition with emphatic particles, 24 f.
Prayer for rain, 23, 27
Precative perfect, XXIV, XXXIX, 19 f., 23, 26 f., 44, 54 f., 58, 65 f., 94, 118, 157, 169, 184, 188, 215, 241, 250, 252, 268, 273, 286
Predestination, 271
Preposition balanced by *mem,* 259
Prepositional phrases, 237
Prepositions, XXVI
Prepositions with afformative *-n,* 285
Presence of Jacob, 152
Profession of faith, 87
Pronominal suffix in construct chain, 25, 214 f., 237
Psalm, Canaanite, 175
Psalms, royal, 7 ff., 13
Psalms, dating of, IX f.
Psalter, structure of, XXX f.
Psalter, theology of, XXXV ff.
Psalterium Novum, 55
Punic, 17, 176, 241
Pyrgi, 176
Qal passive, 19, 97, 105 f., 196, 300, 310
qatala, third person masculine singular, XVII, XXXVIII, 61
Qumran Hodayot, XXX
Qumran Scrolls, XV, XLII, 11, 87, 222

Ras Shamra, XV, XVII, XVIII ff., XLII
Ravenous monster, 215
Rejuvenation, 173
Relative clause without relative pronoun, 113, 213 f., 307
Resheph, 235
Resurrection, see also Afterlife, Immortality, XXXVI, 4, 99 f., 183, 222 f.
Return to Sheol, 39, 58
Rhyme, 45, 297
Royal psalms, 7 ff., 13
RSV, XXV, 8

Samaria Ostraca, 45
scriptio defectiva, 18, 27, 31, 58, 87, 89, 99, 109, 114, 164, 292
scriptio plena, 65, 189, 268
Shaphel, 213
Sheol, snares in, 258
Shift of person, 134
Shift from singular to plural, 34 f.
Sitz im Leben, XLIII
Slander, 34, 41, 117, 119, 210, 219, 237, 249, 251, 297
Stars, 175 f.
Stichometry, 289, 301
Storehouses of rain, snow, etc., 201
Style, 115, 166, 169, 190, 197, 215, 282
Subjunctive, 57, 142, 162, 240 f.
Suffix balanced by energic ending, 77
Suffix functioning as article, 98, 191, 298

Suffix interposed in construct chain, 110, 293
Suffix omitted with name of part of body, 88f., 95, 184, 271, 284
Superlative, 139
Superscriptions: see also Titles of Psalms, 15 f.
Suzerainty treaty, 17
Syllable-counting, 13
Syncope: see also Aphaeresis, 143, 148

Tarshish, 291 f.
Textual criticism, XXII
Third-person feminine plural verb in *-āh,* 274
Third-person masculine singular *qatala,* 26, 115
Third-person singular suffix *-ī/y,* XXI, 10 f., 81, 112, 114 f., 140, 168, 197, 218, 257
Titles of Psalms: see also Superscriptions, XVII
Tyrian robe, 274 f.

Ugaritic, classification of, 30, 66, 124, 158, 197, 211, 223, 229, 252, 262

Vastness of nether world, 111
Versions, XXIV ff., 301
Victory over flood, 180
Vocative *lamedh:* see also *lamedh vocativum,* XXXI
Vulcan, 109

waw adversativum, 10
waw emphaticum, XXV, 24, 30, 88, 116 f., 157, 189
waw explicativum, 18, 303
Weapons, divinely made, 115 f., 272
Wings, imagery of, 107, 221
Wisdom psalms, 80, 227, 296
Wolves, metaphor of, 97
Word division, XXII, 258
Wordplay, 32, 47, 56, 105, 228, 252, 286, 297, 310
Wordplay, theological, XXIX, 17, 113, 285
Wortfeld, 221